Y0-BVO-609

AFRICA 1880-1980
AN ECONOMIC HISTORY

AFRICA 1880–1980
AN ECONOMIC HISTORY

PETER LIONEL WICKINS

1986
OXFORD UNIVERSITY PRESS
CAPE TOWN

Oxford University Press

OXFORD   NEW YORK   TORONTO
MELBOURNE   AUCKLAND   NAIROBI
DAR ES SALAAM   CAPE TOWN   PETALING JAYA
SINGAPORE   HONG KONG   TOKYO   DELHI
BOMBAY   CALCUTTA   MADRAS   KARACHI

AND ASSOCIATES IN
BEIRUT   BERLIN   IBADAN   NICOSIA

ISBN 0 19 570416 9

Copyright © 1986 Oxford University Press

OXFORD is a trademark of Oxford University Press

Printed and bound by Citadel Press, Lansdowne, Cape
Published by Oxford University Press, Harrington House,
Barrack Street, Cape Town 8001, South Africa

CONTENTS

MAPS

In Memoriam

H. M. Robertson

(1905–1984)

PREFACE

In an earlier volume, *An Economic History of Africa*, I attempted a survey of the economic history of the continent of Africa from prehistoric times until the late 19th century. That dwelt upon its unchanging or scarcely perceptibly changing features: the methods of agriculture, the trade patterns within Africa and between Africa and the outside world, the handicrafts and the economic aspect of political and social arrangements. That is not to say that Africa was in a state of torpor for centuries or millennia; rather, as I was at pains to show, there was a constant process of adaptation to new circumstances. None the less, the peasant of Ancient Egypt would not have been mystified by the cultivation practised in the Nile valley in the 19th century; nor would the tropical farmer of the 14th century have found much difference in the agricultural methods of five hundred years later, even though not all the crops were the same; traffic across the Sahara and the slave trades of the Atlantic and the Indian Ocean remained essentially unaltered for centuries for all the shift of routes and change of imports and numbers of enslaved; and the manufacture of cloth and utensils altered hardly at all. In short the book of which this is the sequel concerned itself with the *longue durée* of African economic history. In contrast, the present volume is filled with the *conjonctures* and *événements* of the last century. Although much to this day continues to be done in time-honoured ways, Africa was transformed during that century. The whole world, caught up in a process of accelerating metamorphosis, has of course been equally subject to the most far-reaching change. But for Africa the change has been an effect of, a response and reaction to, external forces and influences and it has been compressed within so brief a period. Railways were built in a continent unfamiliar for the most part with wheeled transport; minerals were exploited on a scale previously unimagined; foodstuffs and industrial crops were exported in large and increasing quantities; population, after declining under the shock of slaving, conquest and often brutal plundering, began that expansion so alarming to the social engineers of our day; modern government with its ability and urge to intervene in economic processes was established. During that same period Africa passed through political convulsions remarkable for their rapidity and drastic character. Within those relatively few years the continent was shared out, vanquished, drawn into international conflicts of little immediate concern to itself and relinquished. Large tracts of Africa were brought under European sway barely twenty – even ten or fewer – years before the process of withdrawal began. Since decolonization, itself in some cases accompanied by bloodshed, cruelty, hardship and bitterness, there has been a turbulent history of understandable, though naïvely optimistic, endeavours to secure both affluence and equality within a generation or two; often heroic, yet still inadequate, economic achievement; wars across, wars within the old colonial boundaries; corruption, massacre and economic retrogression; revolutions and coups d'état; tyranny of right and left; and famine. By comparison even Latin America has enjoyed a century's tranquillity.

In my first book I adopted an arrangement suited to the slow pace of economic change in Africa. It made sense to treat separately agriculture, trade and industry over a very long time-scale. Now, however, it is essential to convey the volatility of recent African economic history. It is for this reason that I have chosen a chronological approach. I have no patience with models that affect an omnibus explanation of economic history. During the last twenty years the study of economic history has witnessed a series of attempts to analyse economic development or regression in terms of a set of rules – or, perhaps a more suggestive metaphor, in terms of a chemical formula – applicable to the most diverse societies and situations. Unquestionably these models, at least the less doctrinaire, contrived and esoteric ones, have been stimulating and none has failed to leave behind it a worthwhile insight. Such, however, is the complexity of human behaviour and circumstances that to force the infinite variety of economic history into simplistic theories with their poverty of variables, even the multi-causal models, is sterile and unrewarding. Not a single model so far devised has been capable of explaining more than one set of experiences and even that in a partial manner. Forsaking models does not mean a return to the history of the annalist, nor a renunciation of analysis and explanation. What happens is indeed susceptible to cautious and tentative explanation, especially what happens in economic history, where motives and forces are perhaps less baffling, though rarely straightforward. But to make dogmatic or even only confident statements is to fly in the face of human experience. If there is any place in the world that has been the victim of facile dogma and stereotype it is Africa. At least its historiography can be liberated from doctrinal bigotry.

There is no claim here to objectivity, only to a striving for dispassionate appraisal. It is African history seen through the eyes of a European to whom it seems self-evident that the overwhelmingly important fact of African history in the last century has been the impact of Europe upon Africa or, more precisely, that of European governments and of individual Europeans – capitalists, soldiers, politicians, officials, missionaries, settlers – but not that of elusive abstractions – Capital or Imperialism or Neo-colonialism. Indisputably an African-oriented history would be different from mine, though not *ipso facto* less partisan or prejudiced. A graver danger than bias in an enterprise of this sort is plain error. I have no claim to expert knowledge of a tithe of all that I have presumed to discuss. It is not humanly possible to achieve complete accuracy, and together with the risks of blunder there is the danger of distortion through false emphasis. There is an unavoidable random element in even the research of the monographist. One reads this source, not that, because one is aware of the first and not the second; and in the last analysis one is dependent upon what has been written, unable to penetrate areas where there is no surviving evidence or no literature, and even ignorant of the very existence of topics perhaps more significant than those that readily find their way into discussion. This book is largely dependent upon sources in English, and that in itself is a cause of bias and false perception.

I have chosen to cover the economic history of the last century in a series of essays on successive decades. At first sight this may seem intolerably artificial, almost a return to the narrow vision of the Anglo-Saxon Chronicle. It is, I think, much less absurd than may appear. The objections to this method are those which can be raised against all periodization, even the most widely accepted and apparently obvious. While the treatment of any particular chronological segment seems to capture the essence of that time-span, it does so only at the expense of taking the slowly changing continuities as given, and I have been acutely conscious of the disadvantage of slicing into decades long-term developments, such as demographic trends. To some extent we are the prisoners of conventional periodization. We all think we know what is meant by the Middle Ages and each century of European history since the twelfth, with its alleged renaissance, has meaning for us. It is not only centuries that conjure up automatic associations. In a context admittedly not primarily of economic history we are accustomed to references to and discussions of the Nineties of the last century and the Twenties, Thirties and Sixties of this, each with its supposed distinctive flavour. Almost every decade of the last century of Africa's history has been profoundly affected by some great event or process such as war, depression or political upheaval, and that gives some justification to a periodization which, after all, like all such methodological tricks, is mostly for the convenience of the historian. History is the record of change through time and the decade is an accepted way of sub-dividing time. The diachronic method provides the simplest and least pretentious model of all, sensitive to rapid change over a continent which shared broadly similar experiences.

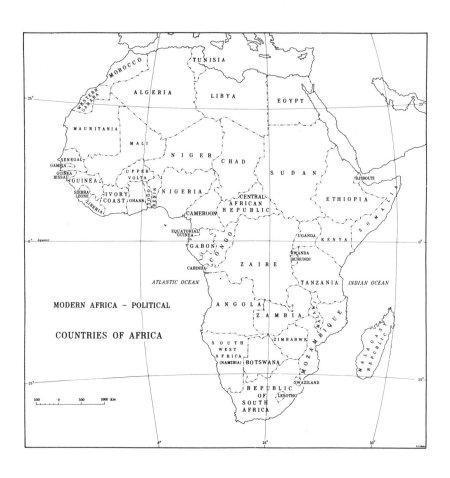

MODERN AFRICA – POLITICAL

COUNTRIES OF AFRICA

500   ·0   500   1000 Km

x

CHAPTER I

1880-90 (PARTITION)

The partition of Africa did not begin in 1880, nor did it end in 1890, but it proceeded at an accelerating pace during the 1880s. Britain and France gained most territory. Their association with Africa, though not so long as that of Portugal and Spain, was, none the less, of long standing. Their pre-1880 colonies on the Atlantic side of the continent were Sierra Leone (British) and Gabon (French), with their settlements for released slaves (Freetown, 1792, and Libreville, 1849), and Senegal (French) and Gambia (British). There were, too, several long-established forts and trading posts, such as Cape Coast Castle (British), Assinie (French) and Grand Bassam (French). In addition France and Britain had founded several small protectorates (the current euphemism for territorial acquisitions) in West Africa in the less spectacular imperialism that preceded the scramble – Lagos (British in 1861), Porto Novo (French in 1863) and Cotonou (French in 1868). In East Africa, France possessed a number of small islands – Mayotte, Nossi Bé and Réunion; while Britain ruled Seychelles and Mauritius (seized from the French in 1794 and 1811) and exercised a powerful influence in the sultanate of Zanzibar.

In South Africa, Britain annexed the Cape of Good Hope in 1814 and Natal in 1843, imposing its rule on those white natives of Africa, the Dutch-speaking Afrikaners, as well as numerous black and brown ones, and it had not ceased to extend its territories since. In the 1880s a protectorate (not altogether unwelcome to a people fearful of Afrikaner – Boer – conquest) was proclaimed over Basutoland (1884), and Galekaland and Tembuland were added to the Cape Colony in 1884. In 1886-1887 Zululand, where the British had sustained a severe defeat at Isandhlwana in 1879, was annexed. The attempt, however, of the late 1870s to bring the Boers north of the River Vaal under British administration was abandoned in 1881 after a brief war in which Britain suffered reverses. The British contented themselves with cutting the Transvaal Republic off from the outside world by the annexation of St Lucia Bay (added to Natal) in 1884 and Bechuanaland in 1885.

France had already appropriated a considerable section of North Africa with the conquest of Algeria between 1830 and 1845. The scramble for the rest of northern Africa began with the imposition of a French protectorate over Tunis in 1881 (despite, or perhaps because of, strong Italian influence there) and the British occupation of Egypt in 1882. Egypt had already been since 1878 under the tutelage of an Anglo-French Dual Control, but France, for reasons of internal politics, declined to participate in military action to suppress a nationalist rising and the Dual Control was terminated in 1883, though various European powers kept rights of intervention in Egyptian administration. The British occupation did not encompass Sudan, Egyptian since 1820. This, overrun from 1881 by the followers of the religious leader Muhammed Ahmad, the Mahdi, was abandoned after the fall of its capital, Khartoum, in 1885. Not long after its occupation of Egypt, Britain stated its intention of withdrawing as soon as possible and in 1883 signed a convention with Egypt undertaking to leave in three years from then. Although there is no doubt that Britain's Liberal party government of 1880-1885 had no wish for permanent responsibility for the administration of Egypt, the promise was not honoured, and the withdrawal from the Sudan proved to be only temporary.

Events started moving somewhat earlier in tropical Africa. In 1876 Leopold II of Belgium, in an address to a geographical conference meeting at Brussels under his auspices, spoke of the need for a crusade to open central Africa to civilization. The outcome was the founding of the International Commission for the Exploration and Civilization of Central Africa (the International African Association), presided over and financed by Leopold himself. In 1882 the Association became the International Association of the Congo. In the meantime, in 1879, H. M. Stanley the explorer set out on an expedition on behalf of the Belgian Committee of the Association, established trading stations (including Stanleyville in 1883) and negotiated with hundreds of chiefs treaties recognizing the jurisdiction of the Association. Another agent, or nominal agent of the International Association, was P. S. de Brazza, active north of the Congo organizing a protectorate on behalf of France. In West Africa the French began that penetration of the interior which was to link their West African and North African possessions. In 1883 a post was set up by Captain Gallieni at Bamako on the Upper Niger, deep in the western Sudan. The British came to be confined to two small coastal enclaves, Gambia and Sierra Leone, and two larger ones, Gold Coast and the enormous and populous territory that came to be called Nigeria. Britain established a protectorate over the River Niger Districts in 1885, the area in the vicinity of Lagos as far as the River Benue.

It was the international rivalry over Leopold's claims to the Congo that was one of the reasons for the convening of the Conference of Berlin in 1884-1885, a gathering of fifteen states which laid down the rules for the acquistion of territory. Leopold's rights in the Congo were recognized, and he was proclaimed sovereign of the Congo Free State in 1885, a state quite separate from Belgium, with its own administration and police and comprising a large part of the Congo basin. The initiator of the Berlin Conference was the German Chancellor, Prince Otto von Bismarck. Although Germany had had trading interests in West Africa since the middle of the 19th century and from the 1860s in East Africa, Bismarck had not been enthusiastic about colonies; but he bowed to, or took advantage of, those who were, or perhaps simply changed his mind, and Germany did very well from the partition. Even before the Conference of Berlin the substantial territory of Kamerun and the much smaller Togoland, both in West Africa, and South-West Africa (1884) (with the exception of Walvis Bay, annexed by Britain in 1878) were acquired; and after the Conference Germany annexed in 1885 the territory it called German East Africa, dividing a vast region with Britain, which proclaimed a protectorate over Zanzibar in 1890 and over the whole of its East African sphere of influence in 1895 as the British East African Protectorate. In the Indian Ocean, Madagascar fell to the French after a war lasting from 1883 to 1885. English merchants and missionaries had been more active there than French and even after the occupation of the capital their influence remained and was eliminated only with difficulty. The British did rather better in the Horn of Africa – British Somaliland in 1884, to which northern Somalia was added in 1887 – than the French – Djibouti in 1886. The Italians got Eritrea in 1885 and Italian Somaliland in 1889. Ethiopia (Abyssinia) escaped annexation.

Portugal and Spain, which had the longest history of colonization in Africa, survived as colonial powers despite their weakness in international politics. Spain obtained or retained possessions that were relatively unimportant – part of the western Sahara, Ceuta and Melilla on the Mediterranean, Fernando Po and Spanish Guinea; but Portugal retained the very large colonies of Angola and Moçambique, as well as Portuguese Guinea and a number of off-shore islands, including São Thomé in the Gulf of Guinea. The territory assigned to Portugal by the Berlin Conference and by international agreement in 1891 was far in excess of what it effectively controlled and what its European status entitled it to. Portuguese claims were recognized only because greater powers for their own interests chose to acquiesce in them.

The partition of Africa formed part of a renewed surge of European domination in the world, in fact the last, since European power reached its highest point in the closing decades of the 19th century and the first of the 20th. Europe had been expanding ever since the great German migration to the eastern part of the continent in the 12th century and the age of the Crusades. The powers of western Europe moved into every power vacuum that they encountered: South America in the 16th century, North America in the 17th and 18th, India in the 18th and 19th, Australasia in the 19th.

In the late 19th century Africa, China and South-East Asia lay open to European penetration with the conquest of malaria by quinine and of distance by steampower, with improvements in weapons and with the collapse of effective government, notably that of the Ottomans and the Manchus. To separate the explanation for the partition of Africa from that for European aggression elsewhere in the world is parochialism; to separate European imperialism of the late 19th century from its earlier manifestations is to obscure the underlying continuity of Europe's relationship with the rest of the world over the centuries.

Before the scramble for Africa, during the first three-quarters of the 19th century the British and French empires were already expanding vastly, establishing certain national interests that swayed governments irrespective of their political stance. Imperialism had a momentum of its own, not merely requiring further acquisition of territory to safeguard what was already held, but, as empire appeared to be a demonstration of national power and prestige, inspiring those without one to acquire one. India was the principal imperial interest that Britain came to cherish, of great economic value both for its own sake and for its rôle in Britain's trade with China. British exports to Asia by the last quarter of the 19th century were worth more than exports to the United States or western Europe. India was of particular importance to the British cotton textile industry, which maintained a powerful lobby. It is understandable that Britain was concerned for the security of the route to India and beyond – hence the annexation of the Cape of Good Hope and Aden (1839) – and that the Suez Canal (opened in 1869) was considered of vital interest to Britain. In 1875 Great Britain acquired a controlling interest in the Canal and concern for that investment, as well as other investments, provided a subsidiary motive for intervening in Egypt, a motive, however, that was not powerful enough to induce France to join in the occupation, though French investments were greater.

Few would dispute that economic advantage or supposed advantage was at the heart of empire-building. To suggest that British imperialism in Egypt stemmed from its strategic importance for the route to India rather than to protect economic interests in Egypt itself simply substitutes a more remote economic reason for the more immediate one. What is more to the point is that the economic reasons for empire were diverse and that one was more significant than another in a particular instance, but never the only one. The search for markets and sources of raw materials was always a motive for colonization, though its strength varied according to the prevailing economic circumstances or the dominant economic philosophy, broadly mercantilist or *laissez-faire*, more narrowly protectionist or free trade. The argument that there are different types of imperialism linked to particular stages of economic development has never commanded universal or even majority acceptance. There is said, for example, to be a nexus tying together the concentration of business ownership, the dominance of financial institutions over industrial enterprises, falling profits, the export of capital and imperialism. It has been amply demonstrated that the most active imperialists were not those with the greatest degree of concentration of business ownership and that there was no close correlation between capital exports and the acquistion of new colonial territory.

Obviously special factors came into play at particular times and in particular areas. In Egypt the growth of nationalism, coming to a head with a rebellion led by Ahmad Pasha 'Urabi, threatened European lives and pockets and the Suez Canal. In West Africa the preliminaries to annexation were quite different. There Anglo-French rivalry and mutual suspicion were paramount and the struggle for the profits of the export trade an additional factor. It was not only broadly conceived national interests that were decisive. Missionaries, explorers, businessmen, colonial officials, colonial politicians and plain adventurers could exercise influence with metropolitan governments and even present them with a *fait accompli*. Such people were often popular heroes whose exploits appealed to beneficiaries of the extension of schooling in the later 19th century in Europe and the readers of the new cheap and undemanding newspapers that were being published. These heroes were not necessarily the product of the unscrupulous manipulation of public opinion, but often genuine idealists uninfluenced by personal profit, though actuated by mixed motives. Very often, however, the views of men on the spot had less to do with policy than international relations within Europe itself or with the clash of domestic interest groups for which imperialism or anti-imperialism was a means of winning public support for other ends.

Annexation did not necessarily mean immediate effective control. In the 1880s the situation varied widely from region to region. In some areas the process of colonization had not even begun, while in others pacification, i.e. making claims to rule effective, was the dominant preoccupation of the colonial authorities. In some cases European powers took over ancient political entities, particularly in Mediterranean Africa and modified them; in others the colonial frontiers bore no relation to existing political boundaries and an entirely new administration had to be built up. Egypt continued to be ruled nominally by its khedive and there was no sudden diminution of his authority. Even before the occupation tight foreign controls had been imposed. These had resulted from Egypt's indebtedness, and the predominant economic problem in the eyes of the new occupying power was to ensure the free flow of interest payments to foreign investors and the eventual settlement of the accumulated debt.

Although they assumed effective responsibility for the administration of Egypt, the British did not have an entirely free hand in controlling its finances. There were several international organizations with powers over revenue and expenditure, the most important being the Caisse de la Dette, founded in 1876 with British, French, Italian, Austrian and (from 1886) Russian and German commissioners. These were the legal representatives of the holders of Egyptian government bonds and they received certain items of revenue earmarked for debt servicing. They had the right to sue the government in international tribunals, the so-called mixed courts, set up in 1875, a right which could be exercised in the event of an infringement of the Law of Liquidation of 1880, which provided for the payment of interest to foreigner creditors. In fact, the British Treasury was so strict in its supervision of administration – thus guaranteeing the solvency of the Egyptian government – that the commissioners of the Caisse had no cause for anxiety. The British officials responsible for administration were kept on a tight financial rein. No loans could be contracted without the consent of the commissioners and any revenue in excess of interest payments and administrative expenses was supposed to be used for the liquidation of the public debt.

Undoubtedly debt servicing imposed a heavy burden upon the Egyptian economy. Annual interest charges accounted for 39 per cent of ordinary government revenue in 1880 and 41 per cent in 1890, and although they fell thereafter, they remained very onerous. Nor did they constitute the only regular drain of resources from Egypt. There was a fixed tribute payable to the Ottoman government, which was the nominal suzerain of the Egyptian state, as well as the upkeep of the army. Altogether non-productive government expenditure took half of all revenue in the 1880s. At first there was nothing for debt redemption, little for development. In 1888 the European powers agreed to the establishment of a reserve fund from which the government could draw for extraordinary expenditure, though subject to the consent of the commissioners of the Caisse. Sir Evelyn Baring, later Lord Cromer, the British Agent, or chief administrator, from 1883 to 1909, was of the opinion that the Caisse acted 'as an obstacle to progress, and occasionally as an agency for the manifestation of hostility towards England'. Some money was found for irrigation and other measures designed to assist production of cotton, the export of which was important for the economy and state income. There were no more ambitious development projects like those favoured by the earlier khedives.

Egypt's fiscal recovery depended very much upon the proceeds of exports, 40 per cent of which went on paying the government's creditors. The chief export was cotton. This had a very ancient history, but it had been particularly encouraged in the 19th century. Rural unrest associated with the 'Urabi rebellion disrupted production and marketing and it was only in the latter part of the decade that, with the return to stable conditions and an improvement in the water supply in the Delta, production recovered and the area devoted to cotton reached and passed earlier dimensions. Most of it was grown in Lower Egypt, where about a third of the total cultivated area was given up to it, though the Fayyum in Upper Egypt was growing in importance. Most of the cotton and cotton seed produced was exported, with Britain taking about half. The new British administration resumed the policy of the khedives of encouraging and helping cotton producers. Measures to improve the quality of seed, the distribution of improved seed and the dissemination of advice on eradicating cotton-worm were undertaken by the government. More important, however, were the higher standards of efficiency achieved in the irrigation system. Old canals were cleared and new ones dug. Dykes and the Delta barrage, which dammed the river north of Cairo, were repaired. Changes were made in the administration, including the abolition of the corvée, the public duty to do work on the canals and dykes, maintenance of which was now put out to private contractors. The government's programme of the 1880s economized on labour and enlarged and cheapened the water supply in Lower Egypt. A further improvement, which aided cotton exports, was the result of private enterprise, not government action. The Association Cotonnière d'Alexandre (later the Alexandria General Produce Association), founded in 1883 by the cotton merchants and brokers, established grading standards, thus increasing the confidence of foreign importers in Egyptian cotton.

Large-scale commerce, finance and industry, and the professions as well, were dominated by foreigners, among whom Greeks and Italians were prominent. They settled mostly in the towns, especially Alexandria, Cairo and Port Said, where they formed a substantial proportion of the population and enjoyed a standard of living that was much superior to that of most Egyptians. Nothing was done to prevent their buying land, but in 1884 Europeans held only about 92 000 hectares (220 000 feddans) and foreigners as a whole in 1887 about 94 000 hectares (225 000 feddans), i.e. a little more than 5 per cent of the total of some 1,6 million hectares (3,92 million feddans) of privately owned land, a proportion that in due course grew larger, but far from overwhelming.

In contrast, in Algeria, where conquest began much earlier, encountered much more resistance and was intended to be permanent, French settlement was encouraged and aided. Its status was somewhat ambiguous. It was not a colony, nor a protectorate. On the other hand, although it had the same local government system as France, being divided into three departments, each with its prefect, and subdivided into arrondissements and communes, it had a governor-general. Until 1871 this was a soldier and the territory came under the authority of the war ministry, to which the departmental prefects were also responsible. In 1871 a civil governor-general was appointed and Algerian affairs were transferred to the French ministry of the interior, though a large zone remained under direct military control. Ten years later, in 1881, the ministry of the interior lost its responsibility, when a decree placed under the authority of the appropriate French ministers the different government services operating in Algeria. The effect of this was that the governor-general lost his power to the Algerian lobby in the French parliament, a group composed of the representatives of the European settlers in the territory, the *colons*. The so-called *rattachement* of 1881 inaugurated the heyday of assimilation, when Algeria, despite the presence of some four million unenfranchised native Algerians, was treated just as though it were a part of France.

French settlement in Algeria was officially encouraged from 1848. Private, or free, colonization always existed side by side with official colonization and assumed a growing importance, but no European settlement would ever have taken place on the scale it did without official support, which made available land that the Muslims would not otherwise have parted with, and constructed roads and other public works. The system of land tenure found by the French was complicated, but broadly land was of three kinds, privately owned (*milk* land), tribal (*'arsh* land) and state land, each about a third of the 14 000 000 ha of the Tell, or coastal region. The colonial government took direct charge of much of the state land (notably all the land defined as forest) and permitted the sale of privately owned land to immigrants and even the sale of tribal land to the government in the military zone or to individuals in the civil zone. In addition thousands of hectares of uncultivated *'arsh* land were expropriated for European settlement. Tribesmen were confined to just enough land needed for survival (*cantonnement*). In the latter part of the Second Empire of Napoleon III French policy was more sympathetic to Muslim interests. In 1863 *'arsh* land was declared inalienable and vested in the *duwar* or clan, a policy which aroused resentment among the settlers without reconciling the Algerians to the earlier loss of so much land.

In the early years of the Third Republic, founded in 1870 after the fall of Napoleon III, there was a much harsher attitude. In 1871 a revolt led to large-scale confiscations and in 1873 a law was passed to facilitate the acquisition of land by colonists by permitting the conversion of communal land into individual ownership subject to French law. In a land sale to a European it was up to those with claims to the land to protest against the sale and it was the vendor who took the responsibility of ensuring that the land sold was free of other claims. Individual land-holding and free alienation of land were concepts that were quite foreign to tribal thinking and social organization and the way was opened for encroachment by speculators taking advantage of tribesmen whom they persuaded to apply for separate land-holding or who, in the process of tribal disintegration which inevitably followed such an application, were unable to comprehend what was happening. The social repercussions were grave. Separation set in train legal processes that were beyond the understanding and resources of many Algerians, and the result was large-scale dispossession. It is estimated that between 1883 and 1889 their ignorance and poverty, which made recourse to the law difficult, cost tribesmen 40 per cent of their land.

Between 1871 and 1885 just over half a million hectares of land were devoted to official colonization, but only 33 000 heads of families were settled on the land, and of these, despite the policy of settling on the land refugees from the French provinces of Alsace-Lorraine (lost to Germany in 1871), only 17 000 were new arrivals from France, the rest either Frenchmen already resident in Algeria or foreigners. Immigrants were attracted from Italy, Spain and Malta, and in addition Jews, granted French citizenship in 1870-1871, tended to identify themselves with the European community. Not all – probably less than half – those arriving from metropolitan France held on to the plots they had been granted. Some sold out, others rented them to Muslim tenants. Farms were small. In 1878 a ceiling of forty cultivable hectares was set for each farm belonging to a group of farms, one hundred for an isolated one. The *colons* complained endlessly of the inadequacy of their holdings, the shortage of land for their sons, and the policy of reserving a large proportion of land grants for the immigrants from France. In practice farms tended to be larger than the official limit and the average farm size increased. Algerian-born settlers succeeded in enlarging their access to land, often by exerting pressure upon their parliamentary representatives.

Although by 1889 the European rural population stood at some 200 000, having doubled since 1872, this fell far short of the hopes of the French government after the suppression of the rebellion of 1871. There was a continuing drift of settlers to the towns, which became predominantly European. In 1883 Parliament was asked to authorize a loan of 50 000 000 francs to establish 175 settler villages on 300 000 hectares of land to be compulsorily purchased. This project, which was condemned as unjust even by some advocates of colonization, was narrowly rejected. Thus in the 1880s official colonization slowed down. 400 000 hectares of land were allotted to official settlers in the period 1871-1880, 176 000 hectares between 1881 and 1890. Colonization was not cheap, costing 4 000 000 francs a year between 1877 and 1881 and 3 000 000 a year between 1882 and 1891.

The Algerian *colon* cultivated the same crops as those of southern Europe – wheat, barley and oats, vines, potatoes, early vegetables and tobacco – thus competing with French agriculture. Tree crops included olives, figs and oranges in the Tell, and dates in the south. Esparto grass, used in the manufacture of textiles and paper, grew extensively but could be exploited only where transport facilities existed. The possibility of growing cotton was mooted from time to time but nothing came of it. Algerian wine was admitted into France duty-free from 1867 and production increased markedly during the phylloxera attack on metropolitan vineyards in the 1870s. A similar pattern of colonization evolved rather later in Tunisia, where legislation made possible the purchase of land by private individuals. In 1881 over a third of a million hectares were expropriated, mostly tribal land.

European colonization, together with population growth, caused land hunger. In Algeria many peasants who had fallen into debt, were compelled to take up share-cropping on very unfavourable terms. Share-croppers (*khammès*) had to provide their own equipment, animals and seed, and in return for their work on the proprietor's land received a proportion of the harvest varying from a fifth to a third in the case of cereals and usually half in the case of tobacco and fruit. There were *khammès* cultivating twenty or thirty hectares and enjoying a tolerable standard of life, and sometimes smallholders who had been forced by misfortune into dependence, escaped after a few good harvests had restored their position. The typical *khammès*, however, lived wretchedly.

The only other area of considerable white settlement was South Africa, where the white population in 1876 was about 320 000, of whom 220 000 were in the Cape, the rest in Natal and the Boer Republics of the Orange Free State and Transvaal. The black population within these territories numbered then about 1,2 million. The advance of the Boers and the frontier wars that were the outcome of the conflicting interests of European and African resulted in extensive annexations for the benefit of the settlers. The time came, however, when the Africans proved to be too numerous to be extirpated or exterminated, and the conquerors were compelled to recognize that some provision was needed for the conquered. It became the practice to set aside special areas for the indigenous people, the so-called native reserves, which were of varying size, but usually broken up into fragments, among which, for the sake of greater control, European settlements or outposts were interspersed. The British colonial authorities in the Cape of Good Hope excluded Europeans in principle from the Transkeian Territories from 1864, and that same year in Natal the Crown vested in a Native Trust those areas of the colony that had been set aside for the inalienable possession of the native inhabitants. Zululand was later

(1897) so divided that three-fifths of the land was reserved for Africans, whose interests were safeguarded by the Zululand Native Trust. In the territories controlled by the Boer Republics the situation was somewhat different. In the Transvaal scant regard was paid to African needs until, at British insistence, a standing Native Locations Committee was appointed in 1881. Eventually rather more than 800 000 ha were set aside for exclusive African occupation. In the Orange Free State, where warfare had much reduced the African population, three small areas were reserved.

Not all Africans lived in these reserves. Thousands found themselves living on land that had been appropriated or, crowded out of often scanty reserves or escaping from government demands for labour or from the sometimes arbitrary rule of government-sanctioned tribal chiefs, over-flowed on to unoccupied white-owned land, where they preserved their traditional economy. The presence of these Africans aroused equivocal feelings in European breasts: resentment at the existence of 'squatters' ignorant of or uninterested in the conquerors' laws, gratification at receiving some kind of rent, in cash or kind, for land that would otherwise have remained unutilized, satisfaction at the availability of a pool of labour, and fear that overgrazing would destroy the fertility of the soil. Displeasure was the emotion that came to predominate and the tendency was to force Africans out of European areas or to compel them to remain on terms that gave maximum advantage to whites and maximum hardship to blacks. Increasingly Africans were permitted to stay only as labour tenants, i.e. they paid a labour rent of a certain number of days a year.

Until the development of the diamond and gold-mining industries there was only a trickle of European immigration and the white population was largely dependent upon natural increase for its growth. Most lived on the land. In the 18th and 19th centuries there was plenty of this available and the acquisition and holding of farms were subject to only rudimentary legal formalities. Most were held on a lease known as a loan place, for which a small annual rent was nominally payable. Gradually the authorities had asserted their will, so that by 1880 perpetual quit-rent had become the normal tenure. By then, however, it was beginning to give way in the Cape Colony and Natal to freehold through the redemption of quit-rents by a lump sum spread over a period of years. An Act of 1887 in the Cape Colony made new land grants subject to public auction at a minimum price. In the Boer Republics tenants turned into owners and quit-rent into land tax.

In the first two centuries of the Cape Colony's existence the typical farm was as big as 2 500 hectares, but by the 1880s there was no longer enough land left for farms of such generous proportions, except marginal land suitable only for extensive pastoral farming. The authorities in the Cape and Natal favoured close settlement to encourage European immigration, reviving an older practice. The Natal Land and Immigration Board in the 1880s offered free passages to immigrants and the right to buy small farms (of up to 280 hectares) on instalments. Such small-scale farming enjoyed only a mixed success. It required a high degree of skill lacking among farmers accustomed to the subsistence methods characteristic of South Africa. None the less the trend was towards smaller farms. Partible inheritance was the law and large families the custom. Estates were divided and subdivided until sometimes there were fragments too small to support their owners. White landlessness grew among Boers and a substantial client group emerged, the *bywoners*, who, without land or at least adequate land, entered into a relationship of dependence upon their better-off neighbours, for whom they performed services in exchange for access to land. The land situation was aggravated by the acquisition of great tracts as a speculation by individuals and land companies, such as the Natal Land and Colonization Company. Speculators did not use the land themselves, frequently leaving it to black squatters, and were more interested in the possibility of mineral exploitation, especially gold.

The development of diamond-mining at Kimberley after 1867 and gold-mining on the Witwatersrand from 1886 presented two sorts of opportunities to whites on the land. They could either move into mining themselves or into one of the urban occupations that came to serve the mining industry; or they could provide food for the new and expanding urban market dependent upon mining, especially maize for the large black labour force. Lacking as they did industrial skills and even elementary education, unwilling to compete with blacks in unskilled work, most whites were unable to seize the new opportunities for urban employment, and at the same time, without capital, agricultural, business and management skills and even the inclination to produce for the market, they (particularly in the Transvaal) were slow to respond to the agricultural opportunities. Boers preferred the adventure and easier, though more uncertain, rewards of prospecting and hunting. Thousands of them engaged in transport. Good money was to be made by a man who could get together enough capital to purchase a wagon and a span of oxen. The railways put an end to transport-riding and moreover facilitated the importation of cheap grain and other foodstuffs from overseas.

Most farmers, even those with adequate land, had a poor standard of living, the result of low productivity, but there were exceptions. The growth sectors, such as ostrich farming and sugar planting, had a record of innovation and enterprise. The chief farm exports in the 1880s were wool, ostrich feathers and mohair. Sugar was grown with some success in Natal after a long struggle to survive. In the 1870s it was an important export which contributed to the development of the colony. The chief market was the Cape. In the 1880s, however, despite the development of the railways, which enlarged the internal market, the Natal sugar industry was in difficulties because of falling prices and overseas competition, especially from Mauritius, later from German beet sugar. Sheep farming was concentrated in the Eastern Province of the Cape of Good Hope, where there were some 13 million woolled sheep by the end of the 1880s (and 3 million woolless ones), but the Orange Free State was gaining importance, with over 5 million. The Cape government took steps to raise farming standards. Viticulture was scientifically studied at Groot Constantia from 1885 and an agricultural school was opened at Stellenbosch in 1889. There was, however, a terrible setback in the wine industry in this period through the ravages of phylloxera.

By the 1880s the Boer frontier had passed beyond the territory of the Boer republics. Some trekkers succeeded in establishing themselves as farmers on the southern plateau of Angola, at Huila, which had enjoyed a shadowy existence since 1845. Angola had attracted a trickle of Portuguese and other white immigrants throughout the latter part of the 19th century, some granted land by the government and subsidized during the first five years of settlement. Officially-sponsored land schemes had little effect. Immigrants preferred hunting and trading to farming, which they practised on a virtually subsistence level. Not all the land that was assigned to them was sufficiently fertile to ensure an adequate return and there was a lack of trained agronomists. The plateau was thought to be too high for growing high-value crops such as coffee, and until the construction of roads and railways, transport was not good enough for the marketing of bulky, low-value ones. Some settlers, as soon as the period of government subsidies expired, became, after selling or abandoning their plots, which they had never seriously attempted to develop, itinerant traders among the African pastoralists. Even those who stuck to farming combined it with trade in order to survive at all. Conversely it was not unusual for traders to save enough money to buy a piece of land to supplement their trading income. Some combined trade with the raising of cattle, for which they had no land of their own, but which they grazed on tribal land.

The most prosperous part of Portugal's African empire was the small islands of São Thomé and Principe in the Gulf of Guinea, where cocoa was grown on plantations with forced labour. Although slaves were emancipated in 1876, *de facto* slavery persisted long after that. The so-called contract workers of the estates were actually bought from African slave traders, who obtained them mostly from Katanga, Kasai and Barotseland, though some came from estates, known as *prazos*, in the Zambezi valley in Moçambique. In theory contracts were for a fixed period of service (usually five years) at agreed wages, but in practice a contract was a life sentence. The death rate on the islands was high.

The Atlantic slave trade went on well into the second half of the 19th century and it was only the abolition of slavery in Cuba in 1886 and in Brazil in 1888 that eventually caused it to wither away. Two problems remained: the Arab slave trade in East Africa and the continuation of indigenous slave-owning. Attempts were made in the 1870s to curb the East African slave trade through treaties imposed on the Sultan of Zanzibar. Although the slave markets were closed, slaving went on. Not all slaves were sent overseas. The Arab clove plantations of Zanzibar and Pemba were dependent on slave labour. Slave-holding was also common among Africans in West Africa, especially in the Muslim areas. Although colonial authorities were committed to its abolition, they were inclined to act with caution because of the disturbance precipitate emancipation was likely to cause to economy and society. It was thought to be inexpedient to deprive of slaves those who used them for the production of export crops or chiefs whose authority was enlisted to assist in administration. The problem, too, of providing the necessary machinery for the identification, release and rehabilitation of slaves was no light one. From 1887 the French colonial authorities, who were dealing with rather larger numbers than the British were, established villages in the interior for the resettlement of liberated slaves, but these were shunned by the intended beneficiaries because they simply provided a pool of unpaid labour for local officials.

The substitution of the export of raw materials for the export of slaves as the chief economic activity in West Africa was a spontaneous response of Africans to the changing character of European demand. African small-holders had at their disposal under-utilized land and labour that permitted the production of, in addition to food, commercial crops which, in some cases, were already cultivated for food. For some – palm produce and rubber – capital requirements were slight. Sometimes colonial governments, in order to raise revenue or to assist private interests, tried to coerce Africans into providing wild and cultivated products that would fetch a good price on world markets; sometimes they relied upon persuasion and gave help. Very often exports grew amidst official indifference. Probably the chief contribution of government to production consisted in the suppression of local wars and raids, often the accompaniment or result of slaving, and in transport improvements.

Exports of palm oil from various points on the West African coast, but principally the Niger Delta, rose markedly, though from a low base, in the first half of the 19th century. Soap, candles and lubricating oil provided the early demand, later on the tin plate industry. Palm oil exports from Lagos in the 1880s varied between about 7 000 and 9 000 metric tons, but they competed with other types of oil from various parts of the world. Exports of palm kernels grew much more rapidly. These found little local use, but were used increasingly in Europe in the manufacture of margarine and cattle cake. Exports from Lagos trebled from the late 1860s to the late 1880s, from some 12 000 metric tons to some 36 000 metric tons.

Ground-nuts were a source of cooking oil and an ingredient of margarine and could be used for making soap. Though grown over a very wide area, they were cultivated for export chiefly in Senegal and Gambia. Intensive cultivation in Senegal followed the opening of the Dakar – St Louis railway in 1885. The Muslim Mourides community started to go in for ground-nuts in a business-like manner at the end of the 1880s. Exports, chiefly through Dakar, rose from 15 000 tons in 1872 to 40 000 in 1885 and to 60 000 tons in 1894.

Africans could participate in the world economy not only by the cultivation of cash crops, but also by collecting and hunting and pastoralism. The hunting of elephant for the tusks and rhinoceros for its horn was an ancient practice that became more efficient with the introduction of firearms. Other animals were slaughtered for their skins. Efficiency brought but short-term profit and long-term extermination. Collecting, too, was by no means new and there was no rigid distinction between it and cultivation, e.g. in oil palm harvesting. Rubber was collected in some places on native initiative with the encouragement of merchants who advanced credit and in others under European compulsion. Demand grew *pari passu* with the manufacture of bicycle and motor tyres and electrical insulation. Hitherto the chief source of supply had been Brazil. Africa attracted attention as a source of supply in the 1880s after an attempt made by speculators to corner Brazilian supplies. Most came from the Congo and West Africa. In the 1880s exports from Gold Coast reached 681 metric tons, from Congo Free State 131 metric tons (in 1889).

The expansion of cash crop production provided an important contribution to the growth of Africa's overseas trade. International trade from the later 1870s expanded more slowly than it had done in the previous quarter of a century, including trade in primary produce. Industrial countries were importing larger quantities of foodstuffs, an important component of African exports, but the trade in foodstuffs no longer grew faster than the trade in manufactures, which had been the case earlier in the century. In the long term the rate of growth of the volume of primary products entering international trade did not alter very much, though in the case of individual territories there could be striking fluctuations from year to year.

The exports of the colony of Nigeria were worth less than half a million pounds in 1881, rose to nearly £700 000 in 1884 and fell again to less than

£500 000 in 1887 and 1889. Exports from Senegal rose from 16 million francs in 1878 to 28 million in 1882, fell to 21 million in 1883 and fluctuated below 20 million francs after 1884, falling to 13 million in 1890. The exports of the Gold Coast were worth £393 000 in 1878 and £601 000 in 1890, but were below £400 000 half the 1880s. In 1880 the exports of Tunisia earned 11 million francs, in 1881 22 million and in 1882 only 11 million again. Egyptian exports retained much the same annual value throughout the decade, between £E 10 million and £E 13 million. The highest value of Algerian exports in the 1880s was 219 million francs in 1887, the lowest 142 million in 1881. The value of exports in 1890 was exactly the same as it had been in 1880 (178 million francs), but because of their tendency to go up and down the export figures of individual years cannot be usefully compared with one another. What can be noticed is that Algeria normally had an unfavourable balance of commodity trade, as did Tunisia. Given the movement of European settlers and capital into these countries, that is hardly surprising. Egypt, with its debt problem and strict financial controls, maintained a very favourable balance of trade. In the tropical colonies the value of imports tended, like that of exports, to be very irregular.

In the last quarter of the 19th century world prices were falling. Until the early 1880s this favoured the primary producers because the prices of manufactured goods fell more than those of raw materials. Thereafter the terms of trade moved against Africa. Different products had a different price history. African vegetable oils were badly affected by the increasing use of the Suez Canal, which gave an advantage to Indian vegetable oils and Australian and New Zealand animal fats. In the course of time, however, the Canal was of value to the eastern side of Africa as ships passing through it began to call at the Indian Ocean ports, and the whole of Africa benefited from the declining transport costs of the 19th century, the result of growing shipping capacity and increasing competition.

Africa's trade with the rest of the world was an insignificant proportion of total world trade. Even the imports of Britain from Africa, though its chief trading partner, amounted to less than 5 per cent of all British imports. Moreover, the bulk of African exports came from a relatively restricted part of the continent. European plantations on the off-shore islands of São Thomé and Fernando Po in the west and Mauritius and Réunion in the east had an importance quite disproportionate to their size. The most important British trading partner of the continent was Cape Colony, the exports of which increased greatly in value with the development of diamond-mining. Exports of diamonds and, after 1886, gold accentuated the importance of South Africa to the world economy and widened the gap between that region and the rest of the continent. In 1870

South Africa and West Africa were conducting an external trade of more or less equal value, but by the end of the century South Africa's gold exports had increased so rapidly that West Africa was left far behind.

Though eclipsed by gold exports, the export of vegetable and animal products from Africa grew rapidly, and imports correspondingly. However marginal African trade was to the European economy, it was of growing importance to the African economy. The growth of foreign trade outstripped the growth of GNP and it became an increasingly important component of GNP. This growth was precarious in that it was dependent upon the production of a limited range of primary products. By the 1880s four-fifths of Egypt's exports were made up of cotton as its other major product, wheat, declined in the face of increasing world competition in grain production and the growing popularity of cotton as a cash crop. There was a similar dependence on ground-nuts in French West Africa and palm products in British West Africa.

Given the high degree of dependence upon the export of a relatively small range of primary products for the purchase of manufactured goods from overseas, the economic well-being of Africa became sensitive to the rise and fall of the demand for its primary products and the movement of industrial prices. The trade cycle, technological change in the industrialized world and the adventitious appearance of competing sources of supply and competing substances all had their influence upon African prosperity. It was impossible for myriads of primary producers to keep up prices by agreed restriction of output. Their response was rather, though not invariably, to maintain aggregate income by expanding output and exports.

The overseas trade of Africa was controlled by outsiders or expatriates. In Egypt and North Africa trade was shared between foreign-based firms and firms run by minorities. In East Africa Indians and Arabs had long been dominant, but were losing their dominance with the increasing influence of European traders. In South Africa local export-import businesses developed in Cape Town and other ports. In West Africa there had been a thriving African mercantile community since the days of the slave trade, but this had always had to deal with European middlemen, and in the later 19th century it came under increasing pressure from European-based firms, which tended to become fewer, but larger and more powerful. The collection and export of palm produce, previously handled by African merchants, fell increasingly into their hands as they penetrated ever deeper into the interior and established a network of trading posts. The rivalry between European and African merchants sharpened as the prices of primary products fell, and European merchants became more and more impatient with the restrictive practices of African middlemen.

In the 19th century and later it was commonly thought by economists that international trade benefited all partners. By specializing in the production of those goods where they enjoyed a comparative advantage, trading partners were able to obtain imports more cheaply than they could make them themselves. The very process of trade facilitated the diffusion of technology and skills and the international movement of capital. Such advantages accruing from foreign trade were not thought to be confined to the export sector, but to be spread throughout the entire economy. The classical argument is that trade, by widening the existing internal market through its demand for raw materials, provides a 'vent for surplus', i.e. an external outlet for produce not required for home consumption, and that increases the division of labour in the exporting country, thereby raising the general level of productivity. Land and labour that would otherwise have remained unused because of the imperfect domestic market (lack of currency or transport), are drawn into production and produce is exported without any reduction of domestic consumption. Development is assisted by the accumulation of capital, growth of population and changes in taste which are all encouraged by the growth of international trade. A modification of the argument suggests that resources are under-utilized, not because the market is rudimentary, but because the terms of trade between agricultural products and manufactures are not sufficiently favourable to the farmer to induce him to give up leisure in the interests of increased output. International trade is able to provide manufactures that are cheap enough to make additional production worthwhile, which was not the case with the products of local handicraft industry.

This optimistic view of trade has not been universally held. The supposed advantages of trade are dismissed by some critics. In practice its effects have been disastrous, especially when it has been the result of the penetration of foreign enterprise. Imports of capital into the colonies have been used only to develop resources for export and led to the atrophy of the rest of the economy. The result has been the formation of a foreign-controlled enclave attached to the industrial trading partners, bestowing few benefits on the indigenous economy, but adversely affecting traditional production, agricultural and industrial, and established social relations. The profits of foreign enterprise have been largely drained away to the capital-exporting countries. Cash crop production has brought with it the evils of monoculture: soil erosion and neglect of food crops, leading to famine and dietry deficiencies. Farmers have had to sell their crops to, and buy their imports from, trading and processing firms, mostly foreign, with monopsonistic and monopolistic advantages. What income there has been has not been saved and invested at home, but spent on imported foreign manufactures that have ruinously competed with indigenous production, or perhaps been invested abroad. Africa has become the exploited periphery of an exploiting centre, the industrial countries of western Europe and America. Between centre and periphery there is an unequal exchange of products. The terms of trade have always favoured the centre, once again because of its monopolistic and monopsonistic position. In Marxist terms international trade is a means of extracting surplus value from the underdeveloped countries. The only ones to gain within Africa are a local élite, sometimes indigenous in origin, sometimes foreign, in a better position through landowning, superior education, government employment, or participation in commerce, and displaying no interest in promoting manufacturing. Some critics have emphasized the deleterious effects of colonization, Africa's loss of the power to determine its own destiny. Others would argue that economic backwardness and inequality are the inevitable consequences of the operation of Capital.

There is an element of truth in both the favourable and the critical views. It is true that idle land and labour were put to use for the production of a surplus. This surplus was exchanged for imports, an increasing proportion of which was made up of investment goods. There was growing investment in transport and building. Division of labour was promoted through specialization in export production and the provision of services to those engaged in that specialization. On the other hand, the disadvantages of national dependence upon the export of a small range of primary products and the difficulty of escaping from that dependence to a more diversified and adaptable economy became all too apparent. Colonial rule retarded diversification, particularly into industry, by preventing the protection of infant industries. Metropolitan countries, whether they expounded free trade like Britain, or were protectionist like France, did their best to ensure the free entry of their own products into the territories they controlled, though giving colonial producers of foodstuffs and raw materials free entry into the metropolitan markets.

France, apart from a brief phase in the Second Empire, had never been as wedded to free trade as had Britain, and it is argued that protectionism was another aspect of the European policy that manifested itself aggressively in imperialism. Britain, however, remained still firmly in favour of free trade. In the 1880s, even earlier, there was something of a reaction against it and a renewed interest in imperial economic co-operation for the sake of creating a common market populous enough and with sufficient resources to hold its own against the United States and Germany. The Fair Traders advocated tariff protection against imports into Britain of foreign goods, particularly manufactured goods and free entry of empire products in return for preferential treatment for British exports to imperial markets. These ideas found little support with the electorate because they would have meant higher food prices, were impracticable because Britain was vulnerable to foreign retaliation and were unenthusiastically received in self-governing colonies, which were rather inclined to protect their own infant industries against British competition.

As far as Africa was concerned, Britain felt no need to interfere with the existing trade pattern, being dominant in the trade of its colonies. Indeed, by giving internal self-government to the Cape Colony and Natal, Britain permitted them to erect tariff walls against its own products. In 1884, for the first time the Cape introduced a tariff explicitly aimed at giving protection to colonial industry and, more particularly, agriculture. However, the protective aspect of the new duties was still of smaller importance than their revenue purpose. After 1889, when a customs union was formed, income from customs had to be shared with the Orange Free State. Natal and the Transvaal Republic remained outside the union, the former because it feared a loss of trade if it accepted the high tariff of the Cape – mostly 12 per cent *ad valorem* – and the latter because, having failed to persuade the coastal colonies to give it a share of their taxes on imports, it intended to divert trade from the British-controlled ports to Lourenço Marques.

International agreements did not always permit colonial powers to monopolize the markets of their dependencies. France went as far as it could. Metropolitan tariffs were applied to Algeria in 1884. The free movement of goods between France and Algeria had long been permitted. Similar privileges were more difficult to obtain in Tunisia because of prior British and Italian treaty rights. In their equatorial colonies the French, seeking not merely to secure free entry of their own products into the territory which they controlled, but also to exclude as far as possible competing goods, encountered the limitations imposed by the Congo Basin Treaty. The area covered by the treaty extended beyond the geographical basin of the river and included not only the Congo Free State and the French Congo and much else of French equatorial Africa, but the whole of, what later became, Kenya, Uganda, Tanganyika and Nyasaland, parts of Angola, Moçambique, Sudan, Ethiopia, what later became Italian Somaliland and a small part of what was to become Northern Rhodesia. Amongst other provisions, including the safeguarding of free access to the resources of Africa and free navigation of the Niger and Congo rivers the treaty provided for completely free trade within the Congo basin as defined. This was modified by the Brussels treaty of 1890 permitting the imposition of customs duties, not exceeding 10 per cent *ad valorem*, for revenue purposes, to apply to all without distinction.

The real trading pattern that emerged in the colonial period did not, however, conform exactly with the sentiments and requirements of international agreements. The colonial relationship restricted free trade despite the free trade provisions of the Congo Basin Treaty, and it did so even without the imposition of discriminatory taxation or other administrative means of controlling the direction of trade. Political ties tended to engender economic ties. Colonial administrations and settlers would be more likely to import from their metropolitan country than from a foreign source. Britain and Italy, which had a substantial share of Tunisian trade before the French annexation, were quickly eliminated during the 1880s. On the other hand Britain was providing two-fifths of Egypt's imports and taking two-thirds of its exports.

In West Africa the Dutch and Portuguese were squeezed out of trade during the 19th century, though this was partly a function of their declining position in world trade. Britain and France were predominant, with Germany rapidly growing in importance. These were the chief colonial powers. Hamburg and other north German ports took large quantities of palm oil, a good deal from Kamerun, and Germany was also a major importer of palm kernels for cattle food, re-exporting the oil to Holland for manufacture into margarine. Britain was the biggest trader, operating over a very extensive area, while France, the principal importer of ground-nuts, did most of its trade with Senegal. With the spread of colonial rule, Britain found itself losing ground in the Congo, Dahomey and the Ivory Coast, but equally was able to maintain predominance in the Niger valley.

In the early 1880s French commercial interests made a determined effort to break into the British dominated Niger valley, but without success. The Compagnie française de l'Afrique équatoriale, founded in 1880, and the Compagnie du Sénégal, founded in 1881, after establishing branches in the Niger delta and up river as far as the Benue, were bought out in 1884 by the National African Company, formerly the United African Company, founded in 1879 as the result of a merger of a number of British firms trading along the Niger and renamed in 1882. The National African Company, chartered by the British government in 1886 as the Royal Niger Company, though a private company, received with its charter sovereign functions which permitted it to maintain its own armed forces and conclude treaties with African rulers. By participating in local political conflicts it greatly increased its influence.

Companies like the Royal Niger Company, i.e. companies combining commerce with politics and administration, were founded elsewhere in Africa: the Imperial British East Africa Company (1888), the British South Africa Company (1889), the German East African Company (1883) and the German Colonial Company for German South-West Africa (1885). The South-West Africa Company did not retain its administrative functions for long, but the others did, acting as surrogates of the colonial powers and using private capital for quasi-political ends. None the less, they all differed from one another as much as they resembled one another. The Royal Niger Company was the only true trading enterprise among them and, despite the cost of its political rôle and fierce competition, it made a profit. Dividends were not large in the 1880s, the period of the National African Company and competition with the French companies. No dividend was paid from 1885, a year of loss, until 1888. During this period, however, there were big investments in trading stations and steamboats and the purchase of the property of the Compagnie française de l'Afrique équatoriale. Improvement in profits was the result of the charter, which permitted the Company to levy customs duties and in practice, in spite of the obligation of maintaining free trade, to exclude competition and thus force down prices paid to producers. The chartered companies had no exclusive commerical rights. Freedom of trade was enshrined in the Act signed by the nations attending the Berlin Conference. In practice this was persistently infringed. The Royal Niger Company made it difficult for competitors to operate.

The German East Africa Company was a product of the 'Konquistaran-illusion' of Karl Peters and the Society for German Colonization. Peters' hopes were illusory because, being himself without personal resources or business interests of his own, he was compelled to submit to the Company's financial backers. At first, before Bismarck's conversion to imperialism, private capital was reluctant to come forward at all. The state would go no further than the offer of moral support. Although the purchase by the crown of half a million marks' worth of shares, which made it the biggest shareholder, did have the effect of eliciting contributions from other quarters, industrialists, financiers and the landed aristocracy, the Company's resources remained meagre for the task it set itself. It hoped to make its profits from leasing mining, plantation, railway and banking concessions. There was an element of illusion in this too. No profit could be made before the conquest of the territories to which it laid claim and which it then had to administer and provide with an infrastructure. For this its capital was far from adequate. The Company's charter empowered it to collect customs and taxes within the German protectorate, but as long as the Sultan of Zanzibar dominated the coast revenue was likely to be low. The Company could get no income until the interior was developed; the interior could not be developed without sufficient income.

The Congo Free State was run in much the same way as the territories acquired by chartered companies. It was a private empire using private capital (organized by the Comité d'Etudes du Haut Congo which Leopold formed in 1888) for private profit. The state claimed the ownership of all land, though taking care at first not to interfere with the activities of existing traders engaged in the purchase of rubber and ivory. There was genuine free trade from 1885 to 1891 and a rapid growth of exports from 1,9 million francs in 1887 to 8,2 million in 1890.

The British East African Company was the chartered successor of the British East Africa Association, which obtained a concession to administer the mainland territories of the Sultan of Zanzibar in 1887. Unlike Peters, its directors were businessmen, its president William Mackinnon, the founder of the British India Steam Navigation Company, which started a monthly mail service to Zanzibar in 1872, and its vice-president Thomas Brassey, the railway engineer and contractor with various other business interests. Nevertheless, the fact that philanthropic interests, particularly those concerned with the elimination of slavery, were prominent among shareholders, was an indication of the non-commercial aspect of its objectives. Acquisition of territory for future exploitation rather than the more effective organization of existing trade was Mackinnnon's predominant motive, just as it was Leopold II's. Like its German counterpart, the British company lacked the financial means for the tasks it set itself.

The British South Africa Company was interested in gold rather than cash crops or commerce. To all appearance gold was more important than politics. For, although its objectives included the laying down of railway and telegraph lines and the fostering of European settlement and the development of trade and mining and its charter of October 1899 (to run for twenty-five years) gave it the power to make treaties, promulgate and enforce laws, levy taxes, maintain a police force and undertake public works, the Company had no permission to annex territory and its area of operation was ill-defined, simply west of Portuguese East Africa and north of the Transvaal. It was formed ostensibly to exploit the concession of mining rights ceded to Charles Rudd, an agent of the British-born Cape businessman and politician, Cecil John Rhodes, in 1888 by Lobengula, the king of the Matabele and suzerain of the Mashona, who had very soon repented of his action. Faith in the existence of gold deposits across the Limpopo was nourished by the remains of old workings and the recent discoveries in the Transvaal. Rhodes was not the only one jockeying for power in Lobengula's territory, but it was he who received the support of the British government. No doubt the hopes entertained of finding gold were genuine enough, but the Rudd concession was as much a pretext for the extension of imperial authority as a means of private enrichment. For the British it was a way of restricting Boer ambitions. But many British businessmen were affronted by the monopoly that Rhodes and his associates had acquired.

The capital that Rhodes put into the British South Africa Company was founded on South African diamonds. In its early years diamond-mining in Kimberley was open to small prospectors, but unbridled competition and rising costs – as mining went deeper and became more dangerous – forced out the small man. Throughout the 1880s there was a struggle for control of the industry among a small number of companies. Between 1886 and 1889 Rhodes, with the help of French and British capital, built up the De Beers Consolidated Mines Limited and, to maintain prices, sought to create a monopoly, which was achieved in 1893 with the establishment of a Diamond Syndicate. The trust deed of De Beers gave the management of the company wide powers over its resources and Rhodes used them to invest in projects where political aims were as influential as the desire to diversify the company's activities to reduce dependence upon a commodity subject to sudden price changes. Capital went not only into the British South African Company, but also farming – fruit, wine, cattle – railways and coal, copper and gold mining.

In 1878 diamonds (worth £2,1 million) displaced wool as the principal export of the Cape Colony. They were the chief reason for a boom in the South African economy in 1879-1881. New companies were floated for various purposes and banks were generous in granting credit. At the same time wool and ostrich feathers were fetching good prices. The First Boer War of 1880-1881 was good for business in the Cape because of expenditure by the British government. When the war ended depression descended, aggravated by drought and by a recession in the British economy. But it was diamonds that were largely blamed for the collapse of the boom. Investors lost confidence in diamond shares, and banks, which were widely held responsible for the speculation, reduced their credits.

South Africa was rescued from depression by the discovery of gold on the Witwatersrand in 1884. It profoundly affected the economy, reinforcing the earlier effect of the diamond rushes of 1867 and 1871. The ranks of the white population were swollen by immigrants, mostly from Britain. Large-scale foreign and domestic investment was stimulated; large numbers of Africans were recruited to work in the mines; employees had to be housed and provided with goods and services; investment in railways became more attractive; and a new market for agricultural produce was opened. The peculiar nature of this primary product gave South Africa an exceptionally secure income. The fixed price of gold saved the country from the fluctuations of revenue characteristic of other primary produce exporters. Gold very soon became the chief earner of foreign exchange and the main contributor to public revenue, and so the chief prop of the entire economy. By the early 1890s exports of diamonds were worth an annual average of £3,7 million, but the value of gold exports through the Cape Colony reached £4,0 million a year.

South Africa's gold was not alluvial, easy to win, but particles embedded in hard rock for the most part deep underground. Great difficulties of a technical nature had to be overcome. At first the outcrops of ore were exploited but it was not long before mining at great depths was called for, posing problems of ventilation and drainage; and it was necessary to provide transport, machinery and power and both expert and unskilled labour. However, the deposits were the richest in the world and the problems of exploitation were soon solved. The Macarthur-Forrest cyanide process permitted the economic extraction of the metal. Coal deposits were discovered within reach of the gold-mines in 1887. Little difficulty was experienced in mobilizing capital. By the end of 1887 two hundred or so companies had been formed. By 1888 forty-four mines were in operation, with a nominal capital of £6,8 million and a gold output worth a million pounds a year. Up until 1881 about half the capital for diamond-mining was subscribed in the Cape Colony and a good deal of the early capital requirements for gold came from within South Africa, including the diamond companies. But Rhodes, who used European finance for his struggle to gain control of the diamond industry, floated his gold-mining company, Gold Fields of South Africa Limited, in London.

Excessive optimism resulted in speculation and inevitably in a loss of confidence and a collapse of gold and land company shares on the London stock exchange. Gold shares worth £24,8 million in early 1889 fell to £9,4 million a year later. Land company shares worth £30,1 million in 1889 were worth £18,6 million in 1890. This led to a banking crisis in South Africa, causing the failure of many small businesses and a general recession in 1890. Gold-mining entered a critical phase. Far more capital was needed than at first realized, with a much longer gestation before profits – genuine, not speculative – could be made. More efficient management, with more rational organization, and a higher level of mining engineering had to be introduced. The industry turned increasingly to foreign investors.

Before the development of gold-mining in South Africa interest had been attracted to the gold deposits of the Gold Coast after the defeat of the Asante and the capture of Kumasi in 1873. A French company was floated in 1878 to prospect for gold at Tarkwa, where there were already numerous small mines being worked. English-based companies followed. As early as 1881 there were seven companies registered for gold-mining and prospecting. The problems, however, were formidable, especially transport. Heavy machinery had to be dismantled and carried by porters, who brought the gold back in armed caravans. Output was meagre and wastage among companies high. There was a strong speculative element in company flotation. The effect upon the economy of the Gold Coast was slight. Gold-mining was not an important influence in drawing Africa, apart from Southern Africa, into the world economy.

Mineral exploitation in the long run provided a powerful incentive to railway construction. Railways were built to serve mines and mines provided them with their most important source of income. South Africa exemplified this connection first. One of the difficulties in starting a railway was deciding its destination in the absence of inland towns, except in Egypt and the western Sudan. It was not until Kimberley and Johannesburg grew that the idea of railway building on a big scale could be entertained in South Africa. The first railway was begun as early as 1858, but as late as 1873 there were still only a hundred kilometres of line. In the 1880s nearly two thousand kilometres were built. With the opening of, first, the diamond-mines, then the gold-mines the construction of lines from the Cape ports of Cape Town, East London and Port Elizabeth and the Natal port of Durban into the interior began. The Cape railway reached Kimberley in 1885. The Transvaal then asked the Colony to extend its line, but, not realizing the impending economic transformation of the South African Republic, it refused. When it changed its mind, it was too late. The Boers refused permission for the extension to the Witwatersrand to be built and they revived instead an earlier agreement (1875) for a railway from Delagoa Bay, which had hitherto made no progress owing to lack of capital, but which had the great advantage for the Transvaal of reducing dependence upon British colonial ports and for the Portuguese of opening up a wider hinterland for Lourenço Marques. In 1889 the Moçambique line was completed as far as the Transvaal border and the remaining section entrusted to the Netherlands South African Railway Company.

In South Africa much traffic was taken by sea from Cape Town to the other Cape ports and Durban and beyond, and back, but there was a shortage of navigable inland waterways. In other more favoured parts of Africa goods could be moved readily into the interior by water. In West Africa the Niger delta and the Niger itself, together with the Benue, afforded hundreds of kilometres of navigable water, and on the River Congo and its tributaries, the Oubangui and the Kasai, it was also possible to navigate for more than three thousand kilometres. Other inland waterways provided rather fewer, but by no means unimportant, opportunities for vessels, in some cases for those of considerable draught. In West Africa there were the Gambia and Senegal rivers and in East Africa the Great Lakes of Victoria, Tanganyika, Albert and Nyasa. Since time immemorial these natural waterways had been used by canoes and sailing vessels. These boats, however, even the West African canoes, which could be fairly big, were small by European standards and slow. There were other disadvantages, too. Meandering courses, seasonal changes in water level, impassible stretches (in the case of the Congo the first three hundred kilometres of its lowest reaches) and shallow mouths all made the rivers less useful, while the lakes were all remote from the coast. Some of the first colonial railways were designed to supplement the inland water system, to circumvent the obstacles to river traffic. The first railway in West Africa (opened in 1885), running a distance of 260 km between St Louis, the port at the mouth of the River Senegal, and Dakar, was built by the French to replace the less than satisfactory river communications. The first railway in Central Africa was planned to connect Matadi on the coast of the Congo Free State with Stanley Pool, where the Congo became navigable. A survey was carried out in 1887 by the Compagnie du Congo pour le Commerce et l'Industrie, of which the moving spirit was the soldier-cum-entrepreneur Colonel (later General) Albert Thys, who was actively concerned in most of the companies formed to exploit the Congo. Construction was entrusted to the Compagnie du Chemin de Fer du Congo and begun in 1890.

Egypt was endowed with an excellent highway in the Nile, plied by river traffic for millennia. Like all natural waterways, however, it had its disadvantages in its cataracts and wandering course. The first Egyptian railway was built long before the colonial period, in 1856, between Alexandria and Cairo, a distance of 200 kilometres that could be covered in seven hours by train instead of forty-two by river steamer. Subsequently a network of branch lines was built in the Nile delta and connected with the Suez Canal at Ismailia and a line was constructed along the Canal by the Suez Canal Company (opened in 1891). Upper Egypt had a separate railway system. Its 350 kilometre line along the Nile reached Assiout from Cairo in 1874. The southern system also had a short line to the north of Cairo, built in 1872. This joined the existing Cairo-Alexandria railway eighty kilometres south of Alexandria.

Railways also came relatively early to North Africa. The first in Algeria were open to traffic in 1871, between Algiers and Oran and between Philippeville and Constantine. In Tunisia, before the annexation, a French company began a line which ran along the valley of the Medjorde to join with the Algerian system, with which a junction was effected in 1884, and Bizerta was linked with Tunis, from which a metre gauge line was very gradually, over the next thirty years, extended southwards. In 1886 Algiers was linked to Constantine and the western system reached Tlemcen in 1890. The principal Algerian line ran parallel to the coast with branch lines to the principal ports. Railway construction in the Atlas range presented problems. Much construction work had to be carried out and traffic was slowed by steep gradients and sharp bends.

Most railways had some military or administrative purpose and in some cases this was the overriding consideration. In Senegal a railway was begun in 1881 to link Kayes on the River Senegal to Koulikoro on the Upper Niger primarily for the movement of troops to the interior of the western Sudan. The eradication of the slave trade and slavery was certainly one motive. The value of railways for that purpose was recognized by the Brussels Conference of 1889. They would not only promote settled conditions, but would also reduce the need for porters, who were so often slaves, and encourage the substitution of legitimate commerce for slaving. But frequently railways had more to do with empire-building for its own sake. When the French administrators Louis Faidherbe and Louis Brière de l'Isle conceived in the 1870s the ambition to link Senegal with Algeria in a great sweep of French-ruled territory, the railway was to provide the link. In the event, there was no immediate result as far as railway construction was concerned. A similarly ambitious project was the railway which was started in Luanda in 1886. It was called the Grand Trans-African Railway, indicating that at least one motive for its construction was the establishment of Portuguese rule from the Atlantic to the Indian Ocean, joining Angola and Moçambique. Despite its name it never got beyond about 450 kilometres inland. More modest in aim was the first track laid in the Egyptian Sudan. It was designed to facilitate the movement of troops from Wadi Halfa southwards after the Mahdist revolt and was put down (in 1884-1885) and operated by the Anglo-Egyptian army. When the British decided not to proceed with the suppression of the rebellion, the railway was abandoned to the Mahdists until the re-conquest began in 1896. Another Sudanese line, begun in 1885, in the early stages of the Mahdist rebellion and planned to run from Suakin on the Red Sea coast to Berber, south of the 5th cataract of the Nile, was abandoned amidst Mahdist attacks and excessive haste and disorganization.

Before the development of the motor vehicle railways were the most efficient form of overland transport and it was not until after the First World War that a great deal was done to improve the road network. However, a beginning was made. In Egypt, for example, in the 1890s steps were taken to improve rural roads. Algeria, in contrast, was precocious in its road building. By as early as 1860 there was an extensive road system, designed primarily for the movement of troops. In South Africa road construction programmes were implemented sporadically from early in the 19th century, and by 1880 Cape Colony was comparatively well-off. It was the beginning of gold-mining and the increase of traffic with the Witwatersrand that was the stimulus for development in Natal. The Transvaal and Orange Free State were much slower in road building. Like railways, roads were expensive to build and much of the country was too backward economically to need them.

Of an importance comparable with that of railways was the introduction of the steamship and telegraph. Steamships could guarantee
regularity and, as their engines grew in efficiency, carry a great deal more
than sailing ships. It was only very slowly, however, that the sailing ship
was superseded because it too increased in size with the introduction of the
iron hull, and improvements were made in design and handling. It had
one great advantage over the steamship: it had no fuel costs and problems
of bunkering.

The sailing ship could hold its own chiefly on long hauls transporting
cheap bulky cargoes where low freight rates were of greater importance
than the speed or regularity offered by steam. In the Mediterranean the
steamship made an early successful appearance on the short runs between
European and African and Near Eastern ports. As early as the 1830s the
British companies P and O and the Oriental Steamship Company, the
French company, Messageries, and the Austrian company, Lloyd, were all
running regular services to the eastern Mediterranean, including Alexandria. Steamships also started operating in the 1830s between Toulon and
Algiers and steam services were rapidly extended from various European
Mediterranean ports and London to different places in Algeria, Tunisia
and Morocco, and also from one point in North Africa to another
(particularly valuable, given the importance of coastwise trade), to give a
very comprehensive service by the 1860s. By 1890 well over a million tons
of shipping were entering Alexandria and Algiers a year.

The steamship was ideal for mail and for passengers who wanted speed
and regularity, not only those bound for Mediterranean ports, but also
those on their way to India and the East, since these could travel overland
to Suez and catch there the British India Steam Navigation Company's
ships. With the opening of the Suez Canal in 1869, which like the Red Sea,
could more readily be navigated by steamships, direct voyages became
possible from Europe to India and beyond. Soon after the opening of the
Canal the British India Company began a monthly mail service to
Zanzibar and in 1890 the Deutsche Ost-Afrika-Linie inaugurated a service
between Hamburg and German East Africa. The tonnage using the Canal
(four-fifths of it British) came to exceed that passing round the Cape in the
course of the 1880s. It is doubtful whether Egypt gained much from the
Canal's success, however, once the khedive's shares passed into the hands
of the British government in 1875. What is more, the overland route lost its
importance and ceased to yield any income. Moreover the ships sailing the
Mediterranean, as indeed those serving the coasts of sub-Saharan Africa,
were largely European. At that time only Europe possessed the technical
and organizational ability and capital to run ocean-going shipping.

For the West African routes the African Steamship Company was formed in 1851 and in 1868 the British and African Steam Navigation Company, both of Liverpool. They called at the Gambia; Freetown, which was a coaling station and the only safe and convenient harbour for several hundred kilometres along the coast; Gold Coast, where goods and passengers had to be landed in surf boats; and Lagos, which had a good harbour. By the mid-1880s well over a million tons of British shipping visited West Africa annually, a tenfold increase in twenty years. French ships plied between Bordeaux and Dakar and the Gambia; German between Hamburg and the Gold Coast and Lagos. The shortage of good harbours restricted the number of ports of call. Some harbours were improved by government, particularly in North Africa (e.g. Algiers, Oran, Tunis and Bizerta) and Egypt (Alexandria and Suez, both greatly improved before the British occupation) and its southern neighbour (Port Sudan, though not until 1906), and to a lesser extent elsewhere (e.g. Dakar and Cape Town). The problem of harbours did not affect the shallow-draught steamboats which came into increasing use along the navigable stretches of the rivers, such as the Cuanza in Angola between Luanda and Dondo, a distance of 320 kilometres, plied by river steamers from 1869 until they were superseded by the railway. In some cases small steamships were dismantled, sent into the interior and put together on navigable stretches of river and on lakes, such as Nyasa and Victoria.

The combined effects of larger vessels and increasing competition among shipping companies were to push down freight rates markedly. Exceptions to this were the services between Algeria and France, reserved to French ships from 1889, and services to Angola, effectively reserved to Portuguese ships by government protection. Two companies subsidized by the government operated ships between Portugal and its colonies, Unias Mercantil and Empresa Nacional de Navegação. Subsidies were available elsewhere chiefly in the form of mail contracts provided by imperial governments. But competition was fierce and cartels, known as shipping conferences, were formed to mitigate it. A conference among the shipping lines serving South Africa was formed in 1883, and in 1886 it introduced the system of deferred rebates, which entitled the shipper to a delayed refund of part of the freight charges provided he did not make use of non-conference ships in the interval, a method of constrained loyalty unpopular among South African merchants. There were several British companies running a service to South African ports, the principal ones being the Union Steam Ship Company, which had held the Cape mail contract since 1857, and the newer Castle line. In 1881 the Clan Line, which traded to India via Suez, also started a direct service to South Africa. These companies took over much of the South African coastwise trade as well as the external trade.

Already by 1880 Africa, or at least its ports, had been drawn into the international telegraph network. The techniques of submarine telegraph were perfected in the 1860s and Algeria was connected with France as early as 1861, and in 1870 Egypt with India. A cable was laid along the east coast of Africa in 1879, connnecting Aden, Zanzibar and Durban. Cape Town, which already had a line to Kimberley since 1876, was linked to Europe via West Africa in 1886. The Cape Verde Islands became important as a telegraph cable station (and also as a bunkering station). They had little other significance. Both east and west coast cables were operated by private companies subsidized by the British government – the Eastern and South Africa Telegraph Company (east coast) and the Africa Direct Telegraph Company (west coast). The internal telegraph system was developed in West Africa in the course of the 1890s. Like the railway, the telegraph had as much military and administrative significance as economic. A line was laid between Suez and Suakin in 1882 for political reasons. However, the rapid transmission of commercial orders and information, such as news of fluctuations in international prices, and even money was of great economic importance. African exports and imports were affected, either stimulated or depressed. The tramp steamer was assisted in its irregular passage by the receipt of instructions by telegraph and direct connection was made between buyer and seller.

Railway construction, mining and white agriculture set up a demand for labour. As European towns grew, domestic servants, municipal workers and general labourers in commerce and industry were also required. Without cheap labour the gold-mines of South Africa could not have functioned and commercial agriculture could not have survived. The attraction of European employment for native workers varied widely according to conditions of work and pay. The diamond-mines of Kimberley were a magnet to labour resident several hundred kilometres away during the early years, but were less attractive when the workers were housed in compounds under strict surveillance to prevent theft. White farm-work was not popular. In black Africa men who offered their labour were interested mostly in temporary employment. Although few were insulated from the money economy, not many were wholly dependent upon a cash income. Most African wage earners were migrant labourers who, after a spell of work in the monetary sector, returned to their villages, where they engaged in subsistence agriculture. Certainly most unskilled workers fell into that category. A view that commanded widespread support among employers was that all migrants were target workers with fixed targets and that therefore the supply of labour varied inversely with the size of the wage paid. The target worker had some particular objective in view, e.g. to pay taxes, to make a marriage payment, or to make a particular purchase. The money required to meet that objective was the worker's target. Once the target was reached, the worker preferred his leisure, so that the length of time he was prepared to work depended upon how quickly he could earn what he wanted to save. If he could earn enough from the sale of his agricultural produce, he would not work for wages at all. If he did enter wage employment, the higher his wages, the sooner he would reach his target and stop working. From this it was argued that the higher the wages that were paid, the smaller the labour supply would be. From the point of view of employers it was better to pay low wages in order to ensure an adequate supply of labour.

The whole argument had a core of truth. Migrant workers did tend to be target workers, and it is possible that in the early days of contact between Europeans and Africans higher wages did adversely affect the labour supply, because wage-labour was so repugnant, wants were so rudimentary and demand so inelastic that higher wages had the effect of reducing the period spent in employment. If, however, this was once true, it soon ceased to be so, and generally speaking the shortage of labour resulted from low wages and poor conditions rather than from quixotically generous wages.

One reason for the impermanence of much of the African labour force was the persistence of communal land holding. Even if the subsistence farmer favoured selling his land and taking up permanent paid employment, he could not do so in the absence of individual ownership. It was not possible to sell land, only resign rights in it, and few were willing to do that. Land was a means of security, while paid employment was not only alien but also precarious. As long as there was little land hunger, pressure of population on land would not drive people out in search of wage employment. Apart from local shortages over most of Africa, land was abundant, though the quality was often poor. Rights in land were very widespread and there was reluctance to sever connections with the countryside. Even in Europe in the 19th century, without communal land rights, the urban working class maintained a link with the land. In Africa the hold of the land upon people was generally very strong indeed and wage labour was regarded as something temporary. Therefore the amount of labour available tended to be seasonal, fluctuating according to the demands of agriculture. Wage labour was regarded as a supplement to the proceeds of farming and was readily abandoned. Those workers who were not target workers were seasonal, dividing their time between town and country. Many Africans spent years in towns only to retire eventually to the country. Even permanent urban workers might have farms. The typical African wage earner was a temporary sojourner in town or a seasonal migrant. Most migrants travelled from a distance. People living near centres of employment could usually earn what cash they wanted by growing food for towns or export crops.

European employers complained constantly of the low quality of black labour, its inefficiency and low productivity. They alleged that African workers needed constant supervision because of the lack of interest they displayed in their work. Although there was substance in the complaint, since migrant workers were likely to be inefficient, especially target workers who made only one expedition into the modern sector of the economy and were not worth training, low wages had probably as much to do with the inferior quality of labour as well as its inadequate supply. There was a vicious circle. Labour was unproductive because wages were low, wages low because labour inferior. There was also a lack of understanding between labour and management, the result of racial differences. Added to this was the difficulty of communication and the disincentive of constant disparagement. Management did not understand the reasons for poor performance and its policies tended to perpetuate the evils. The widespread belief in the inherent inferiority of Africans inhibited experimentation in selection and training. There were climatic restraints upon effort, such as high humidity, compounded by poor health and inadequate food. In the towns health was a particularly serious problem because accommodation tended to be bad and overcrowded.

That Africans were not reluctant to work or indifferent to its rewards is amply demonstrated by the enormous growth of the production of export crops in West Africa. What they did object to was unskilled work for colonial governments or expatriate employers. They saw no virtue in work for its own sake and associated unskilled manual work with slavery. Africans, accustomed to the seasonal and customary rhythm of subsistence agriculture, had no experience of the discipline of continuous and regular work under the supervision of men of no traditional authority, nor of wage labour outside the family and the community. In the early colonial period there was distaste for the long absences from home that working for Europeans entailed. Money and European goods (even if they could be supplied when there was only a rudimentary system of distribution) were often unfamiliar, or at least the taste for them was very quickly sated. In contrast leisure, or idleness as it seemed to European observers, was highly valued.

At this period the problem of finding suitable labour for European enterprise was largely confined to South Africa, where development came earlier than in tropical Africa. The quality and permanence of labour was not of great moment. Unskilled labour employed for relatively short periods met the needs of the time. The problem was getting a sufficient supply even of that, especially for mining and white agriculture. To begin with diamond-mining was not, it is true, a big employer of labour. The typical unit of production was a single white prospector, colonial born or

immigrant, working alongside a black labourer or so. With the concentration of ownership the independent small white entrepreneur disappeared and the demand for black labour grew, though there remained a
place for the white man in the diamond industry as an artisan or
supervisor. The gold industry was conducted almost from the beginning
far beyond the capacity of the small prospector, on a large scale, using
expensive equipment and requiring a huge amount of black labour and a
considerable number of white employees.

Gold-mining was unattractive to blacks because of the conditions of
work and poor wages, and that was true also of commercial agriculture.
Wages were low partly because profits did not permit paying higher wages
and partly because of the conventional view about target workers. Black
cultivators preferred to subsist on tribal land or, as squatters, on state or
white-owned private land, meeting their needs for cash in more congenial
ways than labour in mine or on white farm, by selling to the market or by
transport-riding. The latter came to an end with the completion of the
railways, and in production for the market, black farmers were unable to
complete on equal terms with white. In the end Africans were forced into
the rôle of unskilled contract labourers. In the meantime, in the absence of
an adequate supply of local labour, employers and governments sometimes
turned to external sources. British and Belgian labourers were brought to
South Africa to work on the railways, but white labour was expensive and
had to be handled more tactfully than black. The Natal sugar planters
brought contract workers from India, with the colonial government
contributing to the costs. The practice began in 1859, was interrupted in
1866 as the demand for labour fell, and started again in 1874, continuing
until 1911, when the Indian government prohibited further contracts.
Most of the immigrants chose to remain in Natal after the expiry of their
contracts, seeking work in agriculture (including sugar planting) and
commerce and a wide variety of other employment. A substantial proportion of the labour force in the coal mines was drawn from the Indian
population.

In some respects the labour situation in French North Africa was similar
to that in South Africa. There was a demand for labour by European
enterprise and a racially divided working class. In South Africa the white
working class was composed of English-speaking immigrants, many of
them with skills, and Afrikaans-speaking emigrants from the soil; in French
North Africa it was made up mostly of foreign settlers, Maltese, Italians
and Spaniards. In both cases there was a degree of competition for work
between settlers and natives. There the similarity ended. In North Africa
there was no great employer like the gold-mines. The chief employer was
settler farming and North Africa did not experience the same labour

shortage characteristic of South Africa. Another factor was that in North Africa the white working class expected the same protection of labour legislation as that enjoyed by workers in France, of which Algeria was in some respects an integral part, especially in the period of *rattachement*. The practice thus arose of applying French labour laws to Algeria either immediately or after some delay. Thus as early as 1884 a law on trade unions covered Algeria as well as metropolitan France. The French government was faced with a certain moral dilemma, whether to treat native workers in the same way as white ones, a situation little to taste of European employers. To begin with, however, the problem hardly arose because most native wage labour was employed on farms and fell outside the scope of labour legislation.

The protection of native labour had a low priority in the colonies in the 19th century. Colonial governments saw as their task the provision, within the limits of their resources of money and manpower, of the conditions that facilitated economic enterprise, so that, as far as possible, each colony should pay its own way. Such a limited aim might involve injustice and hardship for the indigenous population – especially forced labour and the seizure of land – but, on the other hand, could bring benefits. On the credit side were the abolition of the slave trade and inter-tribal warfare, the establishment of usually efficient and incorruptible and increasingly paternalistic government, the construction of railways, roads and harbours, and the beginning of health, educational and agricultural services.

Such innovations made possible an increased life expectancy, the spread of literacy and the expansion of agricultural production, mining and trade, by no means all carried out by expatriates, and opened a wide range of new occupations and opportunities for talent. Nevertheless, such advantages as the colonized derived were, in the early colonial period at all events, the by-product of colonial policy. The authorities were much more sensitive to expatriate interests in the development of urban facilities, railways and roads. They hoped that European enterprise and, in areas suitable for white settlement, European immigrants would be enticed to Africa, so that a market for manufactured goods would grow up and the colonies would be economically viable. Metropolitan governments did not expect to subsidize their colonies, though there was sometimes a departure from that unwritten rule with varying degrees of generosity. Subsidies to mail services were one such exception. A cheap and efficient postal service had strategic and commercial advantage for the imperial power and in any event was far from financially burdensome. At the end of the nineteenth century Britain was spending only about £40 000 a year on steamer services throughout the entire colonial empire. Total British expenditure on the dependent empire as a whole came to rather less than £100 000 in

1879–1880. Although this was rising and more than doubled during the decade, it amounted to very little per capita. Colonial governments had to act within the limits of exiguous local resources.

In the early colonial period the most expensive item of colonial expenditure was the construction of railways. Many were built directly by government. In South Africa this was the case in Cape Colony and Natal, and the Transvaal government had a substantial financial stake in the Netherlands South African Railway and considerable powers of control. Private enterprise was reluctant to sink capital into such risky and slowly maturing undertakings without generous inducements. The Portuguese Grand Trans-Africa Railway was guaranteed a minimum gross revenue per kilometre, a formula which made it worthwhile to make the line follow a roundabout route and gave no encouragement to look for freight. The government of the Congo Free State was compelled to promise lavish, ill-defined land grants in 1886 to the Compagnie du Congo pour le Commerce et l'Industrie for the Matadi-Stanley Pool line. The company was to recover its investment from both railway revenue and the exploitation of its land. The form that payment to the company was to take illustrated the financial embarrassment of the Congo Free State. Leopold's territorial ambitions, which extended to the Upper Nile, and the costs of administration, pacification and a war against the Arabs of the Upper Congo were a heavy burden upon his personal fortune. The only sources of local revenue were taxes on exports, particularly ivory and rubber, and state commercial enterprise, and the profits of trade and export taxes were far from enough to cover the king's expenditure. Import duties, which in the situation of the time were by far the most promising source of tax revenue, were prohibited by the General Act of the Conference of Berlin. Leopold was able to achieve some relief from the 10 per cent import duty allowed by the Brussels Act of 1890. In the same year he persuaded the Belgian parliament to make a ten year, interest free, loan of 25 million francs to the Congo Free State, in return for which he made a will bequeathing the territory to the nation. Soon afterwards the financial situation began to improve as the profits from state trade and exploitation grew.

In Algeria the native inhabitants to a considerable degree paid for their own subjugation. After the insurrection of 1871 the Berber Kabyles were given eight years to pay the enormous sum of over 36 million francs. More money (nearly 11 million francs) came from the repurchase by its original owners of land confiscated as a reprisal but not wanted for European settlement. It took nearly twenty years to pay off these great debts, impoverishing the three-quarters of a million people implicated in the revolt. These extraordinary payments were quite apart from the regular taxation paid by native Algerians, who were liable both to the traditional taxes and to the taxes imposed by the authorities on settlers and natives alike. The former were complicated, inequitable and prone to corrupt assessment, falling upon harvests, lands and beasts, but also including the obligation (*prestation*) of furnishing labour and the labour of camels and oxen, both commutable to a money tax. The latter were both direct (e.g. property taxes) and indirect (e.g. customs). Less than a fair share of the contribution by Muslims to the public revenues was disbursed on services for them. Despite, however, the financial burden imposed on the natives, Algeria still did not pay its way. After the *rattachement* of 1881 the Algerian budget (apart from the three departmental budgets) was included in the general French budget. After 1882 it was the practice to list revenue raised and sums disbursed in Algeria in an annex to the annual French budget and this showed that more was spent there than collected.

In South Africa hut taxes went back to 1875 in Natal and 1884 in Cape Colony. Africans also contributed indirectly to revenue through the taxes imposed on imports. Although their tax burden was disproportionate to their means and to the public services they received in return, their share of taxation was small in total. The chief sources of government revenue were customs duties, various legal charges, quit-rent and, after 1886, profits from the railway. Diamonds made a big difference to the Cape. During the first decade of mining revenue quadrupled because of increased imports, legal and commercial transactions, land transfers and the sale and lease of crown land. In the 1880s revenue ran at well over £2 million a year. In comparison Natal, with a revenue of £0,7 million by the end of the decade, was poor. The Boer Republics were still poorer, but of course the Transvaal Republic became much richer as a result of gold production.

An early task of colonial government was to establish as far as possible uniformity in the currency system. Sterling circulated in the British colonies of South Africa and in the Transvaal during the British occupation of 1877-1881. When the Transvaal Republic was restored in 1881 it inherited a huge public debt and a prohibition on the issue of paper money by the terms of the Pretoria and London Conventions of 1881 and 1884. From this predicament it was rescued by the development of the gold-mining industry, which gave the government plenty of gold for a trustworthy currency. In West Africa there was a mixture of foreign coins and local commodity currencies in use and the rate of exchange between them varied over time and space. In the 1880s the British authorities attempted to introduce order by restricting the variety of coins taken as legal tender and fixing the rate of exchange between acceptable foreign coins and sterling and between sterling and cowries, manillas and other local currencies. Sterling coins, however, were treated with some suspicion

by the more conservative traders in palm produce, who preferred the old
semi-bartering arrangements, and were not much use for local petty trade
because of their relatively high value, and barter was still the principal
form of trade in West Africa until after 1900. In Egypt in 1885 a new
currency of gold, silver and copper coins was issued. The French napoleon,
the pound sterling and the Turkish pound were also recognized as legal
tender, but in practice the British pound came to predominate, driving out
of circulation not only the French and Turkish coins, but even the
Egyptian pound itself.

Algeria had its own currency, issued by the Bank of Algeria (1851),
which also became the bank of issue for Tunisia in 1904. Its francs were
convertible at par to metropolitan francs. From 1878 the French Treasury
maintained a current account at the Bank of Algeria at sufficient level to
meet all demands for French francs. The Bank also acted as a commercial
bank. In the 1880s it pursued a policy of easy credit to European farmers,
most of whom were planting vines with blithe optimism. Short-term bills
were repeatedly renewed until, in the end, the Bank was compelled to
foreclose; so that much of its capital was immobilized. Another source of
credit for Algerian farmers was the Land and Agricultural Bank of Algeria
(Crédit foncier et agricole d'Algérie), founded in 1880, later renamed the
Land and Agricultural Bank of Algeria and Tunisia. It lacked state
authorization, but in practice was closely linked to the Land Bank of
France, which supplied it with funds for loans. Loans were also made
directly by the French Land Bank itself. Like all land banks these
institutions made mortgage loans, i.e. advanced money on the security of
land.

Apart from Algeria, Egypt and South Africa, European-style banking
had scarcely begun. In South Africa most of the banking business was
taken over by British-based banks, the so-called imperial banks, which
expanded at the expense of the locally based, so-called colonial banks. Of
the imperial banks, the Standard Bank had been active in the Cape
Colony since the 1860s, though it had been unsuccessful in extending its
operations to the Boer republics. The Orange Free State had its own
national bank, the National Bank of the Orange Free State, chartered in
1877. In Egypt, as in South Africa, banks with European connections went
back to the middle years of the century. One of the earliest was the Bank of
Egypt, founded by a Greek in 1855 and backed by British interests. This
soon became deeply involved in government finance. The Anglo-Egyptian
Bank was founded in 1864. Although it raised its capital in London and
enjoyed the support of British interests, the initiative came from Europeans
resident in Egypt. Its original purpose was to finance trade, especially in
cotton, but it found greater profits in the floating of public loans and

providing the government with short-term credit. Elsewhere there was a French bank operating in West Africa, the Banque du Sénégal, founded in 1854, while the Portuguese Banco Nacional Ultramarimo, founded in 1864, had a branch at Luanda.

Widely recognized and convertible currencies and the banks which issued paper money and advanced credit were features of economic modernization that was still largely restricted to the periphery of the African continent. Railways, modern administration and the international economy had scarcely begun to penetrate the interior. In the 1880s Europe declared its intention to divide Africa up, tried to justify the morality of partition and defined the rules that were to govern the distribution of territory. Conquests had still to be completed and colonial government to be enforced.

CHAPTER II

1880-1900 (CONQUEST)

In the 1890s the European partition of tropical Africa was more or less completed. An Anglo-French Convention settled spheres of influence in West Africa in 1890, an agreement which put Sokoto, whose sultan had once dominated the Fulani emirates of the western Sudan, in the orbit of the Royal Niger Company, and the northern and eastern boundaries of Sierra Leone were settled between Britain and France in 1895. The 1890 Convention was not implemented without friction, but the frontier was finally fixed between Nigeria and Dahomey in the Convention of 1898. British and French subjects were guaranteed equal treatment in the navigation of the Niger, trade and taxation. In East Africa agreements were made between Britain and Portugal (1891), Britain and Italy (1891), Britain and the Congo Free State (1894) and Germany and Portugal (1894) to fix boundaries. In 1894 an understanding was reached between France and Leopold II on the Congo frontier.

In East Africa the British and Germans asserted their control over the enormous territories to which they laid claim. This was not achieved without the resistance of their inhabitants. In 1897 the British had to contend with an insurrection in Buganda, subsequently incorporated into Uganda, and at the end of the decade hundreds of Africans lost their lives in a protest against German taxation. Madagascar had to be more thoroughly conquered and in 1896 it was annexed by France. In 1899 an Anglo-Egyptian Condominium was set up in the Sudan after its reconquest from the Dervishes and a dispute between representatives of Britain and France – the Fashoda incident – that was settled in Britain's favour, putting an end to French ambitions of trans-continental dominion. The Italians were less fortunate. Their attempt to annex Ethiopa ended in failure at Adowa in 1896, or rather was postponed for forty years. In West Africa, the French maintained the momentum of their penetration of the interior, taking Timbuktu in 1893 and completing their conquest of Dahomey the same year. They reached Lake Chad in 1900. In the Gold Coast effective British control over the interior was secured by the establishment of a protectorate over Asante in 1896, and in the 1890s the Royal Niger Company made effective its claims over the Fulani emirates and in Yorubaland.

So-called pacification had its effect upon population. In Madagascar it declined rapidly during the long period of French military operations. The population of the Anglo-Egyptian Sudan suffered a setback in the closing decades of the century as a result of the Mahdi's revolt and the subsequent reconquest of the territory. There is some evidence that in East Africa it was not until after the First World War that the earlier population decline was arrested and reversed. Apart from casualties in fighting, in the closing years of the century there were some severe famines, epidemics and epizootics. Some of the diseases were new to Africa, introduced from Europe, e.g. influenza and measles; others were endemic only to parts of Africa, notably sleeping sickness, but spread by intruding strangers. Particularly severe afflictions were the sleeping sickness epidemic of the turn of the century, which swept away thousands of people, and the rinderpest outbreak which destroyed innumerable cattle in the early 1890s. In the less turbulent regions of Africa, however, there was evidence of population growth.

Statistics of population are sparse outside Egypt, French North Africa and South Africa. In those countries the population was undoubtedly growing from the late 19th century, even sooner. The evidence seems to suggest that the population of Algeria, which, after declining through colonial warfare, plagues and famines, was fast recovering by the middle of the century, suffered a severe setback as a result of a famine in 1867 and the revolt of 1871, but by the census of 1882 had already passed its 1860 level and thereafter there was rapid growth, particularly in the early years of this century. The Tunisian population seems to have started to grow again in the 1860s. The growth rate, due partly to European immigration, was in the order of 1 per cent a year until well into this century. Libya and Morocco, conquered later, had a rather different experience. In Egypt, where there was no prolonged process of conquest and famine less likely than in areas dependent upon rainfall for cultivation, the population was growing throughout the 19th century (though subject to periodic sharp contractions through plague and cholera attacks, the latter continuing with decreasing virulence until the end of the century), attaining a 1,5 per cent annual growth rate in the later 19th century. In South Africa the population of the Cape of Good Hope increased from 0,7 million in 1875 to 1,5 million in 1891 (0,3 million whites), that of Natal from 0,4 million in 1881 to 0,5 million in 1891 (0,04 million whites), that of the Transvaal from 0,8 million in 1880 (0,4 million whites) to 1,2 million in 1904 (0,2 million whites) and that of the Orange Free State from 0,4 million in 1880 to 0,5 million in 1891 (0,04 million whites).

The South African population was also becoming more urban. By 1890 37 per cent of the white population was living in towns. Johannesburg was growing particularly rapidly. Between 1890 and 1896 the white population rose from 13 to 39 thousand and the total population of the town to 61 000.

The same trend was to be seen in Algeria, with its growing towns of Algiers and Oran. Where exceptional urban growth occurred it was largely due to an influx of foreigners or the establishment of new towns by European settlers. Generally speaking there was no appreciable drift from country to town and urban population grew at much the same rate as total population.

Changes occurred in the administration of some of the colonies. The British Colonial Office took over the running of the Niger Coast Protectorate from the Foreign Office in 1899 and in 1900 the territories of the Royal Niger Company. In 1895 the eight French colonies in West Africa – Senegal, Soudan, Guinea, Ivory Coast, Dahomey, Mauritania, Niger and Upper Volta – were grouped together under the Governor of Senegal as French West Africa (L'Afrique occidentale française, AOF). In 1891 the French parliament, hitherto apathetic, began to feel uneasiness about the treatment of the Muslim population in Algeria. Its attention was drawn to the colony by the settler agitation in support of a demand for financial autonomy, a departure from the earlier insistence upon assimilation. A senatorial commission of inquiry was appointed and Jules Cambon was appointed governor-general with instructions to resist settler pressure. Jules Ferry, who led the senatorial team that pursued its investigation on the spot, came out in favour of decentralization with the appointment of a governor with strong powers. This would end the manipulation of the metropolitan legislature by the settler representatives able to capture important positions in government departments and parliamentary committees concerned with Algerian administration and use their votes to exert an influence quite disproportionate to their numbers. In 1896 administration was transferred from Paris to Algiers (dérattachement). However, Ferry's death in 1893, the loss of public interest and colonial obstruction deprived the reform movement of its impetus. Although the policy of assimilation was not resumed, the French government from 1898 followed the path of appeasement, and in 1900 Algeria was granted fiscal autonomy. In theory the separation of the Algerian budget was supposed to bring home to the colonist that expenditure was dependent upon revenue and to require the territory to borrow in its own name money for development projects. But military expenses remained the responsibility of the French government and there were various other expenses (e.g. certain civil service pensions) that fell to the metropolitan government, individually small but in total not inconsiderable. In return a small fraction of Algerian revenue was appropriated by the French government. The Algerian budget was drawn up by the governor's council, chosen by the largely settler electorate.

The number of new settlers in Algeria continued to decline. Between 1891 and 1900 fewer than a hundred villages were established or enlarged, compared with 107 in the preceding decade and over 250 in the period 1871–1880. In the 1890s 120 000 hectares were allotted to settlements. The drift of French immigrants from the land went on still, their farms falling into the hands, for the most part, of Algerian-born Europeans but also into those of foreigners. Some settler farms were sold to relatively well-to-do native Algerians, but more Muslim land was bought by Europeans than the other way round, and in 1898 a commission for the protection of native landownership was set up to moderate the rate at which native land was being alienated, but it had little result. The European rural population increased in size, but only slowly, standing at some 210 000 in 1901 (out of a total European population of half a million), compared with a little fewer than 200 000 ten years earlier. Europeans, enjoying a far higher standard of living than Muslims, occupied most of the professional and skilled jobs in administration, manufacturing, commerce and the service industries.

Tunisia was attracting increasing numbers of immigrants. The scale of settlement was not so great as in Algeria, but, whereas immigration into Algeria ceased after 1900, it continued into Tunisia until 1920. Most Europeans in Tunisia lived in the towns, dominant in industry, commerce and finance. The minority living on the land, went in for olives, wheat and wine.

Most of the European immigrants into Tunisia were Italians, who preferred the French territories of North Africa to Italy's own colony of Eritrea. Yet, as the Eritrean highlands appeared to be suitable for white settlement, thinly populated and temperate in climate, a scheme for state-supported small-scale peasant agriculture designed to help solve the problem of peasant landlessness in Italy was attempted. From 1893 a few hundred families were settled on 20–25 hectare plots, with equipment and cattle, which they were supposed to pay for gradually, and the promise of title to the land after five years if they cultivated it. The project was largely a failure. After ten years of colonization there were barely more than a hundred colonists left, living in fear from the native inhabitants. The Eritrean plateau was not in fact sparsely populated but only temporarily vacated during a period of disturbance, and the Eritreans started to return to their lands. The only market for agricultural produce was Massawa on the coast, with which communications were primitive.

In a much more important region of European colonization, South Africa, the frontier of white settlement was extended across the Limpopo. In 1890 the pioneer column of the British South Africa Company invaded Mashonaland, which, together with Matabeleland, was renamed Southern Rhodesia, and new white towns grew up, notably Salisbury and Bulawayo. In 1891 the Company's charter was extended to cover the territory which came to be Northern Rhodesia, and it undertook to subsidize temporarily the administration of Nyasaland, which had been put under British protection in 1889.

In East Africa the German East Africa Company relinquished its administrative functions to the German government, receiving compensation in the form of money, land, mineral rights and the right to establish a bank of issue. The Company lacked the capital to develop the territory and the means to gain effective control of the interior and administer it properly. It made little headway in commerce, unable to compete with the German trading firms of Zanzibar. The British East Africa Company was similarly ineffective and short of funds. It surrendered its charter in 1895. The Royal Niger Company also lost its charter in 1900, but it retained in effect its commercial monopoly, and it was in a strong financial position because it received generous compensation for its earlier administrative expenses. New competition was difficult to establish because the Company controlled the existing trading centres. The new government would permit only the leasing of land and rents were high.

New chartered companies came into being. The Compagnie du Katanga was chartered in 1891 to forestall a possible British occupation of Katanga, where a geological survey by the Société générale du Belgique had revealed the existence of a very rich belt of copper, 350 km long and 25 km wide, stretching beyond the frontier of the Congo Free State southwards into Northern Rhodesia. As payment for its administration of the territory, it was granted one-third of all the public land in freehold (some 15 million hectares), together with a ninety-nine year right to exploit minerals. A subsidiary company, the Compagnie du Lomami, was given a large tract on the Lomami river in 1896. In 1900 administration of Katanga was taken from the Compagnie du Katanga and handed over to a Comité spécial composed of four representatives of the Congo Free State and two of the Compagnie. The Comité's revenues were divided between state and Compagnie, in the ratio of two-thirds to one-third.

In Moçambique two companies were chartered in 1891, the Moçambique Company and the Nyassa Company. The British South Africa Company was very influential in northern Moçambique, but the British government, for diplomatic reasons, intervened to thwart an attempt by associates of the Company to take over the Moçambique Company. The two Portuguese companies administered large territories and their obligations included the promotion of European settlement on the land, and the Nyassa Company had to build a railway to Lake Nyasa, in both of which objectives little was achieved. Of the two, the Moçambique Company was the more profitable and longer lasting, reaping advantage from the transit traffic to Southern Rhodesia. In Angola the Moçamedes

Company (1894) exercised similar administrative powers over a wide area without contributing much to its development.

In the 1890s a new type of private enterprise emerged, the concessionary company, which paid for the privilege of exploiting lands which had been appropriated by the colonial state. At first Leopold II attempted to exclude private interests and operate a personal monopoly. In 1891 the Congo Free State reserved to itself the collection and sale of rubber and ivory, which, however, aroused so much protest from private interests, Belgian and foreign, that the state modified its claims, and the monopoly was confined to a specified (but still very extensive) zone. Exploitation of that zone was conceded to the Société Anversoise du Commerce du Congo and to the Anglo-Belgian India Rubber and Exploration Company (ABIR). Each paid the state an initial lump sum plus a tax on the forest products which they collected, rubber, copal and ivory. In 1896 a special area, the Domaine Privé, was set aside for exploitation by the state itself and in 1901 the thirteen companies operating in the free trade region were combined into another concession company, the Compagnie du Kasai. Leopold II held 50 per cent of the capital and the company had virtually the exclusive right to buy rubber in the Kasai basin. An increasingly restrictive interpretation was made of the rights of natives to land, confining them to the land they were actually occupying and cultivating, and the sale of rubber to anyone except the state or the concession companies was made a criminal offence. The latter made very large profits and exports increased rapidly. Ivory continued to be of great significance, reaching a peak of 67,8 per cent of the total value of exports in 1892, but falling steeply after 1895 to only 11 per cent in 1900.

In the French occupied territories the problem of budgetary deficits which had to be underwritten by the metropolitan government induced it to grant similar concessions to private companies operating in its territories. The first grants were made in 1893, carving out immense fiefs in French Congo and Ivory Coast, permitting the exclusive exploitation of forests for periods of up to thirty years without payment to the French state. There were public protests and the concessions were withdrawn in 1895-1896, but the concessionaires had to be compensated with substantial estates in freehold (up to a third of a million hectares for each) and in cash or tax relief. In 1899 a further batch of concessions was issued, to forty different companies in the French Congo. To forestall public opposition the concessionaires were required to pay rent (which was, however, only small) and 15 per cent of their profits and to help provide certain services, such as river boats and telegraph. About a third of the French Congo was involved, one concession covering an area of 140 000 square kilometres. Each concessionary company received sole right to rubber and ivory, which were their chief interest, and other natural products, but not minerals, for the period of thirty years, with the opportunity to claim permanent freehold of all the land that it developed. The criterion of development was undemanding, little more than a token cultivation.

A similar grant of lavish concessions was found in the German colonies of South-West Africa and Kamerun. In the latter two big concessions (one for 50 000 square kilometres) were made to speculators looking for profits from wild rubber. In the former, one third of the territory was conceded to six companies, including the German South-West Africa Company. One of the six was a British company, the South-West Africa Company. The cosmopolitan character of capital and management in both chartered and concessionary companies was a striking feature. British companies and capital participated in enterprises in Moçambique (including the Moçambique Company) as well as German South-West Africa. Most of the capital in the French Congo came from Belgium; and yet French capital went into the Moçamedes company of southern Angola.

The expectation that these concessionary companies would contribute to developing the colonies was somewhat optimistic and naïve. They were undercapitalized for that purpose and in any case lacked the inclination, having their sights set rather on quick profit. Those of the Congo Free State and the French Congo became notorious for the brutality of their methods of enforcing the delivery of quotas of wild latex. Most colonial authorities made use of a degree of coercion even if they stopped far short of the barbarities of the Congo. European officials also sought to expand output by means of encouragement, example and assistance. Even at its most benign, however, their policy was not altogether disinterested. Revenue was related to the volume of exports.

Revenue was hard to come by. In the 1890s most of the income of Nigeria came from duties on spirits, mostly from Germany, but increasingly from Holland. The Brussels Act of 1890 established a prohibition zone between latitudes 20 degrees North and 22 degrees South, but did not concern itself with the areas where the liquor trade was already being carried on, beyond attempting to curb it by fixing a relatively high minimum duty on imported spirits. The effect in Angola, however, of import duties on spirits was simply to encourage the manufacture of rum from locally produced sugar, and that was used in the wild rubber trade. By the end of the century 15 million litres were being distilled annually. This affronted foreign opinion and in 1899 an excise tax was imposed. As that was not effective in curtailing the liquor traffic, distilling was prohibited. This meant that Angolan sugar had to find an outlet in Portugal, already oversupplied with sugar from Moçambique. Some of the sugar grown there was also turned into alcohol, but the southern part of the colony fell outside the prohibition zone of the Brussels Convention. In 1902 local distilling and brewing were forbidden in the interests of Portuguese wine exports, but the law could not be enforced.

Not all cash crops were as troublesome as wild rubber and sugar could be in their different ways. Cotton presented fewer problems, at least in Egypt, where there was a marked expansion of production during the last years of the century. The area under cotton in Egypt increased from the early 1890s. In 1893-1894, 0,9 million feddans (378 000 ha) were devoted to cotton, in 1895-1896, 1,0 million (420 000 ha) and 1,2 million in 1899-1900 (504 000 ha). The growth was more rapid in Upper Egypt, though, with 105 000 feddans (44 100 ha) under cotton in 1900-1901 (compared with 53 000 feddans in 1893-1894), the south remained relatively unimportant. The expansion can be attributed partly to the pacification of the countryside after the disturbances associated with the 'Urabi rebellion and partly to the greater water supply as a result of the irrigation works constructed in the 1880s. Prices must have exerted an influence, but not the chief one. Their movement tended to be erratic: £E 2,9 a kantar (about 45 kg) in the late 1880s, falling to £E 1,8 in 1893-1894 and 1894-1895, recovering to £E 2,2 in 1895-1896, but, before finally returning to the £E 2,0 level, collapsing in 1897-1898 to £E 1,5, the lowest point during the period 1880-1914. Farmers continued to plant cotton because, even when the price fell, it was still the most profitable crop and it was easy to market. They were also influenced by the power of custom, which made it difficult to change an accepted crop rotation in response to short-term price movements. There was an underlying trend to substitute a two-year crop rotation, with cotton grown every other year, for a three-year rotation, with cotton grown every third year, a trend which was responsible for much of the increased area of cotton cultivation; but once that change was made there was no going back to the old system. The movement of rents possibly had more effect on planting decisions than the rise and fall of prices. When rents rose in the latter part of the decade, tenants may have sought in cotton cultivation the additional income needed. Yet another influence was the priority given by the government to cotton in the allocation of water.

Total output of cotton doubled during the 1890s, though there were yearly fluctuations. In 1889-1890 the volume of production was 3,2 million kantars (142 000 metric tons), in 1899-1900, 6,5 million (289 000 metric tons). This helped to counteract price falls. The annual average value of exports of Egyptian cotton was £E 7,5 million in the second half of the 1880s, £E 8,5 million in the first half of the 1890s and £E 9,6 million in the second half. Exports of cotton-seed brought in a further £E 1,6 million in 1894 and £E 1,4 million a year in 1895-1899. Increased output was due not only to the extension of the area of cultivation. There was also the effect of the introduction of a better variety of cotton in the late 1880s, with a higher yield and less risk of cotton-worm attack. The improved water supply also affected yield. In the 1890s yields exceeded 5 kantars per feddan, compared with less than 4 in the 1880s, though from the end of the decade they started to decline.

Compared with US output (2,2 million metric tons in 1900) Egypt's was small. Egyptian cotton, however, was long-staple and had special uses, e.g. in the manufacture of sewing thread and fine fabrics. Nearly half Egypt's cotton went to Britain, but a growing proportion, though still small (only 5,6 per cent in the late 1890s), was going to the United States itself. Egyptian cotton sold for considerably higher prices. Rural incomes per capita rose markedly in the later 1880s and early 1890s (though so did the incidence of bilharzia as the irrigated area expanded), but by the end of the century they were beginning to fall. An increasing amount of land was falling into the hands of bigger landowners and foreigners. The area held by owners of 50 and more feddans increased from 2,0 million feddans in 1894 to 2,2 million in 1900, and in the last ten or fifteen years of the century foreign holdings more than doubled in extent, to 11 per cent of the cultivated area, nearly a quarter of all big estates, though much of the foreign-owned land was being reclaimed for future sale. Some of the land on the market was sold by the state, part of it also falling into the hands of the smallest cultivators, those with less than five feddans, who increased their total holding from 0,9 million feddans in 1894 to 1,1 million in 1900.

The 1890s were an important period for the development of Gold Coast cocoa farming, though even in 1900 exports still amounted to only 530 tons, compared with some 10 000 tons from São Thomé and Principe. Exporting began in 1891. Elsewhere it had always been a plantation crop; in the Gold Coast it was a peasant crop. Its success was a remarkable achievement. For not only was it not a food crop, it was also unfamiliar and did not give an immediate yield. Cultivation required some foresight and entailed some risk. One favourable factor was that the cocoa harvest coincided with the slack period of the farming year, so that family labour could be used. Although a number of individuals, African and European, and groups, official and missionary, experimented with cocoa cultivation, the basis of the Gold Coast industry was laid by migrants moving from the Accra region in the south-east, where land was in short supply, westwards into the forest belt, which had the necessary fertility and humidity, and their purchase of land from local chiefs, who, having no tradition of cash crop agriculture, had no use for it themselves. The settlers brought with them capital accumulated in the production of and trade in rubber and palm oil, in which they had long been engaged, and they were familiar with buying land. The European trading firms played a passive rôle, providing export services, but taking no active part in production or collection.

Cocoa was cultivated as a substitute for palm produce, the prices of which were declining. On the whole cocoa production was more profitable than palm produce, which, given the lower prices, was relatively expensive to transport. Only production near the coast was able to bear the high transportation costs. The maximum distance from the coast for palm production was about 65 kilometres, with most being carried on within a 40 kilometre range, compared with a distance for cocoa growing of about 120 kilometres.

Cocoa owed nothing to begin with to railway building. The producers made their own transport arrangements. The harvested product was carried by hired porters and only the high price made this possible. These cocoa pioneers were few in number and distinguished by their enterprise and response to market opportunities and their willingness to migrate, invest resources and take risks. Their original investment must have been substantial: purchase of land, costs of migration and land clearance, and working capital. The cost of the land was shared by the family or by a group of partners and apparently paid in instalments. None the less considerable expense and risk were involved. The pioneers were able (despite their inferior productivity) to break into the world cocoa market partly because of lower production costs, partly because transport costs were lower to the main centres of consumption than from South America and the West Indies. The family labour of West African cocoa farms cost less in cash terms than the hired labour of Latin America and the Caribbean, where cocoa was a plantation crop, though in the course of time African farmers began to employ wage labour, which came seasonally, mostly from the poorer areas around the forest, from the northern Gold Coast, Togo and Dahomey.

Cocoa farming also began in the western parts of Nigeria, in the neighbourhood of Ibadan and elsewhere. The earliest cocoa farmers were Lagos merchants looking for an alternative to unrewarding palm products. Subsequently capital came from a wider range of sources, handicrafts, farming or trading or loans from kinsmen. Land was rented rather than bought and the wealthier farmers often employed others less well-off as labourers. Profits were invested in extending cocoa production, education and housing, but not in other commercial or agricultural activities. The industry developed more slowly than in the Gold Coast. In 1900 exports were less than half (202 tons) those of the Gold Coast. In both colonies assistance was forthcoming from government botanical gardens, which distributed seeds and seedlings, but official encouragement was of small importance compared with local enterprise.

At first sight coffee would appear to have been a more likely crop for Africa than cocoa, as it is indigenous. Arabica, the best quality, originated in Ethiopia and there are many other African varieties, including liberica, indigenous to, and named after, Liberia. There was from Ethiopia a centuries-old export of coffee, an expensive luxury, but Arabia adopted the coffee bush and eclipsed Ethiopia as a producer even to the extent of giving the variety its present name. Similarly *coffea liberica* was introduced into Indonesia and the West Indies. It took a long time for African coffee to gain world importance. Like cocoa it benefited from the fall in palm produce prices and some European plantations were started in West Africa in the latter part of the 1880s. In Liberia coffee cultivation was begun much earlier by black American immigrants and it reached a peak of output in the 1860s. In 1894 an estimated 445 metric tons were exported, being the principal earner of foreign exchange. Very small, but variable, quantities were also exported by the Congo Free State (46 metric tons in 1890, 34 in 1900, but less than one in 1896), but it was important for the early colony, earning in 1891 1,6 million francs, with rubber earning only 2,3 million. Angola was producing in the late 1890s several thousand tons a year (9 000 in 1898), but even that was a minute quantity compared with the output of Brazil, some 600 000 tons at the end of the century.

A not so large, but still considerable, gap between Africa and South America was to be seen in rubber production. At the end of the 19th century Brazil was exporting some 30 000 metric tons. The amount of wild rubber collected in Africa reached a maximum in the early part of the present century – output in the Congo Free State increasing between six and seven fold in the course of the 1890s – but even the Congo Free State, the biggest producer, managed only some 5 000 tons in 1900. Nigerian output reached 3 100 metric tons in 1896, then fell. French West African exports reached 2 900 tons in 1900, those of the French equatorial colonies rather more than a thousand. Rubber collection was viable only because of its rising price, enabling it to bear the high transport costs which curtailed the export of other raw materials far from the coast. To the extent that it was a free and spontaneous activity it was encouraged by the credit advanced to the producers and middlemen by coastal merchants who wanted to make sure of their supplies.

Wage labour and cash crop production, though by world standards still very restricted, extended the use of money. Colonial governments were influential in the expansion of the money economy because they paid their considerable work force in cash and preferred to collect taxes in cash. European coins increasingly displaced the old local currencies, which were depreciating in value as their volume in circulation grew and which consequently were becoming inconvenient for use in all but the smallest purchases. Africans engaged in the production or sale of export crops saw the advantage of European silver coins, which were of sufficient, but not excessive, value for their purposes, including the purchase of land, and permitted the buying of imported goods without the restriction on freedom of choice implicit in the traditional moneys. The old established European firms tended to resist the transition to modern currencies because, having mastered the intricacies of barter and the local currencies, they preferred the old ways as a means of discouraging new entrants into the trade. The fact that the Germans were willing to pay in silver helps to explain why they were able to capture an increasing proportion of the Lagos produce trade.

In South Africa an important development was the minting by the Transvaal government in the 1890s of a gold, silver and bronze currency based on sterling and known as Kruger coinage. This was made possible by the recovery of the gold-mining industry from the financial crisis of 1889. New companies were started and by the end of the century the South African Republic was the biggest gold producer in the world, contributing more than a quarter of total world output. Output in 1888 was 228 ounces, in 1898, 3 823 ounces. During those ten years the value realized rose from £967 000 to £16 240 000. More competent engineers and managers and better equipment were brought in and the work was reorganized in the light of the experience of the earlier years of exploitation when quick and easy profits had been expected from shallow mining. In the 1890s profit came increasingly from what were known as the deep-levels and it has been argued with some plausibility but amidst much criticism, that it was the mining magnates whose interest lay chiefly in the deep-levels who, because of their desire for a compliant government in the Transvaal during the long period when new mines were being developed, were behind an unsuccessful putsch by a leading figure in the British South African Company in 1895, the Jameson Raid.

After the 1889 crisis dividends began to be paid that were genuine profits, not sums distributed at the expense of working capital simply to raise share prices for speculative reasons. The crisis affected organization. Many small enterprises failed and the surviving companies, while retaining their separate shareholders and managements, began to associate themselves with a holding company or group, such as Rand Mines Ltd, set up in 1893 by Wernher, Beit and Company with shares in a number of mining companies. The group helped its members to meet their capital requirements, gave expert advice and provided bulk purchasing, secretarial and other services. The Transvaal Chamber of Mines, founded in 1887–1889, promoted still further co-operation among the mining companies, representing their interests in contacts with the outside world, with government and labour, disposing of considerable powers and controlling a number of subsidiary organizations.

Deep mining and the use of the cyanide process for extraction required capital investment far in excess of what was originally anticipated. The sharp increase in British private capital exports to Africa from 1893 was due in large measure to the gold-mining boom in South Africa. New British portfolio investment in Africa rose from £2,6 million in 1893 to £14,9 million in 1895, fell back again to £9,6 million in 1896 but rose to a new height in 1899, £21,3 million. 1899, 1903 and 1904 were the only years before the First World War that new British investment in Africa exceeded that in North America and those were the years of high investment in the gold-mines. £12,8 million went to South Africa in 1899. The 1890s on the whole, however, were a trough in the waves of British capital exports and the expansion of investment in Africa during that period ran counter to the trend. French foreign investment, on the other hand, increased in the 1890s, particularly towards the end of the decade, when it exceeded a thousand million gold francs a year, maintaining that rate during the early years of the 20th century. Not a great deal, however, went to Africa. It is estimated that France's total external long-term investment at the end of the 19th century amounted to some 28 000 million francs. About 70 per cent of that was in Europe, only 5 per cent in the French colonies, most of it in North Africa and Indo-China. About 10 per cent was invested in Egypt, including the Suez Canal, and South Africa. German capital exports also picked up in the mid-1890s after some severe losses to investors in the early part of the decade. As in the case of France colonial investment subsequently grew in importance, but was always relatively small. Total German investment in the whole of Africa never reached a tenth of total external investment, more than half of which was in Europe. In the 1890s the main areas in Africa of German investment were Egypt, especially the Egyptian public debt, and South Africa, where German capital went into the gold-mines and railways of the Transvaal.

In the course of the 1890s the Transvaal gold-mines became linked by rail to the coast. More than 4 000 km of line were laid in the decade. The mines were the most powerful economic force in southern Africa, influencing not only the Transvaal, but also all the other territories of the region. It was for the benefit of the Transvaal that Lourenço Marques and its railway, which between them took most of the investment that went into Moçambique, were developed. In North Africa, too, mining stimulated railway building, in this case phosphates, used for the manufacture of phosphorus and in the iron industry. The first deposits were discovered in Algeria as early as 1873, but exploitation of the richest known deposit was begun in the 1890s after a narrow gauge railway was built from Tebessa to

Bône in 1888. Similarly a railway from Sfax to the Gafsa area of southern Tunisia in 1899 permitted the exploitation of Tunisian phosphates, discovered as early as 1885, but 200 km from the coast. Other railways from Gafsa to Sousse and from the High Tell to Tunis (1906) enlarged output, which soon overtook Algeria's.

The difficulties encountered by railway engineers were formidable. Great distances, endemic diseases, geographical obstacles – the Mau Escarpment in East Africa, the tropical rain forest and the coastal swamps of West Africa – and occasional hostility from people whose territory was violated, all slowed down the rate of rail construction and put up the costs. The Beira Railway to Southern Rhodesia across northern Moçambique proceeded at the rate of 50 kilometres a year. Given the immense costs and the low level of economic activity in the vast expanses across which the railways ran, it is little wonder that private enterprise, deterred by the expense and unimpressed by the potential profits, did not clamour for the honour of bearing the torch of economic progress.

The British government took a relatively long time to reconcile itself to sinking money into railway construction in Africa. In any case its West African possessions were comparatively well served with water transport. With the appointment of Joseph Chamberlain to the Colonial Office in 1895 there was a change in policy. It was then that the West African lines were started, partly to secure British commerce in the interior against French competition. The Uganda Railway, too, was started in 1896 (but finished as far as Lake Victoria only in 1902), running from Mombasa on the coast of Kenya to Kisumu from where it was possible to reach Buganda by steamer or dhow. Non-economic motives continued to play a part in initiating construction. The wish to suppress the slave trade in East Africa was one motive for building the Uganda Railway, and the Anglo-Egyptian campaign for the reconquest of the Sudan was responsible for the rebuilding and extension of the line from Wadi Halfa. It was pushed on as the troops advanced, first to Abu Hamed between the fourth and fifth cataracts, thus cutting off a loop of the Nile, then to the confluence of the Nile and Atbara. In 1899 it reached Khartoum.

In South Africa, although they certainly performed a useful function economically, the railways suffered from excess capacity as the result of rivalries between colonies and ports. The prize was the traffic of the Witwatersrand. The shortest route from the coast was the one from Lourenço Marques on Delagoa Bay. Progress on this was very slow, chiefly owing to lack of funds, and it was with considerable reluctance that President Kruger of the South African Republic, compelled by his need for money, permitted (in exchange for a loan) the construction of a line from Johannesburg to the River Vaal, where it would meet the Cape railway system via the Orange Free State. Thus the Cape railways were the first to connect the Witwatersrand with the coast (1892), giving the Colony a great, though temporary, advantage. The Pretoria-Delagoa Bay line opened in 1894. The Natal Government Railways reached Johannesburg in 1895. The situation then was that there were three railways competing for Transvaal freight, though within the Republic itself the entire system was controlled by the Netherlands South African Railway Company, which could manipulate traffic by the rate it charged on different lines. In this competition all the advantage lay with the line from Lourenço Marques. The Cape was worst off because it had three lines operating and its approach was through Orange Free State, the interests of which also had to be considered and which in fact took over its section of the line in 1895 after the Jameson Raid. The Cape's debt was large and its revenue heavily dependent on the railways. Natal was better off because its route was shorter and its debt smaller. A rate war was started in 1895 which severely strained relations between Britain and the South African Republic and which did little to further Cape interests. The Cape share of Transvaal traffic went down and down, followed by the Natal share. In the meantime the British South Africa Company pushed ahead with its railway into Southern Rhodesia in order to strengthen its hold on that territory. Refused right of way through Transvaal, the Company had to lay its tracks through Bechuanaland. It reached Bulawayo in 1897. Salisbury was joined to Bulawayo in 1902. The Company also built and operated the Beira Railway, which reached Salisbury in 1898, before the line from the south.

Not all railways were politically inspired or bedevilled by politics, sometimes having a quite explicit economic purpose. Nearly a thousand kilometres of narrow-gauge railway were laid down in the Nile Delta to facilitate the movement of cotton. Much of the North African railway system was composed of narrow-gauge line built for transporting minerals. In West Africa a line was begun in 1898 from the coast of the Gold Coast at Sekondi to Tarkwa (finished in 1901 and extended to Obuasi in 1902) for the benefit of the gold-mining industry. Whatever their original main purpose, however, all railways could serve other interests as well.

Vague ideas were entertained of a Cape to Cairo railway through British-controlled territory. Cecil Rhodes was the best-known advocate of that somewhat romantic and impracticable scheme. His negotiations with the British government for the extension of his Rhodesia railway northwards to Lake Tanganyika were unsuccessful. There was in fact little co-ordination even between British territories and each line had an *ad hoc* character. Different gauges were used in different areas. The Egyptian state railways adopted the standard British gauge of 4 feet 8½ inches, but even in Lower Egypt that was not used everywhere. Apart from the cotton railways, a section of the Canal railway between Port Said and Ismailia was narrow gauge. It was converted to standard gauge when it was taken over by the government in 1902. Another narrow-gauge railway in Egypt was built (completed in 1898) and run by the Kena-Asswan Railway Company in Upper Egypt. By 1897 Qena (Kena) was the southerly terminus of the state railway system which ran from Cairo through Assiout (320 km from Cairo and 240 km from Qena). It took over the Qena-Aswan line in 1926 and converted it to a standard gauge. A further Egyptian development was that linking the Upper and Lower Egyptian railway systems in 1896 by a short line in Cairo between the two termini. The essential framework of the Egyptian railway network was completed by the end of the 19th century – a trunk route along the Nile to Qena, supplemented by branch lines in the Delta (standard and narrow gauge), a line to the Fayyum Oasis (dating from as early as 1869) and lines to and along the Suez Canal.

The Uganda Railway was constructed on the metre gauge and Lord Cromer advised the adoption of the same gauge in the Upper Egypt. Instead a 3 feet 6 inch (1,06 metres) gauge was employed both in Upper Egypt (until conversion to British standard gauge after the First World War) and the Sudan. Although this happened to be the standard gauge of the South African system, the decision to adopt it in the Sudan had nothing to do with the Cape–Cairo railway dream, being influenced rather by local military needs. In general, there was very little comprehensive planning of railway systems. The trunk routes ran from the established ports into the interior, and such inter-territorial lines as were built were normally between contiguous colonies under the same flag.

At least partly because of intensive railway construction the labour problem became more acute in the 1890s. The demands of the South African gold-mines also grew. The pressure of demand caused wages to rise, and to some extent the stimulus to wage labour was the growing taste for European goods and services, e.g. utensils, clothing, farming implements and European-style housing and education, an indication of a rising standard of living (though a taste for some European commodities, e.g. spirits, did not obviously represent an improved level of civilization). Wages, however, did not rise sufficiently to draw into the labour market all the workers that were required. Consequently a high degree of compulsion was used. Getting their subjects to work was regarded by many colonial officials as their chief administrative function. Without the labour of the colonized, not only could public works not be carried out, but mines and plantations could not function. Besides, wage-labour contributed to colonial revenue since only people who worked for a wage could pay taxes in cash. Taxes levied on Africans (hut tax or capitation tax) were primarily to raise revenue, but also had the effect of increasing the labour supply when blacks could not earn the requisite cash from their own farms. An example of more direct, though not very effective, compulsion was the additional tax imposed by the Cape Colony in 1894 by the Glen Grey Act on those Africans who had not spent at least six months of the year in wage labour. General Joseph Gallieni, Governor-General in Madagascar between 1896 and 1905, used taxation to force people into work.

The cost of labour was much the most expensive item in South African gold-mining costs. About a third of total expenditure went on black labour. Given the fixed price of gold, profits were dependent upon keeping costs down, and the easiest way to do this was to reduce the expense of finding and paying black workers, who were less able to resist than skilled, articulate and organized white workers. This was one of the first tasks of the Transvaal Chamber of Mines, and the obvious way to do so was to eliminate the competition for labour which was pushing wages up, and to bring down the cost of recruiting, which involved payment to recruiting agents and the cost of bringing workers to the Rand. Collaboration among employers was not easy to obtain because they tended to break ranks when labour needs became pressing, and the fixing of wages itself affected the labour supply. However, agreements were made on standardizing wages and conditions of employment and these had some effect. At the same time the system of recruitment was centralized to reduce the capitation fees charged by recruiters and the sharp practices of those who cheated both workers and employers. In 1896 the Native Labour Supply Association was formed (reorganized in 1900 as the Witwatersrand Native Labour Association) to recruit for all the Rand mines. It was not able to establish a recruiting monopoly either in the Transvaal itself or in the British colonies, but enjoyed some success in Moçambique in eliminating competitive recruitment. Moçambique was the chief source of supply, providing about half the total. The African labour force on the gold-mines increased from 14 000 in 1890 to 97 000 in 1899.

All colonial authorities made use of one or more methods of compulsion to secure labour, but some had a worse reputation than others. In the Portuguese colonies force was used in an arbitrary and indiscriminate way and it persisted much longer, until many years after the Second World War. Labour was requisitioned from chiefs by officials on behalf of private employers in return for a capitation fee. Britain was one of the severest critics of Portuguese labour policy, despite the fact that so many workers in the gold-mines were recruited with Portuguese permission in Moçambique. Another much criticized government was that of the Congo Free State where a labour tax (*prestation*) was introduced. The system was open to abuse. There was little restraint upon the officials of the state and the employees of the concessionary companies. They were free to extort as much labour as they thought fit and pay it as little as they felt inclined. As they themselves were poorly paid and supplemented their salaries with the commission they could earn on the ivory and rubber they obtained, they had an incentive to use harsh methods, e.g. the use of black troops to terrorize people into supplying them. Such measures, reported by missionaries, created a scandal in Europe. A Commission for the Protection of the Natives, appointed in 1896 by the Congo government in response to criticism and composed of missionaries, turned out to be more for the sake of impressing international opinion than for effecting genuine reforms.

Labour taxes were found also in German, French and Portuguese colonies. Ten or a dozen days' labour a year was the usual requirement. In the French colonies the obligation was imposed on whites as well as blacks, but as a rule it was possible to commute the labour tax for a money payment, and was thus an important source of revenue. As in the Congo, it was a system open to abuse (by inadequately supervised private companies as well as by officials) and, therefore, criticism, but the French did not abolish it until 1946.

Some justification for the use of forced labour was found in tribal custom, which allowed for service to a chief (tribute labour) or to the community (communal labour). The purpose of tribute labour was to support the chief in his office and to enable him to perform his public duties, such as hospitality to strangers and the relief of the hungry in time of dearth. But with the spread of a money economy chiefs became acquisitive and the system was abused. Tribesmen found themselves compelled to cultivate their chief's land, not in the tribal interest, but purely for his personal gain; or even sent off to work as contract labourers on the mines, either individually or, as was sometimes the case in South Africa, in age-regiments. The attitude of the colonial authorities varied. The French upheld the rights of chiefs. The British sometimes did, especially in West Africa, but sometimes prohibited tribute labour, especially in Kenya, and at other times commuted it for salaries, as in Barotseland (Northern Rhodesia). The trend in British policy was towards abolition or commutation. Unpaid labour became increasingly inappropriate in an expanding money economy.

Communal labour, paid at standard rates, was adopted by colonial authorities chiefly, but not exclusively, for public works and porterage (for private employers as well as for colonial civil servants). In African customary law the communal obligation was left vague, but under colonial rule it was defined by statute and fixed at so many days - sixty being quite normal - a year, usually paid, It was no longer, as it had been in the old days, just for maintaining pathways between villages, but for the construction of modern roads and railways, entailing absence from home. Critics of the system raised many objections, alleging that there were few safeguards for the protection of conscripted labour. There were no regulations governing the methods of recruitment and no health regulations. Statutory limitations were not necessarily respected. Sometimes there were high death rates, especially on railway construction. Rural life was disrupted by the departure of the able-bodied men.

Two other forms of forced labour were military conscription and penal labour. The Congo Free State used nominally military labour for building railways and this practice continued after the Belgian government took over the territory in 1908. The French used military conscripts either as soldiers or as labourers, the latter falling into the so-called *deuxième portion*. Penal labour was exacted from criminals, tax defaulters and vagrants. When it abolished slavery in 1848, France used vagabonds for public works, and Portugal, after the abolition of slavery, compelled vagrants to do two years work for the government or a private employer. Punishment for tax defaulting was a useful source of labour in most colonies. In fact, the British authorities accepted labour in lieu of tax in some colonies.

Despite compulsion most colonial authorities were short of labour for important public works, particularly railway building. Demands for labour in situations where capital was short and labour productivity low could be enormous. Governments were forced to import labour in spite of the expense and health risks. The Germans in East Africa toyed with the idea of bringing in Chinese, the French actually did so for railway building in the French Congo, also importing labour from Indo-China and Cuba. Britain used indentured labourers from India in East Africa, some thousands of whom settled there after the completion of their contracts, and the Congo Free State obtained workers from China, Barbadoes and Liberia.

Although European governments in Africa resorted, in order to secure a labour supply, to all those expedients which troubled consciences in Europe and which involved force and, to say the least, discomfort, they none the less increased their pressure upon slave-holding, even when it appears to have taken a relatively mild form. The arrival of the British East Africa Company was followed by a stricter enforcement of earlier anti-slavery treaties, and by the end of the 1890s the movement of slaves into Zanzibar was more or less at an end. The plantation economy of Zanzibar, as well as Arab trade, suffered a severe blow, though it was not until 1907 that slavery was made illegal. In West Africa, more especially in the French colonies, slave-owning persisted well into the twentieth century.

Short of condoning slavery, colonial governments saw it as part of their function to ensure the labour supply and very often they accepted the obligation of providing railways. Beyond these commitments they were unwilling to go. They did not see it as their duty to foster colonial manufacturing. On the contrary, part of the purpose of colonies was to provide captive markets for metropolitan industry. Colonial economies were regarded as complementary to the metropolitan economy, exchanging raw materials for manufacture. Far from wanting to encourage import substitution, colonial governments looked with favour on increasing external trade. The chief aim of tariff policy was to maximize revenue. Customs duties were the main source of revenue and there was no wish to discourage imports. Colonial authorities were less likely to give protection than to compensate for the competition of local manufacturers with metropolitan goods by imposing an excise tax on domestic products. Humanitarian interests, too, were suspicious of colonial industrialization, though for a quite different reason. They were opposed to any measures designed to force natives into the labour market. The development of industry, wherever it occurred, took place almost invariably in spite of metropolitan policy rather than because of it. There was no incentive for expatriate trading firms or metropolitan manufacturers to start industries in the colonies. There were no high tariff walls to surmount and the colonial market was small. No driving force towards industrialization existed within most colonies. The equipment used in the production of cash crops was simple and inexpensive, such things as hoes, cutlasses and axes. There was thus low investment spending, offering no stimulus to a domestic capital goods industry.

Colonial rule and external trade were damaging rather than helpful to native industry. African craft manufacture, especially in the metal trades, became subject to increasing competition from cheaper and superior European manufactures. However, craft industry, e.g. the making of textiles, leather goods and pots, was very resilient and, especially in the interior, enjoyed some protection from the higher transport costs paid by exotic products and from entrenched taste and habits.

The most primitive form of modern industrialization in Africa was the processing of primary products before export. Sometimes this was unavoidable to reduce weight which would have otherwise made export uneconomic. Cotton had to be ginned, timber sawn and oil extracted from palm fruit (though not from the kernel). Certain perishable products had also to be processed, hence the tinning of fish. More purposefully, in Egypt and North Africa efforts were made by pre-colonial governments to foster import substitution, in Egypt in the 1820s and 1830s, Tunisia in the 1840s and Morocco in the 1880s and 1890s. The obstacles were formidable both in the pre-colonial period and after: meagre, and at that time unexploited, deposits of coal and iron; lack of skilled labour at all levels; the narrowness of the local market (either smallness of population or low per capita income or both); the reluctance of native and foreign investors to make long-term industrial investments when there were other more secure outlets for capital in trade, government, railways and land; the concentration of bank loans on trade and mortgages; and foreign competition, against which no protection was possible in the absence of political independence. Egypt saw some progress. In the 1890s some twenty new manufacturing firms, engaged in making textiles, cement, cigarettes and processed foods, were founded by foreigners, resident and non-resident. Algeria, with its European population, seemed set for early industrialization. That it did not take place can be attributed largely to the absence of tariff protection and the hostility of French manufacturers who exploited the Algerian market and of those European farmers who feared a loss of labour. The customs union with France was beneficial less to the general public than to vested interests, including, apart from certain French industrialists, the big import firms in Algeria, which had no interest in promoting local manufacturing, and those settlers who produced for the French market, especially wine-growers. French manufacturers were able to force the closure of textile, carpet and ceramic factories.

South Africa, with its long-established European population and its cultural links with industrializing Europe, had a further advantage which Algeria lacked, greater distance from Europe and a greater degree of independence, though it too suffered from a small market and, despite great progress, by European standards a rudimentary transport system. The first industries were food processing, brewing and distilling, clothing, furniture and wagon making, boat building, tanning and construction and the manufacture of building materials. They were most advanced in the Cape, where to some extent they derived, in addition to the protection afforded by distance from European centres of production, a fortuitous protection from tariffs designed primarily to raise revenue. As late as 1891, however, there were fewer than 20 000 men and women employed in industry in the Cape Colony and only some 300 of the 2 000 factories and workshops were using engines of any sort. The development of mining and the railway network had little immediate effect upon the growth of manufacturing in South Africa. The Transvaal Republic gave concessions for the making of explosives and cement, but generally capital, skilled labour and entrepreneurial talent went rather into mining. Nevertheless, the enlargement of the internal market permitted economics of scale that enabled local manufacturers to compete sucessfully with products brought long distances from overseas. Costs would further be kept down by the cheapness of unskilled labour. While low-paid labourers were impecunious customers, the increasing, and increasingly prosperous, white population helped to restore the balance. A significant proportion of the profits of mining remained inside the country, the share of relatively highly paid settlers who had made their homes in the country from which they drew their income.

South Africa got over its gold crisis of 1889–1890 relatively quickly. It was, however, a short-lived recovery. The economy went into recession in 1897, following a collapse of gold share prices at the end of 1895. Politics had something to do with the depression, the tension between Britain and the Transvaal after the Jameson Raid. Farming was adversely affected by a severe drought in 1896 and the outbreak of rinderpest. International trade during the 1890s was generally rather sluggish, though appearances were deceptive. World manufacturing output grew somewhat slowly in the early part of the decade and although it accelerated in the latter part, much of it was due to the rapid expansion of American industry. As a very large proportion of American output was for the internal market, there was no corresponding expansion in world trade in manufactured goods. Thus the slow growth of international trade as a whole was due to the deceleration of trade in industrial products rather than to a general recession. World trade in primary products continued to grow throughout the decade, though with some fluctuations, and Africa was much more affected by the prosperity of its chief industrial trading partners.

Britain and France, Africa's most important trading partners, were in depression in the early 1890s. The response of France to economic difficulty was to raise tariff walls and strengthen imperial preference. In 1892 it applied its highly protective Méline tariff to Algeria and in 1898 was able at last to introduce tariffs into Tunisia that discriminated in favour of itself. Obstacles remained, notably the 1885 Berlin Treaty and the Anglo-French Convention of 1898, which prevented imperial preferences in Ivory Coast and Dahomey and also in the British colonies of Nigeria and the Gold Coast. But it was not difficult for an imperial power to tighten its grip upon the trade of its colonies. Germany, for example, enlarged its share of the trade of its colonies, though, of course, colonial trade was still only a tiny proportion of its total trade. India lost most as a result of the expansion of German trade with German East Africa. In the second half of the 1890s, as Germany's share of imports rose from a little more than a quarter to almost half, India's share dropped from nearly a half to less than a fifth.

Britain's share of African trade declined. Although to some extent this reflected its deteriorating position in world trade, it went further and faster in those territories that came under a different flag. The cause of protection became a serious political issue. Joseph Chamberlain was the most passionate advocate of an imperial free trade with tariffs walls against foreigners. But a proposal in 1897 to implement this was rejected by the self-governing colonies, which would go no further than imperial preference. For the idea of giving free entry to British manufacturers was unwelcome to them. In the Cape Colony Cecil Rhodes, the Prime Minister from 1890 to 1896, opposed higher tariffs altogether, whether in the interests of British manufacturers or for the sake of local industry. Protection conflicted with the aim of securing the biggest share of the important transit traffic to the Transvaal. In Britain itself the taxation of foreign food imports in order to give preference to foodstuffs from British colonies was as unpopular as ever with the electorate when four-fifths of food imports were being supplied from foreign sources.

Cartels, trusts, amalgamations and other forms of business concentration came into increasing favour with the businessman of the developed world, though in the United States and Germany rather than Britain and France, in the closing decades of the 19th century. European firms operating in Africa showed a trend away from family organization and partnership towards limited liability and pooling arrangements. In Nigeria the number of trading firms was reduced in the 1880s to three important ones, Alexander Miller Brother and Co. and the Royal Niger Co., which had close ties with each other from the days of the United African Company, and the African Association, the result of a merger in 1889 of several smaller firms operating on the Lower Niger. Among the three companies competition was keen, but in 1893 the Royal Niger Co. purchased some of the assets of the African Association, which received in turn shares in the Company. In 1899, when the charter of Royal Niger Co. was about to lapse, it negotiated an agreement to share Nigerian trade with Alexander Miller and the African Association, and that remained in force for ten years. It was both a territorial division, with the parties to the pool undertaking to confine their activities to their existing spheres, and a profit sharing arrangement. A similar pool in the Gold Coast was formed in 1905 by the African Association and other firms operating there, also a profit sharing arrangement. Matching this suspension of commercial competition, more cartels of shipping companies were formed and companies became larger through amalgamation. In 1890 the British steamship lines operating to West Africa were taken over by Elder, Demster and Co., which in 1895 joined with Woermann-Linie in a shipping conference. In 1900 the dominant members of the South African Shipping Conference, the Union and Castle Lines, amalgamated as the Union-Castle Company, subsequently (1911) taken over by Elder, Dempster and the Royal Mail Steam Packet Company.

Banking in Africa was dominated by firms controlled from Europe or at least with strong links with Europe. British-based banks began operations in West Africa in the last decade of the century. The Bank of British West Africa was chartered in 1894, with currency issuing rights and a *de facto* virtual monopoly of the profitable movement of British coins into West Africa. It opened branches throughout British West Africa as well as in Monrovia, the capital of Liberia. It was owned by British-based banks, including the Standard Bank, and was linked with others through common directors. In South Africa, as a result of the over-extension of credit in the share boom of the late 1880s, several of the locally-based, or colonial, banks collapsed, leaving only four, three of them being taken over in 1890–1891 by the African Banking Corporation of Britain, the last of the imperial banks to start operations in South Africa. In the Transvaal the government-chartered bank, the National Bank of the South African Republic (1890), had the backing of the Deutsche Bank. It was given the sole right to issue notes. In Algeria the charter of the Bank of Algeria was renewed in 1897. As a condition the French government required a stricter credit policy. Its headquarters was removed to Paris to make it less open to local pressure, and the management was brought under close state supervision. Moreover, the Bank had to make an interest-free loan to the state, pay a yearly tax and perform certain services free of charge.

The close connection between European and African banks brought both advantages and disadvantages. It was a source of financial strength, without the burden of rigid centralization, since a good deal of discretion was given to local head offices of British banks. None the less, this connection resulted in the provision of a service directed primarily at expatriate interests and the investment of surplus funds in Europe. For that reason the development of banking was to a considerable degree in direct proportion to the size of the European population. Branches tended to be opened only in towns where expatriate enterprise had already established itself. The native population had little to do with them either as lenders, because the banks were uninterested in small deposits, or as borrowers, because they were not thought to be very creditworthy. In any case, British banks, in accordance with British banking practice, were primarily interested in the provision of short-term credit, for which there was comparitively little demand. In West Africa in particular, where the European population was very small, the absence of suitable local borrowers reinforced the tendency to invest in London. It was further strengthened by the need of the banks for liquid assets to cope with severe fluctuations in bank deposits that reflected movements in commodity prices, and these could most easily be obtained in London.

In the latter part of the 1890s the economy of Europe was buoyant. This

owed something to armaments, rearmament to increasing international
tension and international tension to imperialist rivalries in Africa. These
disputes over empire were settled, though not always without crisis, at least
without conflict. The biggest war of the decade was the protracted, bloody
and expensive, but eventually successful British attempt to conquer the
Boer republics, the Second Boer War of 1899-1902. It was a war that
helped to isolate Britain in Europe and to strain relations particularly with
Germany because of the too obvious expression of German sympathy
towards the Boers. Nevertheless within Europe international relations were
still comparatively fluid. After the dismissal of Bismarck in 1890 by the
new German emperor, William II, who introduced into European politics
a greater degree of instability, Germany was on worse terms with Russia,
thus reinforcing Franco-Russian ties, but it was still far from certain in
which direction Britain would go. Its African differences with Germany
were more easily settled than its suspicions of Russia in the Near, Middle
and Far East were assuaged.

The Boer War was no bad thing for the British economy. It contributed
to the boom experienced towards the end of the century. It had mixed
effects upon the South African economy. One result was the improvement
of the Eastern Telegraph Company's cable service between London and
Cape Town. In times of crisis the British Treasury was willing to modify its
habitual parsimony. Imperial war expenditure was very beneficial to the
Cape and Natal, but the economy of the Boer republics suffered a severe
setback, what with the virtual suspension of gold production and the
devastation of farm land. On the whole, however, the 1890s were a good
decade for Africa, including South Africa. South African exports grew at
an annual average rate of 7,7 per cent in the first half of the decade and 6,1
per cent in the second. The corresponding figures for imports were 8,6 per
cent and 11,5 per cent. Exports had an average annual value of £14,2
million in 1891-1895 and £19,2 million in 1896-1900; imports £13,9
million in 1891-1895, £23,9 million in 1896-1900.

Despite a relative decline in Britain's trade with Africa, in absolute
terms in 1900 Africa was importing a great deal more from Britain (£19,7
million in value) than it had been at the beginning of the decade (£13,1
million). More striking figures were those for 1888 (£8,8 million) and 1901
(£24,4 million), a two to three-fold increase over a dozen years. The
volume of British goods imported by Africa would indicate a certain level
of African prosperity. As a market for British exports Africa surpassed the
United States for the first time in the late 1890s. However, the importance
of African trade should not be exaggerated. For one thing the overtaking of
the USA as a customer for British goods owed much to the fact that
America was importing comparatively fewer British goods as its own

manufacturing industry developed, and in any case Africa was a far less significant British market than Asia or the industrialized countries of Europe. Secondly, South Africa absorbed much the biggest proportion of African imports from Britain. Tropical Africa was yet to become a market of any size. As an exporter, too, it was still of minor importance. Of the total exports of Asia and Africa (including South Africa, but excluding Egypt and North Africa) in 1899 Africa contributed only 19,2 per cent and more than half of Africa's share was South Africa's (12,9 per cent). The contribution of no individual colony in Africa exceeded 1 per cent of total Asian and African exports. As late as 1898 Africa's share of world cocoa exports was only 13 per cent, of which 11,5 per cent came from São Thomé and Principe. Only in palm oil and gold (mostly from South Africa) did Africa dominate the world.

The total imports of sub-Saharan Africa in 1897 amounted to £37,3 million and exports to £28,3 million. Of the imports Southern Africa accounted for £23,9 million and of the exports £20,4 million. The Portuguese colonies were next to Southern Africa as the biggest importer of goods, to the value of £5,3 million in 1897. Angola, with exports worth £1,1 million, more than covered the cost of its imports, but Moçambique, with imports worth £4,3 million and exports only £0,2 million, had a very unfavourable balance of commodity trade. British West Africa was the most important exporting region after Southern Africa, with exports worth £2,9 million, the value of imports being about the same. The French colonies accounted for 5,7 per cent of total sub-Saharan imports and 6,1 per cent of exports; the German colonies 2,9 per cent of imports, 1,9 per cent of exports.

Whether or not Africa, like other developing regions in the world, was getting more value for its exports, or less is a vexed question. The common view is that from the latter part of the 19th century until the Second World War Africa's terms of trade deteriorated constantly, i.e. a unit of exports was able to buy a decreasing amount of imports. The evidence seems rather to suggest that from the second half of the 1890s until the Great Depression of the early 1930s there was no conspicuous worsening of the terms of trade for primary products, possibly even a slight improvement. The price of manu- factured goods appears to have been fairly stable. At the same time freight rates continued to fall. Not only did Africa pay no more, possibly even less, for its imports, transport costs of its exports, which, because of their bulk and low unit value, were comparatively onerous, declined, bringing down the prices of its commodities without reducing the return to the producer, but rather increasing it by encouraging bigger sales. Not all commodity prices behaved in the same way. Increasing competition was forcing some down, but others, such as the price of cotton, were rising.

CHAPTER III

1900–1910 (CONSOLIDATION)

In the years before the First World War of 1914–1918, European powers extended and strengthened their hold upon the African territories which they claimed, Portugal slower than the others because of the inadequate resources of the metropolitan and colonial governments. African resistance was both refusal to submit to colonial rule and protest against colonial practices such as forced labour, one of the causes of the Maji Maji rebellion of 1905 in German East Africa and the revolt of the Herero and Hottentots in German South-West Africa between 1904 and 1908. The Bamato uprising in Natal in 1906, which caused some alarm among whites, was an aspiration to freedom from European rule and a protest against its methods. A series of campaigns and punitive expeditions was undertaken by the different colonial powers and colonial boundaries were the subject of a further round of conventions and other agreements. France and Spain enlarged their power in Morocco. The sultan, deeply in debt to French creditors, was an obvious target for imperialism. In 1904 France made agreements with Britain and Spain making provision for a partition of Morocco and in 1905 France imposed a scheme of reform under its guidance. Soon after William II paid a visit to Tangier to offer German support for the sultan's independence. At German insistence an international conference was convened at Algeciras in Spain. Morocco was the occasion rather than the cause of this diplomatic conflict which contained hints of war. Europe was beginning to divide rigidly into two opposing camps, and in the alignment Britain and France were beginning to settle long-standing differences, chiefly of a colonial provenance. Germany hoped that the conference on Morocco would weaken the Anglo-French Entente of 1904. It failed to do so, as Britain at Algeciras supported French claims in Morocco, and in 1907 Britain reached a similar accommodation with Russia. These ententes were not directed against Germany, but none the less were symptomatic of changing international relations. A very real possibility of a general European war was beginning to emerge.

In 1908 Austria-Hungary annexed the nominally Turkish province of Bosnia in the Balkans, precipitating a crisis that involved Russia, which demanded compensation in the form of the opening of the Black Sea straits to its warships, and Germany, which gave unconditional support to Austria-Hungary early in 1909. Although Russia drew back, Europe came near to violence and the annexation of Bosnia was itself a threat to

European stability because it aggravated the problem of Slav nationalism within Austria-Hungary, contributing in the end very directly to the outbreak of war in 1914. Moreover, this continental tension was accompanied by an acceleration of the naval arms race between Britain and Germany, reaching a new pitch in 1909, when there was a public outcry in Britain demanding an enlarged naval shipbuilding programme to match a supposed German expansion.

Anti-foreign violence and demonstrations in Morocco served as a justification for the French occupation of Ujda, Casablanca and Rabat in 1907. German opposition, though it had not been able to keep the French out, had secured at Algeciras the principle of freedom of economic opportunity. The extent of international interference was illustrated by the character of the new State Bank of Morocco, set up as a result of the conference. Although it had its administrative headquarters in Paris and two-sevenths of the capital was French (half state, half private), its registered office was in Tangier and the balance of its capital was subscribed by twelve different governments, all European, except Morocco itself. It acted as the Moroccan government's agent, had the first option in floating governments loans and had the sole right of issuing banknotes.

Control of currency was a sign of sovereignty. When Britain occupied Tansvaal in the Boer War, the Pretoria mint was closed and in 1903 the notes of the National Bank of the South African Republic (which became the National Bank of South Africa) ceased to be legal tender. Kruger coins retained their legal status in the Transvaal and the Orange Free State (temporarily the Orange River Colony) and in fact in 1911 became legal tender in the Cape and Natal, but in 1906 the imperial coinage regulations were applied to the Transvaal.

In British West Africa the authorities continued their battle against the old moneys, which people still preferred because they were divisible into very small denominations. The official exchange rate in Nigeria was 300 cowries to the penny, and the penny was too large an amount of money for purchases of food. Even the bronze farthing introduced into Nigeria in 1903 was unpopular because it was too big. In 1902 the rate of exchange was fixed in Nigeria between sterling and manillas and Maria Theresa dollars and these were no longer allowed to be imported. By the First World War the use of manillas and cowries was confined to the very poor and to the conservative. Manillas ceased to be legal tender in 1911. A new local coinage of bronze and aluminium was minted in 1908 and this caught on because the coins were pierced with holes so that they could be strung together like cowries and they were of sufficiently low value for the smallest of purchases. Currency notes remained the prerogative of the Bank of British West Africa until 1912. In French West Africa the Banque de l'Afrique occidentale was formed in 1901 with currency issuing rights. It took over the old Banque du Sénégal.

The use of colonial money spread more slowly in East Africa than in West. In both British and German colonies the silver rupee was the circulating medium. This was because of the great volume of trade with India carried on by Indian merchants. The Indian rupee coin was made the standard coin in British East Africa in 1898 and the rate of exchange was fixed at 15 rupees to the pound sterling in 1905. In Uganda cowrie shells were demonetized as early as 1901 and in East Africa the Germans introduced the heller coin in 1912 for small change. In Madagascar, where there was no bank of issue, the circulating medium was the French five franc silver piece.

Rationalization of the currency was one aspect of more formal and more intrusive administration. Private empires were dissolved. The most conspicuous example was the Congo Free State, a by-word in Europe for cruel exploitation. Protests about the behaviour of the concession companies led to the appointment of an International Commission in 1904, and the ABIR and Anversoise concessions, against which the most serious charges had been made, were terminated in 1906. The report of the International Commission came out in 1908 and largely confirmed the truth of the accusations, more especially the allegations about the companies in which the state had a large share. Forced labour limited in theory to forty hours a month was imposed far beyond that limit. The security of tenure and pay of company employees and government officials depended partly upon their success in rubber collection and there was no proper control of African subordinates. Thus in 1908 the Congo Free State was taken over by Belgium and about a third of the 27 million hectares granted to private companies in freehold was repossessed by the state.

Colonies of different colonial powers made little contact with one another. Each colonial empire was administered as a totally separate entity. France continued with its policy of reserving for itself as best it could the trade of its colonies. In Britain, with a more buoyant economy than in the 1890s, the cause of protectionism lost ground. In 1902 Chamberlain left the Conservative government to campaign for tariff reform after failing to persuade it to continue a duty on corn imports, imposed for revenue during the Boer War, with a new purpose of facilitating imperial preference. The upshot was a split in the Conservative party and electoral defeat in 1905. None the less, Chamberlain's campaign was not without its effects. After 1903 the South African colonies gave preference to imports from Britain and to certain other parts of the empire in return for similar privileges: Canada in 1904, Australia in 1906 and New Zealand in 1907.

Within each empire an attempt was made at co-ordination and co-operation. Although external economic links were with the metropolitan countries, not with one another, some colonies were grouped together for certain purposes. The Federation of French West Africa was given a governor-general in 1904 with his capital at Dakar, and in 1910 the French Central African colonies of Gabon, Middle Congo and Ubangi-Shari were grouped together as French Equatorial Africa (L'Afrique équatoriale française, AEF), with a governor-general and a capital at Brazzaville. Since each federation controlled the collection and expenditure of most indirect taxation, the object was perhaps at least partly to subsidize the poorer colonies from the comparative wealth of the richer ones. Such a grouping was less feasible in British West Africa, where the British enclaves were separated by French territory. However, Britain went as far as it could. Lagos was merged with Southern Nigeria in 1906, and Northern Nigeria, which became a protectorate in 1902, added to them in 1914, largely to subsidize the poor north with the revenues of the more prosperous south and thus relieve the British taxpayer.

In South Africa, when the Boer War was concluded in 1902, the former republics became crown colonies, but the imperial government did not delay long before relaxing its control. Where government was in the hands of Britons abroad, there was no necessity for its close control. The only difference between South Africa and Canada, Australia or New Zealand lay in the size of the indigenous population handed over to settler administration and in the size of its alien white group, the Afrikaners. Some sort of agreement was necessary between the four colonies, if only to ensure a common market and an equitable division of revenue from railways and customs duties. In 1903 a customs union composed of the Cape, Natal, Transvaal, Orange River Colony, Rhodesia and the protectorates of Basutoland, Bechuanaland and Swaziland was brought into existence. Within six months there was disagreement. Eventually Natal threatened to withdraw, but another conference, held in 1906, patched up another compromise. The British High Commissioner in South Africa, Lord Selborne, urged the merits of political association as a means of facilitating agreement on customs and railway tariffs. Advocates of political union pointed out the added advantage of cheaper government and more equitably distributed fiscal burdens. The Union of South Africa thus came to be formed in 1910. The Act of Union made provision for eventual inclusion of Rhodesia and the protectorates, but they never joined, though they remained part of the customs union. The new state was a self-governing dominion with a constitution in which clauses were entrenched with the aim of safeguarding the existing franchise of blacks in Cape Colony, rights which were not extended to the other colonies, now provinces of the Union.

The Boer War was not the last of the colonial wars, but over a large part of Africa the new political dispensation was completed. Greater stability was followed by a resumption of population growth. It is generally assumed that population increase was attributable to a fall in the death rate as a result of better food supplies and the reduction of disease and that the birth rate was consistently high, especially among Muslims. It is possible, however, that the latter was influenced by the demand for labour, e.g. for cash crop farming. It is impossible to make any confident statements about population numbers over most of Africa. There is every reason to believe that population was increasing in Nigeria, where the total was estimated at 15 million in 1900 and 19,9 million in 1921. In the colonies of South Africa there were fairly accurate censuses. Total population was put at 5,1 million in 1904 and 5,9 million in 1911.

Increasing numbers, together with the alienation of land to Europeans, resulted in subdivision of holdings, landlessness and rising land values. In Egypt, although the population growth rate was actually slowing down, it was still about 1,5 per cent a year in the first decade of this century and the number of owners of land was increasing. In 1900 there were 913 000 landowners, in 1910, 1 391 400. In 1900 there were 761 000 owners of five feddans (2,1 ha) or less, in 1910, 1 247 000. The area of land owned by these farmers increased in total, from 1 113 000 feddans (467 894 ha) in 1900 to 1 370 000 (575 934 ha) in 1910, but the average plot fell from 1,46 feddans to 1,10 feddans. At the same time the percentage of cultivated land owned by big landowners (50 feddans or more) increased from 43,9 to 45,0 (1900-1910). Five feddans of land were considered to be the minimum for self-sufficiency, but the census of 1907 showed that one rural family in five had no land. Those with none or little had to make ends meet by working for their more fortunate neighbours.

A number of factors favoured population growth. It was not only a question of a cessation of slavery and violence – a slow and long drawn out process – and more effective administration. Transport development was of great importance, permitting greater participation in production for the market, and therefore rising incomes, and improving the distribution of food. Ocean shipping continued to expand both in tonnage and in range of services. The number of ships entering Cape and Natal ports increased from 3 000 in 1898 to 4 100 in 1910, the tonnage from 7,9 million to 11,4 million tons. Africa was still, however, comparatively insignificant. Over the period 1909-1913 East African ports accounted for only 5,2 per cent of the tonnage passing through the Suez Canal. Britain took the biggest share of the freight to and from African ports except where it encountered discrimination. German shipping capacity was expanding rapidly and German firms secured for themselves a substantial share of the African market.

Although they began to rise after 1910, freight rates during the first decade of the century were lower than they had been in the 1890s. The shipping conferences were unable to charge whatever they thought fit. For there was the constant threat of the interloper, leading to either a rate war or admission of the newcomer into the ring. In 1904 the South African Shipping Conference was reconstructed after the Houston line was taken in and in 1907 new pooling arrangements were made in West Africa to accommodate Hamburg-Bremen-Afrika and Hamburg-Amerika. The tendency was for existing companies to extend their services or start new ones, adding a further impetus to the trend towards cartelization. The Union-Castle line started a service to East Africa and Natal via Suez in 1910. While lines serving South Africa extended their routes to East Africa, those in the East African trade expanded their operations to Moçambique and Natal. By the outbreak of the First World War in 1914 there was an East African Conference. Such were the complaints of shippers against shipping rings that the British government appointed a Royal Commission on the subject. Its majority report in 1909 accepted that on balance conferences were inevitable and excusable, ensuring regular services and stable rates.

After 1900 many of the railways already started were completed and new ones begun. In Egypt a line was built along the coast westwards to Abu Haggag, a distance of 240 km, and another, a narrow gauge one, to Kharga (the Great) Oasis. Both were private lines, but were later acquired by the government. The French laid down the line from Conakry in French Guinea to the Upper Niger (1899–1914), chiefly for the export of rubber, and in the Horn of Africa a French firm, the Compagnie du Chemin de Fer Franco-Ethiopéen, completed by 1918 the line from Djibouti to Addis Ababa that had been abandoned by the Compagnie impériale d'Ethiopie when it went bankrupt in 1907. In South-West Africa the Swakopmund-Windhoek railway was opened in 1902. In German East Africa the Central Railway, from Dar es Salaam to Kigoma (on Lake Tanganyika), was built between 1904 and 1914 and the Northern Railway reached Moshi, connecting it with Tanga, in 1911. In Britain West Africa the railway from Lagos to Kano, started in 1896, was finished in 1911; that from Sekondi to Kumasi in the Gold Coast in 1903; and that from Freetown to Pendembu in Sierra Leone, begun in 1896, in 1906.

In Rhodesia the railway was extended from Bulawayo to the coalfields of Wankie, then (in 1907) via Victoria Falls to Broken Hill in Northern Rhodesia, where zinc had been found. Since traffic was not sufficient to cover the costs of operation, the British South Africa Company made an agreement with the Congo Free State for its continuation to the border, thus providing a route for the export of the copper which it was hoped would be mined in Katanga and at the same time revenue for the

Mashonaland Railway Company. The extension was completed in 1909 and a link to Elizabethville in 1910.

Other railways were started in the Congo Free State/Belgian Congo at this time. Two stretches of the Chemin de Fer du Congo supérieur aux Grands Lacs africains, designed to provide communications where the Upper Congo and Lualaba were not navigable, were built before 1910. Work by the Compagnie du Chemin de Fer du Bas-Congo au Katanga (BCK) on a line which was to run from Port Francqui on the River Kasai to Sakania, a distance of nearly 2 000 kilometres, was begun in 1909. The Benguela Railway was planned in 1909. It was to run from Lobito Bay in Angola to the Congo frontier, where it was to link up with the Bas-Congo-Katanga system. The entire line was to be just over 2 000 kilometres, 650 of which would be in Belgian territory. It proved, however, to be so costly that by 1914 only about a quarter of its length had been put down.

In South Africa, after the Boer War, the competition between the colonial lines and ports did not abate. If the Cape and Natal hoped that, as a result of the conquest of the Transvaal, they would get the Delagoa Bay traffic from the Rand, they were disappointed. The Portuguese were able to secure, by the so-called *modus vivendi* agreement, a substantial share of the freight, chiefly because the need for Moçambique labour for the gold-mines compelled Britain to pay that price for the right to recruit contract workers.

Agreements such as the *modus vivendi* were valued because it was so difficult to make railways pay. Some were subsidized. In 1904 France undertook to pay an annual subsidy to the Algerian railway companies, to take the place of the state guarantee of interest payments to the share-holders. The subsidy was to decrease over the years, but not to lapse until 1946. Despite this help construction was often held up by lack of funds. The German government was chief source of the capital of the Central Railway of East Africa and most of the Northern Railway was constructed by the government. When the Dahomey railway from Cotonou to Tchaourou was built, the colonial government was responsible for the roadbed, the Compagnie des Chemins de Fer en Dahomey for the track and rolling stock. Between 1900 and 1904 the colony spent just over six million francs, all out of local tax revenue.

Nowhere was there a comprehensive network of railways. But they were no mean achievement. Several were over a thousand kilometres in length, including the Dakar-Bamako, Lagos-Kano and Dar es Salaam-Kigoma lines. The costs were heavy in terms of colonial taxation, forced labour and alienated land for the exploitation of concession companies. Distribution of railway mileage was very uneven. South Africa was much the best served. Less well off, but still better provided than most were Algeria, Egypt, the

Belgian Congo and South-West Africa. In West Africa the wealthier coastal colonies – Nigeria, Gold Coast, Ivory Coast and Senegal – did much better than their poorer neighbours in the interior, where, however, to some extent river and lake navigation reduced the need for railways.

Because railways were so often planned, financed, equipped and managed by aliens and stopped far short of providing a complete network, their construction and operation did not have such beneficial effects upon the African economy as they did upon the economies of Europe and North America (though their infuence is considered by many historians nowadays to have been exaggerated in the past). African railways depended upon foreign capital rather than upon the mobilization of local savings; they imported their rails and rolling stock and did not stimulate local manufacture; and they employed expatriate managers and skilled workers, not local ones. Although they did have the effect of enlarging the market and breaking down local monopolies – and in Europe and America that fostered regional specialization and more efficient production for the benefit of all – in Africa it was more often for the benefit of overseas merchants and manufacturers than African ones. The railways mostly connected the interior with the coast rather than different regions with one another. When local enterprise did benefit, it was often settler rather than indigenous enterprise, e.g. white farmers. At first some railways were hard put to it to find any freight at all. In the absence of branch lines, roads and wheeled transport, only the land immediately next to the track could take advantage of their services. In East Africa the railway ran for long distances through arid thorn-scrub, sparsely inhabited and infested with tsetse fly, and were for a long time operated at a loss. The Umtali-Beira railway was initially narrow gauge. It had little traffic to begin with because of the slow development of Rhodesia. If anything, there were too many railways. So many were under-utilized – those to the Transvaal, those from Luanda and Beira.

Yet railways were not without their effects. In areas where waterways were inadequate or entirely lacking, and animal transport little used in the absence of roads and the endemic presence of trypanosomiasis, human porterage was the only form of transport. Railway freight charges were far lower than charges for porters and made possible the movement of bulk goods previously unable to bear the costs of transport, and at the same time released their labour for other employment. In West Africa the cultivation or collection of vegetable products for export became worthwhile in inland areas. The Dakar-St Louis railway facilitated the transport of ground-nuts. Freight rates were by no means low on the Uganda Railway in the first years of its operation, but all the same permitted for the first time exports from the interior beyond the narrow coastal belt, other than slave-carried ivory. Where railways were built primarily for non-economic motives, administrative or strategic, as in the case of the Uganda Railway, the colonial administration, under pressure from the imperial authorities, were spurred on to encourage economic activity simply to make the railway pay. In a small way, too, railways did contribute to the development of industry and urbanization. Nairobi, for example, began its modern existence as the up-country site of stores and workshops during the construction of the Uganda Railway. In South Africa, De Aar became both a railway junction and a repair centre, as did Bulawayo in Southern Rhodesia. In Egypt repair shops were set up in Cairo and Alexandria.

Railway construction needed a lot of labour. Up to five thousand labourers were working at a time on the Dahomey railway. They were all recruited from the chiefs within the colony. Labour in sub-Saharan Africa was mostly contract with a high turnover and not much re-engagement. Although wages were low, it was not cheap labour owing to the high costs of recruitment, including transporting recruits, and it was rarely adequate either in quantity or in quality for the needs of railway construction, mining and agriculture, the chief employers. Even before the First World War, the idea was mooted of stabilizing the labour force by encouraging migrant workers to take their families to their place of employment. A strongly contrasting but not new solution was the importation of indentured Chinese labour, and this was tried in South Africa, where there was a shortage of mine labour after the Boer War. Chinese indentured labour, however, was an experiment that proved to be short-lived, partly because of the passionate hostility that it aroused in Britain and partly because the supply of inexpensive black labour once again improved. The Chinese labour was strictly contract labour, admitted for a defined period and then repatriated. The South African authorities had no wish to see the growth of a permanent Chinese population in the country, as had happened in the case of the Indian indentured labourers.

Contract labour in South Africa incurred a great deal of criticism among philanthropists in Europe and America and missionaries in Africa. Recruitment for the mines was carried on in conformity with recognized rules. The element of direct compulsion was small and conditions of work, though falling far short of comfort, were regulated and wages, though small, were regular. None the less, in 1907 the Aboriginees Protection Society in Britain condemned labour recruitment as a mild form of slavery. The Portuguese, themselves subject to sharp criticism, complained repeatedly about the harshness of service for Moçambican Africans working in the mines and the high mortality rate. A more cogent criticism was that labour recruitment seemed to indicate that colonial administrators and entrepreneurs looked upon Africans merely as plantation or mine-fodder. The

Portuguese sold labour from Moçambique like any other commodity. This colony was looked upon as a labour reservoir with no other exportable commodity of importance. This was an attitude apparently shared by the British. The Portuguese did indeed have reservations about exporting labour, but less because of doubts abouts its morality than that of a fear that Moçambique's own development would be retarded by labour shortage.

Moçambique was the chief source of mine labour. After 1909 sometimes as many as 100 000 workers were recruited in the territory out of a population of perhaps two million. The rules governing recruitment were laid down in the *modus vivendi* of 1901. The Portuguese did very well out of it. They charged the recruiters fees which were an important part of the colonial budget, and the contract workers were able to earn the money to pay their taxes, as well as bring back savings that were spent in Moçambique. Wages were kept low in the interests of maintaining the profitability of the low-grade mines. Mortality rates were high, as much as 67 per thousand in the period 1901–1910, but many workers from the tropical zone of Moçambique were already suffering from tuberculosis at the time of their engagement, and the mortality rate did gradually decline. Despite the uninviting contract terms, Africans preferred them to even more poorly paid work at home. The mines recruited all over southern Africa. In Southern Rhodesia they met competition from local labour demands. In 1903 the British South Africa Company set up a Native Bureau to recruit contract labour for farms and mines. It looked to Moçambique among other places but encountered opposition from the Witwatersrand Native Labour Association.

An element of force was almost always present in the recruitment of contract labour. This was exerted formally by official policy through taxation. In the Belgian Congo this was deliberately fixed at so high a rate that it was difficult for an unmarried man – who did not enjoy the help of wives – to earn it through traditional methods of agriculture. In 1901 British East Africa also resorted to this device for obtaining labour. A hut tax of two rupees was introduced and later raised to three rupees, supplemented by a poll-tax to apply to non-householders. Informal pressure was exercised by means of dubious recruiting practices, which were encouraged by the inadequacy of the controls maintained by colonial authorities. Often recruiters made disreputable arrangements with chiefs. In the Belgian Congo recruiters went in for holding women hostage until the men agreed to volunteer for contract. Examples of such activities could be multiplied. The contract labour system, moreover, had undoubted drawbacks apart from the question of the application of force. Recruiting tended to be indiscriminate. Whole districts were sometimes denuded of labour. This was a common complaint in Moçambique among those who resented recruitment for the Rand. Normally young and able-bodied men were recruited, resulting in population disequilibrium in many villages.

The Portuguese came under severe criticism for their use of contract labour in the cocoa plantations of São Thomé and Principe. Normally they simply denied the existence of anything improper, and in any case were reluctant to remedy the situation because the islands were their only colonies that were actually paying their way. The most celebrated exposure of labour conditions was made by an English journalist, Henry W. Nevinson, in a series of articles in *Harper's Magazine* in 1905 and 1906, afterwards published as a book, *A Modern Slavery*. In Benguela he visited the office of the Central Committee of Labour and Emigration for the Islands, where slaves became contract labourers (serviçães) and found ample evidence of slaving and slavery. Such was international outrage that São Thomé cocoa was boycotted. The Portuguese responded with a decree of July 1909 which brought recruiting agencies under greater control. As regulations concerning health and wages were introduced, the situation began to improve. An increasing number of men were recruited in Moçambique on genuine short-term contracts, repatriation of men whose contract had expired began and the mortality rate fell from the very high level of 20 per cent a year.

Action was taken by other imperial governments, too, against the excesses of compulsion. Bernhard Dernburg, in charge of German colonial affairs from 1906 to 1910, disliked it and in German East Africa contracts were restricted to 180 days, raised to 240 days in 1913, at least for workers on the rubber plantations. In 1908 the British government condemned forced labour throughout the Empire and forbade conscription for private employers. An ambiguous situation developed in the British colonies. Since colonial officials were allowed to use taxation and persuasion to get labour for employers, confusion arose about the permitted level of taxation and the degree of persuasion, which at its most overbearing could be tanta-mount to coercion. Methods of officials varied widely. But government put limits upon compulsion. White settlers in East Africa pressed in vain for heavier taxation and for confiscation of African-occupied land in order to force peasant farmers into wage employment. The government was unwilling to raise taxes to a level disproportionately higher than those being paid by Europeans, and in any case was unconvinced of the effectiveness of taxation as an instrument of coercion. It steadfastly resisted land expropriation for that purpose.

Generally speaking labour law was rudimentary in Africa before the First World War. Algeria was probably the most advanced, simply because it was the beneficiary, though usually after some delay and subject to some modification to suit local conditions, of French legislation to protect workers. In 1903 a Consultative Labour Commission was set up and in 1909 the governor-general was empowered to appoint inspectors of labour. The sections of the French labour code, the first of which were enacted in 1910, were gradually extended to Algeria. How effective this legal machinery was in protecting native Algerian workers is not entirely clear.

Most often in sub-Saharan Africa labourers were black, employers white, but not always, employers sometimes being black too. In West Africa, where wage-earning dated to pre-colonial times, though on a restricted scale, chiefly for porterage, migrant workers were used increasingly after 1900 for cocoa harvesting or cultivation in the Gold Coast either on piece rates or on contract. However, where there was access to slave and client labour (as in Asante), this was used by chiefs and merchants going in for cocoa cultivation. Domestic slavery was under pressure from colonial governments. Between 1905 and 1907 about a third of a million native-owned slaves in French West Africa were freed. The process of emancipation was helped, in British as well as French West Africa, by the development of road transport, which lessened the need for slaves for head-loading. It was mainly in the poorer parts of the French colonies that resettlement posed a difficult problem. Elsewhere ex-slaves found openings in trade or the production of cash crops.

The export of cash crops continued to expand. Until the 1920s Africa – principally West Africa – was furnishing virtually the whole of the world's supply of oil palm products. Exports of palm oil from Nigeria averaged 53 thousand metric tons a year over the period 1900-1904, 65 thousand in 1905-1909 and 77 thousand in 1910-1914, as much again being consumed at home. Palm kernel exports rose from an annual average of 119 thousand metric tons in 1900-1904, to 128 thousand in 1905-1909 and to 171 thousand in 1910-1914. The proportion of total African – therefore, in effect, world – exports of palm oil from Nigeria was 67,7 per cent and of palm kernels 53,8 per cent in 1909-1913. The chief constraints upon the export trade were inadequate transport, shortage of labour and the rather poor quality of oil extracted by the farmers themselves. The Germans, who were the biggest customer for palm produce, not only from their own colony of Kamerun, but also from Nigeria, were active in developing small machines for extracting better quality oil and also for cracking palm nuts to release the kernels. Machine crushing and extraction, however, were slow in spreading. European-owned mills depended upon local supply and farmers were reluctant to abandon their traditional methods, inefficient and wasteful as they were.

Sierra Leone was an important producer of palm kernels, with an output not far short of the whole of French West Africa. It accounted for an annual average of 14,2 per cent of African output in 1909-1913. In the Gold Coast, however, cocoa replaced palm produce, and also rubber, as the chief export in terms of both volume and value. In 1908, 12 946 metric tons of cocoa beans were exported, 6,7 per cent of world exports, despite the fact that their price was tending to fall from 1896, while that of palm kernels was tending to rise. The expanding production of the Gold Coast was itself probably a factor in the declining price of cocoa in the world. Cultivation reached 160 km inland after the construction of the railway to Kumasi in Ashanti.

A substantial amount of profit from cocoa was ploughed back into the industry, permitting the great expansion of cultivation. Some went into house building, the construction of roads and bridges and education. Expenditure on imports did not rise appreciably, even during the cocoa boom of 1901-1911. None of the profit seems to have gone into other productive investment. Cocoa farmers tended to put their savings into money-lending at high rates of interest or into land, the acquisition of which, because of the prestige attached to landowning, was a possible inducement to undertake cash crop farming.

Largely as a result of cocoa, national income in the Gold Coast grew at an estimated 3,77 per cent a year during the first decade of the present century. Cocoa was also started in the Ivory Coast, by immigrants from the savanna, some of them traders with capital to invest, others prepared to work for a share of the crop. They bought or, more usually, rented land and employed either family or wage labour. In Nigeria after 1900, following the pacification of Yorubaland, migrant farmers extended cultivation into the forest belt. The export of ground-nuts began from Nigeria largely as the result of railway construction to the north and greatly expanded from Senegal and Gambia.

The price of cotton continued to rise steeply until 1913 and the value of exports of cotton and cotton seed from Egypt grew very quickly. By 1914 over 90 per cent of the total value of Egyptian exports was derived from the sale of cotton, compared with about 75 per cent at the start of the occupation. In 1902 a new dam was completed at Aswan to regulate the autumn flood down the river, and its height was subsequently raised. Yet cotton production grew rather more slowly during the years immediately preceding the First World War. Although the area devoted to cotton cultivation continued to expand, yields began to decline. There was a particularly bad harvest in 1909. Irrigation was bedevilled by inadequate drainage and excessive cultivation, which caused weed and insect infestation and loss of fertility. The latter could be remedied by the application of chemical fertilizer, which, however, could be afforded only by wealthier farmers. None the less, substantial, if uneven, expansion of agricultural production occurred, though per capita production and real income declined with the increase of population.

Cotton cultivation never enjoyed much popularity in West Africa and was never a significant West African export in relation to total world production and to total West African exports despite encouragement from public authorities and private organizations. Most influential was the British Cotton Growing Association, which was formed in 1902 (and chartered in 1904) to develop cotton growing within the Empire and thus safeguard British supplies, threatened in the 1890s when American cotton was attacked by the boll-weevil. The president was Sir Alfred Jones, the West African shipping magnate, and it was to West Africa that the Association turned. To begin with the emphasis was upon European plantations but these were not a success owing to the shortage of labour and the high cost of European supervision. Consequently the Association turned to small African cultivators. Cotton cultivation was not new, nor cotton exporting: in the late 1860s, during the American cotton famine, half a million kilograms had been exported annually through Lagos, but production for overseas ceased when American supplies picked up again and prices fell. Now the Association guaranteed a price and with the help of colonial subsidies provided a range of services: research, distribution of seed, advice, ginning and transport to the coast. In due course the work of research and development was taken over by colonial Agricultural Departments and the colonial subsidies ceased. The chief cotton exporting region was southern Nigeria. The climate was unsuitable in Gambia and Sierra Leone; in southern Gold Coast cotton could not compete with cocoa; and in the interior regions of the Gold Coast and Nigeria transport costs were prohibitive before the spread of the railways. Cotton was grown in northern Nigeria, but mostly used by local manufacturers.

Southern Dahomey experienced a boom in maize exports, which rose from 207 tons in 1904 to their maximum of 20 000 tons in 1908. This was the result of rising world prices, facilitated by the development of the railway. Most was bought by German merchants. Maize farming was combined with oil palm production and the expansion was accompanied by an increase in the output of manioc for domestic consumption. Since, however, its maize was of uneven quality and comparatively dear, Dahomey was a marginal source of supply, called upon only when world demand could not be met from the chief exporting areas. Conversely Dahomean exports had a high export price elasticity: only an exceptionally high world price could persuade farmers to plant more or divert supplies from domestic consumption, though exports could also be influenced by the price of palm products on world markets. The French authorities made no attempt to provide storage facilities or in other ways to ensure for Dahomey a permanent share of the international trade in maize.

There was a revived interest in rubber during the early years of the century, especially between 1908 and 1910, and new companies entered the trade in West Africa, where the older firms were still active, collecting wild rubber as one of their lines of business. The new flurry was the result of increased demand and an inadequate supply of wild rubber, which still came principally from South and Central America. British capital was mobilized to develop new sources of supply. Most investment went into plantations in Ceylon, Malaya and Sumatra as an alternative to the collection of wild rubber. In South-East Asia planting enjoyed great success. Some – by no means a negligible amount – of the capital went into tropical Africa. Twenty-six companies were floated to operate in West Africa (Liberia and Ivory Coast, in which, unlike British territories, substantial concessions were obtainable, and British West Africa), though some were more concerned with making profits – sometimes fraudulently – from the sale of shares during the speculative boom in rubber shares in 1909–1910 than with the production of rubber. In West Africa only a small amount of cultivation was carried out and often as a sideline of firms engaged in other activities, such as trade. Wild rubber continued to predominate but because it involved high labour costs and was often difficult to collect, it was on its way out. In its heyday African wild rubber collection (mostly from West Africa and the Congo Free State/Belgian Congo) was of considerable significance, accounting for 25,33 per cent of the total output of wild rubber in the world. When the price of rubber fell not long before the First World War, it rapidly lost importance. The rubber companies, often incompetently managed, scarcely paid a dividend. African wild rubber could not compete with the cheap high quality rubber of the plantations of South-East Asia. It was not up to the increasingly strict standards of the tyre manufacturers, and at the same time the new cocoa industry was presenting an alternative source of income. Moreover, the trees and vines from which it was derived were recklessly tapped and thus destroyed.

From East Africa the export of hides and skins helped to fill the commercial vacuum created by the abolition of the trade in slaves, slave-transported ivory and slave-cultivated copra and grain. The construction of the railway into Uganda permitted the export of bees' wax and ivory, as well as hides and skins. But these exports were not sufficient to rehabilitate the region, and ivory was a diminishing asset. In Uganda the cultivation of all sorts of crops was tried by native smallholders before the emphasis finally settled on cotton and coffee. In Kenya the authorities, after toying with the idea of bringing in Indian smallholders, who, it was presumed, would set a good example to African cultivators, soon became convinced that only European settlement would permit the economic development of the protectorate and enable it to support itself. In the event, Indians, including those who settled in East Africa after completing a term as indentured labourers on railway construction, were discouraged from settling on the land and only a few did so. Instead planting, mixed farming and ranching were carried on mostly by Europeans. Partly for that reason wage-labour on European farms was more common than independent cultivation for the market, giving a lower level of income among Africans than that attained in Uganda.

The people of East Africa did not have the same advantages as the West Africans, who had cash crops ready at hand, one – palm produce – that could be collected virtually without cultivation, and another – ground-nuts – long familiar as a food crop. From these it was a relatively short step to the cultivation of crops for the market. Moreover, there were incentives operating in West Africa, with its long history of commercial contact with Europe and its familiarity with, and taste for, European goods, that exerted scarcely any influence in East and Central Africa. Possibly, too, the nature of the social system was of some significance. The fact that peasant cultivation of cash crops – primarily cotton – took on in Uganda much more than in Kenya may have had something to do with the presence in Buganda of a vigorous ruling class and the predominance in Kenya of an acephalous society. In Kenya the Kavirondo farmers of the Lake Victoria basin, who were unenthusiastic about cotton growing, went in for maize production for the internal market and they grew simsim, an important export crop before the First World War. But the export of simsim died out and maize for the market became primarily a settler crop.

As in West Africa cotton was urged by the authorities and the Cotton Growing Association. Encouragement does not seem to have been any less in Kenya, where it had little success, than in Uganda, where it had much more. The greatest initial impetus came from the world shortage in the early years of the century. Seed was imported from Egypt and the United States and distributed in Uganda by the Church Missionary Society, the government and the Uganda Company. A powered cotton gin was set up by the Uganda Company in Kampala and some hand gins were sold cheaply or given away. The industry got under way surprisingly quickly, but the problem of maintaining a standard of product acceptable to cotton manufacturers had to be overcome before Uganda could become a producer of any significance. In 1908 the government took away the hand gins and insisted on the exclusive use of government-issued seed. The industry survived, with an increasing output of improved lint. It was this achievement that was largely responsible for the quadrupling of colonial revenue between 1903 and 1910. The total value of exports rose from less than £100 000 in 1906 to £500 000 at the outbreak of the First World War.

Small-scale cotton cultivation developed in German East Africa at the same time. The rôle of government was important. When cotton prices fell in 1908, it encouraged growers to persevere by guaranteeing a minimum price. Exports were worth 2 million marks in 1912. Cotton was only one of several crops that were tried, with varying success. In time native farmers became responsible for the bulk of coffee, copra and ground-nut exports. Ground coconut was also sold for local consumption.

Sometimes the production of cash crops was at the expense of food production for home consumption. In Egypt the area devoted to beans and barley declined throughout the later 19th century and the period up to 1914. The consequence was a growing dependence on imported foodstuffs. In the quinquennium 1885–1889 Egypt had on average a net export of cereals per annum worth £E 194 000; in the quinquennium 1905–1909 an average net import per annum of £E 2 501 000. But naturally there was a tendency for fluctuations to occur. Mere pressure of population was probably a more significant factor in food imports than the excessive shift to cash crop cultivation. Smallholders gave priority to the production of food and animal fodder, regarding cotton as a source of extra cash income for the payment of taxes or rent and the purchase of things that had to be bought. Cotton was only one crop of a two or three year cycle of some four or five crops. Even on the large estates it was not permitted to oust other crops.

At the same time as dependence upon imported foodstuffs grew, an increasing proportion of total output of cash crops was coming from a shrinking proportion of all those engaged in production. In Egypt before the First World War some 70 per cent of all cotton produced was grown on estates classified as large (over 50 feddans) and medium (5–50 feddans). There can be little doubt that the superior income derived from these estates from cash crop sales was one factor in the ability of the large and medium landowners to protect to a considerable extent their estates from subdivision or, perhaps, to build them up through the absorption of fragments that they were able to buy.

In Egypt on the large estate cotton was sometimes cultivated with hired labour, but some big landlords had a permanent pool of labour on their estates in the form of service or labour tenants, who were granted small plots for growing food and fodder and perhaps some cotton, in exchange for their labour and that of their families. There is not much evidence of the substitution of farm machinery for labour. There was a considerable annual migration from Upper Egypt northwards to the Delta for work in the cotton fields. Large numbers of those without land or owning plots too small to provide a livelihood worked for the big owners, and sometimes for the small at the busiest times of the year. Wages tended to fluctuate according to market prices and harvests, but were generally at a low level, while rents tended to be high. Working capital was a problem for the small man. Those leasing land from big landlords were provided with seed and fertilizers, but many had recourse to money-lenders, and chronic rural indebtedness became a serious social problem. Cotton cultivation remained less widespread in Upper Egypt, where there was less perennial irrigation, yields were lower and big estates were somewhat less common.

To meet the needs for cheap credit of poorer peasants burdened with debt and hungry for land, an Agricultural Bank was especially established in 1902 in Egypt. The government's intention was to lessen the threat of rural violence. In practice, however, the Bank did more business with medium and large landowners, and loans tended to be for land purchase and debt repayments rather than for improvements and inputs. The trouble with the small man was that he was less credit worthy.

Co-operative agricultural credit banks became numerous in Algeria after 1900. The number of local banks increased from 92 in 1905 to 259 in 1913 and the number of regional banks, which controlled the local banks, increased from 25 to 41. Their own capital resources were meagre, but they were able to offer cheap and easy credit by means of advances from the Bank of Algeria. The intention of the French government in 1897 to restrict credit came to nothing. Loans were either short-term or long-term, up to 25 years. They were supposed to be subject to a legal limit, but were frequently much bigger. Credit was also available from the Land Bank, though this confined itself to medium-term loans on a restricted scale. The commercial banks and the Bank of Algeria lent money freely. The Bank of Algeria's loans rose from 16 million francs in 1901 to 57 million in 1911. Loans from these various sources were used for working capital and investment in new equipment, but were also used to buy land, sometimes as a speculation. The easy availability of money helps to explain the great success of Algerian colonial agriculture in the pre-war period, especially in wine growing.

Capital was only one of the problems of the farmers. Another was skill and knowledge. Colonial authorities with varying success tried to raise the standard of indigenous agriculture. Concern was also shown by private individuals and groups, religious and commercial, with or without government support. Missionaries, anxious to promote material as well as spiritual well-being, were active in popularizing export crop production, such as cotton in Uganda, arabica coffee in Kenya and cocoa in the Gold Coast, and in encouraging better farming methods, such as manuring, and the use of better implements, such as the plough. The most obvious example of commercial enterprise that encouraged African cash crop production, through research and technical and marketing assistance, was the British Cotton Growing Association. Among public bodies was the Kolonial wirtschaftliche Komitee, which did valuable work in the German colonies. The Germans were noted for their excellent schools of agriculture and centres of research, especially the Amani Biological-Agricultural Institute in East Africa (1902). Similarly the British colonial authorities were active in testing plants and trees in their research stations and in supplying farmers with seeds and seedlings. In this regard much work was done in England at the Royal Botanical Gardens, Kew. The other colonial powers – French, Belgian, Italian and Portuguese – likewise maintained in their colonies and at home institutions for research into agriculture and animal husbandry. The findings of research and experiment were disseminated by means of extension services. There was considerable success during the colonial period in the development and use of new crops, new implements, disease and pest controls, and new techniques of production, though in these early years investment in colonial agriculture was still modest.

It was, however, not only help that colonial governments gave. Compulsion was also employed, such as enforced cultivation of crops. This served a dual purpose, to provide export crops, usually at a lower than market price that represented a tax on cultivators, and an adequate supply of foodstuffs and to educate Africans in the use of better techniques, a purpose emphasized by France and Belgium. In the Congo Free State, where the educative aim did not exert much influence, there was compulsory cultivation of cash crops, and after the Belgian annexation the compulsion remained, though the methods of collecting and marketing were reformed. The most important compulsory crop in the Belgian Congo was cotton, for which there was a guaranteed market and a guaranteed, if low, price. In their West African colonies the French tried to enforce the cultivation of cotton and cocoa before the First World War, but without much success. In the British colonies powers were usually taken to enforce adequate cultivation of food crops, but there was no enforced cultivation of cash crops, only the application of persuasion.

The response of African cultivators to the opportunities for cash crop farming was influenced by – and in turn influenced – the extent to which European agriculture was introduced into Africa. The attitudes and calculations of political authorities were also important, as were the climatic conditions regarded as tolerable by prospective European settlers, for whom, it was assumed in the 19th century, a healthy decent life in the tropics was possible only on high land several hundred metres above sea level.

Expatriate agriculture necessitated the confiscation of land. Conquerors have rarely felt any compunction about seizing as much land as they have thought fit. Successive rulers of Egypt and North Africa helped themselves, and in the more sparsely populated regions of sub-Saharan Africa, where large areas seemed, however mistakenly, to belong to no one, few qualms were felt at the large-scale expropriation of unutilized or underutilized land. The consideration shown towards native inhabitants varied. The large-scale seizure of land characteristic of the 1880s and 1890s for state exploitation or leasing to concessionaries tailed off, though very large grants were still possible. In 1904 a million hectares in the basin of the Busira in the Congo Free State were bestowed in freehold – the so-called Bus-Block – upon the Compagnie du Chemin de Fer du Congo to honour the undertaking of 1886 to the Compagnie du Congo pour le Commerce et l'Industrie. The land was entrusted to the Société anonyme belge pour le Commerce du Haut-Congo (SAB). All three companies were inter-connected and Albert Thys was intimately involved in them.

Early grants of land in West and Central Africa were mostly used for the collection of forest products, though some plantations were established, e.g. rubber plantations in Kamerun, some of them British-owned. German colonial policy, however, became stricter, at least towards foreign enterprise. In 1910 most of the 5 000 hectares allocated for purchase by Anton Jurgens, the Dutch margarine manufacturer, was declared inalienable native land. Other land was bought at a price and the project was a financial disaster.

Expatriate farms and plantations were rare in British West Africa, but not unknown. Land was communally owned in theory, though family occupied land was recognized as private property. Customary law in the Gold Coast allowed chiefs to sell tribal land in order to pay tribal debts and it was through this loophole that migrant cocoa farmers bought land. In Ashanti the colonial government permitted only the renting of tribal land to ensure that chiefs did not lose their power through loss of control over land distribution. In practice there was nothing to prevent chiefs alienating or leasing up to 50 square kilometres of land at a time. A good deal of land sold or leased was for mining rather than planting, and there was extensive alienation to gold-mining companies in 1900-1901. Some land was acquired by European business interests for timber cutting or for rubber production, mostly the collection of wild rubber. In Nigeria the Native Lands Acquisition Order of 1903 kept a much tighter rein on such land transactions. Foreigners were not allowed to buy land there, though a few entrepreneurs, native as well as foreign, did acquire land on lease. W.H. Lever, the British soap and margarine manufacturer, began an agitation in 1906 for permission to start plantations, but without success, although there was in fact something to be said for large-scale production. Farming standards in some agricultural sectors were not high. Increased production was achieved more by extending the area of cultivation than by improving the productivity of the land. Farmers had few resources to fall back on in difficult times and little cash to spare for fertilization and pest control. The quality of the produce tended to vary. The success of plantations in Malaya and the East Indies proved to be a serious threat to some West African products. However, the situation was complex. With some crops, small farmers were very successful, notably cocoa, and with others, e.g. ground-nuts, they had a very great advantage over the plantation. British officials who came under pressure from Lever and the British Cotton Growing Association certainly did not accept the argument that the plantation was more efficient than the system of peasant production. The latter was thought to be more firmly based than European enterprise, developing spontaneously and self-supporting in labour. While European plantations were dependent upon expensive expatriate managers and often upon the use of compulsion in obtaining local labour, the costs of production of peasant farming were very low, and it could be much more rapidly expanded than European enterprise. Certainly shortage of capital, labour and technical competence limited the success of much European agricultural enterprise.

Practice varied in East Africa. In Uganda the Baganda chiefs were converted into landowners by the Uganda Agreement concluded by Sir Harry Johnston, the special commissioner of the Foreign Office, in 1900. Some of them set themselves up as planters, growing rubber and coffee. The British government took over about half the total land of the kingdom as crown land, but set aside some 23 000 sq. km. for the king and the chiefs, altogether about 3 700 people. Those of them who chose to go in for commercial farming sometimes used the tributary labour of their followers, now transformed into tenants; others allowed their tenants to commute their labour into cash and then employed wage-labour. Most of the landowners, however, were unwilling to farm themselves and preferred to live on their tenants' rents. That was the situation in Buganda; in Toro and Ankole only small areas were granted to the rulers and a few prominent chiefs, and the government asserted its own claim to uncultivated land.

With few exceptions the Africans in Kenya were left in possession of the land they were actually occupying. Expropriation was unnecessary since the Highlands were sparsely inhabited except near Lake Victoria and the eastern districts. The unfairness of the land division in Kenya was that the much more numerous and faster growing African population was excluded from the large part of the Highlands reserved for Europeans, but to a considerable extent left unused. The East Africa (Lands) Order in Council of 1901 accorded to Africans only rights of occupation, cultivation and grazing, without freehold title, so that deserted land fell to the crown. Under the Crown Lands Ordinance, 1902, the Commissioner of Lands was permitted to lease land containing African settlements and the land occupied passed to the lessee if it was abandoned. In practice, colonial officials allowed lessees to turn Africans off the land they had leased if they paid compensation for their cultivation and houses. A report made by Sir Percy Girouard, governor of the East African Protectorate, recommended in 1909 the setting aside of inalienable African reserves, but little was done before the First World War to implement its recommendations.

In Algeria there was a revival of official settlement. Between 1902 and 1907 government money, largely borrowed, was spent on this object at the rate of more than $3\frac{1}{2}$ million francs a year, and, although thereafter the rate of annual expenditure fell, it still amounted to 1,8 million francs in 1913. A different type of settler was aimed at, one with some capital of his own. Land was sold rather than given and farms were somewhat larger from the outset, up to 200 hectares in the less favoured south previously used largely for pastoral farming. Free grants, for which there was some demand, continued, but were less numerous than land sales. In the ten years 1902-1911 some 174 000 hectares were brought under settlement. Despite these efforts, however, the European population of the countryside declined by a fifth between 1901 and 1914. Some settlers were unable with the capital they had to survive on even the larger farms now allowed officially. It was this that helped the trend towards amalgamation of properties and the emigration of unsuccessful settlers from the land. To that extent official policy failed. Yet the establishment of very many settler villages throughout the country, even in remote areas, contributed to its economic development by providing centres of economic activity. In Tunisia, where private enterprise was given a freer hand, there were more settlers making their own arrangements and they took with them more capital. But the proportion of Frenchmen among the colonists was smaller.

Among Muslim farmers in Algeria the number of small and medium proprietors remained stable, but as a proportion of the agricultural population they were declining, from rather more than half at the beginning of the century to rather less than half before the 1914-1918 war. About three-fifths of rural families were farming less than ten hectares, thought to be the minimum for subsistence. The proportion of *khammès* remained much the same, at about a third, but their situation was deteriorating. Fewer proprietors took on share tenants, preferring to buy a French plough and cultivate their land more intensively themselves, and competition for places increased, bringing down the share tenant's return for his labour. In effect *khammès* tended to be depressed into hired labour paid in kind, worse off than the regular workers in European agriculture. Yet they were not the bottom layer of rural society. For beneath them were the landless unemployed. The rural proletariat was increasing. It was recruited partly from the Arabic-speaking nomadic sheep herders, partly from Berber-speaking highlanders, though Spanish and Moroccan labour was also used on European farms. Wages from farm employment were an important source of income for native Algerians. The number of male agricultural labourers on European farms, which in 1901 was about 151 000, about 13 per cent of the total male rural population, had risen by 1914 to 210 000, 18 per cent of the total male rural population. 41 per cent of native agricultural workers were in viticulture, 31 per cent in cereal cultivation. The ranks of the rural proletariat were swollen by smallholders who lost their land and by share tenants unable to find plots.

In South Africa most European immigrants made for the big towns, especially on the Witwatersrand, though some did look for farms and thus aggravated the competition for land. European farming over large parts of the country was depressed as a result of the devastation wreaked during the Boer War. Thousands of families were left destitute by the British policy during the war of burning farms to crush guerilla resistance. The so-called poor white problem became the subject of official concern. Between 1902 and 1906 some 80 000 hectares of land were acquired in the southern Transvaal for distribution to small white settlers, but such schemes could only be a partial solution and in any event enjoyed only indifferent success. After the war, however, because of the development of the railways and extension of the market, maize production in South Africa increased and, helped by preferential railway tariffs, maize farmers begun to export. Maize production in the Transvaal, 0,1 million tons in 1904, was 0,3 million in 1911 and in the Orange Free State it increased during that period from 0,03 million metric tons to 0,1 million. In 1908-1909 the South African colonies exported 0,1 million metric tons. But harvests and exports tended to fluctuate with the weather.

The effects of the war upon black agriculture were mixed. Although they too suffered from the widespread destruction, the war presented new opportunities. Many settled on deserted Boer farms and were able to cultivate food to sell. Others worked for the military authorities for wages that rose during the war. After the war the numbers of black tenants paying in cash and kind apparently increased at the expense of labour tenancy. This, and the accompanying shortage of labour on white farms, gave rise to renewed legislative assaults in the colonies upon squatting, share tenancy and other forms of independent black farming. These were for the most part without effect, and the question of black landholding was a burning issue which the first Union parliament had to consider.

Elsewhere in sub-Saharan Africa the conflict of interests between white and black agriculture had barely begun. Early in the century not much more than a trickle of settlers was as yet arriving in Southern Rhodesia, German East Africa, Kenya and German South-West Africa. In Southern Rhodesia white farming was slow to develop. Early settlers were inspired chiefly by hopes of riches from gold-mining. When these hopes were disappointed old and new settlers turned to the production of maize and tobacco for (in the absence of an internal market of any size) export. European farmers settled along the newly-built railways, though these did not run across the more fertile sections of the country. The production of tobacco reached 1,3 million kilograms a year by the beginning of the First World War.

By 1911 the white population of German East Africa was just over 3 000. It included Boers from South Africa, German ex-soldiers and former employees of German companies. The administration was cautious in its attitude to white immigration. Europeans could buy land only after demonstrating their serious intention of developing it, though this rule was sometimes evaded. In 1914 only one per cent or a little less of the total land area was occupied by Europeans. They tended to be concentrated in particular areas, such as the Mount Meru area and there some of the tribal land became overcrowded as the scope for expansion was restricted by white intrusion. Poor communications and the smallness of the internal market for foodstuffs made small-scale mixed farming hazardous.

The earliest plantations in German East Africa were for coffee, but after a promising start in the Usambara district in the 1890s its output declined during the early years of the century and it became chiefly an African peasant crop. There were experiments in various other crops. Two very large cotton plantations of more than 300 square kilometres each were started by German cotton manufacturers, but did not last very long, defeated by ignorance of local conditions, disease and high costs, including the cost of European management. Rubber cultivation, too, was encouraged by rising prices. As early as 1906 some 1 265 hectares had been planted, mostly in the Tanga-Pangani area. Some British capital was invested. Initially profits were made, but yields were poor and production costs were higher than in South-East Asia because of the higher cost of labour in relation to its productivity. In 1912 exports passed the million kilogram mark, worth more than £300 000. It was, however, a relatively brief boom. East African wild rubber was of poor quality, and unable to compete with the South-East Asian plantation product. Sisal in German East Africa in contrast was a great success once a suitable hybrid had been developed. It was an ideal crop for plantations, which alone could give the economies of scale that were essential for success. At the same time it was a hardy plant and demand for it remained fairly constant, though prices did fluctuate according to world supply. It was used for making twine for agricultural purposes and it was superior to competing products. Cultivation began in 1893, but it was some years before fibre was being processed. In 1911 sisal exports were worth $4\frac{1}{2}$ million marks, out of a total value of exports of 22,4 million marks. Plantations were run by companies based in Germany and by individual planters.

In Kenya in the early years the emphasis was on sheep farming and wheat growing, partly because at that time coffee, for which the lower slopes of the Highlands were ideal, and most other tropical produce (except cotton, which could not be economically grown in Kenya on European plantations) were not fetching good prices, and partly because the British and South African entrepreneurs, Lord Delamere and the East African Syndicate, representing interests in London and Johannesburg, who were prepared to put up money at a time when British investors generally were not attracted to East Africa, favoured European-style farming undertaken by white immigrants. The East African Syndicate was granted 1 300 square kilometres in the Rift Valley in 1903, but its experiments in wheat and sheep were not very fortunate. Both fell victim to disease, and it took decades of persistent experimentation by Delamere and others to develop a disease-resistant strain of wheat. Sheep and wheat never became of enormous importance, partly because there was only a relatively small area of land where they thrived. Similar difficulties were encountered at first with cattle, which were especially susceptible to East Coast fever, but in the end a high quality beast was developed from crosses of local and exotic breeds. But even after the experimental period and its successful outcome the dairy and cattle farmers were unable at first to stand on their own feet and could make a living only by virture of having a protected domestic market, primarily of urban Europeans and, to a lesser extent, Asians. In time an export trade in meat, meat products and hides developed, though not all originating from European farming. Stock-farming predominated in terms of area.

Following the example of the Germans, British companies were floated, some of them by enterprises already engaged in agriculture or trade in British East Africa, to start rubber plantations along the Kenya coast. The experiment enjoyed little success. Yields were even lower than in German territory and the quality just as poor, and plantation rubber from Kenya was unable to compete in the depressed world market in the immediate pre-war years. Rubber in Uganda proved to be more, though not appreciably more, profitable. There cultivation was combined with the collection (licensed by the colonial authorities) of wild rubber, but the whole operation was on a small scale.

Europeans were not the only foreigners to settle in East Africa. Indians immigrated in large numbers, engaging there in trade and performing an indispensable rôle in the marketing of African products and distributing imports. The traders were mostly Muslim Gujeratis and Hindus from the Bombay region and Kathiawar who moved inland from Zanzibar and Mombasa, bringing little capital but a commercial enterprise that was rarely met among Africans. They were also more than a match for white immigrants. European settlers had great difficulty in establishing them-selves in British East Africa. In agriculture the market for food was small and African cultivators could grow maize and vegetables more cheaply. Only men with fairly substantial resources were able to farm successfully in Kenya. Mixed farming could be profitably undertaken only on a com-paratively large scale and plantation agriculture demanded considerable capital and gave only slow returns. Kenya did not turn out to be a place for mass European immigration. Not only did initial investment and running costs in farming require large resources, but, because of the social tone set by the gentleman immigrant, a relatively high standard of living was expected. Apart from trade and farming there was nothing to which the small settler could turn his hand, at least in the early days. Even if he were prepared to work for wages, it would have been socially degrading and economically unfeasible for him to attempt to compete with blacks and Indians. Few settlers were very wealthy and only those who worked hard and knew their business could really prosper. None the less, the European population firmly established its dominant rôle in the economy.

The economic situation of the British East African Protectorate was discouraging, even desperate, as late as 1909. Exports in 1908–1909 were worth only £157 000. Not everywhere in Africa did so badly. The world economy was generally buoyant in the opening decade of the century, though many countries experienced recession in 1900–1901 and 1907–1908. International trade expanded rapidly, especially till 1905, and some African countries took advantage of this, particularly West Africa and, on account of the rapid rise of cotton prices, Egypt. South Africa suffered a post-Boer War depression from 1903 until 1909, largely the result of internal factors, the wartime devastation of farming and disagreement among the different territories on the question of railways and customs. The recovery after 1909 can be attributed partly to the settlement of political differences by the unification of the former separate colonies in 1910. The renewed prosperity of gold-mining was also of great importance.

Africa's trade remained of relative insignificance. In 1913 its share of world exports was still only 3,7 per cent and of world imports only 3,6 per cent. South Africa, Algeria and Egypt were far ahead of the rest of the continent in the volume of overseas trade, with Algeria's worth £47 million in 1913 and Egypt's £60 million in 1910. (World trade in 1913 was worth £8 360 million.) But the gap between them and the rest of Africa, though still wide, was beginning to close. The value of Egypt's exports in 1899 was $75,9 million and in 1913 $156,3 million. Nigeria, exporting goods to the value of $8,5 million in 1899 (11 per cent of the value of Egypt's) exported in 1913 goods to the value of $33,0 million (21 per cent of the value of Egypt's). World prices for Africa's staple exports recovered strongly and the terms of trade again moved in its favour, though not all exports fared equally well.

Africa's long distance trade fell increasingly into the hands of European commercial companies as they extended their trading posts into the interior. During the early years of this century there was a steep decline of the trans-Saharan trade, which was an exchange of British cotton goods and other European manufacturers at Kano and other points in the western Sudan for feathers, skins and ivory. The most westerly route to Morocco decayed earliest, even before the end of the 19th century. The most easterly route, from Benghazi to Wadai proved to be the most resilient, longer lasting than those of the central Sudan to Tripoli. A variety of reasons explains the decline. The most important was the increasingly cheaper rates on the sea routes to West Africa, but the growing insecurity of the desert routes, the result of banditry, political rivalry and the disturbance of the *status quo* by the French also contributed to their falling out of use. The desert routes kept going as long as they did partly because of the skills and experience of Tripoli merchants in the Sudan trade, but more because of the higher costs of transporting across the savanna and forest by donkey and ox, goods which had been brought by sea. Freight brought from the north was carried more cheaply by camel. Transport costs for goods imported by sea dropped as colonial administration became more effective. River steamers were introduced and, more importantly, the railway was constructed to Kano.

European capital investment in Africa, already growing in the 1890s, became even more pronounced after 1900. There was an influx of foreign capital into Egypt. Most of it went into mortgage companies which lent money on land and into land companies selling land on credit. This had unfortunate results. Competition to buy land pushed up its price. In 1905-1907 there was a boom, much of it of a speculative nature. In 1907 came collapse, with the failure of many businesses and restrictions upon credit by foreign banks. Considerable losses were incurred by big landowners who had borrowed freely to buy land and consequent resentment against foreign business interests for acting, so it was thought, in a disreputable way and against the British authorities for failing to take action to alleviate the crisis. A recently established National Bank was not, despite its name, a bankers' bank, could not influence prevailing interest rates and had no control over the money supply. It was therefore powerless to prevent or mitigate the crisis. The authorities tended to pursue a *laissez-faire* policy in finance and commerce, neither encouraging nor discouraging foreign investment.

The soundness of the Egyptian economy and the apparent security offered by British rule made Egypt a good investment opening. Foreign investment soon resumed after the 1907 crisis. Foreign private capital invested in companies operating in Egypt rose from £E 24,6 million in 1902 (out of a total of £E 26,3 million invested in Egyptian companies) to £E 92 million in 1914 (out of a total of just over £E 100 million). Although the average return on investment in the private sector was low – less than 5 per cent as a rule – there was a substantial drain of capital from the country into the pockets of foreign investors, representing a burden on foreign exchange earnings that added to the problem of servicing the foreign-held public debt. By the First World War foreigners were drawing in interest and dividends some £E 3 184 000 a year, compared with £E 1 360 000 in 1902. In 1914 total private foreign investment stood at some £E 200 million, plus some £E 86 million of a total public debt of £E 94 million and the Suez Canal shares, valued at £E 14,2 million, all held abroad. Wealthy Egyptians, displaying a marked propensity to consume imported luxuries, were unenthusiastic investors. In so far as they did invest it was in land or in foreign companies. In 1914 only 8 per cent of all money invested in joint-stock companies was in Egyptian-run enterprises.

French interests held the largest share of foreign private capital invested in companies in Egypt (excluding the Suez Canal), 46,3 per cent in 1914, overwhelmingly in mortgage companies. British interests controlled 30,3 per cent, fairly well spread over mortgage companies, banks, land companies, transport and canal companies and manufacturing, commercial and mining companies, mortgage companies claiming the biggest proportion. A further 14,3 per cent was held by Belgian interests, largely in land companies. 92 per cent of all foreign capital was French, British and Belgian owned. Most of it was tied up in land.

There was little foreign private capital invested in Morocco or Libya before the First World War, though the sultan of Morocco continued to borrow fairly freely (but on a much smaller scale than the Egyptian khedives), partly to meet debts incurred through personal extravagance, partly to finance development projects and partly – and chiefly – to pay indemnities that were imposed by Spain and France in 1909. With the extension of French power in Morocco, French capital began to flow in and there was a considerable accumulation of foreign capital, mostly French, in Tunisia and Algeria, coming from both capital imports and reinvested profits of foreign residents. The majority of this investment was in land and agricultural improvements.

In sub-Saharan Africa much the largest proportion of total capital investment went into South Africa. There was a marked correlation between imports of private capital and, on the one hand, the size of European settlement and, on the other, the extent of the exploitation of minerals. South Africa gained on both counts and so, to a lesser degree, did the Rhodesias. In Belgian Congo there was relatively little white settlement, but the development of copper-mining in Katanga attracted foreign investment. In British East Africa, apart from that of the East Africa Syndicate, there was little investment before about 1910. Private investment depended mostly on what expatriate firms engaged in mining or the export of staples thought desirable.

The commercial banks operating in Africa continued to exist primarily to meet the needs of expatriate firms, colonial authorities and individual officials and settlers. They were still not much used by the native inhabitants. The close connection between banking and the needs of expatriate commerce is shown by the founding in 1900, with funds from the Niger Company, the African Association and Alexander Miller Brother and Company of the Anglo-African Bank, renamed the Bank of Nigeria in 1905. In 1912 it was sold to the Bank of British West Africa, in which, however, the Niger Company maintained an investment.

Capital needs for those starting up peasant cash crop production were not large and if they could not be met from family resources or other economic activities, such as trade, or money-lenders or mutual help associations traditional to some tribal societies, savings could be built up through share-cropping or employment by established producers. The banks were not interested in loans to farmers or native traders, who would be unable to offer satisfactory security; nor did these people put their savings into the commercial banks, which charged heavily on current accounts. Post Office savings banks began to operate after 1900, but branches were at first only in the main towns and interest was low. By the First World War there were several thousand depositors in the Gold Coast and also in Nigeria, with a few hundred in German East Africa. A start was made in Egypt in 1904, but amidst some controversy because of the Muslim prohibition of usury. The government was able to draw support from the opinion of the liberal Grand Mufti of Egypt which distinguished between usury – excessive interest – and dividends, i.e. a share in legitimate profits.

The biggest consumer of private capital was undoubtedly gold-mining in South Africa. Although it was virtually brought to a standstill by the Boer War, after the war the industry soon recovered and there was a boom in gold share prices and an influx of capital. Gold output returned to its pre-war level by 1906, the result of the greater exploitation of the so-called deep levels. Outcrop production was reduced to comparatively slight significance. Many of the old-established mines went out of production, being replaced by new mines at greater depths. In the latter part of the decade the number of independent mining companies was reduced as the result of mergers, not a new phenomenon, but at an unprecedented rate. Many deep level companies that had reached the producing stage but were unable to proceed further because of shortage of working capital, were absorbed by producing mines able to provide the necessary funds to bring them into production. In the immediate aftermath of the 1902–1903 boom, capital was hard to come by. The producing mines which were thus able to extend their holdings safeguarded their future without the great risks attendant upon new ventures. The diminishing number of mining finance houses that controlled the producing companies collaborated to keep down costs, but remained independent in their policy.

The so-called Far East Rand began to be vigorously exploited just before the First World War. Even by the end of that war there were only eleven mines there compared with thirty-eight on the central Rand, but they were far more profitable and, although these were deep mines and costs were rising, their profits were going up. During the pre-war period the tonnage of ore milled rose, partly as a result of improved plant, and, despite a fall in the average grade of ore milled, the total profits of the industry increased. An increasing proportion of capital needs was met from undistributed profits, though for development purposes the industry remained dependent on imported capital, a large amount of which entered South Africa in another expansionist boom of 1908–1910. By 1910 a quarter of its national income could be attributed directly to the output of gold. By 1913 nearly a third of a million people were employed in mining in South Africa, chiefly in gold-mining. Only 36 000 of them were white. Coal, exploited to meet the needs of the gold-mining industry and the railways, which in turn facilitated the mining of hitherto inaccessible deposits of coal, grew in importance. South Africa, previously an importer, began to export coal, chiefly from the Natal mines via Durban.

Elsewhere in Africa, the Gold Coast, Southern Rhodesia and the Belgian Congo were important producers of gold, although their total output fell far short of South Africa's. Production in expectation of profit while the Witwatersrand mines were out of action through the Boer War was a powerful influence at the beginning of the century. In 1901 an English company re-opened ancient workings in Egypt near Imbaraq on the Red Sea. In the Belgian Congo production began in 1905. In Southern Rhodesia the authorities, the British South Africa Company, thought in

terms chiefly of mining by biggish companies. A large number was floated
in an atmosphere of considerable speculation and some fraud. Prospecting,
however, near old workings revealed no gold-field of any consequence.
The companies, with their inefficient management and high costs, were
able to pay only low dividends. Conditions best favoured the small man.
Since gold was generally found in good agricultural land, mining could be
combined with farming and there were enough trees to provide the rather
small fuel needs. After 1903, when Rhodesian mining shares collapsed on
the London market in sympathy with the depressed state of those of the
South African mining companies, the British South Africa Company
showed increasing sympathy for individuals and syndicates. Thereupon
output rose from less than £1 million in 1904 to £3,9 million in 1916.

Gold-mining in the Gold Coast got under way at the turn of the century,
helped by the completion of the Sekondi-Tarkwa railway. More than 300
companies were floated in 1900-1901, though only a few of them ever
produced any gold (thirteen in 1904). Four thousand concessions were
obtained from chiefs, some of whom took advantage of the gullibility and
ignorance of prospectors. Concessions overlapped, resulting in much
litigation and chaos. Some of the companies, however, gained mineral
rights over extensive areas, notably the Ashanti Goldfields Corporation,
which controlled 2 600 square kilometres. The railways made a big
difference to output, which by 1903 reached 71 000 ounces and by 1915
462 000 ounces.

Apart from gold, Africa was not noted for its mineral production at this
time. Tin had some importance in Nigeria. By the end of the 19th century
conditions were sufficiently peaceful to permit exploitation, but investment
capital and entrepreneurs were slow in coming forward. The Niger
Company, which retained a half share of the mineral rights in the northern
part of Nigeria when it lost its charter, did some prospecting itself and
leased out the more promising areas of the Bauchi plateau. By 1908 there
were 70 companies, but none paying a dividend, and three-quarters of
them went bankrupt. In 1909 there was a boom fostered by the Champion
Tin Fields Company, which did no mining itself, but promoted other
companies. Until the construction of the Lagos-Kano railway ore had to
be carried by porter and river boat, but after 1911 it was necessary to carry
the ore only some 60 km to the railway at Rigachikun. Then exports began
to exceed the thousand ton level.

Some iron and phosphates were mined in Algeria and Tunisia and
copper in South Africa (in Namaqualand since the middle of the 19th
century and at Messina in the northern Transvaal from 1906), but little
else. Hopes were entertained of mineral discoveries in East Africa. In
1902-1903 a survey was carried out by the East Africa Syndicate. Except

for a big deposit of sodium carbonate at Lake Magadi nothing of importance was discovered. This disappointing outcome was repeated in Moçambique, where a survey was made by the British Imperial Institute on behalf of the Moçambique Company. Some coal was mined near Tete and shipped out on the Zambezi during the six months of the year when the river was navigable.

There was considerable scepticism among mining experts about the prospects of ever extracting any copper in Katanga, where a prospecting monopoly was granted by the Comité spécial du Katanga to Tanganyika Concessions Limited. This company was founded by Robert Williams, an English engineer and businessman and associate of Cecil Rhodes, and it was also subsequently awarded the concession for the construction of the Benguela Railway. To exploit the deposits which were located, Union minière du Haut-Katanga, in which Tanganyika Concessions had a substantial interest, was created in 1905. It was not until 1911, however, that any copper was produced.

Capital imports into Africa for manufacturing were small. In West Africa the expatriate trading companies had little interest. Local capital went mainly into land, internal trade and building. The most precocious industrial development south of the Sahara outside South Africa occurred in Southern Rhodesia. Brewing, the repair and manufacture of mining machinery and of rolling stock were started very soon in Salisbury and Bulawayo. More important, however, in terms of value added were food processing, sawmilling and furniture manufacture and, above all, the processing of tobacco. In South Africa the most dynamic industries before the First World War were explosives and cement. These products, and fertilizers too, were manufactured by African Explosives and Chemical Industries, established through the amalgamation of existing small explosives firms. The rotary kiln was introduced in 1904 for making cement and by 1914 South Africa had an output of $1\frac{1}{2}$ million bags. But the processing of farm products remained the most important sector of manufacturing industry. Some clothing was made and there was some production of boots and shoes.

The South African colonies, with a large measure of self-government, were able to pursue a tariff policy favourable to domestic industry even before the formation of the Union. But there were conflicting interests and when the South African customs union was formed in 1903 the needs of internal industry had to be balanced against the policy of imperial preference, the influence of the gold-mining industry, which wanted its inputs admitted free of duty and, like commerce, was opposed to agricultural protection in order to keep down the cost of food for its labour force, and the pressure of farmers who wanted to preserve the South

African market from foreign imports. Above all there was the fiscal consideration. Customs duties were the main source of revenue and the colonial governments wanted to extract maximum income without going so far as to discourage imports altogether. The result was a compromise which gave some protection for manufacturing and agriculture. When a new Customs Convention was made in 1908, at a time of depression, tariffs were raised partly to yield more revenue, partly to accord greater protection. But imports from Britain and other parts of the Empire retained their preference.

To prevent competition with British industry was the preoccupation of British officials in Egypt. To protect Lancashire cotton yarn and piece goods from the effects of a revenue-yielding customs duty, excise duties were imposed on Egyptian cotton products. On occasion local enterprise was helped with a little protection, but generally the government was loath to offend British interests. In spite of this official reluctance to offer much encouragement, total capital in industry more than doubled between the beginning of the century and the outbreak of war in 1914.

Egypt and South Africa were the most developed parts of Africa and able to pay for their own government, more than pay for its own government in the case of Egypt. There revenue continued to grow, though latterly at a slower rate. At the same time the proportion of government expenditure given up to servicing the public debt continued to fall, from 32 per cent of ordinary revenue in 1900 to 25 per cent in 1910, though debt charges actually grew absolutely, from £E 3,6 million in 1900 to £E 3,9 million in 1910. About an eighth of foreign exchange earnings went on national debt interest payments. The reduction of the burden upon revenue permitted the allocation of more funds to services and development projects. On the other hand, military expenditure rose as war approached, though, with increasing revenue, its share of national expenditure remained much the same.

Many colonies at the beginning of the century were far from paying their own way, which was the hope and intention of imperial governments. The Congo Free State was saddled with very heavy debts (as much as 137 million francs) when it was taken over by Belgium in 1908, not because it could not be self-supporting, but because so much profit was taken out of the territory by Leopold II and the concessionary companies. In 1909 the colonial government was permitted to raise a loan of 6,4 million francs, but no other aid was forthcoming. The Germans subsidized their colonies, more generously from 1906, when Bernhard Dernburg became the first Colonial Minister, and very large loans were contracted, some 250 million marks. French West Africa was able to accumulate a small reserve from current revenue, but French Equatorial Africa received a small subsidy from the metropolitan government. The British were compelled to give financial support to poor colonies in the form of advances, grants-in-aid and loans. In 1901 payments ranged from £280 000 to Northern Nigeria (part of it to pay for the West African Frontier Force) to £40 000 to British Central Africa (Nyasaland) and £22 534 to the Northern Territories of the Gold Coast. These sums were not lavish and by 1910 had in most cases been reduced. The Algerian budget was subsidized for the benefit of the settlers, but the tax burden on the native inhabitants grew at the very time their ability to pay was declining. The yield of the traditional (or Arab) taxes fell continuously from 1887, when it reached 21 million francs, down to 15 million in 1910, but the total amount paid by native Algerians rose, according to one estimate, from $35\frac{1}{2}$ million francs in 1901 to $44\frac{3}{4}$ million in 1911, an increase outstripping the rate of population growth and occurring during a period when Muslim property in land and beasts was decreasing. An investigation in 1912 concluded that Muslims owned 38 per cent of total property, movable and immovable, but paid about 71 per cent of total direct taxation.

Colonial governments derived most of their income from customs duties and, to a lesser degree, from export levies. In some colonies traditional taxation was retained side by side with the new. It was not necessarily as harsh as in Algeria. In Northern Nigeria it was made less burdensome, more equitable and more directed to public purposes. However, it was taxes on trade that were favoured, partly because they could be used in a discriminatory way to impose a particular trade pattern, but more because they were the best source of revenue. Direct taxes were paid by settlers and assimilated Africans and these tended to yield increasing amounts. Increasing revenue came from the earnings of public utilities. Railways not only began to pay their own way, but even assisted revenue by increasing the tax capacity of those benefiting from them. But it was trade that counted most. Even in the colonies of settlement government receipts from customs were most important. Therefore they were at the mercy of movements in the international economy. Apart from its direct effect upon revenue through the level of income from customs, the state of trade had indirect effects by raising or lowering income from other sources. When trade was bad railways were sometimes unable to earn enough money to meet operating and depreciation costs, still less to pay capital charges. Direct taxes on the mass of the population or even excise or sales taxes were difficult to assess and collect given the limited use of money in the early colonial period, the rarity of individual land tenure and of wage-labour and the probem of getting information about individual incomes. It was for the sake of revenue that colonial governments were so anxious to promote crop exports. Where there was individual landholding, taxes on land were possible; elsewhere taxes on heads or houses were common. Poll taxes might or might not be graduated and were levied on smallholders and self-employed as well as those in wage-labour. Sometimes such taxes were a device to compel reluctant subsistence farmers to undertake wage-labour or cash crop cultivation. In fact, in the economy where money did not circulate widely, taxes, at least at first, were payable in labour or kind. They presented severe problems of administration and collection. Moreover, though onerous to individuals, they contributed relatively little in most colonies.

A large proportion of total investment in Africa was government investment in railways and other public works. Even in South Africa, where so much capital was attracted by private enterprise, a very substantial proportion of total investment came from government. In those territories where there were no minerals and almost all investment was in infrastructure the government share of the total could be much larger. It was generally large in French Equatorial Africa, rather smaller – with some exceptions, such as Sierra Leone – in British West Africa, especially in the Gold Coast and Nigeria because of the investments of the big trading companies, and in the Rhodesias, where the British South Africa Company exercised administrative functions over a long period, in the Portuguese territories, where a considerable amount of British private capital flowed, and particularly in the Belgian Congo, where there was private investment in railways and, later, mining, though here the government had in fact a large stake in private enterprises.

Shortage of investment capital could be overcome to an extent by raising loans on the European money markets, but this was thought to be something exceptional. Financial orthodoxy required a balanced budget, the meeting of all payments from local taxation. Borrowing by French colonies before the First World War was far from heavy. AOF raised four loans between 1903 and 1913, totalling 346 million francs, for railway construction, port development and other public works, military and civilian. The French Congo borrowed 21 million francs in 1909, partly to pay off a debt contracted in 1900 and partly for public works. A loan of 171 million francs authorized in 1914 for the construction of a railway from Brazzaville to the sea was not taken up until after the war. As a result of this restraint debt servicing was not onerous. British colonies wishing to borrow could enjoy the protection of the Colonial Stocks Act. The safeguards provided made colonial issues attractive for the investor, but fixed interest rates were a burden to the debtor colony even when the sums borrowed were small. Loans tended to favour only the more prosperous colonies, which had the ability to service their debts, and borrowing tended to fluctuate with the state of trade.

Imperial unwillingness to invest in colonies helps to explain why relatively little development occurred. A large proportion of the colonial budget was set aside for the payment of the civil service and police. Smaller amounts were allocated to public works, agriculture and education. After the provision of various services the surplus available for investment was very small and, moreover, investment was the first casualty during periods of depressed trade and the low revenues that that entailed.

CHAPTER IV

1910–1920 (THE GREAT WAR)

For Africa the immediate pre-war years were on the whole a prosperous period of rising imports and exports. While exports of British capital to Africa did not keep the same high levels of 1902–1910, they were still substantial, up to £12,9 million in 1914. Although rubber prices went down and rubber production fell off, cocoa and cotton continued to do very well. It was after 1910 that coffee and sisal in British East Africa began to become a significant contributor to its exports and its economic well-being. Coffee became important as a result of a steep increase in prices on world markets following the devastation of coffee bushes in Ceylon by disease. If anything, dependence upon coffee in Kenya became too heavy; for it was not always grown on land wholly suited to its cultivation. Nearly half the European landholders came to rely on it, either because they grew it themselves or because they grew maize for those who did. It was maize that became the staple crop of most white farmers who did not have the resources for plantation cultivation or had land in those parts of the Highlands where coffee was out of the question. Large quantities were exported, though its chief contribution to exports was indirect, through the feeding of African workers on the plantations. It was competitive on external markets at least partly because it was carried on the railways at concessionary rates and, even with that help, only at the cost of depleting the fertility of the soil, for there was no crop rotation. Flax was tried in areas unsuitable for coffee, but it was not worthwhile when prices were low.

European production of coffee and maize in Kenya had a discouraging effect upon African commercial farming. As in South Africa legal hindrances were placed in the way. White farmers wanted independent cultivation by blacks confined to the land set aside for them and only for subsistence. In its most extreme form, the European attitude towards the reserve was to regard it merely as a recruiting ground for labour for expatriate enterprise. The result was a combination of a stagnant traditional agriculture with an expanding (though not always efficient) white agriculture. Hostile to African cash farming because it competed with them both in the market and for land and labour, settlers were able to exert pressure on the government in favour of their interests. The priority given by the colonial authorities in Kenya to plantation agriculture had much to do with the absence there in the early years of peasant production of coffee, though taken up with much success by African farmers in Uganda and German East Africa. Either because they were deprived of the opportunity of producing regularly for the market or because they found it an easier and surer way of acquiring money needed for taxation and satisfying undemanding tastes for consumer's goods, agriculturists neglected their own land and went to work on white farms for shorter or longer periods. Pastoralists, on the other hand, the Masai and the Nandi, tended to operate outside the new system almost entirely.

Just as the colonial economy in Kenya was at last finding its feet, the war broke out. It was not only East Africa where its adverse effects were felt. Africa was the scene, even the proximate cause, of some of the pre-war international crises, and some would argue that the war itself was the inevitable product of the imperialist competition characteristic of a late phase of capitalist development. In 1911 Germany dispatched a gunboat to Agadir in Morocco to protect its interests in a territory where the French had been spreading their influence since the crisis of 1905 and the Algeciras conference of 1906. War seemed very near indeed, but a compromise was reached confirming German recognition of French claims in Morocco in return for two strips of territory in the French Congo. Such bargains were possible in Africa, where the sovereignty of pieces of land could be transferred from one colonial power to another without regard for the feelings and wishes of their inhabitants. Clashes of interest in Europe, however, were less readily soluble than colonial disputes in Africa and war, when it finally broke out in August 1914 between France, Russia and Britain (joined by Italy in 1915), on the one hand, and Germany, Austria-Hungary and Turkey, on the other, had more to do with the internal problems of Austria-Hungary and the mechanics of European diplomacy and military organization than with the peripheral issues of colonial quarrels.

By 1914 the partition, though not the conquest, of Africa was completed and on the whole it had been for the colonial powers a process of compromise and accommodation with more bluster than danger. It was very shortly before the war that the final stages (if the Italian annexation of Abyssinia in 1935 is excepted) were reached, the Italian annexation of Libya and the acceptance by the Sultan of Morocco of French and Spanish protection, imposed as a response to threats of German intervention (1912). These assumptions of sovereignty, however, were merely claims that had to be substantiated by subjugation. Marshal Lyautey subdued Morocco between 1912 and 1914, but the process of conquest in Libya took twenty years to complete.

Not even South Africa, with its large population of European stock and its internal self-government, was consulted when Britain declared war on

Germany in August 1914, and it participated in the face of opposition so bitter that there was a brief rebellion by a section of the Afrikaans-speaking whites. Still less were the views of the subject peoples of Africa considered. For a long time before the outbreak of the war some French colonial administrators and experts had looked to the African colonies, especially AOF, as a reservoir of military manpower. Black troops had long been used in colonial warfare, but in the immediate pre-war period it was proposed to employ them to offset the declining birthrate in France during an age of mass conscript armies. It was hoped that they could, in addition, make a contribution to the colonial economy at the end of their service. In 1912 a law was passed legalizing conscription. Although it was supposed to be implemented only if there were not enough volunteers, force was in fact used. In 1912-1913 some 16 000 men were recruited, but during the war this contingent was expanded enormously. Estimates of the total numbers recruited in AOF and AEF go as high as 181 000, of whom perhaps as many as one in three perished. Many of those who died lost their lives in the defence of France.

In addition to Africans who went to France to fight, many thousands went there to work, especially Algerians, attracted by the higher wages there. This too was not new. For, as early as 1914, there were ten thousand working there, three-quarters of them in the mines of the Pas-de-Calais. In July 1914, however, travel permits were abolished and this facilitated migration. Indeed, Algerians and Tunisians were specially recruited for war work. After the war this immigration into France intensified.

It was in Europe that the great battles took place. Germany, hoping to achieve a quick victory across its own frontiers, attached little importance to its empire. When war broke out, it suggested the neutralization of Africa, for which some basis could be found in the Berlin and Brussels Acts. This offer, however, was not accepted and the Allies attacked the German colonies. Togo was soon overrun and South-West Africa relatively so, but Kamerun took nineteen months to capture and the German colony of East Africa put up a prolonged and resourceful defence. These campaigns were fought largely with African troops at African expense. South Africa took a leading part in the campaigns in South-West and East Africa. The war and the 1914 rebellion cost it £38,0 million and only a fraction of that sum was paid from taxes, although these were increased. The Gold Coast spent £60 000 on the Togoland invasion and another £10 000 was given to the imperial government immediately after the outbreak of the war as a gesture of support. After the Togo campaign West African troops and porters were sent to participate in the fighting in East Africa, and casualties, through disease as well as wounds, were very high. In East Africa itself some 63 000 Ugandans were recruited for the carrier corps.

The numbers of casualties and the financial cost incurred by Africa were small compared with the vast expenditure of life and money in Europe, but in proportion to population and resources in Africa the burden was a heavy one.

Economically the war had mixed effects. Obviously it dislocated the international economy by its disruption of existing patterns of production and trade as industry in the developed countries shifted from the manufacture of civilian goods to military needs and as some commercial links were broken and others strengthened. The wartime shortage of ships restricted the international movement of goods, and that became especially acute as a result of German submarine warfare in 1916 and 1917. Sometimes essential supplies were severely reduced. Algeria was short of coal, petrol, sugar and rice, a predicament aggravated by military requisitions and periodically poor harvests. The volume of African imports fell and during the early part of the war so did exports. In the Gold Coast, although the annual value of exports from 1915 to 1917 exceeded their value in 1913, the average annual value of exports over all the war years was below the 1913 level. In terms of volume, a truer reflection of trends than value because of the effect of price changes, wartime exports recovered the 1913 level only in 1917. The value of imports declined more sharply, only half the pre-war level in 1917 and barely more than a third in 1918. The value of Nigerian exports was £7,0 million in 1913, £4,9 million in 1915; the value of exports from British East Africa £1,5 million in 1913, £0,7 million in 1915. Because of the East Africa campaign, however, imports into Uganda and Kenya continued to rise. In the case of South Africa imports fell from £41,8 million in 1913 to £31,8 million in 1915 and exports from £66,5 million in 1913 to £34,8 million in 1915. In terms of volume, imports did not recover until 1920, though exports began to pick up towards the end of the war. British exports to the whole of sub-Saharan Africa fell from £38,6 million in 1913 to £31,3 million in 1915, though British imports from Africa continued to grow.

Because of the Allied command of the sea, trade between Germany and Africa was brought to an end, and that itself was a blow to Africa, as Germany was an important trading partner, sometimes a very important one, e.g. in the Gold Coast, where it was the second largest. German firms operating in British colonies were first closed down and their stock sold and subsequently put into liquidation. One victim of anti-German feeling in the British colonies was the Basel Mission Trading Company in the Gold Coast, which was closed in 1918. Though a Swiss institution, it had German ties, some German employees and alleged pro-German sentiments. It was then expropriated and its assets handed over to a philanthropic body, the Commonwealth Trust Limited. After the war the seizure was successfully challenged by the Swiss government and it was the Gold Coast which had to bear the heavy burden of a quarter of a million pounds compensation to the trading company.

The USA, which was neutral for a large part of the war, and Japan, which, though on the Allied side, was remote from the war, helped to fill the commercial vacuum left by Germany. An increasing number of American sailing ships put into West African ports. However, the chief firms to gain from the disappearance of the Germans were French and British. Those in West Africa did particularly well out of the war. They bought up the stock of the liquidated German firms and were able to take advantage of rising prices to gain exceptional profits. They had privileged access to scarce shipping space. A few small African enterprises tried to exploit the favourable situation, but could make no headway against expatriate firms with their greater resources and their connections with sources of supply and markets in Europe.

The effect of declining imports was reinforced by increasing internal demand. The expeditionary forces had to be supplied, as well as a larger labour force engaged in mining and manufacture. Pressure of demand forced up prices, but of equal influence was the increased volume of money in circulation. Gold coins ceased to circulate and their place was taken by banknotes or treasury notes which were printed in ever larger quantities. In the Gold Coast the volume of money in circulation was five times as great in 1918 as it had been in 1913. Further contributory factors were bigger shipping and insurance costs and in some cases tariff increases to compensate for the decline in customs revenue resulting from the contraction of trade and to help meet higher wartime expenditure. Rising prices, especially the prices of foodstuffs, brought much hardship. Price controls were introduced in some colonies, but sometimes only partially and belatedly, e.g. in the Gold Coast, where the price of imported food was fixed in 1918.

In Algeria the government in 1916 adopted compulsory purchase of produce, which angered farmers, and price fixing, which was not very effective. Between 1914 and 1918 the cost of living more than doubled in some regions, more than trebled in others. Speculators bought up grain to hoard and resell when prices had risen. Wages failed to keep pace with prices. In the countryside there was a labour shortage on European farms, where wages were very low, and this adversely affected production; while in the towns there was acute unemployment owing to the stagnation of some sectors of the economy such as public works and a continued movement off the land. Total grain production, which had reached its highest point just before the war, levelled out until the latter part of the war. Wheat production exceeded a million metric tons for the first time in

1911. In 1918, 1 340 000 metric tons were harvested, but output fluctuated from year to year, and in 1919 there was a bad harvest (572 000 metric tons). Very similar quantities of barley were produced. South Africa was a much smaller wheat producer (exceeding 200 000 metric tons only in a good year) and was still dependent upon imports from Australia and elsewhere. Maize, however, was produced in ever greater quantities on white farms devoting an increasing area to it, 1,7 million hectares in 1917 (though an exceptional year) compared with 0,8 million hectares in 1911. In four of the six years between 1915 and 1920 output of maize was more than a million metric tons. Native farming made little progress. That was also the case in Algeria, where Muslim output showed a downward trend.

Public works and administration were everywhere a wartime casualty, damaged by shortage of funds and personnel. Capital imports ceased and Europeans joined up in large numbers. In Uganda an attack of rinderpest which raged uncontrolled by the depleted veterinary service, killed 200 000 head of cattle. The shortage of skilled man-power also had an effect on trade and agriculture, with merchant firms, plantations, and other enterprises deprived of managers, though this had the advantage of presenting new job opportunities to local talent. One casualty of the war was the Benguela Railway. Work on that was suspended in 1914 when Robert Williams ran out of money. Negotiations with the Deutsche Bank for further capital were broken off at the outbreak of war.

There was not a complete suspension of public works. Some pre-war projects were completed. In Tunisia the north-south railway trunk route, which had reached Sfax in 1911, was extended to Gabès in 1916. In the Gold Coast Accra was linked to Koforidua in 1915, giving the greater part of the cocoa districts in the south-east access to rail transport. In East Africa and Egypt there was a certain amount of road and railway construction in connection with the war. A military railway was built to the Mediterranean coast from El Qantâra on the Suez Canal to Gaza in Palestine. In the Gold Coast there was a good deal of spontaneous road construction by chiefs and villagers. The first Ford lorries had been imported into West Africa just before the war. Their high clearance and their lightness made them ideal for the indifferent roads. Goods vehicles registrations in the Gold Coast rose from 29 in 1914 to 213 in 1919 to 586 in 1920.

Because of the amount of fighting that went on there, East Africa was particularly badly affected by the war. Soldiers and carriers returning home took with them smallpox, meningitis and plague. External trade was disrupted not only by the general shortage of shipping, but also by the disorder into which Mombasa had been thrown by the demands of the war, and internal trade by the requisition for military purposes of most of the steamers which plied Lake Victoria. German East Africa, blockaded and much fought over, was severely damaged economically. European and native farms had been neglected as men were drawn into military duties. The Germans, ingenious in the manufacture of essential supplies no longer obtainable from Europe, produced a wide range of medicines and foodstuffs at the Amani Agricultural Research Institute. But agricultural output fell, overseas trade ceased for a large part of the war and internal trade was disturbed. In some districts there was a decline in population. There was a setback to education, medicine and scientific research.

Some groups were very well off as a result of the war. Apart from speculators, there were all those engaged in the production and sale of commodities for which there was increased demand. Exports of North African tobacco and wine to France ran at a high level during the war. Not all those who made money in Algeria and Tunisia were European. There were Muslims who prospered from the sale of wool, growing or curing tobacco and manufacturing olive oil. Even the simple producer of olives, figs and dates was able to take advantage of high wartime prices. Indeed, there is some evidence that the Arab and Berber population as a whole derived a net benefit from the war. Inflation was offset by the considerable sums of money paid to the families of those in military service and the remittances of those in war work in France, and in 1918 the Muslim community was relieved of a heavy fiscal burden by the abolition of the so-called Arab taxes. However, farmers did not always benefit from higher prices. Gold Coast cocoa producers were in difficulties in the war. This was partly because of plant diseases, but also because they got a rather poor return on their crops. In 1916 a cocoa export duty was imposed and the oligopsonistic European cocoa buyers shifted the burden of this to the farmers in the form of lower cocoa prices.

In most cases the war was a stimulus to increased production. Over the whole period, despite wartime conditions, Ugandan exports of cotton, coffee and hides increased in volume and, more especially in value. Palm produce exports from Nigeria fell when the war broke out because Germany was no longer able to buy, but by the end of the war the 1913 levels of oil and kernel exports were recovered as Allied demand grew. Nigeria also became an important world cocoa producer. Output was 4 500 metric tons in 1910, declined to below 4 000 tons in 1911-1912, but rose to 5 000 tons in 1913 and 16 000 tons in 1916. After that it fell back again except in 1918, when 26 000 metric tons were produced. Nigeria's contribution to total world exports of cocoa rose from 0,7 per cent in 1908 to 3,8 per cent in 1918, part of a general expansion of West African cocoa exports. The percentage of world cocoa exports coming from Africa rose from just over a quarter in 1908 to nearly two-fifths in 1918. Production in

São Thomé was falling, but very unevenly and it still was greater than that of Nigeria. It was as low as 14 000 metric tons in 1917, but as high as 55 000 in 1918. The contribution of the Gold Coast to world exports rose from 6,7 per cent in 1908 to 24,6 per cent in 1918 and continued to rise after that. The volume of African exports of cocoa beans more than doubled between 1908 and 1918, from 48 000 metric tons to 105 000. Exports from the Gold Coast in 1917 were 91 per cent up on 1913. Cocoa's contribution to the value of total exports increased from just under 50 per cent in 1914 to almost 70 per cent in 1916. Ivory Coast and Togo were also becoming significant – though still small-scale – exporters. This expansion of cocoa production occurred despite fluctuations in prices and a general price decline. The average annual price of Gold Coast cocoa fell from £61,5 per ton in 1913 to £34,5 in 1917. Much of the growth of cocoa and other exports can be attributed to pre-war investment rather than to wartime demand. There were many products of which the output could not be expanded readily. Cocoa bushes and olive trees took several years to mature. Not all the cocoa beans that were grown were harvested and not all those harvested were sold. Transport problems, internal as well as external, and price fluctuations influenced marketing.

Rubber was much in demand for its military uses. This reversed the drastic downward trend of prices from 1911 and presented an incentive to revive flagging production in Africa. It was not an opportunity that was seized. In Nigeria production, which had fallen below 1 000 metric tons in 1912, did not reach that figure again until 1925. Output in the Belgian Congo reached 3 000 metric tons only once during the war and the downward trend since the beginning of the century was maintained.

Metropolitan countries looked with increased interest at colonies as sources of raw materials not only in the short-term for war production, but also in the long-term. Ideas of imperial self-sufficiency gained ground. In Britain, where the first important departure from the principle of free trade was made in 1915 with the introduction of the McKenna duties on imports, primarily with the aim of conserving shipping space, a pressure group calling itself the Empire Resources Development Committee began to agitate for imperial preference. In 1919 Britain imposed duties on palm kernels and tin leaving West African ports and gave a rebate on assignments to the United Kingdom. Another move was the appointment of an Empire Cotton-growing Committee in 1916 to promote cotton-growing. In 1920 it became a permanent body under government supervision and renamed the Empire Cotton-growing Corporation. It was supported by a levy charged on British cotton imports and it worked very closely with the Cotton Growing Association, which started to confine itself to ginning, transport and marketing. More general in its terms of reference was the Colonial Development Committee, created in 1919, composed of politicians, civil servants and businessmen (including Sir Owen Phillips, later Lord Kylsant, the shipping magnate). Its task was to make enquiries, examine proposals and advise government.

In France in 1917 the Colonial Minister, André Maginot, presided over a conference of interested businessmen and officials which made proposals for increasing production in the colonial empire for immediate needs and in the interests of long-term development. On the eve of the war the French empire accounted for only 10 per cent of France's external trade, and much of what its empire supplied to France it could well have done without. A fifth (in value) of all French imports from the colonies was wine from North Africa, which caused deep resentment among French wine farmers. Three-fifths of colonial exports to France were made up of foodstuffs. For certain commodities there was a more or less substantial dependence on the Empire – phosphates (55 per cent of total needs), oil seeds (28 per cent of needs) and rubber (14 per cent of needs). But less than one per cent of France's requirement of raw cotton came from the colonies, and it was that sort of failure to co-operate that the government hoped to remedy.

It is curious that at the very time France and even Britain were thinking of closer economic ties between colonies and metropolis, Portugal for a brief period in its imperial history relaxed the bonds. In 1910 the monarchy was overthrown and the republic experimented in colonial autonomy. At first it was a granting of greater latitude in administration, but in 1920 Angola and Moçambique received financial autonomy. However, the result was rather the enlargement of the power of the governors and high commissioners, and these followed one another in rapid succession, each lasting scarcely longer than the republican ministries in Portugal.

Portugal fought in the war against Germany and this participation, together with political instability, made it difficult to implement serious colonial reform. The war also hindered plans for increasing colonial exports to France and Britain. Shortage of shipping put a certain limit upon exports but to some extent the problem could be solved by the processing of produce before export. In Senegal ground-nuts, in Nigeria palm kernels and in Uganda cotton seeds were milled. In Uganda the lead was taken by Asian entrepreneurs.

Another stimulus to African industry was the virtual protection of local industry by the disruption of the usual supplies of manufactures. Import substitution was encouraged, and its most common form was food processing, such as flour milling, and simple consumer's goods, such as soap. Old handicraft industries were revived, e.g. textiles, and new industry developed, especially in parts of Africa where there already existed an industrial base – South Africa and Egypt. An indication of progress in South Africa is that the value of goods manufactured doubled between 1915 and 1920, though a good deal of the increase was the result merely of rising prices. The contribution of private industry, including handicrafts, to GDP rose from 6,7 per cent in 1912 to 9,8 per cent in 1918. The number of industrial establishments rose from 3 638 in 1915–1916 to 5 287 in 1918–1919, power used from 114 000 to 148 000 h.p. and the manufacturing labour force from 89 000 to 110 000. Yet South African industry was still in a rudimentary stage, either processing local materials in the manufacture of food, drink, tobacco products and leatherwear, or engaged in the further processing of imported semi-manufacturers, e.g. in the clothing and metal industries. There was no local iron and steel industry of any consequence and there was no textile industry apart from the manufacture of blankets with imported woollen yarn. In some respects manufacturing in Egypt was more advanced. There industry expanded in terms of output and numbers involved, though, apart from a limited manufacture of arms in the workshops of technical schools, there were no qualitative changes as a result of the war. There was, however, a change in government policy. As late as 1915 a British firm offering to manufacture uniforms in Egypt was refused government help because the long-standing official belief that state-aided industrialization would bring no general benefit to the country; but in 1916 the government appointed a commission to investigate ways of overcoming wartime shortages and promoting industry. Although the commission's recommendations (1918) had no immediate effect, their acceptance by the government, recognizing the need for industrial growth to give work to an increasing labour force and reduce dependence upon cotton, was of importance. At this stage industry was still by and large old-fashioned. Half the seventy or so thousand manufacturing establishments employed fewer than four workers each, most of them only one. About two-fifths of the industrial labour force worked in food processing, another two-fifths in clothing and weaving. Only some 30 000 workers were employed by modern factories out of the 400 000 who derived their livelihood from industry.

Although war undoubtedly made an impression upon industrial development, it was of less significance than other influences that existed before and continued to exist afterwards. In the long run the fortuitous protection afforded by imports declining in volume and increasing in price was not so important as formal protectionist policy. South Africa's Customs Tariff Act in 1914, introduced just before the war, was criticized by local industrialists as a betrayal of their interests. Nevertheless, it had a protectionist aspect and it is noteworthy that as early as 1910 Lever

Brothers thought it worthwhile to begin soap manufacturing in South Africa because tariff protection and preferential rates on the railways enjoyed by local manufacturers after the establishment of the Union made the market very competitive for overseas producers. Having secured access to the market in that way, the firm proceeded to assume a commanding position by buying up local producers or by entering into price fixing arrangements to its advantage. That sort of development had nothing to do with the war, and indeed the war itself hindered, as well as helped, industrial growth. Wartime difficulties took the form of shortages of capital equipment and imported raw materials and fuel, though these were lessened by the use of local materials and concentration on the manufacture of products which made relatively small technological demands.

Manufacturing industries which started or grew in the exceptional circumstances of war sometimes had difficulty in surviving in peace time. Processing raw materials before export was not always worthwhile. Local milling of palm kernels was uneconomic when oil prices were low. Part of the profit lay in the sale of a by-product, oil cake, for which there was no local demand and for which transport costs to overseas markets were too high to justify its export. Shortly before the war Lever Brothers started crushing palm kernels in Nigeria, but soon abandoned it. Although it was resumed after the outbreak of war because the palm kernel oil price rose, it had to be given up once more in 1920 when oil prices again fell. Another problem was the opposition of metropolitan interests. French firms protested against imports of colonial vegetable oil. Once the war was over, all colonial manufacturers had to face the resumption of the competition of imported products. Not all wartime ventures were able to withstand it.

There were important developments in mining immediately before and during the war. In 1911 Union minière du Haut-Katanga at last went into production. Mining was simple because there was only a shallow covering of soil. It was the treatment of the ore and its export that presented the problems. It could not be concentrated, but had to be smelted directly. Smelting itself was difficult and at first, despite the high copper content of the ore, production and transport costs exceeded the value of the product. Although the completion of the railway from Beira to the new mining town of Elizabethville made production possible, the distances were immense. The Benguela Railway remained uncompleted and until 1928 most Katanga copper was exported southwards and even after that a very substantial proportion went that way under a guarantee given by Union minière in return for assured supplies of coal from Wankie in Southern Rhodesia. A thousand metric tons were produced in 1911 by a single smelter. Further smelters were brought into service just before and during the war, and output increased rapidly and unit costs declined. In 1914

11 000 metric tons were produced, 23 000 in 1916 and 28 000 in 1917. In 1918 Union minière paid 22 million francs in dividends.

Coal output at Wankie passed 500 000 metric tons by 1920. This was substantial compared with parts of Africa where production was just beginning – Algeria (8 000), Nigeria (184 000) and the Belgian Congo (2 000), but minute compared with South African production, which grew rapidly but irregularly. The Transvaal and Natal accounted for most. Cape output, never very great, declined and, although Orange Free State output was approaching the million ton mark by the end of the war, it was coal of not very good quality. The prosperity of the coal-mining industry was related to that of gold-mining and of the general state of trade. Ships and locomotives were important customers and the wartime diversion of shipping from the Suez Canal increased the demand for South African coal for bunkering. With a total output of 10,9 million metric tons in 1920, South Africa was at much the same level as Canada and Australia.

A new deposit of phosphate rock was mined in the Sétif area of Algeria before the war. Output was exported through Bougie, to which a railway was built. Exploitation was also extended to the Gafsa region of Tunisia after a branch railway was constructed to the main line at Sfax. Algerian output varied widely from year to year, as much as 739 000 metric tons in 1911, as little as 165 000 in 1918. Tunisian production also varied, but at a higher level, 2,1 million metric tons in 1913, 815 000 in 1919.

New mineral discoveries included manganese in the Gold Coast in 1914 and alluvial diamonds in north-eastern Angola in 1912. In 1917 the Companhia de Diamantes de Angola (Diamang) with Portuguese, French, Belgian and American participation, received an immense concession from the government. South-West Africa also began exporting diamonds just before the war. In 1920 Angolan production was nearly 100 000 metric carats and that of Belgian Congo 215 000 metric carats. South African production reached 6,8 million metric carats in 1913, thereafter falling never to recover the same level. It was by far the biggest in Africa or, indeed, the world, well over 90 per cent of total world output before the war. None the less, the South African diamond-mining industry was in difficulties. There were disputes among the partners of the Diamond Syndicate and a drop in demand as a result of the war. But in 1916 demand recovered and the Syndicate handled the output of all the big South African producers, as well as that of South-West Africa, which came under South African Administration during the war. It was only after the war that production in Angola and Belgian Congo seemed to pose a threat to the South African domination of the market.

In 1919 diamond production in South-West Africa, which was nearly a fifth of total South African and South-West African combined output, was taken over by the Consolidated Diamond Mines of South-West Africa, behind which was Ernest Oppenheimer. He was the leading figure in the newly-founded (1917) Anglo American Corporation, which had interests in diamonds, gold and coal, including mines in the Far East Rand, the development of which was the chief objective of the new corporation. Anglo American was registered in South Africa, but it drew upon American investment and it acquired interests in London-based companies operating in South Africa. It was never run as a monolith. It was Oppenheimer's policy to leave its increasingly diverse interests separate, but linked together in a web of great complexity.

The contribution of mining to net domestic product in South Africa fell from 27,1 per cent in 1911-1912 to 25,2 per cent in 1921-1922, losing ground to all other sectors (agriculture, manufacturing and services). This was partly due to the difficulties of gold production. These had already appeared before the war. Essentially it was a question of the falling grade of the ore being mined, which brought down average profits per ton of ore. One partial solution to the problem was to bring down costs, and that above all meant lower labour costs. Almost the only practicable way to do this was to reduce the cost of recruiting black contract workers and to lower their wages. The recruiting system was tightened up in 1912 by the establishment of a joint agency with exclusive rights to operate within the boundaries of South Africa and the protectorates of Basutoland, Swaziland and Bechuanaland. The monopoly, however, was not made complete until 1919. With regard to wages, a system known as the maximum average was introduced to prevent piece-work payments from rising about a certain level in all the mines. The other partial solution to the cost problem was to mine higher grade ore. However, the exploitation of the deeper levels was held up by shortage of capital. The war not only cut off overseas investment, but also forced up working costs as prices rose. More and more mines were classified as low-grade as profit margins contracted. Some relief came through an increase in the gold price. A premium was added to the normal price, raising it by a quarter in 1919-1920, but that offered a brief respite only. The crisis came to a head in the early 1920s.

The war ended in November 1918. Its psychological impact had been profound, not least on individuals who had served in armies overseas. Not all Africans had been reluctant soldiers. Those in the French colonies who had, or who hoped to acquire, citizenship were anxious to display their loyalty to France. When in 1916 a new law of compulsory military service was applied to the most gallicized parts of Senegal, it was not unpopular. But casualties were very high and survivors took back home novel ideas and new points of view. These were not necessarily hostile to colonial authority, though forced recruitment did help spread anti-colonial sentiments which found wider and deeper acceptance because of economic hardships such as rising prices, falling real wages and, in some cases, loss of export markets for primary produce. The burden of taxation increased. In Kenya revenue from hut and poll taxes rose from £105 000 in 1909-1910 to £279 000 in 1919-1920. In Northern Rhodesia the ten shilling poll tax was extended into those parts of the colony where hitherto the less onerous three shilling hut tax had been customary. Where there was no direct taxation, as in the Gold Coast, the burden fell upon producers of exports and consumers of imports and of certain local products subject to excise. Export duties on cocoa and palm kernels were introduced and railway freight rates were raised. Even then total revenue fell towards the end of the war because of the reduction of imports. In Southern Nigeria the steep drop in the quantity of imported alcohol, from over 80 000 hectolitres in 1913 to some 13 000 hectolitres in 1916, reducing revenue from that source by two-thirds. As in the Gold Coast, export duties were imposed on cocoa, palm oil and palm kernels. As revenue still did not match needs, direct taxation was introduced in parts of the protectorate from 1918, in the form of a graduated capitation tax.

In tropical Africa there were numerous and serious anti-colonial rebellions. Some were a protest against wartime hardships, particularly conscription and forced labour in French Africa, where considerable force had to be used to suppress them. Others were more complex in their origins. The 1915 insurrection and death of John Chilembwe, a mission-educated and American-trained evangelist in Nyasaland, made an impression upon both blacks and whites quite disproportionate to the numbers involved in the uprising. Although he was certainly protesting against the war, there was more to Chilembwe's revolt than that. He had long been a critic of expatriate enterprise and an advocate of indigenous commercial agriculture and business, and he had already come under suspicion for his radical views.

Trade unionism received a considerable stimulus from the war owing to the rise in prices and the increased demand for labour. Protests were common straight after the war, sometimes taking the form of strikes. The first trade unions in Africa were formed in South Africa among British immigrants. They were craft unions of skilled men for the most part and, given the demand for skills, they were in a fairly strong position, with members able to run a union and give it financial support. There was a good deal of unrest before the war among white miners, not all of whom did have scarce or indispensable skills. A strike of 1907 was broken by the management through the introduction of Afrikaans-speaking rural emi-grants, landless poor whites. In order to preserve their bargaining power, the unions opened their doors to the newcomers and this solidarity among white workers, together with the political influence they exercised, won for them great advantages. In 1911 the Mines and Workers Act reserved a privileged place for whites in the mining industry and in 1913 the South African Mine Workers Union obtained recognition from the employers. On the eve of the war there was a great deal of violence on the Rand, but during the war there was greater collaboration between workers and management, shown particularly by the acceptance of the closed shop principle and an agreement of 1918 committing the mine-owners to maintain the *status quo* in the racial distribution of work.

White example was soon followed by Indians and blacks. In 1913 Mahatma Gandhi was behind a general strike among Indian workers in Natal. After the war a black union, the Industrial and Commercial Workers Union of Africa, or ICU as it was called, was launched by a Nyasaland immigrant, Clements Kadalie, with the help of white sympathizers in Cape Town in 1919 and almost immediately attracted attention by its partici-pation in a largely unsuccessful dock strike. It was not, however, easy to organize black workers. Migratory labour was so common that trade unionism had to struggle. Migrant workers were neither committed to wage-labour nor wholly dependent upon it. A trade union could be effective only with a stable committed work force. Other obstacles were the slow progress of industrialization, the size of the labour surplus, widespread illiteracy and the existence of tribal and family loyalties that competed with trade union loyalties. In the early days workers were disposed to seek help from their tribal headmen in industrial disputes rather than confide in trade unions. But attempts by employers to handle industrial relations through tribal elders in the work force were not a success. The paucity of transport and communications made it difficult for union headquarters to maintain contact with branches and for union officials to maintain contact with one another. Employers were generally hostile and this hostility was aggravated by racial differences. It was difficult for unions to get competent and responsible officials. Members distrusted officials and were unwilling to pay their subscriptions. They were quickly disillusioned if the formation of a union was not followed by an increase in wages. But as trade unions became more common and effective, they could take advantage of the African propensity to conform, which satisfied the problem of collecting dues. Fulfilling accepted social obligations was a strong influence in most African societies and this was sometimes reinforced by intimidation. Some trade unions tended to intrude into politics and were therefore likely to be suspect to colonial authorities.

There was little improvement during this period in the position of indigenous labour. One of the few advances was the introduction in Algeria in 1919 of the eight-hour day, at the same time as in France, a measure that was, however, more likely to benefit European workers than native ones. On the whole, there was deterioration in Africa. There were exceptional demands for labour for wartime purposes and conscripted workers experienced an exceptionally high mortality rate. Two thousand carriers are said to have died of cold in German East Africa in 1916. The rate of losses, through disease and desertion, among porters serving with the Belgian Congo forces was 242 per thousand between June 1917 and March 1918, higher than the wastage among black soldiers and much higher than the peacetime death rate for porters employed, e.g., by the Tanganyika Concessions Company (12 per 1 000). Apart from wartime labour requirements, the ordinary demand for labour went on, and in some respects the pressure upon natives to take employment in European enterprise increased. By a decree of October 1914 Africans in the Portuguese colonies were liable to be compelled to take up public or private work under a variety of pretexts, e.g. if they were judged to be vagrants. In Kenya, although a Labour Commission of 1912-1913 rejected, to the displeasure of settlers, taxation as a means of forcing men into the labour market, during the war, with greater settler influence, the government was persuaded in 1917 to agree to the use of moral pressure to get Africans out to work, and this was confirmed after the war by the Northey Circulars of 1919-1920 which imposed an obligation on officials and chiefs to help the process of recruitment, a policy that was endorsed in 1920 by the Colonial Secretary of the day, Lord Milner. The best that can be said for these practices in various colonies is that, at least in theory, labour conditions were regulated, with minimum standards set.

Black grievances were not only, or chiefly, to do with labour. In South Africa land was a burning issue. After the formation of the Union the Natives Land Act of 1913 scheduled, i.e. defined and made inalienable, the existing African reserves, which at that time constituted just over seven per cent of the total area of the country. To secure in perpetuity a certain area of land for the African people was, however, only one aspect of the measure. The more pressing purpose was to prevent any African from farming independently beyond the boundaries of the reserves, though the intention was expressed to add to them in order to compensate for the loss of this right. Further land purchases outside the reserves were forbidden, as well as the renting of white land for money or kind (though not for labour). This restriction was the result partly of an exaggerated conviction that black landholding was spreading rapidly at the expense of white and partly of the assumption that independent black farming deprived white agriculture of labour. The intention was to clear Africans from settler land unless they were working for the white farmer either as wage-earners or as labour tenants. In the event the Act was not rigorously applied, partly because too many white interests were likely to be damaged if they were. One modification was dictated by the African franchise rights in the Cape Province (based on a property qualification) entrenched in the Act of Union, which would have been curtailed had the prohibition upon African land purchases been enforced. However, though ineffective to begin with, the Act was the foundation of the policy of racial segregation and later apartheid and it served doctrinaire racialism as well as seeking to solve an economic problem.

The Act of 1913 scheduled 5,1 million hectares in the Cape, 2,3 million in Natal, 0,9 million in the Transvaal and 0,6 million in the Orange Free State. A commission - the Beaumont Commission - was appointed to recommend how much additional land was to be assigned to Africans in the different provinces. When, however, it proposed in 1916 that some 7 million hectares of extra land should be thus allocated (1,1 million in the Cape, 1,5 million in Natal, 4,3 million in the Transvaal and 0,1 million in the Orange Free State), there was vociferous protest from white opinion. The parliamentary Select Committee on Native Affairs rejected the Beaumont Commission's recommendations and, as a result, Local Committees were appointed to revise them. They reported in 1918, suggesting rather more land for blacks in the Cape (1,3 million ha), rather less in the Transvaal (4,0 million ha) and in the Orange Free State (none at all) and a good deal less in Natal (0,3 million ha). Although the allocation in Natal was thus drastically reduced, the Local Committees offended intransigent white views, while blacks complained that their share of the land was inadequate. The undertaking to provide Africans with more land was not honoured until 1936, and then not fully. From 1918, however, the government by administrative order allowed individual Africans to buy or lease land recommended for African occupation by both the Beaumont Commission and the Local Committees and from 1922 land recommended by the Local Committees alone.

Practice in South Africa influenced the British colonies of settlement. In Kenya, in 1915 the Crown Land Ordinance gave the governor the power to set aside reserves, but it was not the intention that these should be permanently secured to their inhabitants, and the possibility existed that land would be taken from them in the interests of European settlement. It was not until some years after the war that there were serious attempts to give security to tribal land. During the war the settlers exercised a powerful influence on policy through their representatives on the advisory War Council, which threw its weight on the side of strengthening the European position in the colony, in particular by settling ex-soldiers on the land after the war. The Resident Natives Ordinance of 1918, like the South African Natives Land Act, sought to reduce Africans living on white land to labour tenants. In Southern Rhodesia the British South Africa Company was permitted by its 1889 charter of incorporation to make grants of land to settlers, provided that due regard was paid to the laws and customs of the people, and the imperial government made some rather feeble attempts to regulate land grants. The overthrow of Lobengula, as king of the Matabele, in 1893 and the crushing of the rebellious Matabele and Mashona in 1896–1897 put the country virtually at the mercy of the Company and the pioneers. The British government confined itself merely to requiring the Company to set aside what was described as sufficient land for African occupation. Thus, as in South Africa, it was a question not so much of the quantity of land that should be allocated to white settlers and expatriate companies as the amount that should be left at the disposal of the displaced inhabitants. A land commission set up in 1913 delimited 204 reserves with a total area of about 8,5 million hectares for some half a million Africans, though these retained the so-called Cape privilege of purchasing land outside the reserves. Some 32 million hectares were available for purchase by both Europeans and Africans.

In North Africa there were no legal restrictions on the purchase of land by natives, and after the war Muslims were buying more land from Europeans than they were selling. Many had saved money during the war from military service, war work in French factories and the sale of agricultural products during a period of rising prices. Land prices were high and colonists were all too willing to take advantage of them.

In territories not obviously suited to white settlement, the land question was not that of setting aside reserves for natives, but of making provision for European agricultural enterprise wherever the demand arose. In the Belgian Congo the Huileries du Congo belge, an Anglo-Belgian enterprise in which Lever had interests, was permitted in 1911 to lease up to three-quarters of a million hectares of land in five 'circles', with the promise of ultimate freehold tenure of a minimum of 150 000 hectares. In return the company undertook to provide certain public services, guarantee minimum exports and pay minimum wages. Its most important site was at Kinshasa, near Leopoldville, and it gained a reputation for efficiency, making the Belgian Congo an important exporter of palm oil.

In regions of white settlement white farmers were much better placed than black for getting credit from public institutions, commercial banks and co-operatives. Co-operatives were very often organized by the government and in any event subject to government supervision. In South Africa co-operative laws authorizing the provision of advice and loans by the authorities were passed in the pre-Union colonies between 1904 and 1910, but farmers were slow to respond and early co-operatives were prone to collapse through mismanagement. The establishment of the Land and

Agricultural Bank in 1912, which took over the assets of the pre-Union colonial land banks greatly extended access to capital and strengthened the co-operative movement by making funds available to co-operatives. Starting with an initial capital of £2½ million, which was doubled in the course of the first fifteen years of its existence, the Land Bank lent money for buying land and stock, settling earlier debts and making improvements such as fences, dipping tanks, silos, boreholes and windmills.

Events in Southern Rhodesia followed the South African path. In 1909 an Act was passed providing for the registration of co-operatives and in 1912 the British South Africa Company set up the Rhodesian Land Bank Limited, which lent money on mortgage.

Credit for blacks was either unavailable or available from suspect sources. In 1910 the French started Sociétés indigènes de Prévoyance in West Africa. These grew out of earlier government arrangements for the loan of seeds at rates of interest lower than those charged by private creditors. They were found firstly in the ground-nut growing area of Senegal and Guinea, but in 1915, during the war, membership was made compulsory. Some regarded them simply as a means of raising additional taxation and facilitating administrative control. Certainly there was little that was spontaneous in their formation and administration.

In Egypt the credit position of the poorest farmers was weakened by the passage of an Act which had been intended for their protection. This was the Five Feddans Law of 1912, which forbade money lenders and foreign banks foreclosing on loans made to owners of less than five feddans (most of the peasants), having the effect of cutting them off from credit. The gap left by the inevitable withdrawal of these creditors was partially filled by agricultural co-operatives, the funds of which came from large owners who, in many cases, were prominent in nationalist politics.

The war caused much discontent in Egypt. Cotton prices were kept down and many landowners found themselves in difficulties, unable to get credit from the banks and forced to turn to the money lenders. A moratorium was declared in 1914 on debt repayments, but the mortgage banks attempted to maintain pressure for the repayment of loans. The rise in prices of food, clothing and fuel afflicted not only the labouring classes but even the urban middle class, many of whose members were products of western education and beneficiaries of the new employment opportunities that economic development had made available. These people were especially susceptible to the ideas and ideals of nationalism. There was much social distress. Thus the enemies of colonial rule gathered their strength to bring it to an end, while colonial subjects sympathetic to the culture of the metropolitan nations pressed for rewards, which inevitably meant participation in government and privilege. Colonial powers had much to be grateful for in the support, albeit sometimes reluctant and even forced, given to their war effort, and were made aware of new pressures for reform. British administrators in Africa, though less so than in India, were compelled to face the possibility of a time limit to their rule, and French officials recognized (e.g. in the loi Diagne of 1916) the need for hastening the process of conferring full rights upon those who threw in their lot with the metropolitan power. Although it scarcely appeared so at the time, the process of decolonization began before colonization itself had even been completed. It was in Egypt that the two processes seemed almost to overlap: in 1914, after the removal of Germany from a position of influence, the British *de facto* protectorate was made formal, and not many years later (1922) the first grant of limited autonomy was made.

More important, perhaps, than the rumblings of colonial discontent was the effect of the war upon the balance of economic and political power in the world. It left Europe exhausted and, after the Russian Revolution of 1917, ideologically divided. It was the United States, by then the most powerful industrial nation in the world, transformed from debtor to creditor, which tipped the balance in favour of the Allies by its intervention in the war. Although the colonial empires appeared to be as strong and enduring as ever, European hegemony was sapped. Political doctrines incompatible with colonization gained ground: Marxism, nationalism, Muslim revivalism. The principle of self-determination enunciated by President Wilson of the United States on behalf of the subject peoples of Europe could have a colonial interpretation.

President Wilson had been an advocate of a League of Nations, but when one was established in 1920, the United States did not in fact become a member. Its primary purpose was to settle international disputes peacefully, but for Africa its most important purpose was its guardianship of the former German colonies. These were taken away and shared among the European Allies as League of Nations mandates. German South-West Africa fell to South Africa, Ruanda-Urundi (formerly part of German East Africa) to Belgium, Tanganyika (the bigger part of German East Africa) to Great Britain, and Togoland and Kamerun to Britain and France, between which they were partitioned. South-West Africa was a C class mandate, the only one of that class. It was administered by South Africa as part of its own territory without the requirement of giving to other members of the League the same economic privileges as those enjoyed by the mandatory power. The other African mandates fell into class B. Rights of supervision of the administration of the mandates were vested in a Permanent Mandates Commission and the countries administering class B mandates undertook to respect native interests in land legislation and to prohibit forced labour except for essential public purposes.

After the war countries set about the task of recovery. A pressing need was to restore the international monetary system. The war threw monetary arrangements into disarray just when in Africa they were becoming settled. In British West Africa the currency was put on a more regular footing just before the war by the appointment in 1912 of the West African Currency Board, with its headquaraters in London and local representatives in Africa. It issued coins, minted in London, convertible into sterling at par, though not legal tender in Britain. In 1919 a similar board was established for East Africa. It was part of a general process of associating Kenya and Uganda in joint services, viz a postal service (1911) and a customs union (1917).

Currency was thrown into confusion in East Africa by the war. The Indian rupee, which was legal tender, ceased to have a fixed exchange rate with either gold or sterling. Pounds and rupees fluctuated in value separately from each other as economic conditions in Britain and India changed, causing monetary disturbance in East Africa, which used both. The rupee appreciated against sterling and the pound fell in value from 15 rupees to 8 rupees by 1919. This was against the interests of those who exported to Britain, new settlers from Britain bringing sterling capital and those who had borrowed rupees at their old value and now had to repay their debts in rupees at their enhanced value. Wages rose in real terms and therefore added to the burden of the white employers. To secure stability and to allay the discontent of European settlers, the government fixed the exchange rate at ten rupees to the pound and introduced a new coin, the florin, to replace the rupee, which, however, continued to be legal tender pending the issue of sufficient florins to take the place of rupees. While not restoring the pre-war position, this at least stopped the further loss of value of sterling. But as it happened, the value of sterling did not continue to fall against the rupee. On the contrary, it was the rupee that lost value, returning to the old parity of 15 to the pound. The imperial authorities resisted settler pressure to revert to the pre-war position and found themselves faced with an influx of rupees seeking the far better exchange rate in East Africa. In 1922 the rupee was demonetized and East Africa went on to a shilling standard. This, however, required the exchange of rupees in circulation at the rate of two shillings each. One of the first functions of the East African Currency Board was to buy up existing stocks of depreciated rupees. This turned out to be a costly operation.

The monetary history of British West Africa was less disturbed, but not without its problems. In 1920 alloy coins replaced the silver coins that had previously been issued by the West African Currency Board. The new coins, unlike the old silver coinage, had little intrinsic value and as token coins, had to be covered by securities held by the Currency Board in

London, 90 per cent in gilt-edged British securities, 10 per cent in bullion. This had both advantages and disadvantages for the colonies. Colonial assets were held in Britain instead of being put to work in the colonies themselves and the requirement of full cover for coinage had the effect of reinforcing the impact of trade cycles. Since the volume of money in circulation varied according to the size of export earnings, as these rose and fell, the money supply was expanded or reduced, thus accentuating the inflationary and deflationary effects of trade fluctuations. Moreover the convertibility of local coinage into sterling at face value strengthened the pressure to trade with Britain and other sterling countries rather than with other partners. On the other hand, the colonies had the advantage of a stable currency and as the money supply contracted in recession, an automatic check on imports to the benefit of balance of payments equilibrium.

South Africa, too, had its currency problems. Like Britain it substituted paper money for sovereigns and the banks were allowed for the first time to print smaller denominations, £1 and ten shilling notes in addition to £5 notes. These were redeemable for gold coins. The problem arose because of the expansion of the volume of paper money and its depreciation against gold. Redemption was increasingly attractive. Although it was illegal to export coins or melt them down, it proved impossible to prevent the smuggling of gold out of the country, especially to India. In order to maintain their gold reserves the banks were compelled to buy gold in Britain, where the entire output of the South African gold mines was exported, and because of the rising price of gold, they had to pay a premium.

The ending of the war brought other problems of adjustment. Although they were not so serious in the less advanced economies of Africa as in the industrialized world, where it was necessary to absorb into civilian employment hundreds of thousands of demobilized soldiers and sailors and to restore industrial capacity to civilian production, Africa had its special problems. Uganda was afflicted by drought in 1918 and, as a result, food shortages, emergency food imports and several thousand deaths from starvation. Algeria, where harvests varied widely according to the rains, after the exceptionally good harvest of 1918, had in 1920 its worst since 1867 owing to drought (2 million quintals). In the drought of 1920 some regions lost two-thirds of their animals. However, the transition to peace was everywhere helped by a short-lived boom as shipping space became available to satisfy pent-up consumer demand. The boom reached its peak in 1920. The price of cocoa, tripling between 1918 and 1920, reached £122 a ton in February 1920. Uganda coffee fetched £160 a ton that year. Nigerian palm oil nearly £100 a ton and palm kernel prices £50 a ton. Cotton prices were at their highest since the American Civil War.

One effect of this boom was the weakening of the case, at least as far as Britain was concerned, for imperial self-sufficiency and planning. There was a post-war reaction against state economic intervention, reflected in the return to office of a coalition government in which the Conservatives were powerful. There was still strong resistance to any departure from free trade and therefore to imperial preference. Loud voices were raised by diverse groups against metropolitan-directed colonial development. The Empire Resources Development Committee was opposed by philanthropic circles, which feared that the sort of colonial development envisaged would threaten land rights and traditional society and economy and would be less for the benefit of the colonized than for its contribution to the British economy. An influential critic was Lord Lugard, formerly governor of Nigeria and an architect of indirect rule in Africa. Most weight of all, however, was carried by the British Treasury, determined to reduce state expenditure in the interest of controlling inflation and reducing taxation. One casualty was the Colonial Development Committee of 1919. Its chances of persuading the Treasury to finance a comprehensive development programme were always slight, and it ceased to meet in 1920. In the event, in the 1920s imperial government aid to colonial administrations rose considerably. Despite the policy of financial retrenchment, the war did have some influence upon attitudes. Feelings of moral obligation were roused by a growing awareness of the economic problems of colonies burdened with debt; by gratitude to them for their contribution to the war effort; and by acceptance of the principles of the League of Nations and of its mandates, which were supposed to justify the acquisition by the victors of the German and Turkish empires. However, although more money was made available, it was spread over an empire enlarged by the spoils of victory and was devoted to aid of an *ad hoc* nature, not to the pursuit of an imperial grand design.

CHAPTER V

1920-1930 (POST-WAR RECOVERY)

The post-war peace settlement was of great significance to Africa. Although decolonization was far from the thought of the colonial powers, the mandate system of the League of Nations did express the view that colonies were a trust, the purpose of which was not merely exploitation in the interests of the metropolitan powers, but the well-being and progress of the colonized. There was some grudging progress towards self-government in Africa. The most important example was the granting of greater freedom to Egypt in 1922. Great Britain, not uninfluenced by the anti-British riots that erupted and were suppressed in 1919, terminated the protectorate and conceded limited independence. Defence, minority interests and transport and communications (notably the Suez Canal) remained subject to the colonial power. Egypt acquired some of the trappings of representative government. In British West Africa a gesture was made in that direction. Between 1922 and 1925 Nigeria, Sierra Leone and the Gold Coast were granted constitutions which admitted elected Africans to the legislative council in each. In French Africa the road to political enfranchisement that was envisaged was the admission of individual colonial subjects to the privileges of the franchise. Relatively few in fact either sought or were granted them.

In the parts of Central, East and Southern Africa ruled by Britain the question of political advance involved the settler communities, European and Asian. With the exception of Southern Rhodesia, these territories had too few whites and too many blacks to justify self-determination for the settlers, though they were, none the less, very influential in the legislative councils that were set up. In Southern Rhodesia the white colonists were considered sufficiently numerous to follow the road already trodden by earlier British colonies of settlement overseas. Internal self-government was granted in 1923 by an imperial government unwilling to take the alternative course open to it of buying out the British South Africa Company, the administration of which was wound up. There was a third course open to the settlers, integration into the Union of South Africa. There were many ties linking the two. The early settlement came from South Africa and the pioneers took with them South African customs and attitudes, not least Roman-Dutch Law. The economic connection was strong. Southern Rhodesia was part of the South African customs union and part of its railway system was run by South African Railways. Despite this, the settlers voted against joining the Union, being mostly of British origin and out of sympathy with the Afrikaans-speaking majority of the South African white population. After their rejection of unification their ties with South Africa weakened. Restrictions were placed by the South African government on the import of Rhodesian meat and tobacco, and in 1934 Southern Rhodesia withdrew from the customs union.

The possibility also existed of constitutional links with the British colonies to the north, particularly Northern Rhodesia. This was first mooted by Sir Starr Jameson during the war, but at that time it attracted little support among the settlers in either territory, the north fearing domination, the south unwilling to subsidize a territory which at that time was still poor. Attitudes changed both sides of the Zambezi during the course of the 1920s as the white population in Northern Rhodesia grew and copper mining developed. Northern Rhodesia was no longer seen in Southern Rhodesia as a financial burden; while Northern Rhodesian whites saw amalgamation with the southern colony as a means of achieving expatriate political control. The British government, however, was unenthusiastic.

A less likely possibility for Northern Rhodesia was either an amalgamation with Nyasaland or a federation with the East African territories of Kenya, Uganda, Tanganyika and Zanzibar, together with Nyasaland. Neither proposal came to anything, apart from periodic conferences of the governors of the six territories. There was little support for federation from any of the racial groups concerned, African, European, Indian or Arab, and in any event was hardly practicable at that time, administratively or economically. What was gradually developed was an increasingly more intimate association of Tanganyika with Kenya and Uganda. It was covered by the new East African Currency Board from 1922, joined the customs union in 1923 and the postal service in 1933. In 1922 Kenya and Uganda Railways and Harbours Administration was set up, an autonomous body responsible to both colonies. Its object was to reduce inter-territorial disputes and resentment.

The post-war world economic boom ended in 1920. The fall in commodity prices, combined with lingering wartime inflation which put up government costs, including salaries of expatriate officials, presented colonial administrations with a fiscal crisis from which only the utmost economy offered an escape. Taxes were raised. In the Gold Coast export taxes and import duties, particularly on luxury goods, were increased. On the whole, however, the West African colonies were let off relatively lightly by the slump. Algeria, though passing through a brief phase of optimism in 1920, suffered considerably worse. The decline of wine and alcohol prices aggravated the effects of the very poor grain harvest of 1920, the first of a series of bad harvests which followed the mediocre one of 1919. The authorities had to buy foodstuffs abroad for distribution. In 1920 they were compelled to raise a loan of 360 million francs to make good a budgetary deficit which had accumulated during and after the war. In the following year the French parliament authorized Algeria to raise a loan of 1 600 million francs for urgent public works postponed as a result of the war.

One of the worst-off colonies after the war was Tanganyika. Although the territory began its period of British rule entirely free of public debt and acquired the German Central Railway very cheaply, its economy had been severely damaged by the war and was not helped by the upheaval of the transfer of administration and the loss of Ruanda-Urundi, thickly populated and comparatively prosperous. Britain was compelled to make grants-in-aid totalling £400 000 between 1920 and 1922, and in addition the colonial government borrowed £3 000 000.

One of the most disturbing effects of the war was the breakdown of the old system of international payments. With the exception of the dollar the most important world currencies, no longer tied to gold, had depreciated. To restore the monetary stability that had facilitated pre-war international trade, most countries were agreed that a return to a fixed gold parity was desirable. The United States went back to a full gold standard in 1919, but other countries found it less easy to restore financial order. Britain was one of the few countries, and the only colonial power, to return to the pre-war value of its currency, then only after a great struggle and not to a full gold standard, but to a gold bullion standard (i.e. the convertibility of notes into gold only for export purposes and in large amounts). France fixed the dollar value of its currency at 20 per cent below its pre-war parity, Italy at 25 per cent below and Belgium at 14,3 per cent below. These were on a gold exchange standard, maintaining a fixed exchange rate with a currency on the gold or gold bullion standard. To ensure a stable currency most governments followed a deflationary money policy, reducing the great volume of currency in circulation.

Metropolitan monetary policy naturally affected Africa, most of which either used the metropolitan currencies or had local currencies firmly tied to the metropolitan ones. In the 1920s France completed its colonial monetary arrangements by authorizing the setting up of banks of issue in Morocco (1924) and Madagascar (1925), both private banks. The former broke the issuing monopoly of the foreign dominated state bank. The establishment of the latter was the delayed result of the disappearance from circulation in Madagascar during the war of the old silver five franc coins. Their replacement by Bank of France notes proved inconvenient to it and it was chiefly for this reason that the Bank of Madagascar was set up with the support of the Bank of Paris. Its headquarters was in Paris, with a branch in Tananarive and sub-branches in various other countries. Besides issuing notes it provided credit at moderate interest to traders.

South Africa was exceptional in having a measure of control over its own currency. As this began to rise in value against gold and British sterling, the South African pound broke away from the United Kingdom pound. In 1920 South Africa got its own central bank mint, when a branch of the Royal Mint was opened in Pretoria, and this meant that the profits of coining now went to the South African government. In 1924-1925 the old Kruger coinage was withdrawn, as well as German silver coins from South-West Africa. In 1925 South Africa, like Britain, went on to a gold bullion standard.

New currency arrangements were implemented against, for the most part, a background of economic stagnation, which undoubtedly the deflationary policies adopted by Britain and other countries helped to cause. Primary produce prices began to fall in late 1920. Kenyan coffee, which had been fetching £120 a ton, dropped to £60 and sisal from £96 to £12.10s. The price of South African wool declined from 32,9 pence a pound to 10,7 pence. The price offered to Ugandan cotton growers fell from 15 cents a pound in the 1919-1920 season to 5 cents in 1921, and the fall of the price of rubber to 10 pence a pound, which barely covered labour costs, threatened to ruin the European rubber planters of Uganda. Prices fetched by Algerian wine and alcohol fell by the end of 1920 to a quarter or less of their level of a few months earlier, and the prices of exports of wool, leather, hides and skins just as sharply. Algeria's loss of export earnings, together with heavy imports of foodstuffs because of poor harvests in 1920-1922, added to the territory's balance of payments problems. The total value of exports (501 169 francs in 1913) fell from 1 689 822 francs in 1922 (with a franc worth only 40 per cent of its pre-war value) to 1 441 577 francs in 1920. Total value of imports (667 305 francs in 1913) stood at 1 357 543 francs in 1919 and 2 535 168 francs in 1920.

The pre-war protectionist trends were intensified in the depressed economic climate. The 1919 Convention of St Germain-en-Laye re-affirmed the principle of equal treatment enshrined in the Berlin Treaty of 1885. In all the League of Nations mandates, with the exception of South-West Africa, the mandatory powers undertook not to discriminate against other members of the League. Within the limits permitted by these international obligations France pursued a policy of imperial preference, especially from the latter part of the decade. The imperial share of French imports increased markedly during the 1920s and of French exports from the late 1920s. The proportion of total French exports going to the French Colonies in Africa was 12,2 per cent in 1926 and 26,9 per cent in 1935; the proportion of total French imports coming from the French colonies in Africa was 9,3 per cent in 1926 and 20,9 per cent in 1935.

Of the others, Italy was able to get favourable treatment for its exports to Libya from 1921 and Portugal in the mid-1920s reverted to its traditional policy of imperial economic integration. The army overthrew the Portuguese government in 1926 and, after some confusion, Antonio de Oliveira Salazar built up personal power, firstly as minister of finance in 1928 and then as head of a one-party state. With fewer treaty restrictions Portugal was able to treat its colonies as captive markets. As usual they were cast in the rôle of producers of primary products and consumers of metropolitan manufactures. Since Portugal's own industrial development was backward, this meant large imports into the colonies of Portuguese wine and cotton textiles, priced artificially high by the discriminatory treatment of foreign competitors. In 1933, 56 per cent of Angola's trade was with Portugual, but this represented a peak. Colonial products were exported to Portugal for re-export and foreign manufactures were re-exported to its colonies by Portugal, which reaped tax advantages.

Britain found itself under greater pressure in its colonial markets. Although Lancashire was able to hold its own in the better kinds of cotton piece goods, in the unbleached lines, in which the USA, Japan and India competed, India surged ahead at the end of the war. In hardware, Britain encountered competition from the United States and Japan and it was not long after the war that Germany re-entered the trade, setting, because of its depreciated currency, prices well below those of the British.

In European colonies of settlement the white communities were sufficiently influential to secure tariffs to protect domestic interests. Shortly after the war the Kenyan government prohibited the import of flour except under licence. This benefited local producers at the expense of mostly Indian exports. The Tariff Amendment Ordinance of 1923 in Kenya gave protection to local producers of wheat, dairy produce and other commodities. South Africa, wholly autonomous, could build whatever tariff walls it wished to safeguard local industry, against British as much as against foreign imports. The Revised Tariff Act of 1925 was a much more comprehensive protectionist measure than any previous legislation.

Another pre-war trend that continued in the 1920s was towards business concentration. Nowhere was this more apparent than in the expansion of the business empire of Sir Ernest Oppenheimer and the Anglo American Corporation. In 1924 Anglo American acquired substantial shareholding in the infant copper industry of Northern Rhodesia and in the same year Oppenheimer joined the board of African Explosives and Chemical Industries Ltd., itself a merger of De Beers explosives interests and competing firms, later linked with Imperial Chemical Industries of Britain. In 1925 he achieved a dominant position in the newly organized Diamond

Syndicate. In 1926 he joined the board of De Beers, becoming in 1929 its chairman and in 1931 chairman of African explosives. Thus Anglo American was powerful in gold, diamonds, copper and the nascent South African chemical industry.

In West Africa a number of firms diminished through failures and amalgamations. Many of the smaller firms, native and expatriate, were ruined by the decline of commodity prices and the survivors closed ranks to reduce competition. More capital was now needed. As communications improved it became expedient to set up branches in the bigger centres, which meant that large stocks had to be carried in a trade where distances were great and turnover slow. Although smaller firms relied upon commercial travellers to sell imported goods to local store-keepers and to collect goods for export, the trend was to domination by a few big firms with extensive organization. By 1930 two-thirds to three-quarters of West Africa's overseas trade was being handled by three big companies, the United Africa Company, the Compagnie française de l'Afrique occidentale and the Société commerciale de l'Ouest africain. The biggest, the United Africa Company, handled nearly half West Africa's overseas trade, including a substantial proportion of AOF's trade. It was founded in 1929 through the merger of the Niger Company and the African and Eastern Trading Corporation, to which were added the West African trading companies belonging to Margarine Unie after its amalgamation with Lever Brothers to form Unilever.

Most of the West African companies had interests in shipping, road transport, agriculture and forestry, and at least some of them had directors who served on the boards of concession companies and banks or had other links with banks, local and metropolitan. Lever Brothers retained interests quite apart from the United Africa Company. In 1923 it set up a subsidiary in West Africa for the manufacture of soap. The reason for doing so was not to surmount a tariff wall against British exports. Although there was a revenue duty on imported soap, it was not high enough to be protective. The motive rather was to utilize the plant which the firm had established in Nigeria for extracting oil from palm kernels by adapting it to the manufacture of soap. The fall of oil prices after the war made it uneconomic to continue to crush palm kernels in West Africa, but locally produced oil could be used for the making of a cheap soap for the internal market, though still in competition with soap imported from Britain (including Lever Brothers' own soap).

While the number of firms in West Africa was growing smaller, in East Africa new British companies were starting up business, attracted by its evident commercial opportunities. Some already had interests in the Far East and Australia or in West Africa and they supplemented the old-established firms of Smith Mackenzie and the British East Africa Corporation. The expatriate firms in East Africa did not dominate the economy. African crops were collected by small Indian traders and the cotton sold to the ginneries, which were European and Indian-owned, for processing and export. European crops were either consigned by the grower to an overseas customer or handled by an export merchant, mostly European, but sometimes Indian, with offices at Mombasa, Zanzibar or Dar es Salaam.

World trade began to pick up as early as 1922 and in many countries there was increasing prosperity until 1929. These included South Africa, where national income in real terms grew at the rate of 7,6 per cent a year, and the West African colonies. The index of the value of Gold Coast exports rose from a base of 100 in 1921 to 222,1 in 1927 and of imports to 171,9 in 1927, both falling thereafter. By the end of the 1920s world trade was growing at least as fast as world output, itself growing rapidly, especially in the United States. The USA and Canada increased their share of world trade from 13,2 per cent in 1913 to 17,5 per cent in 1928. Europe, in particular Britain, did not do so well. Its share of world trade fell, though this decline was due largely to the reduction of intra-European trade. It still constituted the most important trading bloc in the world, accounting for 52,1 per cent of world trade in 1928. Its share of world imports of primary products actually increased in the 1920s. The prosperity of Europe was therefore of great concern to Africa.

Africa's share of world trade increased from 3,7 per cent in 1913 to 4,3 per cent in 1928. Of its primary products it was minerals that did best. But the wartime problems of the South African gold-mining industry persisted. Costs continued to rise, 25 shillings and 8 pence per ton milled in 1920 and 1921 compared with 17 shillings in 1914. Its wage bill went down in 1921, from £11,5 million for white employees and £6,0 million for black in 1920 to £10,6 million and £5,9 million respectively in 1921, but so did output and the size of the labour force. Then in 1922 Britain intimated its intention to return to the gold standard at the pre-war parity. The mining companies, faced with the prospect of a fall in the gold price, proposed to cut costs by increasing the ratio of cheap black workers to expensive white ones, abrogating the *status quo* agreement of 1918. Long negotiations between the Chamber of Mines and the white workers of the South African Industrial Federation failed to reach a compromise and in February 1922 the Action Group, strongly influenced by the Communist Party of South Africa, armed the miners and set up barricades. The army was called in and unions subdued in fierce fighting. Four of the leaders were executed. The failure of the strike enabled the mine-owners to cut wages, substitute some black labour for white and introduce certain new technologies previously resisted by the trade unions, the pneumatic drill and the corduroy process for gold extraction. The outcome was a marked improvement in output and profit. It turned out to be a brief respite. The white miners regained by political pressure what they had lost through industrial action. The process of replacing whites with blacks in skilled occupations was reversed and white wages put up in 1927. These increased costs did not affect the mines with the richest ores, which enjoyed a substantial economic rent. It did, however, mean that a quarter of the forty or so mines in production ceased to pay a dividend. None the less, after a decline in 1922, output continued to rise, from 9 149 ounces in 1923 to 10 716 ounces in 1930. South African production represented slightly more than half the total world production throughout the 1920s, except in 1922.

South African and South-West African diamond output fell in 1920 and 1921 but then rose to a new peak of production (5,4 million metric carats) in 1927, though South Africa no longer had the overwhelming dominance in world production that it had enjoyed before the war. In 1927 it produced 73,7 per cent of the total world output, but the percentage fell thereafter. The problem for the Diamond Syndicate was maintaining the price of diamonds in the face of new discoveries inside and outside South Africa. New deposits were found in Namaqualand in the Cape and in the Transvaal in 1926 and by then there were several producers in Africa: Angola, the Belgian Congo and the Gold Coast (where the diamonds were small and mainly suitable only for industrial use) apart from South Africa and South-West Africa. Control of marketing was helped by such moves as investment by De Beers in Diamang in 1923 and the acquisition of Namaqualand diamonds by Oppenheimer in 1928.

In North Africa the most important development was the exploitation of the rich and easily worked phosphate deposits in Morocco. In 1920 they were taken over by the protectorate government to make sure that, contrary to the mining law of 1914, which had been drawn up in compliance with the 1906 Act of Algericas to ensure equal access to all foreign interests, exploitation was reserved to French nationals. The phosphate mines of Algeria and Tunisia remained privately owned. The Moroccan mines made an important contribution to state revenue and export earnings. For an initial investment of 36 million francs the government earned 635 million francs in the course of the 1920s, apart from indirect earnings. By 1930 output (only 23 000 metric tons in 1921) reached 1,8 million tons and exports brought in 247 million francs. The phosphate mines were run by the Sharifian Phosphate Office and capital was provided by this for the establishment in 1928 of a Bureau de Recherches et de Participations minières, a public body which acquired an interest in the private companies exploiting coal and oil deposits (and later other minerals). Relatively small quantities of manganese, lead and zinc were mined by a limited number of private firms, mostly French, but with some Belgian capital involved. Most of the mineral production, including phosphates, was exported unprocessed.

Nigeria was important for its tin. It was the biggest producer in Africa and tin accounted for about a tenth of exports in the late 1920s. Exports rose from about 8 000 metric tons in 1920 to 12 000 in 1930. More than eighty, mostly small, companies were engaged in the industry in 1927–1928, employing about 30 000 men. Asbestos came chiefly from Southern Rhodesia, the second biggest producer in the world, excluding the USSR; and it was the biggest world producer of chrome ore. But the contribution of these two metals to the total value of Southern Rhodesian mineral output was eclipsed by that of gold. Southern Rhodesia was the biggest African producer outside South Africa, with an output normally between five and six hundred thousand ounces a year, but exceeding 600 000 in 1922–1924. It was a small copper producer, too, but its chief contribution to copper-mining was more indirect, the supply of coal from Wankie to the Copper Belt of Katanga and Northern Rhodesia. Coal output reached a million metric tons in 1928. Other small-scale coal producers in Africa included Algeria, the Belgian Congo and Nigeria, where the mines at Enugu were exploited by the colonial government. South Africa was much the most important source of coal in Africa. In 1929 total production was 13,0 million metric tons.

Perhaps the most conspicuous mining development of the 1920s was the beginning of the Northern Rhodesian copper industry. Preliminary exploration by the British S.A. Co (which had the mineral rights in the whole of Northern Rhodesia) in 1903 showed that deposits lay deeper underground than was the case in Katanga. Between 1922 and 1926 the Company, which until 1912 had granted prospecting licences to individuals, granted six big concessions over an area of more than 300 000 sq km. Two of these made important discoveries, the Rhodesia Congo Border Concession and the N'Kana Concession, and as a result five companies came to control Northern Rhodesian copper-mining: the Roan Antelope Copper Mining Co. Ltd. (1927), the Mufulira Copper Mines Limited (1930) and the Bwana M'Kubwa Copper Mining Company Limited, which had been formed in 1910 but had bought what was known as the N'Kana claim in 1924, all three in the N'Kana Concession; and Rhodesia Congo Border Concession (1927) and N'Changa Copper Mines Limited (1926), both in the Rhodesia Congo Border Concession. Expensive prospecting and costly exploitation necessitated large inputs of capital. The first important developments came in the 1920s with the application of a new process to the relatively low-grade ore of the Northern Rhodesian

Copper Belt. By 1929 production reached 5 000 metric tons, worth £408 000. But during the early 1920s the output of lead, and during the later 1920s the output of zinc, both at Broken Hill, exceeded copper production in value. Overwhelmingly Katanga was the biggest copper producer. After falling to 18,9 thousand metric tons in 1920, output rose continually to 138,9 thousand in 1930.

Prospects for the exports of vegetable products from Africa varied widely in the 1920s. It is uncertain whether in general the terms of trade of primary products deteriorated or improved. What was more important for the individual African territory was the state of the market for its speciality. West Africa's share of total exports of palm oil declined markedly as plantation oil began to compete in world markets, firstly from the Congo, subsequently from Sumatra and Malaya. In the period 1924–1928, although exports rose compared with the period 1909–1913 (from 121 000 metric tons to 188 700 metric tons a year), Africa's share of total world exports fell from 100 per cent to 87,7 per cent. While the Belgian Congo's share rose from 1,7 per cent to 8,9 per cent, Nigeria's fell from 67,7 per cent to 59,5 per cent. Most of the former's exports came from the concession of the Huileries du Congo belge, whose machine-pressed oil was of better quality and consistency than the hand-pressed product.

As the prices fetched by South African wool began to rise again from the very depressed level of 1921, reaching as much as 20,4 pence a pound in 1924, and as output increased, export earnings from greasy wool rose from £7,6 million in 1921 to £16,3 million in 1927. The quantity exported passed the 1921 level (99 000 metric tons) in 1927 (115 000 metric tons), partly because of an increase in the number of woolled sheep (36,1 million in 1927), but also because of an improvement in the average wool yield per sheep. As for South African maize, the annual value of exports varied widely, but it exceeded £2,2 million in 1921, £3,0 million in 1923 and £5,6 million in 1925.

In Kenya cattle and sheep farming by settlers prospered, with the number of cattle increasing from 138 000 in 1920 to 218 000 in 1929 and the number of sheep increasing from 104 000 to 239 000. But it was coffee that became firmly established as Kenya's most valuable product, accounting for a third of the total value of domestic products in 1923 and a half by the end of the decade. It all came from European plantations. Sisal (some 5 300 metric tons a year in the early 1920s, 15 200 in the later 1920s), also European-grown, and coffee (an annual output of some 3 500 metric tons in the early 1920s and nearly 8 000 in the later 1920s) contributed about half of domestic exports in the later 1920s. The African contribution to exports shrank. Settlers were deeply hostile to coffee growing by Africans because they feared its effects on their supply of labour. Almost half European landholders were dependent on coffee and these employed about a third of the total labour force. Colonial officials tended to support the settler point of view. In Uganda and Tanganyika the government attitude was more ambivalent.

In Tanganyika the German sisal planters were not allowed to resume their pre-war activity and their plantations were rented out on a yearly lease to other Europeans, including Greeks. Because of the disruption of estate management and the catastrophic fall in prices in 1920 to less than a seventh of their peak value, it took some little time for exports to recover, though they never lost their place as the chief source of external earnings. By 1924 pre-war output had been restored and by 1929 over 45 000 metric tons were produced, more than twice as much as in 1913. Coffee was a peasant crop and, at least from 1923, when African cultivation received official encouragement, in Uganda too. Both robusta and arabica were grown. This development encountered much European hostility. Settlers in Tanganyika were particularly incensed by the cultivation of arabica by the Chagga in the Kilimanjaro area. Coffee exports from Tanganyika were worth £352 529 in 1924, vying with cotton and ground-nuts as the most valuable export after sisal, and in 1928 output exceeded 10 000 metric tons, most of it produced by Africans. Production in Uganda, mostly robusta, grew more slowly, 2 000 metric tons in 1929. Cotton was still the dominant peasant crop.

In French West and Equatorial Africa in the 1920s the authorities favoured expatriate coffee and cocoa planting, and coffee plantations were started also in the Belgian Congo. But the most successful West African export crop continued to be peasant-grown cocoa. World consumption of cocoa had been increasing at a startling rate since the 19th century. It passed 200 000 metric tons in 1910, 250 000 in 1912, 300 000 in 1915, 350 000 in 1919 and 400 000 in 1921, and reached 548 919 in 1929. Between 1918 and 1928 the Gold Coast's share of world exports rose from 24,6 per cent to 43,5 per cent, that of Nigeria from 3,8 per cent to 9,7 per cent and that of Ivory Coast from 0,2 per cent to 2,8 per cent. The contribution of São Thomé and Principe continued to decline. Prices were volatile, falling sharply after 1920, recovering rapidly from 1923 and reaching the pre-war level in real terms by 1927.

Cotton on the whole prospered. Prices fell sharply in 1921, in Egypt to less than half the 1920 level. They tended to fluctuate throughout the 1920s, with another steep fall in 1926. Even so post-war prices were higher than pre-war ones and output rose. In Egypt, when prices fell, the government tried to restore them by imposing restrictions on the area under cotton and by buying up part of the crop for storage. This was a political decision primarily, testifying to the power of the cotton growers'

lobby. Economically it was futile because the price of cotton was determined by the American crop. Only 6 per cent of world cotton
production came from Egypt and the restriction of Egyptian output could
not influence prices, though it could relieve pressure on competitors a
little. Among the latter were Sudan, Nigeria, East Africa, South Africa
and Southern Rhodesia.

In the Sudan production began under irrigation on the Gezira plain
between the Blue and White Nile. This project was planned before the war,
when the construction of a dam at Sennar had been mooted and a British
guarantee given in 1913 to a £3 000 000 loan. It was viewed in Egypt with
some misgiving, partly because Sudanese cotton competed with Egyptian
cotton, partly because of the diversion of Nile water. However, the scheme
was to be subject to a maximum of 300 000 feddans, a relatively small area,
and in 1929 the Nile Waters Agreement settled the problem of water
sharing. The Sudan government was the proprietor of the scheme, but it
was run by the Sudan Plantation Syndicate, with which a ten year
agreement was signed in 1919, later extended to twenty-five years. Land
was surveyed, registered and rented or bought from the owners and divided
up into 30 feddan tenancies, in the allocation of which local farmers
received priority. Absentee landholding was not allowed, nor the accumulation of too much land by one farmer, a provision since criticized as
unprogressive because it obstructed the development of a native capitalism.
Profits were shared in accordance to local custom, 60 per cent to the
government (and this was shared with the Syndicate, 25 per cent, 35 per
cent) and 40 per cent to the tenants. The Syndicate was responsible for
supervision, loans to tenants, processing and marketing the crop and the
provision of seeds. The first water from the Sennar dam became available in
1925, and although tenants complained about the Syndicate and its
regulations, they soon achieved a measure of prosperity. Jobs were created
for local and migrant workers for weeding, clearing irrigation channels and
cotton picking. In 1929 the original scheme was extended, with a concession
allotted to the Kassala Cotton Company. The success of Gezira made a
valuable contribution to government revenue and external trade.

Cotton in Southern Rhodesia was a European crop, as in South Africa,
where its cultivation went back to the American Civil War, though it had
never been on an extensive scale. Production in South Africa reached
2 700 metric tons in 1929-1930 and in Southern Rhodesia 900 metric tons
in 1925-1926. In Southern Rhodesia the low prices of 1925 discouraged
further cultivation. Nigeria was of much greater importance. Exports in
the later 1920s averaged 6 100 metric tons, compared with 4 000 in the
early 1920s and 2 100 in the later war years. In Nigeria it was a peasant
crop, as in Uganda, where the peasant character of the industry was

confirmed after the war. In the 1920s peasant protest in Buganda led the sympathetic British authorities to fix at low levels the rent and labour tributes which landowners might exact from their tenants. This encouraged landowners to sell parcels of land to small men. After the war there was an influx of poor migrant labourers from outside Buganda so that even the peasant cotton grower was able to employ seasonal labour.

In East Africa much of the cotton crop of 1921, when prices fell discouragingly low, was bought up by the trading firms, the government and the British Cotton Growing Association in order to dissuade growers from restricting future cultivation. Uganda was the chief producer. There, output did in fact increase from the 8 800 metric tons of 1921 to 36 000 in 1924, thereafter fluctuating during the rest of the decade, though never falling below 24 000 tons. Kenya never became important and Tanganyika's cotton boom came later. In the late 1920s Tanganyika was regularly producing more than 4 000 metric tons a year. These lesser producers were all dwarfed by Egypt, where output fell below 200 000 tons only in 1921 and for most of the 1920s exceeded 300 000.

The activities of governments and semi-public bodies like the British Cotton Growing Association played an important part in determining the course of agricultural development, either encouraging or discouraging spontaneous enterprise by native or expatriate. Where there was a substantial white population, the authorities lavished help on the politically influential white farming community. In Kenya and South Africa one form of assistance was preferential railway rates for maize exports, and railway branch lines were often built to serve white farming districts. In South Africa government intervention was decidedly paternalistic, compelling farmers to do what the government thought was in their best interests. It intervened to encourage co-operation, provide credit and impose marketing arrangements. In 1922 the establishment by law of the principle of limited liability for agricultural co-operatives, under the terms of the Co-operative Act, gave a strong impulse to the co-operative movement. In 1926 an Agricultural Credit Act was passed to make short-term credit available to farmers. It authorized the formation of rural credit associations to lend money to their members on the security of stock and crops. These loans were supported by loan companies controlled by the Land Bank, which in practice provided most of the loan funds. Although the loan companies were abolished in 1931, the credit societies survived. In the area of marketing the state in 1923 took powers to impose a levy on locally sold meat to raise funds for the payment of a bounty to meat exporters and in 1925 the Fruit Export Board and in 1926 the Perishable Products Export Board (absorbed in 1930 into the Diary Industry Control Board) were founded for the purpose of regulating production.

In Southern Rhodesia the Land Bank of the British South Africa Company was superseded by a Land and Agricultural Bank set up by the new colonial authorities in 1924, with an initial capital of £300 000. White farmers could obtain credit on easy terms. In 1926, 292 farmers borrowed £329 596 and in 1928 the total value of loans outstanding exceeded a million pounds. Loans were for buying land and equipment and also for working capital. Not all were made directly to farmers. Money was also lent to co-operative companies and societies, to the former of which, in 1925, the principle of limited liability was extended. There was no land bank in Kenya until 1931 and it was only then too that an ordinance regulating co-operative societies was passed. Substantial direct government assistance to the white farming community was not available until the 1930s. However, the Kenya Farmers Association (founded in 1919 but changing its name to the KFA in 1923) virtually controlled the export of maize from the colony, grading and marketing the crop of its nine hundred or so members.

Within the limits of funds available to them, the British colonial authorities endeavoured to improve the quality of agricultural produce and the skills of the farmers. In Nigeria a system of inspection and grading was introduced for cotton exports and demonstration fermentation houses were put up for the cocoa farmers. Experimental plantations were founded, agricultural officers appointed and facilities provided for training Nigerian agricultural instructors. The Agricultural Research Station was opened at Vom in 1925 and the Agricultural School at Ibadan in 1927. French West Africa introduced inspection of ground-nuts and other products in the interest of improving the quality of exports and so getting better prices. Experimental farms were started. In Kenya in 1923 a staff of instructors was appointed to give Africans agricultural training and to run small demonstration plots. Makerere College, founded in Uganda in 1921, was originally meant to train carpenters and mechanics, but shortly afterwards started veterinary and agricultural courses. Government-run agricultural education for Africans in South Africa began in 1928. In Zanzibar the government established a Clove Growers Association in 1927 to bring together growers, both big and small, to pursue common aims, such as bringing down costs. It provided marketing and storage facilities and small loans. By making the payment of a bonus on young clove trees conditional upon membership of the Association, the government ensured substantial membership, which, however, fell off when the bonus was abolished. The progress of rural upliftment in colonial Africa was still very slow. In the mid-1920s only 3,76 per cent of government expenditure in AOF and AEF went on agricultural, veterinary and forest services, working out at £0,7 for every hundred persons. In British West Africa the corresponding figures were 3,03 per cent, £1,5 and in the Belgian Congo

3,19 per cent, £0,8. AOF had 84 agricultural and 19 veterinary officers for a population of more than twelve million. In those parts of Africa where there were considerable European populations, government emphasis was mainly on raising the standards of white farmers, whose labour needs were one factor in shaping policy.

A number of decrees (1919, 1923, 1930) after the war regulated the Sociétés de Prévoyance of AOF. A Société was set up in each administrative district with European officials as president and treasurer. In spite of ambitious aims, in practice their activities were confined to digging wells, making grain stores, lending seeds (at interest) and renting out ploughs and trucks. Insurance against accidents or disasters, though envisaged, was not attempted, nor was marketing. The Sociétés were most successful in Senegal, where they had over a million members by 1926. Attempts to operate farms and industrial enterprises enjoyed little or no success. In 1926 the possibilities of agricultural credit were extended in AOF by a law providing for the establishment of loan funds at district level supported by central funds (Caisses centrales) at colonial level. Members of the Sociétés de Prévoyance were eligible for loans, as well as other agricultural associations to be established. Co-operative societies similar to the Sociétés were organized by the authorities in the French mandated territory of Cameroun. These too were under close government control and supervision.

Partly as the result of the expansion of commercial agriculture, pressure upon land continued to increase in some areas. But sheer population growth was more important. Although on the whole population was still very sparse in Africa, barely more than one per square kilometre in AEF and Northern Rhodesia, in places it was dense, no less than 249 a square kilometre in Ruanda-Urundi, a source of migrant labourers for Uganda. A world-wide influenza epidemic after the war, though it caused millions of deaths, did not have profound long-run consequences. There were some signs of a falling death-rate, e.g. in Algeria, but in countries where there was no obvious downward trend of the death-rate, as in Egypt, the rising population can be attributed to continued high, in some cases rising, birth-rates. The death-rate was relatively high on the whole, though not everywhere significantly higher than in parts of Europe. The rate of mortality among infants in Egypt, for example, was no worse than in Portugal, ranging in the former between 133 deaths of children under the age of a year per thousand living births in 1921 to 159 in 1929 and in the latter between 132 in 1925 and 164 in 1923.

Shortage of land resulted in continued subdivision of farms and landlessness. In South Africa the authorities attempted to stem the black townward flow which they had themselves helped to create with the 1913

Natives Land Act. This was done by the Natives (Urban Areas) Act of 1923. This not only aimed to restrict the movement of black rural emigrants, but also imposed upon municipal authorities the duty of providing adequate, but separate, accommodation. It was influenced by the report of the Tuberculosis Commission of 1914 and the influenza epidemic of 1918, which revealed the slum conditions in which Africans lived in the towns, and it did do something to raise standards of health and housing. Some white opinion was in favour of giving Africans security of tenure in their so-called locations and also of modifying the hated legal requirements of carrying passes. This, however, gave way before the view that towns were white creations and that blacks should be admitted only for the purpose of serving whites. Although it did not control the influx of Africans into towns, the Act did require registration of contracts (up to a point a safeguard for the worker) and gave the goverment powers to deal with those who had no documentary evidence of their right to be in an urban area.

The export economy continued to be the most powerful stimulus to the development of transport and communications. For the export of Union minière copper an additional railway was completed by Chemin de Fer du Bas-Congo au Katanga in 1923–1928. Copper exports by that route were encouraged by freight rates that were kept very low by the Belgian authorities, who wished to retain the profits of copper as far as possible in Belgian hands. It was an inconvenient way. Shipments had to travel part of the way by the Congo and Kasai rivers to Matadi, and that necessitated costly transhipments. A third route for Katanga was opened in 1929, with the completion of the singularly unprofitable Benguela Railway. Until 1931 some Katanga copper was sent across Lake Tanganyika to the railhead at Kigoma for transport to Dar es Salaam.

Although most of the trunk routes of the African railway system had been planned and largely constructed by 1914, after the war, when it became possible to resume building, many were completed or extended, like the Congo railways. The Uganda railway reached Jinja in 1923 and Kampala in 1931. In the more favourable parts of Africa, branch lines were built. By 1930 Kenya was served by a fairly comprehensive network.

Some government investment went into making rivers navigable (e.g. large stretches of the Congo) and improving harbours. Where there was no natural harbour at all, artificial harbours were built, e.g. at Takoradi in the Gold Coast. In East Africa, in the optimistic climate of the immediate post-war period, the colonial authorities were persuaded to begin new harbour works at Zanzibar, once the great distribution and re-export centre of the region, and Kilindini (Kenya), a railway terminus and a newly-developing rival of Zanzibar. But Mombasa, where deep-water berths were built, remained the most important port, through which most exports went. Because of natural disadvantages and shortage of capital Beira found it difficult to handle the large volume of minerals and agricultural products exported from Katanga, the Rhodesias, Nyasaland and Moçambique. The South African ports of Durban (providing the most important outlet for and access to the Transvaal), Port Elizabeth, East London and Cape Town all required deepening. In contrast Lourenço Marques, always busy, and Lobito, always underutilized, were first-rate natural harbours.

Roads for the most part were a later development than railways, at least on any scale, and though in some areas they tended to compete with the railways, e.g. in the Nile Delta, they were intended primarily to supplement the railway system. The impetus for road construction was provided by the large-scale introduction of mass-produced, yet reliable motor-vehicles after the war. Road building was undertaken chiefly, though not exclusively, by colonial governments, which sometimes also provided road transport services. The energy which was applied to it varied widely according to demand, the extent of the waterways, government revenue and the availability of suitable building materials. In the Gold Coast the government was able to enlist the help of cocoa farmers anxious to transport their products and put through a big programme of road building – some 6 000 kilometres – just after the war. One of the best-off territories was Uganda, where there was an adequate supply of suitable stone. Already in the early 1920s there were modern roads capable of use by three-ton lorries. The bicycle gained an early popularity there.

Motor transport, able to offer a more far-reaching and flexible service than railway transport, undoubtedly did much to promote internal trade and to spread more widely European goods. Both forms of transport presented new opportunities both for wage-earners and for entrepreneurs. Although the European or the Asian often pulled out the plums, there was a share of the cake left for African enterprise as well. Africans, especially in West Africa, found scope in the provision of buses, taxis and other transport services – sometimes combined with trade – and in the sale, repair and servicing of motor vehicles. The railways were large-scale employers and a training ground for a new and articulate black proletariat. Labour itself became more mobile and less of it was absorbed in the old labour intensive methods of transport, especially head-loading.

Road building was an important part of extensive post-war public works programmes in the colonies. Although these were financed largely by the colonies themselves, imperial assistance did increase. Enlightened self-interest had much to do with that. Leopold Amery, who was Colonial Secretary in the Conservative government of 1924-1929 in Britain, was sure that the colonial empire could help solve the economic problems of Britain, where six years after the war one worker in ten was unemployed. In 1926 the Empire Marketing Board was created to promote production throughout the empire by means of research and improved marketing and methods of production, especially in agriculture. This was followed by the more far-reaching Colonial Development Act of 1929, passed by the new Labour administration, but along the lines advocated by Amery. It set up a Colonial Development Advisory Committee, charged with the task of spending a million pounds a year on the promotion of agriculture and industry in the colonies, not only for the benefit of the colonies but also in the hope of helping in turn British commerce and industry, though it was realized that the contribution to the alleviation of unemployment in Britain could be only small.

In Kenya annual expenditure on public works doubled in the 1920s, to £0,5 million in 1929, and in 1926 the British government lent £8,5 million to the colony and the Kenya and Uganda Railways and Harbours Administration. In Uganda, with the help of an imperial development loan in 1921, there was money devoted to road building and to the expansion of medical, agricultural and veterinary services. Livestock diseases were brought under better control and African cotton and coffee cultivation was encouraged. There was a gradual shift in emphasis from expenditure upon administration and defence to welfare expenditure. In the Gold Coast the governor, F. G. Guggisburg, drew up a ten year plan for the period 1919-1928 which envisaged the spending of some £25 million upon surveys and research and public works, chiefly railways, roads and harbours. Since the cost was to be met out of the colony's own revenue, and that fell short of expectations, a more modest programme in the end was implemented, but its achievements, including the harbour at Takoradi, were not negligible.

The French government also began to be more active in colonial economic affairs, primarily in the interests of France itself. The ideas of imperial self-sufficiency and division of labour which the war had fostered survived into the 1920s. Albert Sarraut, the Minister of the Colonies, who was to express his ideas of imperial development in his book of 1923, *La Mise en Valeur des Colonies françaises*, formulated a comprehensive development programme for the whole empire with the exception of North Africa, which did not come under his ministry. It was set out in a Bill introduced into the French Parliament in April 1921. Its emphasis was on infrastructure and it included the improvement of port facilities, the extension of the road and railway network, the construction of schools, hospitals and other public buildings and the irrigation of part of the Niger valley for the cultivation of cotton. The Niger scheme was a project envisaged earlier and incorporated into the Sarraut Plan. It was extremely ambitious, proposing the irrigation of three-quarters of a million hectares, the settlement of a million and a half people and the production of 300 000 metric tons of cotton (compared with the current AOF output of 2 000 tons). Money for all this was to come from loans guaranteed by the metropolitan government. In the event the programme had to be curtailed as it was difficult to borrow when the franc was depreciating, the economic climate was unfavourable after the initial post-war boom and France was having difficulty in paying for its own post-war reconstruction. The Niger scheme, which from 1924 aimed to produce rice as well as cotton, survived, but little was achieved beyond engineering studies.

In the Belgian Congo there was considerable investment during the 1920s, including a Belgian government loan used chiefly for the development of transport, but also for agriculture. Far larger sums of private capital entered the colony, especially during the latter part of the decade, more than a thousand million francs a year in 1927–1931. Some of it went into manufacturing, e.g. sugar, chemicals, cement, palm oil and beer. Development was left largely to the big mining and railway companies, in which, however, the state had a financial interest. It was the big companies, particularly the Société générale, which achieved most. Many of the smaller companies with concessions did not have the capital to exploit them.

Shortage of capital was even more of a problem for the Portuguese colonies. In the early 1920s an attempt was made to accelerate development, notably by the construction of roads, railways and port facilities. Something was achieved, but much of the money spent simply went on an enlarged bureaucracy, and the cost was heavy. In Angola there was inflation of the locally-issued money, together with trade deficits, exhaustion of foreign exchange resources and public indebtedness. The restoration of close metropolitan supervision after 1926 and, in particular, the advent of Dr Salazar put an end to extravagant plans for colonial development. Financial stringency in Portugal and economic nationalism that was highly suspicious of non-Portuguese capital meant that funds were not available.

One of the great disadvantages of government-sponsored development was the great increase in public indebtedness. In the euphoria just after the war and in the prosperous times of the later 1920s colonies borrowed on an unusually large scale. Interest was relatively high. The average rate on government external debt in British Africa, excluding South Africa, rose from $3\frac{1}{2}$ per cent in 1913 to 4,85 per cent in 1932. Kenya borrowed £5 million at 6 per cent after the war and used part of it to repay an earlier British loan at 3,5 per cent. Then came the £8,5 million loan of 1926. The

Gold Coast government borrowed £4 million at 6 per cent in 1920 and £4,6 million at 4,5 per cent in 1926, the latter debt redeemable in thirty years. The colony owed £11,7 million in 1926, of which £8,9 million was debt incurred on behalf of the railways. In a similar burst of optimism, Nigeria raised a loan in 1919 at 6 per cent that was redeemable between 1949 and 1979. In the Belgian Congo the public debt stood at 2 539 million francs in 1928. In French West Africa loans raised in 1920 and 1922 paid interest of 5,5 per cent and in 1924 the interest on a further loan was even higher, 6,5 per cent. Debt charges in the British colonies south of the Sahara, excluding South Africa, were five times as great in 1925 and eight times as much in 1935 as they had been in 1913. In the Gold Coast debt transfer reached a peak of 16,3 per cent of revenue in 1926; in the Belgian Congo it accounted for a fifth of ordinary revenue in 1928. South Africa also greatly increased its national debt. The Union, beginning its life in 1910 with a gross debt of some £116 million, had by 1924 a debt of some £208 million and by 1935 £248 million. But it was better placed than any other British territory in Africa because of its superior taxing capacity, less dependent upon taxes on trade.

Some parts of Africa had a burden of debt inherited from the more distant past. Egypt still had a large public debt, but it was much lower than it had been at its peak in the early 1890s. By the end of the 1920s it fell below £E 90 million, and of this £E 15,6 million was held by the government itself as part of its reserve fund. But Tunisia continued to be burdened with heavy debt charges of 50 million francs a year out of a total government expenditure of 207 million francs in the early 1920s. The debt position was just as serious in Morocco, with a quarter of annual budget receipts (some 200 million francs) consumed in debt servicing in the early 1920s. New loans at 5 per cent were incurred in 1918 and 1922. There was much discontent with the burden of taxation.

The recovery of world trade in the mid-1920s improved the revenue position. In the course of the 1920s Tanganyika was able to build up a surplus of £900 000. The Gold Coast could reduce import duties, yet maintain a bouyant revenue and build up a reserve fund. The situation was similar in Kenya, where revenue doubled between 1922 and 1929. Algeria began to recover in 1923 with an end to the run of poor cereal harvests. Revenue rose from 595 million francs in 1923–1924 to 1 873 million in 1930. Egypt throughout the 1920s had a succession of budget surpluses. About half its revenue came from customs duties, the land tax having been reduced to a relatively unimportant source of government income. Dependence on trade for revenue by the 1920s varied widely. In the Gold Coast import and export taxes were important. The government hesitated to impose direct taxation (in effect poll tax) lest it incited resistance. In Nigeria, on the other hand, income taxes (so-called, but effectively only poll taxes) were gradually extended in the southern half of the country in the face of sporadic violence in the south-eastern provinces. The change went hand in hand with the extension of indirect rule (the native authority treasury system) from the north to the south. By 1930 direct taxation was contributing 14 per cent of total revenue in Nigeria. This was very different from the position in AOF. In Guinea the poll tax represented three-fifths of revenue in 1930, in Soudan half. In Senegal only 13 per cent of revenue came from the poll tax in 1930, but the percentage had been higher in the mid-1920s and was to rise again in the 1930s. French West Africa as a whole was self-sufficient financially, but the general revenue of the federation derived chiefly from taxes on trade and had to be used to subsidize the colonies in budgetary deficit. Mauritania was a constant beneficiary. In East Africa, Tanganyika had a high dependence on direct taxation, hut and poll tax, the yield of which exceeded that of customs duties. Uganda, too, derived more of its revenue from the poll tax than from taxes on trade, made up of customs duties and an export tax on cotton.

Not all development was dependent directly upon government revenue. In French North Africa and Egypt a new departure was the establishment of banks for the express purpose of promoting trade and industry. The Industrial Bank of North Africa was founded in 1920 with a capital of ten million francs to make long and medium-term loans to commercial and industrial enterprises. In the same year the Bank Misr was set up in Egypt, followed by the Federation of Industries in 1922. The former, the first bank financed and managed by Egyptians, set up a number of industrial enterprises, including a factory for the manufacture of cotton cloth. Egyptian industry, however, was hampered by a shortage of skilled manpower and by international obligations which prevented the erection of protective tariffs. It was still much under foreign domination. Three-quarters of the ninety members of the Federation of Industries, employing in 1925 some 150 000 workers and with a capital investment of £E 30 million, were foreign.

The Bank Misr was primarily an investment bank, but it engaged in a wide range of financial operations, with branches in the main commercial centres and subsidiaries in France and Syria and Lebanon. It acquired a good deal of the business of the big landowners and cotton merchants, partly because it became the government's agent for the purchase and storage of cotton and partly because it made loans on easy terms. But despite its rapid growth it was far from capturing all business. Foreigners still preferred to deal with subsidiaries of the metropolitan banks. One of these, the Anglo-Egyptian Bank, amalgamated in 1926 with the National

Bank of South Africa and the Colonial Bank to form the Dominion, Colonial and Overseas branch of Barclays Bank. The Colonial Bank was founded early in the 19th century to carry on business in the Caribbean but started operating in West Africa shortly before the end of the war, challenging the monopoly of the Bank of British West Africa. The National Bank of South Africa, which, with the Standard Bank of South Africa, dominated banking in South Africa (the Netherlands Bank, its head office in Amsterdam, being relatively unimportant at that time), found itself in difficulties in 1923 and was glad to accept absorption into Barclays. Like the Standard Bank, Barclays DCO operated in East Africa, chiefly meeting the needs of European farmers.

Capital was brought into Africa by a quickened flow of white settlers after the war. In Libya the Fascist government made strong efforts to settle Italians on the land, mostly in Tripolitania in the 1920s. In 1921 Count Giuseppe Volpi was appointed governor of Libya and he proceeded to make effective Italy's claims to the territory. In 1922 he extended the public domain to all uncultivated land. In Morocco the European population, about 20 000 before the war, reached 150 000 by 1930, about 5 per cent of the total population. The proportion of the European population that was French (about 70 per cent) was greater than in the other French North African territories. European settlers in Morocco farmed about a million hectares of land (about 9 per cent of the cultivated area), more than European-owned land in Tunisia, though the proportion of European-owned land was much higher in Tunisia (about 20 per cent of cultivated land) and very much higher in Algeria (about 40 per cent of cultivated land). The European population of Algeria (833 000 in 1926, 14 per cent of the total population) and Tunisia (214 000 in 1936, 8,2 per cent of the total population) continued to grow, but more through natural increase than immigration. Much the bigger part of the European population in North Africa lived in the towns - four-fifths in Algeria, nearly three-quarters in Tunisia, over 90 per cent in Spanish Morocco.

Like those in Algeria and Tunisia, the European farmers in Morocco grew cereals, citrus fruit and spring vegetables. Cereal output surpassed that in Algeria, where production remained fixed at more or less its pre-war level. There was a rapid expansion of vineyards in Tunisia in the 1920s, but the total area under cultivation never exceeded 51 000 hectares, far short of the Algerian total (400 000 ha by 1939).

The European population of Southern Rhodesia grew slowly. Some land was granted to ex-servicemen, but in the mid-1920s there were barely 40 000 Europeans altogether in the country. White farmers mostly culti-vated maize (producing by the 1930s 2 million bags in a good year) and tobacco. From 1925 Britain gave preference to empire-grown tobacco and this attracted new growers and stimulated output. The crop amounted to 11,3 million kilograms by 1927-1928. The market, however, was unable to absorb so much, with the result that output fell to below 2,7 million kilograms in 1929-1930. Almost all Southern Rhodesian tobacco was grown by European farmers. Other European agricultural interests included the export of beef cattle through Beira and chilled beef, and some citrus fruit was grown.

Africans in Southern Rhodesia took advantage of the right to buy land outside the reserves, and by 1923, when responsible government was granted, some 40 000 hectares in European farming districts had been acquired by blacks. Although this was only a small proportion of the 32,4 million hectares available for purchase, the settler community became alarmed. A commission appointed in 1925 by the Southern Rhodesian government recommended the separation as far as possible of the area held by black and white 'until the native has advanced much further on the paths of civilization'. The British government consented to the principle and it was embodied in the Land Apportionment Act of 1930, which, though segregationist in spirit, could not go so far as to separate European and African areas completely because they were already inextricably intermingled. The Act distinguished the areas in which blacks and whites could obtain land by purchase. The division of land between the races was entirely disproportionate to population size, and the African population grew very rapidly. But the land reserved for European use was not necessarily superior to that set aside for Africans.

White settlement in south Central Africa was extended along the railways north of the Zambezi. European farmers engaged in ranching and maize cultivation for the Katanga mines. When this market was lost through the construction of railways that made it possible to supply the area from Kasai and Kivu, it was replaced by the development of the Northern Rhodesia Copper Belt. Further north, in the Congo, European settlement was not encouraged by the Belgian authorities. Such experiments in European farming as were carried out, did not enjoy much success. In 1930 the European population of the Belgian Congo was only 25 000, a third of it non-Belgian.

In Kenya the post-war boom induced such euphoria that ambitious plans were formulated by the representatives of the European population to sell land on easy terms to ex-servicemen. But even so there were still only just over two thousand active European farmers by the end of the 1920s. Not all the land allocated to settlers was fertile and well-watered. In 1929 only 11,4 per cent of the two million hectares reserved for white agriculture were occupied. There was much controversy about the entire land position, the so-called paramountcy debate. In 1926 the remaining African reserves were proclaimed, but there was no guarantee of their inviolability. It was not until 1930, with the Native Lands Trust Ordinance, that the position was defined. The Ordinance guaranteed the perpetuity of the reservation and entrusted the administration of the reserves to a Central Trust Board on which there were to be nominated unofficial (in practice largely European) representatives. Although, subject to certain controls, Europeans were allowed to lease unoccupied reserve land, a large measure of security for African landholders now appeared to be assured.

In Uganda there were two schools of thought among British officials about the economic future of the protectorate, one in favour of European-owned plantations, the other advocating peasant cultivation of cash crops. The two policies were incompatible because they were in competition for land and labour, and both had very different social and political implications as far as traditional institutions and the division of power were concerned. In the immediate post-war years the tide ran in favour of the European plantation. The Uganda administration did its best to assist planters to secure labour and delayed the introduction of cash crops into labour-supplying districts. In 1920 an imperial veto imposed in 1916 on the sale of African freehold land to non-Africans was lifted and in 1921 the Colonial Secretary, Winston Churchill, accepted the seventh report of the local Land Settlement Committee recommending European access to a very large proportion of the land. In 1923, however, the policy was reversed. The colonial authorities committed themselves to a policy of peasant agriculture. Compulsory labour was abolished except in a limited number of cases. The reason for the change was partly African opposition but more the growing doubt about the viability of plantation agriculture engendered particularly by the fall of coffee prices in 1921 and the decline of European demand for land. Whatever the explanation the change of policy represented a victory for paternalism, for the view of empire as a trust rather than a source of wealth and influence for the imperial power.

In post-war Tanganyika there was some settler pressure for the alienation of land to Europeans. But the governor, Sir Horace Byatt, was opposed to ill-prepared and undercapitalized European plantations. The mandated territory's land policy was embodied in a Land Ordinance of 1923, which declared all land, occupied and unoccupied, public land, to be used for the benefit of the native people in accordance with native law and custom. New grants of land were to be only on leasehold and any lease of more than 2 000 hectares to a non-African was subject to the consent of the Colonial Secretary.

In South Africa after the war, under the Soldier Settlement Scheme of 1919, there were some grants of farms of 65–80 hectares, and some of the ex-servicemen's land grants in Southern Rhodesia were small. The small white farmer, however, could not survive in Africa, or only with great difficulty. In the 1920s the average European farm in Kenya was well over 800 hectares. Small farms were exceptional, though the medium-sized plantation – some 200 hectares – was typical for coffee-growing in the Highlands. In Angola and Moçambique for more than a century peasant settlers, farming usually less than 200 hectares, and sometimes much less, were encouraged and helped by the Portuguese colonial authorities. This immigration, sporadic before the war, became subsequently a significant part of the policy of the metropolitan government, which aimed to divert to Africa part of the stream of emigrants to Brazil in the hope of strengthening its hold upon this territory and enhancing its economic value, though settlement of European peasants in a land filled with African peasants made little economic sense, given the high investment costs involved. In 1920 more than a thousand Portuguese immigrants arrived in Africa, but this was only a fraction of total emigration from Portugal that year (over sixty thousand) and it was a figure not equalled again in the 1920s. Many of those who went to Africa returned home; others settled in the towns. At the end of the 1920s there were only 50 000 whites and mestiços in Angola, some 17 500 whites and 8 000 mestiços in Moçambique, compared with perhaps three million Africans in Angola and three and a half million in Moçambique. The latter colony also had about 8 500 Indians and a handful of Chinese.

The expansion of European agriculture in Kenya and Southern Rhodesia and of mining in the Copper Belt, together with railway construction and the growing requirements of the South African gold-mines in the later 1920s, meant that labour remained perhaps the foremost administrative and political issue. There continued to be a strong element of force in labour recruitment. In Kenya there was an increase throughout most of the 1920s in compulsory labour for public purposes. Between 1923 and 1927 the number of men engaged in compulsory government work almost doubled, to 25 000, and the number of days worked by these forced labourers more than doubled over the same period, from 95 000 to 240 000. The situation was no better in mandated territories than elsewhere despite the moral justification claimed for stripping Germany of its colonies. In the French Cameroun labour was conscripted on a considerable scale for porterage and railway building. In 1926 alone over 10 000 men were requisitioned for extending the railway from the old capital of Douala to the new one of Yaoundé. The death rate was very high, far greater than that admitted by the authorities, which was almost twenty per thousand in 1922. Some improvements in living conditions were effected as a result of repeated complaints from the Permanent Mandates Commission.

Because of the odium attached to forced labour and its inefficiency there was a trend towards making less use of compulsion on behalf of private employers. The Northey Circulars to district officers in Kenya aroused an outcry in humanitarian circles in Britain and they were withdrawn. The tendency was for forced labour to be confined to public purposes and to be more strictly controlled. In the mandated territories compulsion for private purposes was prohibited. In 1920, as Colonial Secretary, Lord Milner, though accepting the legitimacy of the use of persuasion, expressed opposition to forced labour for private employment in non-mandated colonies. These sentiments were echoed by the governor of Southern Rhodesia, Sir John Chancellor, in 1925: freedom of contract was the 'traditional policy' of the government. In the Belgian Congo it was the open policy of the colonial authorities to assist the agencies recruiting labour for the big enterprises, Union minière, Huileries du Congo belge and the Katanga Railway, to the disgust of the smaller employers, who felt that their own needs were overlooked. Increasingly, however, the damaging social and economic consequences of denuding districts of young men began to be appreciated. The Advisory Committees on Labour of 1923–1924 and 1928–1929 recommended that no further mining concessions be granted and that only one-third of the colony be open to large-scale agricultural concessions and another third to small-scale. In the interests of African social organization, limits were suggested to the proportion of adult males to be recruited from any area, whether for distant or for local enterprises. The regulations, which were modified in 1930, laid down that only 10 per cent of the adult males could be recruited for work away from their villages and a further 15 per cent for local employment. Certain areas were temporarily closed to recruitment. Officials were required to abstain from direct assistance to recruiters.

It was always difficult for officials to resist the demands of white employers looking for labour, especially when these were big and powerful. As always there were some notorious scandals in the Portuguese colonies. In 1924 an American sociologist, Edward A. Ross, made a whirlwind tour of Angola and a short visit to Moçambique. His report of 1925 was an attack on all forms of forced labour, including involuntary labour contracts, and it seemed to show that nothing had changed. The authorities vehemently denied the charges, but there seems to have been substance in Ross's indictment.

In some colonies an increasing amount of voluntary labour for private employment was coming forward. In Kenya farm labourers could command better wages during the more prosperous times after 1923, and there was an increase in the number of labour tenants. A growing number of blacks from inside and outside Southern Rhodesia looked for wage employment there, only a fraction recruited by the Rhodesian Native Labour Bureau. Men still travelled long distances to centres of employment. Of the 147 205 men in employment in 1925, 92 072 were aliens, from Nyasaland (where labour recruitment was not allowed by the government), Northern Rhodesia and Moçambique. There was a tendency in the 1920s for the labour supply from Northern Rhodesia to dwindle as copper-mining developed there. Everywhere, through the increasing activities of bush traders, the taste for European goods and the possibility of indulging it became more widespread. Africans were becoming more accustomed to wage employment and the mortality rate in mining was declining, by the mid-1920s to less than ten per thousand in the Transvaal and rather more than fifteen per thousand in Southern Rhodesia.

In the copper-mines of the Katanga, the Union minière embarked upon a policy of stabilizing the labour force. Contract labour was regarded as unsatisfactory. There was never enough and what there was, was of poor quality. Katanga was sparsely populated, and it was inconvenient and expensive to bring in labour from outside. It was necessary to have long contracts owing to the expense of recruiting labour from a long way away and the fact that it took two years for a man to reach his maximum efficiency. But it was difficult to get recruits to accept three year contracts and desertion was frequent. In the 1920s the recruiting position worsened because of the limitations imposed in accordance with the recommendations of the Advisory Committees on Labour. At the same time the government was exerting pressure on employers to improve conditions of work. Accordingly in 1925 Union minière began to reduce its dependence on contract labour. Workers were encouraged to bring their wives and families and settle in the mining towns. Various inducements were offered, such as generous rations in addition to wages, housing, and regular medical attentions for workers and their families, and schools. Contract labour was still used and no pressure was put on a worker to renew his contract, but workers were encouraged to stay on. The policy was successful and workers increasingly re-engaged on the expiry of their contracts. By the late 1930s the average annual recruitment was lower than 2 000, compared with 10 000 in the 1920s. There was an improvement in health and the mortality rate fell. The stabilization policy was expensive, but it paid for itself in higher productivity. Union Minière's example was followed by other big companies, including Huileries du Congo belge.

The trend was towards a more stable and committed industrial labour force. But there was little harmony in industrial relations in Africa. Workers became more militant and better organized. In West Africa public (especially railway) employees, were in the vanguard of the labour movement. There were strikes in both British and French colonies. In the latter, on the Thiès-Niger railway white and black workers were involved. The workers' organization in Sierra Leone was particularly precocious, which is not at all surprising given the alien and mixed composition of the original population of Freetown. In 1925 the African Railway Workers Union began a strike that lasted six weeks and led to a great deal of violence. The Sierra Leone authorities, supported by the Colonial Office, dealt with it sternly. This was ostensibly on the ground that the strikers were public employees. In fact there was a Masters and Servants Ordinance that made it doubtful whether strikes of any sort would be countenanced by the government. No firm distinction was made between strikes and revolts, a point of view typical of all colonial empires at that time.

In South Africa the white labour movement suffered a setback as a result of the failure of the 1922 strike. Slowly trade unionism recovered and fresh efforts were made to form a national organization. Black unionization in the 1920s was more spectacular in its development, though the stir it caused was disproportionate to its real strength. The black labour movement was synonymous with the ICU, which enjoyed an effective existence of ten years and attracted a very mixed following. Severing ties with the Communist Party, which might have provided the stiffening it needed for purposeful action and for efficient, economical and honest administration, it became political rather than industrial, rural rather than urban, African rather than Coloured. It did not penetrate the closed world of the migrant black mine workers. These staged a strike in 1920 that achieved nothing and was their last effective industrial action until after the Second World War.

Force in manifold forms remained characteristic of the South African labour market. The problems were still the same; the solutions involved ever more coercive legislation. Fundamentally it was a question of pushing black workers into work which they did not want and keeping them from work which they did. A series of laws to that purpose emanated from both the Smuts government of the immediate post-war period and the Pact coalition of Labour and Nationalists of 1924. The latter pursued what was euphemistically called the Civilized Labour Policy, but laws in the same spirit were passed before 1924. To keep blacks out of skilled jobs the important Acts included the Apprenticeship Act of 1922, which made it difficult for blacks to take up apprenticeships by imposing educational qualifications beyond the reach of most of them. The Industrial Conciliation Act (a 1924 Smuts measure), which imposed upon unions and management the obligation of negotiating and observing agreements on wages, excluded pass-carrying Africans, and these were by far the majority of blacks in industrial employment. As it virtually established a closed shop, it kept out of employment those who could not gain admission to the many trade unions practising a colour bar. The Pact's Wage Act of 1925 was designed to fix fair wages for unskilled workers in industries where there was no union to negotiate on their behalf. Though overtly non-racial, it was administered mostly for the benefit of 'civilized labour' and discouraged the employment of blacks by taking away the chief advantage of black labour in the eyes of most employers, its cheapness. The Mines and Works Act of 1926 restored to the government powers to make discriminatory regulations which had been lost through the invalidation of earlier regulations made under the 1911 Mines and Works Act. It was government policy to employ whites in preference to blacks in public service, even in unskilled work, and to encourage (e.g. by threatening to withdraw trade protection) private employers to take on whites rather than blacks. To stifle opposition, the Native Administration Act was passed in 1927. It was directed chiefly against the ICU and its flamboyant leader, Clements Kadalie, and had the effect of circumscribing trade union activity among Africans.

The 1920s began with an economic depression and ended with another of very much greater dimensions. It also ended on a foreboding political note. In 1930 the violent nationalist party of Adolf Hitler won 107 seats in the German parliamentary elections. The economic depression of the early 1930s was to strengthen the position of the Nazi Party and to foster economic nationalism everywhere. Although its depth took most people by surprise, for the perceptive observer it was far from unexpected. The prosperity of the 1920s was precarious. There was persistently high unemployment in Britain and some other industrialized countries and throughout the world there was overproduction of primary produce and manufactured goods in relation to effective demand. Output of primary products, through the application of more labour and better methods, was growing faster than the capacity of the chief importing areas to absorb them, especially foodstuffs, for which demand was inelastic. As long as the United States, the dominant international creditor and source of capital, experienced the boom induced by internal demand, an equilibrium could be maintained, but as early as 1928 there were signs of falling American domestic demand; and in 1929 the equilibrium was upset by the collapse of share prices following a period of hectic speculation, which destroyed business confidence and discouraged investment.

CHAPTER VI

1930-1940 (DEPRESSION)

The United States depression spread to Europe in the form of a series of financial crises. A severe blow was struck at the international economy in September 1931 when Britain had to suspend the gold standard, an example followed by many other countries. International investment, initially curtailed by the attraction of capital to the United States by the profits of speculation, more or less ceased after the financial crash there. Britain was no longer able to export capital; the USA, chastened by earlier experience, declined to do so. Balance of payments difficulties became widespread as it became harder to get credit. Most countries adopted restrictive practices in their international dealings, aiming at maximum self-sufficiency. This in turn added to the problems of those dependent upon exports. The process of declining earnings and borrowings weakened demand, and falling prices resulted. Between 1929 and 1931 the value of international trade fell by at least a third.

To the extent that the majority of Africans still engaged in subsistence farming or could fall back on it, Africa was insulated from the effects of the depression. Unemployment and excess industrial capacity were problems that were far more acute in the complex economies of the developed world. None the less, African trade suffered a severe blow and individuals who, in growing numbers, depended upon exports in one way or another, were afflicted by hardship no less than the victims of depression in the industrialized world. The effects of the slump varied in timing and magnitude, however. In most cases they were immediate and severe. Tanganyika's income from sisal in 1930 (£1,1 million) was £313 278 less than in 1929, though exports had increased by more than 4 000 tons. Its coffee earnings fell by a third despite an increase in exports by a third. Nigeria's export earnings from palm oil fell from £3,7 million in 1929 to £3,2 million in 1930, though the quantity exported rose from 132 000 to 136 000 tons, and from palm kernels fell from £4,2 million in 1929 to £3,6 million in 1930, with volume increasing from 251 000 to 260 000 tons. The total exports of the Union of South Africa were valued at £87,2 million in 1929 and £72,9 million in 1930. Diamond production in 1929 came to £10,5 million, in 1930 to £8,3 million and in 1931 only £4,1 million. Egypt's commodity exports were worth £E 52,4 million in 1929 and £E 32,0 million in 1930. In 1929-1930 exports of 6,1 million kantars of cotton earned £E 50,8 million; in 1930-1931 7,2 million kantars earned only £E 31,1 million.

In some countries the impact was less immediate. Indeed, Libya, going through a period of intense investment, actually saw its trade expand markedly in the 1930s. That was exceptional. More common was a delayed effect of varying severity. The exports of the Belgian Congo rose in value from 1,4 thousand million francs in 1929 to 1,5 thousand million in 1930. Then came the fall, with total exports worth 1,1 thousand million in 1931. The value of copper exports fell from 737 million francs in 1930 to only 102 million in 1932. The French North African colonies did not experience the worst effects of the depression until somewhat later in the 1930s, reflecting the course of events in France itself. The exports of Algeria were worth more in 1930 (4,2 million francs) than in 1929 (3,8 million) and fell below the 1929 level only slightly in 1931 (3,7 million). In the case of Tunisia the value of exports fell from 1,4 million francs in 1929 to 1,1 million in 1930, but the value of imports rose from 1,9 million francs in 1929 to 2,1 million in 1930. Elsewhere the fall in export earnings was generally reflected at once in a decline of imports. It was not only the timing of depression that varied. The course of depression was affected by local circumstances. In the Gold Coast the cocoa trees were attacked by swollen shoot disease, which was particularly rampant in the oldest cocoa growing areas. Many smaller farmers went out of business or fell into debt. In the Anglo-Egyptian Sudan the Gezira cotton farms were attacked by disease and production in the early 1930s fell to half the 1925 level. Kenya was assaulted by locusts and between 1931 and 1934 afflicted with bad drought. In Tanganyika in 1930 there were heavy floods and in Uganda in the same year there was a very poor growing season.

The terms of trade moved against the primary producers. For, although the prices of industrial goods fell, those of foodstuffs and raw materials fell still more. The price of sisal, £32 a ton in 1929, fell to £21 in 1930, subsequently reaching only £12 a ton. The price of copper was only £54,611 a long ton in 1930, compared with £75,416 in 1929 and fell to £31,682 in 1932. The average f.o.b. price of coffee at Mombasa fell from 86 shillings a 100 pound in 1929 to 46 shillings in 1931 and, after rallying to 51 shillings in 1932 fell consistently until 1938, when it was only 23 shillings a 100 lb. Uganda cotton fetched 17 shillings a 100 lb in 1929, only 11 shillings in 1931, but remained fairly steady in the following years. Nevertheless, although the deterioration of the terms of trade was plainly to be seen, these sharp price falls of primary products were not quite so startling if viewed in a longer perspective. Although copper prices had been steady during the 1920s, rising at the end of the decade, and their steep decline in 1930 was undoubtedly related to the contraction of manufacturing industry during the world slump, the prices of foodstuffs and industrial crops had been going down several years before the great depression. South African greasy wool, which sold at only 4,2 pence a pound in 1932, and 11,8 pence in 1929, had sold at 16,6 pence in 1925. The fall of the price of Egyptian cotton from 20,36 talaris (talari = one-fifth of £E 1) per kantar in 1929-1930 to 12,04 talaris in 1930-1931 was very great, but in 1924-1925 a kantar was selling for 39,49 talaris. The price of cocoa had been falling ever since 1927, that of ground-nuts and palm oil since 1925. Thus the depression aggravated difficulties which had earlier causes. It obscured a secular trend that was more serious, except in the case of particular commodities, for which there was expanding industrial demand. The problem lay deeper than a temporary decline of industrial activity, however severe. It was rather a question of the relative inelasticity of demand for primary products. The population of the chief consumers – the twelve biggest industrial countries importing three-quarters of primary products entering world trade – had ceased to grow so rapidly, partly because of the falling birth rate, partly because of the high death rate during the First World War; but production of raw materials had been maintained or increased.

Peasant producers in Africa, with government encouragement (as in the Belgian Congo and Tanganyika) responded to lower prices by increasing production. Although this had the effect of forcing prices down further, at least some colonies were able to restore pre-depression export earnings fairly quickly, e.g. Uganda by 1936. In the Gold Coast many cocoa farmers, despite the fall of prices, escaped westwards from the area stricken by disease, to the Ashanti region of the forest belt, which then became the chief producing area. In Nigeria (low as its price was) there were new cocoa plantings in the 1930s, since it was more rewarding than other products. Nigeria soon recovered its 1929 level of export earnings, but not the level of the mid-1920s. The Gold Coast, in contrast, surpassed its 1920s peak in 1937. Just as the onset and severity of the depression varied, so did the rate of recovery, depending upon the composition of the export bundle. Edible oil prices revived in 1935, to some extent because of imports by the United States, where the production of animal and vegetable fats had fallen as a result of the agricultural policy of the New Deal (i.e. the American programme of economic recovery) and a severe drought in the south-western states. The price of cocoa also started to go up in 1934, but remained well below the 1927 maximum. The price of Egyptian cotton reached 16,29 talaris a kantar in 1936-1937. By then world economic conditions were generally showing signs of moving out of depression, but in 1937 came a setback and the more prosperous situation of a decade earlier was not restored. The renewed advance to international recovery came with the pre-parations that began to be made in Europe for war.

In the Gold Coast the depression was shorter and milder than in some other colonies, e.g. Sierra Leone, because there was less dependence upon external trade. The decline of total business activity was not so steep or prolonged as the decline in the value of exports. The vigour of the internal economy was a factor in determining the severity of the effects of the depression. The internal market could act as a shock absorber, as it were. Those sectors of the economy which served it were scarcely affected by the downswing of international trade. Fresh water fishing (e.g. on the Middle Niger) and the raising of cattle and sheep (e.g. in the West African savanna) prospered in the 1930s to satisfy the growing demand for meat. In the Gold Coast, as a result of immunization against rinderpest, first carried out on a large scale in 1930, the numbers of cattle increased markedly (69 000 in 1921, 170 000 in 1941) and were bred in the Northern Territories for sale in the more populous south, though these northerners were not herders by tradition. Southern Nigeria was an important and expanding market, supplied by northern Nigeria and neighbouring French territories. More than 200 000 head of cattle, sheep and goats entered southern Nigeria each year in the 1930s, compared with fewer than 10 000 before the First World War.

Gold was the best remedy for depression. The increase in its price after the devaluation of the pound and the dollar was a stimulus to production and had a profound effect upon the economy of South Africa. Output was 10,4 million ounces in 1929, 11,0 million in 1934 and 12,1 million in 1938. Although its share of total world production was declining (from 53,4 per cent in 1929 to 32,9 per cent in 1938), its export earnings rose (£45,0 million in 1929, £69,9 million in 1933) and its contribution to the value of South African exports (50,6 per cent in 1929, 76,0 per cent in 1933) increased until 1933. In Southern Rhodesia, where small enterprises seized the opportunity and production rose from 561 000 ounces in 1929 to 804 000 ounces in 1937, gold contributed two-thirds of the value of exports in 1933, compared with less than two-fifths in the late 1920s; in the Gold Coast exports of gold accounted for 30 per cent of total exports in 1934; and in the Belgian Congo it outstripped copper temporarily as the most valuable export. In Tanganyika the value of gold produced increased twelve-fold between 1929 and 1936, rising from £38 630 to £490 490, and in Kenya there was a minor gold rush when alluvial gold was discovered in small quantities in 1931.

When Britain went off gold in September 1931, followed by many other countries, South Africa did not do so, attempting to compete in a world of diminishing trade and falling prices with those countries which had devalued their currencies. The government, which was committed to gold for the sake of stability and what was thought to be financial probity, continued to pursue a deflationary policy, restricting credit and reducing public expenditure, and took steps to encourage exports and discourage imports. It was, however, defeated by speculation and growing domestic criticism which saw its austerity programme as an aggravation of existing economic difficulties. In December 1932 South Africa went off gold and its pound was linked to sterling. The Reserve Bank held sterling balances and by the Currency and Exchanges Act of 1933 it was given far-reaching powers over currency, banking and foreign exchange dealings, enabling it to influence the functioning of the economy through exchange and credit controls. Throughout the 1930s there was a balance of payments surplus on current account and an expanding money supply, the result partly of increased foreign exchange holdings and partly of larger gold holdings. The economy was stimulated. With no appreciable rise in retail prices national income increased at the rate of 9,3 per cent a year in the period 1931-1932 to 1937-1938.

The great depression gave a further impetus to protection and economic nationalism. The French in West Africa were freed to pursue such a policy by the abrogation in 1936 of the tariff provisions of the 1898 Anglo-French Convention. Imperial preference took the form of tariffs and quotas on foreign goods, the preferential admission of colonial goods into the French market and privileges for French shipping. It gave the colonies a measure of security for their products, but they had to buy in return relatively expensive French consumer's goods. As a result of such measures, trade links between colony and metropolitan power were strengthened to quite a startling degree. France became by far the biggest purchaser of the exports of its colonies, taking, for example, 48 per cent of Dahomean exports in 1934, and the biggest supplier of their imports. In the mid-1930s its trade with the colonies accounted for more than a quarter of its total trade, though this proportion was less significant if Algeria, with its large French population and its close ties with France, was excluded. Algeria was much the most important French trading partner, accounting for as much trade as the West and Equatorial colonies put together.

Britain adopted comprehensive imperial preference as a result of the Ottawa Conference of Empire countries in 1932. The exports of all the colonies were admitted into Britain duty-free, while those from outside the Empire had to pay duties. It is disputable whether this operated very much to the benefit of the colonies, since Britain was not the only market for their produce and the preferences granted to British goods put up the prices of colonial imports. It is equally doubtful whether Britain gained very much. The colonial markets in tropical Africa were relatively insignificant and in any event limitations imposed by international agreements restricted the degree of preference which could be granted to British goods. Sierra Leone and Gambia were able to introduce tariffs discriminating in Britain's favour and Britain also secured restrictions upon Japanese competition, which became particularly fierce in the 1930s. Quotas were imposed from 1934 on Japanese exports of textiles, shoes and other goods to British West Africa. They could not, however, be applied in East Africa on account of the Congo Basin Treaty, with the result that by 1935 Japan had 88 per cent of the cotton piece goods market in Kenya and Uganda.

One effect of the depression was a decline in the demand for labour, while the increasing need and wish for money provided an adequate, indeed excessive, supply even after the demand for it began to recover. In 1930 and again in 1937 the Natives (Urban Areas) Act in South Africa was amended to restrict the entry of Africans into towns and to expel the unemployed. Although as late as 1930 the Low Grade Ore Commission enquiring into the state of the South African gold-mines was recommending the extension of recruitment into Central Africa because the numbers of men coming forward to work in the mines were insufficient; within a year or two the problem was solved by the depression and the drought which afflicted agriculture. The Native Economic Commission's Report of 1932 painted a sombre picture of rural degradation. For white opinion, however, the poor black problem was eclipsed by the poor white problem.

Population pressure was undoubtedly a factor in the decline of rural living standards in South Africa. In 1936 the population reached 9,5 million, compared with 6,9 in 1921. Throughout Africa population was growing. In East Africa growth appears to have become more pronounced from the middle of the 1920s, by which time the effects of the war were beginning to work themselves out and controls on small-pox and yaws had, or were beginning to, become effective. The rate of growth (at most 1,5 per cent a year) was much less striking than it was to become after the Second World War, but sufficient to raise the estimated population of Kenya from just over 4 million to just under 5 million during the 1930s and of Uganda from $3\frac{1}{2}$ million to just over 4 million over the same period. In certain areas there were signs of congestion and competition for land. In Algeria, after increasing at a rather slower rate during the war and post-war period, population grew very markedly in the 1930s. By the middle of the decade it had tripled since the 1871 revolt. Naturally density varied widely. The 20 million hectares of the north had a population of $6\frac{1}{2}$ million, while the 198 million hectares of the south had not much more than half a million people. Population density even in the north, however, at about thirty-one persons per square kilometre, was not at all excessive by European standards, but, of course, land was unevenly distributed. Morocco, where conquest was completed in 1934, also experienced population growth rates in the 1930s (as high as 3 per cent a year according to census figures, though these were of doubtful reliability) that were exceptionally high compared with those earlier and later. In 1936 the official estimate of the Muslim population of French Morocco was 5,8 million. The European and Jewish population was growing even faster, though total numbers were small in comparison with those of the native Moroccans, only 202 000 Europeans and 162 000 Jews in 1936. These minorities were concentrated chiefly in the towns and in manufacturing, commerce and administration. The colonial cities, especially Casablanca, were growing fast. In Libya, because of the influx of Italian settlers, the European population represented a much larger proportion of the total population than was the case in French North Africa, as high as 5 per cent or more in Tripolitania, over 11 per cent in Cyrenaica, and it was less urban. The native population was small, only 800 000, mostly concentrated in the fraction (less than 3 per cent) of the country suitable for agriculture. The European population of Southern Rhodesia was also growing, from 49 000 in 1931 to 55 000 in 1936, about two-fifths of it residing in Bulawayo and Salisbury, which between them had a total population of some 60 000. In Kenya the white population increased from 16 000 to 18 000 between 1931 and 1936, about half of it living in Nairobi. In the early 1930s the population of Nairobi was already more than 85 000 and that of Mombasa 60 000. There were fewer than 3 000 white farmers.

Generally speaking settlers survived depression less well than natives, being accustomed to a higher standard of living and less able to adapt to mere subsistence. White farmers were burdened with higher costs than black peasants, including the cost of labour, though this tended to be pushed down, and with heavy debts contracted in more sanguine times. Nearly three-quarters of the white workers in the Katanga copper industry were thrown out of work, most returning to Europe. In Kenya and Southern Rhodesia farmers were reluctant to abandon their farms. Some did: the number of Europeans engaged in farming in Southern Rhodesia fell from 4 541 in 1931 to 4 305 in 1935 and in Kenya the area cultivated by whites was reduced from 260 000 hectares to 203 000 hectares. Many of these remaining responded to lower prices by increasing output. In Algeria the rapid expansion of the area under grapes, already apparent in the 1920s, was kept up and even accelerated, reaching 400 000 hectares by the end of the 1930s. Sisal exports from Tanganyika rose from 61 000 metric tons in 1932 to 81 000 metric tons (about a quarter produced by Indians) in 1936. In Southern Rhodesia the output of tobacco increased from 8,6 million kilograms in 1927 to 10,1 million in 1936. Another response was diversification. In Kenya there was a shift from maize to dairy farming and the production of pyrethrum and tea. Yet another response was to turn to the government for assistance.

In Kenya the colonial authorities went to great lengths to soften the impact of the depression on white farmers. A Land Bank was founded in 1931 to grant credit which could no longer be obtained from commercial banks. It obtained its funds by borrowing on the London money market under government guarantee. Its loans were used to a considerable extent to pay off existing debts to commercial banks. Other credit was forthcoming directly from the government under the Agricultural Advances Ordinance of 1930, while the Mortgage Relief Ordinance of 1936 prevented the creditors of white farmers from taking possession of their land on failure to meet interest payments.

White farming in South Africa was in a sorry state, with declining output and stock numbers, the result not only of falling prices, but also drought and the deterioration of the land through overgrazing. The number of white country dwellers reached its peak in 1931, after which the drift from the country, which had started long before, brought about an absolute decline in the white rural population. Some 300 000 poor whites were unable to find an adequate living on the land because of the subdivision of farms through partible inheritance and because of the greater obstacles in the way of migrant farmers who settled with their few cattle and sheep temporarily on the land of others in return for a payment in kind, and the fewer openings for squatters, neither group welcome any longer to landowners who were making more intensive use of their farms.

In the ensuing years the situation of the poor whites improved as, with the expansion of the economy in the 1930s, more white workers were absorbed by other sectors. The poor black problem remained. The tribal reserves continued to deteriorate. Yet there was some slight improvement in the economic situation of Africans. An increasing proportion of the land, even though this was land officially white, was farmed by blacks as more and more whites moved into the towns. Blacks, too, derived some advantage from the growth of the economy. The recovery of the goldmining industry after the devaluation of sterling and the dollar was followed by an enlargement of the labour force. After falling to 204 849 in 1929; it rose to 348 048 in 1939. Fewer workers came from Moçambique. The proportion of the labour force recruited there declined from a half in 1927 to rather less than a quarter in 1933, and although the proportion picked up again after that, it did not regain its earlier importance. To make good this loss of amenable labour that could be put to work in less popular mines, recruitment was resumed in areas north of 22 degrees south. By 1939 this source provided 6 per cent of the black labour force. From the same source Southern Rhodesia was trying to get labour. As the economic situation improved, the government there set up a Free Migrant Labour Transport Service in 1934. It was not a recruiting agency, but an organization providing free transport from Northern Rhodesia, Nyasaland and Moçambique to Southern Rhodesia.

The demand for labour also grew in Northern Rhodesia once the effects of the depression upon the copper-mining industry had worn off. By 1937 the number of African workers was 18 000, compared with 22 000 (nearly a third of the black wage-labour force in the territory) in 1930. It reached 33 000 in 1943. Despite this increasing demand for labour, the mines were never without an adequate supply. The labour force was much more stable as Africans became accustomed to working at the mines and were willing to remain for longer periods.

During this period the pressure of international opinion upon colonies began to be felt more. In 1935 the International Labour Conference approved the Forced Labour Convention (1930) which condemned all labour imposed under threat of punishment, in particular the recruitment of labour by officials for private employment, and regulated more strictly pay and conditions in those instances where labour could still be conscripted. The condoned forms of compulsion were military service, convict labour, emergency services (e.g. measures against locusts and fire) and limited labour tribute to chiefs for communal purposes, but these offered loopholes for the admission of abuses of the spirit of the convention. It was ratified by Britain and, after a more or less prolonged interval, by France (1937), Belgium (1944) and Portugal (1956). Further conventions dealing with recruitment and contracts were approved in 1936 (Native Workers Convention) and 1939. These conventions were enforced with varying degrees of determination.

The British government became more sympathetic to trade unionism after 1929, when the Labour Party came to power with Lord Passfield (Sidney Webb) as Colonial Secretary. In the 1930s labour departments were established in the British colonial territories and experienced trade unionists from Britain were appointed as labour officers with the task of assisting trade union development. The Colonial Development and Welfare Act of 1940 made economic assistance to the colonies dependent upon laws protecting the rights of trade unions. Although there were sporadic strikes, especially just before the Second World War, trade union progress was slow. Few collective agreements were reached by direct negotiation and workers relied upon statutory machinery for wage determinations. Trade unions remained financially weak, unable to employ full-time officials. Part-time officials were vulnerable to reprisal and the quality of leadership was poor. Leaders could retain their position only by resort to violent strike action and insistent pay demands. The formation of a union was likely to be followed immediately by a strike. Sometimes a visiting organizer decamped with the subscriptions.

The labour movement in the French colonies made some progress during the Popular Front government. As in metropolitan France, in Algeria in 1936 there was a series of sit-in strikes which gained substantial wage increases for the workers. The forty-hour week was applied as in France. The beneficiaries of the Popular Front legislation were, in Africa, primarily the settlers. The extension of the right to form unions in Morocco was granted only to European workers. Even in West Africa there was a relatively large white population, concentrated mainly in Dakar, and consequently competition between whites and blacks for better paid jobs. Unions were racially exclusive. However, it was not only settlers who made gains in the later 1930s. Agricultural labourers in some parts of Algeria received in 1936 wage rises of about a third as a result of minimum wage legislation, and in 1937 black unions were allowed in AOF (but not in AEF), the first ones finding their membership among government employees and white-collar workers in Bamako and Dakar.

Racially separate trade unions were found in Northern Rhodesia. The white Northern Rhodesia Mineworkers Union was formed in 1936 to protect the European monopoly of skilled work. Black mineworkers struck as early as 1935, but there was no African union until the late 1940s. In the Belgian Congo there were no unions allowed, and that permitted a substantial transfer on the copper-mines and more especially on the railways of skilled work from Europeans to Africans. Multiracial unions in Africa were rare, but not unknown. The Indian Trade Union of Kenya, founded in 1934, opened its ranks to non-Indians in 1936, when it extended its activities beyond the borders of Kenya and renamed itself the Labour Trade Union of East Africa. Multiracial unions were found in South Africa, where trade union membership grew rapidly in the 1930s. Few trade unions had a constitutional colour bar, though among those that did was the Mine Workers Union, exclusively white. Race remained a divisive issue, partly accounting for a split in the labour movement between the Witwatersrand and the coastal industrial areas, where Coloured and Indian workers entered the textile and other growth industries in such numbers that unions had to be multiracial to have any influence at all. Africans, being legally disabled from joining registered unions, which alone could operate under the Industrial Conciliation Act, were unaffected by that trend.

Next to South Africa the country with the most advanced labour movement was Egypt, where there were big employers, like the Suez Canal Company and the railways, considerable numbers of industrial workers and a history of labour militancy going back to the 19th century.

There were some violent strikes in the 1930s. The army was called in to quell a strike in 1936 at the al-Mahalla al-Kubra textile factory, which belonged to one of the Misr Group of companies. In 1938 the textile workers, then working a twelve hour day, struck against an attempt to compel them to look after more looms.

The depression had a serious effect upon African revenue wherever there was heavy dependence upon taxes on trade. In Liberia it fell by three-quarters between 1928 and 1933. Libya was generating in the early 1930s only about a quarter of its own expenses. In 1934 the value of exports was only 16,2 per cent of that of imports. Morocco had a chronic deficit on its current account, with exports covering a third of imports in 1930. In Egypt revenue fell from £E 41,8 million in 1929-1930 to £E 32,6 million in 1933-1934, but, except in 1930-1931, there was no budgetary deficit and after 1932 there was a favourable balance of commodity trade. The shift of the burden of taxation from land to trade was confirmed by the protectionist policy adopted in 1930.

In the dependent British territories revenue fell from £28 million in 1929 to less than £23 million in 1932. One casualty was the East African Currency Board. Because of the fall in the prices of primary products and, under the pressure of a deteriorating balance of payments, the contraction of the volume of currency in circulation, the Board's reserve fund was reduced so sharply that it covered only 17,6 per cent of currency outstanding in 1931 and 9,9 per cent in 1932. The Board was compelled to strengthen the fund with short-term borrowing in London in 1930-1931, and in 1931 the Colonial Secretary had to give an assurance that East African currency would continue to be converted at the existing parity. The three East African governments – Kenya, Tanganyika and Uganda – stepped in to guarantee sterling loans. In fact further borrowing proved unnecessary. The mere guarantee sufficed to restore confidence, helped by the later slow improvement of the East African economy. The rate at which East African shillings were being redeemed slowed down and there was a gradual increase in the reserve fund. By 1937 the pre-depression position was restored. In 1936 the area of the Board's operations was extended to Zanzibar, where the shilling replaced Indian rupees and local notes. The experience of the West African Currency Board was much less eventful during the 1930s. Its reserve more than covered its currency liability. Britain's West African territories enjoyed a substantially favour-able balance of trade.

The third currency board in British Africa, established in 1938 and covering Northern and Southern Rhodesia and Nyasaland, also had an uneventful career. The process of substituting its currency for Southern Rhodesian and British coins and the notes issued by the Standard Bank and Barclays, DC & O, proceeded smoothly and the Board found no difficulty in adequately covering its issue with sterling securities.

Territories with gold resources naturally recovered most quickly from the fall in revenue. Total ordinary revenue of the Union of South Africa fell from an average of £30 million per annum in 1927–1929 to £27,7 million in 1931. In 1933 it shot up to £37,6 million and the proportion of revenue derived from customs and excise fell from 36,9 per cent in 1931 to 28,1 per cent in 1933. Total government receipts from gold-mining rose from £3,4 million in 1931 to £14,5 million in 1934, a rise from 6,1 per cent of total revenue to 33,0 per cent. This was the result of the imposition of an excess profits tax on the gold-mines from 1933. South Africa thus had no difficulty in balancing its budget without recourse to those expenditure cuts that had such a deflationary effect upon other economies. As a gold producer, though on a smaller scale, Southern Rhodesia was in a similarly fortunate position. Public revenue, after falling slightly in 1931, resulting in a budgetary deficit, soon picked up again, reaching a higher figure by 1934 than in pre-depression years. Customs and excise continued to contribute between 25 per cent and 30 per cent of gross revenue. Another territory with a worthwhile gold-mining industry was the Gold Coast. Although public revenue there contracted very sharply, falling in 1931 to about two-thirds of the 1929 level, from 1931 it recovered, being restored to the pre-depression level by 1936. There was continued heavy dependence upon customs revenue, three-quarters of total colonial income in 1935. A proposal in 1932 to introduce an income tax was withdrawn in the face of nationalist and business protest.

The increased revenue acquired by the South African state from the gold-mining industry permitted the government to spend large sums on subsidizing white agriculture. Its policy was to protect domestic producers and facilitate dumping abroad. Import restrictions and high tariffs forced up domestic prices of dairy products, and exports of sugar, maize and wheat were indirectly subsidized by domestic consumers. Farmers were thus spurred on to increase production and exports and to capture a larger share of the internal market. Commodities produced primarily for export – wool, mohair, fruit and wattle-bark – received direct subsidies. In 1933 a Meat Board was set up with powers to limit production and fix prices. Similar controls were extended to sugar. In 1937 all this *ad hoc* legislation was consolidated in a Marketing Act with the aim of long-term stabilization of agricultural prices. The evidence does not seem to suggest a great deal of success in the achievement of this objective. The government control of marketing was subjected to much criticism as inefficient, an encouragement to high cost production on marginal land and an injustice to low-income consumers.

In South Africa government intervention in marketing was primarily for the benefit of the politically powerful white farming community. In Southern Rhodesia too government marketing policy favoured the white farmer. African competition with European interests was discouraged. A Maize Marketing Board was set up in 1931 to which all maize for sale had to be delivered and which allocated it to a "local pool" for internal sale or to the "export pool" for sale on world markets. Prices paid for maize assigned to the "local pool" were considerably above world prices. In allocating supplies to the privileged local pool, the Board during its early years of operation discriminated in favour of small European producers, who received large quotas in the privileged internal market. African producers, all of whom were small producers, were accorded appreciably lower quotas. With other marketing boards and statutory agencies, established with monopsonistic powers, paying guaranteed prices and arranging marketing, African farmers also received less than Europeans for equivalent products. A flat rate was charged to the African farmer for transport costs irrespective of distance and a levy was imposed on behalf of a Native Production and Marketing Development Fund.

A similar discrimination was found in Northern Rhodesia, where the Maize Control Board, founded in 1936, set the African share of the buying pool at 25 per cent.

An attempt was made in 1936 in Kenya by the white maize farmers to impose compulsory pooling of maize in order to increase access to the domestic market, by now dominated by low-cost African producers, to fix higher domestic prices and to divert some of the African maize to the less profitable export markets to which white farmers had become largely confined. This attempt was successfully opposed by other sections of the white farming community who bought maize for their workers.

In British West Africa a number of marketing schemes was put forward in the early 1930s. The Bartholomew Plan of 1931, which aimed to stabilize cocoa prices in the Gold Coast, was rejected by the Gold Coast government, which argued against official intervention. The Nowell Commission's Report, which appeared in 1938, recommended the creation of collective marketing agencies, but no action was taken until the Second World War. Although the government took no steps to control marketing directly itself, expatriate firms, co-operating in the Association of West African Merchants, had a firm grip on both the purchase of primary products and the sale of imports. In 1934 they concluded the Staple Lines Agreement, and in 1937 the more comprehensive Merchandise Agreement, to share out the import trade. Producers blamed the low commodity prices on the traders, and the cocoa farmers of Gold Coast and Nigeria were sufficiently incensed to withhold their crop on two occasions, in 1930-1931 and 1938.

As the most powerful of all the firms, the United Africa Company, which, indeed, increased its power by taking over a number of competitors, was subject to much criticism. It was accused of keeping down palm oil prices in order to ensure cheap inputs for the soap and margarine factories of Unilever, which had a substantial holding in the UAC. The weakness of West African palm oil prices, however, was due rather to the low price of competing products. Margarine itself was in keen competition with very cheap butter and could survive only by using the cheapest possible sources of oil, which in the early 1930s were whale oil (the production of which more than doubled between 1925 and 1935) and Sumatra palm oil. Low prices for West African palm produce were not in the best interests of the UAC and not of very much advantage even to Unilever as long as there was an even cheaper alternative. The profits of the UAC, such as they were, depended to a considerable extent upon its sale of imported manufactures to the African market, and low commodity prices meant reduced demand for imports.

The UAC was in financial dificulties during the depression and survived only because Unilever sank more money into the company, bringing its share of the ownership up to four-fifths. A reorganization of management thinned the ranks of its expatriate employees and advanced Africans to more responsible positions, and its operations were diversified into, among other things, shipping, motor transport, cotton ginning, mining royalties and rubber planting. In the 1930s it extended its oil palm plantations in the Belgian Congo and started an experimental plantation at Sese in the Gold Coast, partly because of declining supplies of wild palm produce and competition from Sumatra. Not only was cultivated palm oil better in quality, it was also cheaper to produce.

In AOF caisses de compensation were formed for rubber and coffee in 1931, bananas in 1932 and vegetable products in 1933-1934. These compensation funds were built up by levying a surcharge on foreign imports of these products at the ports of entry in France and were then paid out to support produce prices in the colonies whenever they fell below a certain level. On the import side, comités de surveillance were created in 1936 to keep check on the prices of goods shipped to the colonies. A price freeze was imposed in 1937 and again in 1939.

Controls without marketing boards were introduced in East Africa. The Cotton Zone Ordinance of 1933 in Uganda entrusted the purchase of raw cotton to the ginners, who shared out the crop among themselves within each proclaimed cotton zone. The object was to raise the return to the farmers and to that end minimum prices were set, but the elimination of competition for the purchase of the crop strengthened the hand of the licensed traders. Similarly from 1932 controls were imposed on the marketing of coffee. This had to be disposed of through licensed traders for processing in licensed curing works. In both Uganda and Kenya Native Product Marketing Ordinances were passed to raise the standard of other produce through enforced sale to licensed traders at licensed markets where it could be inspected and graded. These measures were unpopular because they were thought to favour European, at the expense of African and Asian, traders.

The co-operative movement made progress in the 1930s. Among the Chagga coffee growers of Tanganyika, the Kilimanjaro Native Co-operative Union Ltd. was formed in 1932, the result of the reorganization of the Native Planters Association, which went back to 1924. This was concerned at first only with marketing, but in the course of time extended its operations to raising the standards of cultivation through training and credit facilities. In Angola and Moçambique there were officially organized and directed co-operatives, intended primarily for the benefit of white peasant farmers. In fact, peasants brought out from Portugal on govern-ment immigration schemes were required to join them. However, there were other voluntary co-operatives, some of them highly successful, operating among white smallholders, especially among dairy farmers on the outskirts of the bigger towns.

In some parts of Africa changes were made in existing systems of land tenure in the interests, so it was thought, of more efficiency in indigenous agriculture. In the Belgian Congo the paysannat system, beginning in 1936, was designed to assist families to use new techniques of planting, fertilizing and crop rotation and also to extend the principle of individual, heritable holding. In Kenya the colonial authorities introduced a pro-gramme of land consolidation and registration, which accelerated in the later colonial period and continued after decolonization. It sought to consolodate land fragments into workable farms, to promote individual title to land in order to facilitate the granting of credit, and to provide extension and credit services.

There was a tendency among peasant cash crop producers towards greater specialization. Increasing neglect of the production of foodstuffs resulted in a need for the ground-nut region of Senegambia to import rice on a considerable scale from the 1930s, mostly from Indo-China in the case of Senegal and mostly from Sierra Leone in the case of Gambia. Ground-nuts competed with foodstuffs for land and labour much more than did cocoa, coffee and palm products. But some of the cocoa farmers of Nigeria and the cocoa and coffee farmers of the southern Ivory Coast were also having to buy food as early as the 1930s.

Another trend was towards larger and fewer farms, though there was no economic advantage in bigger farms. It first appeared in the cocoa industry of the Gold Coast and later in the Ivory Coast and Nigeria. There is evidence, too, to support the view of increasing economic stratification among producers of palm oil and kernels and ground-nuts. Wealthier producers were able to buy expensive equipment such as tractors, which they could also hire out, thus widening the gap between themselves and their poorer neighbours, and they frequently advanced loans to their neighbours and relations. They could afford to manure their land, store grain when it was cheap, sell when its price rose, and used hired labour during the busiest periods of the farming year. These differences, however, tended to be ephemeral as wealth was dispersed through partible heritance. In any event, holdings of the wealthier cash crop producers were not very large, $2\frac{1}{2}$ hectares making a cocoa farmer in Nigeria a substantial producer, and were normally fragmented; nor was there a considerable rural proletariat, since most of those who worked for others either worked for kinsmen or were supplementing the income derived from their own land. Nevertheless, there was an increasing individualization of land-holding and the virtual conversion to freehold tenure because of the increasing demand for land and, where there were tree crops, a need for assured occupation. Not everywhere, however, was the trend to economic differentiation encouraged. In Kenya in the 1930s the world's biggest wattle producing company, with government support, encouraged the production of wattle among the Kikuyu and fixed maximum acreages, which deprived the bigger producers of labour and economies of scale.

Migrant and casual labour increased. In Algeria in the 1930s a quarter of the native peasantry engaged in casual agricultural work, about 450 000 out of 1,8 million. These supplemented the permanent agricultural labour force of some 180 000. There were also seasonal workers numbering some 175 000.

A growing stream of migrant labourers found seasonal employment in West Africa with cocoa and ground-nut farmers and in Uganda with cotton and coffee producers. Peasant farmers depended primarily on family labour but they were compelled to find extra hands during periods of exceptional activity, though sometimes during their own slack periods they were themselves willing to take up wage-labour. Migrants came chiefly from poorer, distant areas, from Kenya and Ruanda to Uganda and from the poor, dry areas in the interior to the more prosperous coastal districts. The migrant worked on various terms: for wages, for a share of the crop, for food and lodging, for a fixed number of months a year or hours or days a week; or he rented a piece of land which he cultivated full time. In the Gold Coast cocoa industry work in return for a percentage of the crop (where the risk was borne chiefly by the landowner) and share-cropping (where the risk was borne chiefly by the tenant, who usually paid a third of the crop) were both very common. Share-cropping gave greater independence and the chance of acquiring a freehold farm. It had advantages for the farm owner short of working capital and unable to run the farm himself, perhaps because of age.

Colonial authorities disliked migrant labour because of the time and energy spent on long journeys, while the absence of young men was harmful to the rural economy and rural culture. In 1934 the Kenya Committee on African Wages (the Carpenter Committee) recommended higher wages, better urban housing, and some sort of protection against unemployment. The committee thought it desirable for workers to 'get away from the enervating and retarding influence of the countryside'. There can be little doubt that enactment of minimum wage legislation had the effect in many colonies of stabilizing the labour force. In the Belgian Congo compulsory pension schemes were introduced for industrial workers.

Agriculture was slow in recovering from the effects of the depression, but, once the worst of the depression was over, mining in Africa entered upon a new phase of expansion, the base metals as well as gold. An attempt was made to keep up the price of tin through collaboration among producers, who formed the International Tin Agreement in 1931. In Northern Rhodesia competition among the copper companies was reduced through the merging in 1931 of Rhodesia Congo Border Concession, N'Changa and Bwana M'Kubwa, which were already closely related. There was an exchange of shares and the united company was named the Rhokana Corporation. By the issue of 7 per cent debentures it raised £4½ million to develop principally the N'Kana claim. The merger was promoted by Rio Tinto, controlled by Rothschilds of London and Paris and by a subsidiary of Anglo American Corporation, Rhodesian Anglo American, which had interests in Rhodesian Selection Trust, a holding company led by A. Chester Beatty and operating various businesses in Northern Rhodesia, and in the British South Africa Company. These two companies thwarted an attempt by American Smelting and Refining Company to get control of N'Changa.

The share of minerals in world exports rose from 15,8 per cent in 1927 to 19,5 per cent in 1937. This was largely attributable to expansion of exports of petroleum (not at that time from Africa) and, to a lesser extent, non-ferrous metals. The United States, hitherto an exporter of copper, lead and zinc, had to depend increasingly upon imports and Europe, too, experienced a growing deficiency of minerals. The fastest copper development was in Northern Rhodesia, which had by 1938 an output double that of Katanga, eventually becoming the second largest producer in the world. Costs of production proved to be relatively low once the overburden had been removed. The demand for iron, too, picked up quickly in the 1930s.

The contraction during the depression of the iron and steel industry in the developed countries was due to its dependence on capital goods, for which demand fell off so sharply, but recovery was equally rapid. Two growth industries in the 1930s were motor vehicles and armaments. Between 1930 and 1932 Algerian iron ore production fell from 1 210 000 metric tons to 253 000, that of Spanish Morocco from 572 000 to 94 000 metric tons and that of Tunisia from 437 000 metric tons to 108 000. South Africa's output was 26 000 metric tons in 1930 and only 6 000 in 1931. Thereafter there was a growth of production, varying in pace and regularity. Algeria and Tunisia restored the 1930 level by 1937, Spanish Morocco by 1935 and South Africa by 1934. By 1934 South African output was growing very rapidly and during the course of the decade it increased fifteen-fold. In the later 1930s French Morocco became a producer of some importance, with an output of 210 000 metric tons in 1939. Iron mining was also begun in Sierra Leone and production of ore rose from 15 000 metric tons in 1937 to 525 000 in 1938.

Manufacturing industry made most progress in the 1930s in South Africa and Egypt and some progress in Southern Rhodesia, Kenya and French North Africa. In Southern Rhodesia the BSA Company invested in food processing, cement (1929), chemical fertilizers (1930) and explosives. In 1938 iron and steel production from scrap was started at Bulawayo. But although there were nearly three hundred factories and workshops of various sorts, they were mostly small and their total production of much less value than that of mining and agriculture. In Kenya industrialization was encouraged by a policy of protection to industries beneficial to white agricultural interests. By the outbreak of the Second World War there were factories producing beer, cigarettes, soap, cement and tinned fruit and vegetables. In Uganda in 1937 the British-American Tobacco Company opened a cigarette factory at Jinja, but Asian investment predominated, especially strong in cotton ginning. In the Belgian Congo there was also some industrial progress. The output of textiles increased from 6,5 million metres in 1931 to 11,5 million in 1939. The amount of palm oil exported grew from 30 000 metric tons in 1929 to 72 000 in 1939. Sugar production rose from 1 086 metric tons in 1930 to 16 000 in 1940. The range of chemicals manufactured was enlarged, with the production of small quantities of compressed oxygen, chlorate of soda, industrial glycerine and carbonic acid. The manufacture of soap was started in the later 1930s. On the other hand, some of the industries established in the 1920s barely reached or failed to reach pre-depression output levels by the end of the 1930s: sulphuric acid 16 265 metric tons in 1930, 1 160 in 1933 and 15 800 in 1940; cement 64 080 metric tons in 1929, 10 644 in 1933 and 35 126 in 1939; and beer 27 000 hectolitres in 1929, 9 000 in 1934 and 29 000 in 1939.

Manufacturing in South Africa expanded in terms of volume and value more rapidly than mining and agriculture. The value of net output of secondary industry grew at an average annual rate of nearly 7 per cent between 1928-1929 and 1940-1941. It became the biggest single contributor to national income. The proportion of GDP derived from manufacturing rose from 9,4 per cent in 1930 to 12,5 per cent in 1940, that derived from manufacturing, construction, electricity, gas and water rose from 13,4 per cent in 1930 to 16,7 per cent in 1940. The physical volume of manufacturing output increased 84 per cent over the decade. Employment in manufacturing, construction, electricity, water and gas rose from 161 000 to 531 000 between 1932 and 1939, but labour tended to be used extravagantly compared with, for example, Australia, which was at a similar level of industrial development.

The most rapidly expanding industries in South Africa were clothing and textiles (blankets, unbleached sheeting and canvas at that stage), metal goods and engineering, and cement and other building materials. In 1936 the South African Pulp and Paper Industries were founded, producing before long sufficient paper to meet domestic needs and using locally produced chlorine and caustic soda. There was a corresponding increase in exports of manufactures, mainly clothing, metal goods and machinery, leather and rubber goods, cars, waxes and paints, mainly to South-West Africa and the Rhodesias. This economic revival stimulated an influx of foreign capital and this was supplemented by increased domestic saving, a growing amount of which evidently came from agriculture. During the 1930s Afrikaner entrepreneurs and financial institutions began to move into industry, which had hitherto been the exclusive preserve of immigrant and English South African capital and entrepreneurship. Foreign firms and local mining companies which diversified into manufacturing, however, continued to play the most important part, followed by the state. It was in 1933 that the state-owned Iron and Steel Corporation's plant came into production, reducing somewhat the heavy dependence upon imported materials. In 1934 output of pig iron, which had been 31 000 metric tons in 1930 and fallen to 10 000 in 1931, shot up to 130 000 metric tons and passed 300 000 metric tons by the end of the decade. Output of steel, which had fallen to 9 000 metric tons in 1933 (43 000 metric tons in 1931), reached 188 000 in 1935 and 368 000 in 1939.

Naturally the earliest industries in Egypt included the processing of locally produced crops, particularly cotton, but also sugar and rice. By the 1930s the entire cotton crop was ginned before export, the oil extracted from the seeds being used either for cooking or in the manufacture of soap and the seed cake exported. Industrialization was aided by the protective tariff policy introduced in 1930 as soon as fiscal autonomy was conceded by Britain. The manufacture of textiles became the most important industry in terms of numbers employed and by 1939, 40 per cent of local demand for cotton cloth was met. Import substitution had proceeded so far by the end of the 1930s that imports of consumer's goods were appreciably lower than they had been before the First World War, and Egypt was wholly or largely self-sufficient in sugar, wheat flour, cigarettes (using imported tobacco), soap, furniture and cement. An engineering industry was started, and by 1939 cars and machines were being assembled. Local and imported mineral oil was refined at Suez. By 1938 exports of manufactures (food and tobacco products, textiles, shoes and clothing) accounted for 14 per cent of the total value of exports.

In French North Africa industry catered to two markets that were to a considerable extent distinct from each other, that of the indigenous population and that of the European settlers. This dualism of demand became less pronounced as European tastes spread, but it still persisted. Europeans were better off, but tended to prefer imported commodities, while poverty limited the effective demand of the much more numerous Muslim population. Most obviously brewing and wine making supplied largely the settler population. The region was far from self-sufficient in consumer's goods, but on the other hand produced some which the local European market was not large enough to absorb, notably wine, and which therefore had to find external outlets. Industrial production grew only slowly before the Second World War. The first factory industries were mostly for food processing, some serving primarily the European population, e.g. canning, others the Muslim population, e.g. the refining of sugar, the consumption of which was very great. Both locally produced and imported inputs were used. There was also some processing of other local products, such as esparto grass and cork in Algeria and phosphates and lead in Tunisia, and there was an early development of import substitution in the case of bulky commodities, such as cement and other building materials, serving mostly the local European market, but also to some extent export markets too. Given the high level of urbanization among the settler population, the construction industry was of great importance. There was some progress in the making of textiles, shoes, chemical products and paint, but there was no heavy industry to speak of, and the engineering industry was confined largely to repair workshops. Very high growth rates in the field of electrical power generating were recorded, but much of the electricity was used domestically and for public lighting. In Algeria, output (much of it from water power) rose from 150 to 278 million kilowatt-hours between 1930 and 1939. In Tunisia production in 1939 was 71 million kilowatt-hours. Morocco, where production was negligible before 1925, almost caught up with Algeria in 1939, with 270 million kilowatt-hours.

French North African industry benefited from protective measures. There was no protection against French competition, but foreign products were subject to discrimination. Protective tariffs were difficult to implement in Morocco owing to the commercial rights of other European powers enshrined in the Act of Algericas of 1906, but there were powerful French interests at work and these were able to get indirect protection by means of various devices, such as compulsory import taxes in cases where foreign producers were alleged to be receiving unfair advantages, subsidies, differential freight rates on the railways and exchange controls. High-cost Moroccan industry was thus safeguarded, though at the expense of the consumer, who had to pay more for his purchases. The beneficiaries, apart from French exporters, whose access to the market was safeguarded, were flour-millers (using expensive wheat grown by European farmers), sugar refiners (using to some extent high cost sugar cane from Réunion and Martinique and beet sugar from France) and cement and textile manufacturers.

Industrial progress in Libya under Italian rule was slight, not only because of the paucity and poverty of the population, but also because of the isolation of the main centres of population, which had easier contact with Italy than with one another. Entrepreneurial activities and positions in management were reserved for Italians. Such industry as developed tended to be manufacture of consumer's goods from imported materials. The processing of locally produced materials was not carried far owing to the backwardness of farming. Industrial establishments were mostly very small, only a fraction employing more than five workers. In their East African empire the Italians gave some encouragement to industry and devoted considerable attention to road construction.

In the British Empire the Colonial Development Advisory Committee, appointed under the 1929 Colonial Development Act and composed of businessmen and former officials, was responsible for recommending to the government the allocation of funds to colonies that applied for assistance for specific development projects. Over the period 1929–1939 £3,6 million was given in grants throughout the entire Empire, £3,0 million lent and a further £1,0 million given to meet part of the interest on loans raised by colonial governments on the open market. The terms of the loans were generous, free of interest in the first years, then subject to a low rate of interest. Only a third of the money spent on the various projects that were approved was spent in Britain itself, though the Advisory Committee was required to direct as far as possible to Britain orders for industrial goods, and there were occasions when colonies were denied access to cheaper foreign alternatives. The 1929 Act was criticized, even within the colonial service, for the small amount of funds made available, the neglect of industrial development and the failure to encourage any sort of comprehensive planning. It did not, as has been suggested, indicate a fundamental change of the old principles that colonial economies should complement, not compete with, the metropolitan economy and that the imperial government should help only those colonies prepared to help themselves.

In the colonies, as the slow recovery from depression began, more money could be set aside for development. Some attempted a more far-sighted view than a mere succession of *ad hoc* projects. In 1936 Nyasaland put forward a four-year development programme, aimed at increasing production, raising standards of health and nutrition and the Africanization of government posts. During the 1930s the protectorate borrowed money for railway construction (over 200 kilometres of track were laid) and to help pay for a bridge over the Zambezi. In 1936 Uganda set up a development committee. The problem, however, remained the shortage of funds. To qualify for aid under the Colonial Development Act, colonies had to commit themselves to bearing most of the cost of development projects. Revenue remained very small even in the later 1930s. In Nigeria government income worked out at only about five shillings per head of population. The lion's share of revenue was still devoted in the 1930s to the support of a largely expatriate administration. In some colonies the debt burden was very heavy, notably in Northern Rhodesia, Nyasaland and, above all, Nigeria. Debt charges (excluding railway debts) absorbed (according to the estimates for 1936-1937) 21,4 per cent of public expenditure in Nigeria, 16,2 per cent in Northern Rhodesia and 15,8 per cent in Nyasaland. On the other hand, the proportion in the Gold Coast was only 3,7 per cent and 1,1 per cent in Zanzibar. The share of the budget taken by administration varied from 29,5 per cent in the large and populous colony of Nigeria to 50,5 per cent in the small colony of Gambia. Defence and pensions to retired officials took at the very least a tenth of colonial income, in some cases a much bigger share (nearly 15 per cent of expenditure in Kenya and over 18 per cent in Nigeria). None the less, the proportion of the budget going to social services was growing, varying between a fifth and a quarter of expenditure, but per capita spending on development and welfare varied widely, less than 2 shillings in a poor colony like Nyasaland, over 7 shillings in a prosperous colony like the Gold Coast.

The extent to which the British Colonial Development Act was inspired by the wish to serve metropolitan interests is a subject of dispute. Undoubtedly that aim influenced the government. A similar motive lay behind France's Niger irrigation project, which was inaugurated by an Act of 1931, the revival of the ambitious schemes of ten years before. It provided for the construction of a barrage near Sansanding, the more immediate irrigation of over a quarter of a million hectares of land for cotton and rice, and the eventual availability of nearly a million hectares for irrigated cultivation. In 1932 the development of the Niger basin, including mining as well as agriculture, was placed under the direction of the Niger Office. Although some experimental studies were carried out, most of the preparatory work was on the engineering side of the scheme rather than the agricultural. The project was a gamble, and one that did not turn out to be very rewarding: a few thousand settlers subject to considerable coercion, an irrigated area only a fraction of the proposed area of cultivation, a few hundred tons of cotton and some thousands of tons of rice, obtained at high cost. A good deal of the money allocated to the scheme was absorbed by a top-heavy administration. Initial cost was met from a loan of 300 million francs raised by the colonial authorities under a metropolitan guarantee. The rate of interest was high and the hope was that the scheme would soon become self-financing. This expectation was not realized.

Expenditure on the Niger scheme was only part of development spending in French West Africa. The Act of 1931 and its amendments authorized a total borrowing of 1 837 million francs. Apart from the 300 million on Niger irrigation, 628 million were earmarked for railways and 227 million for industry and agriculture, some of the latter in connection with the Niger project. Thus, very large debts were incurred, though changes in currency value tended to lighten the burden. By 1937 the share of public expenditure in AOF devoted to debt servicing fell to 13 per cent. In contrast, in AEF the share was 40 per cent in 1937. However, administrative costs in the French colonies, though such comparisons are dangerous because of the different structure of colonial budgets, appeared to be rather lighter than in the British, not much more than a fifth except in the case of the mandated territory of Cameroun. None the less, the principle of French colonial administration remained that development had to be paid for by the colonies themselves. A possibility of greater generosity seemed to arise with the election of the Popular Front government, but the instability of the coalition and the hostility of the Senate put paid to any far-reaching change.

In the Portuguese colonies the Salazar government maintained its policy of financial restraint, but by dint of increased taxation and retrenchment it built up a surplus that was available for public works. A Colonial Fund was established in 1937, not composed of metropolitan donations but rather supplied from colonial revenues. In Moçambique and the Belgian Congo there was considerable railway building in the 1930s and in the latter the public road network was doubled in length. Debt servicing consumed a large part of the colonial budget, 43 per cent of expenditure in 1935. Another 28 per cent went on administration, defence and pensions. Financial help came from the metropolitan government, though this was paid for partly out of the profits accruing to the Belgian government from its investments in mining and other companies in the colony, and a large proportion of the cost of health and education was borne by the missions and private firms.

Colonial development was curtailed by the outbreak of the Second World War in September 1939. This began with the German invasion of Poland. Poland's allies, Britain and France, declared war on Germany, but were helpless to prevent its being rapidly overrun and divided between Nazi Germany and the USSR, with which Germany had concluded a non-aggression treaty. In western Europe, during the winter of 1939-1940, there was no movement by either side. Then in the spring and early summer of 1940 Germany waged a lightning campaign which conquered Norway, Denmark and the Low Countries and forced France out of the war and brought Italy into it on the side of Germany. Hesitating to launch an assault upon Britain, Germany turned its attention in the autumn of 1940 to south-east Europe and the Mediterranean, where Italy was in difficulties in its attempt to conquer Greece; then in June 1941 invaded Russia. Almost the whole of Europe thus became caught up in the war. The colonial empires and the British self-governing dominions were already involved. The scale of the fighting was extended by the Japanese attack on the United States and Britain in December 1941 and the Italian and German declarations of war on the USA. The war assumed a world-wide character.

CHAPTER VII

1940–1950 (THE SECOND WORLD WAR)

Like the First, the Second World War had a profound, though in some respects different, effect upon Africa. Sub-Saharan Africa was not free from military campaigning. Many thousands of Africans served in the armed forces as soldiers or pioneers, some of them outside Africa. In Uganda alone over fifty thousand men served in the army. After the withdrawal of France from the war in June 1940 and the removal of the metropolitan government to Vichy, General Charles de Gaulle formed a Free French movement to carry on fighting. The West African colonies of Niger and Chad declared in his favour and an unsuccessful attempt was made in September 1940 to wrest Dakar from the Vichy government. However, the Free French were successful in Cameroun, the French Congo and Gabon, and in 1942 AOF changed allegiance from Vichy to De Gaulle. In May 1942 Britain invaded Madagascar, which then accepted the leadership of De Gaulle. In the meanwhile Britain and South Africa, which despite much Afrikaner opposition, declared war on Germany in September 1939, engaged in a campaign against the Italian colonies in East Africa and by May 1941 Ethiopia had been freed from Italian rule and the Italian colonies of Italian Somaliland and Eritrea occupied.

It was super-Saharan Africa, however, which saw the most bloody campaigns on the African continent. From Italy's entry into the war in June 1940, Britain (with the assistance of troops from South Africa, Australia and New Zealand) was engaged in defending Egypt against the Italians and, subsequently, their German allies too; then in driving them back through Libya into Tunisia and out of Africa altogether. Additional pressure came from an Allied army that landed in Algeria in November 1942. In May 1943 the remaining Germans surrendered in Tunisia. Africa was free of further fighting. The decisive battles of the war, where the scale of operations dwarfed the battles of northern Africa, were fought in eastern Europe, where the Russians, after their signal victory at the battle of Stalingrad, gradually expelled the invaders, and western Europe after the Allied invasion of the Continent from the south in July 1943 and, more important, from the west in June 1944.

The political repercussions of the war upon Africa, these having in turn economic consequences, were far-reaching. The process of decolonization was begun. On the one hand, Africans north and south of the Sahara were no longer prepared to continue under European tutelage; on the other, the colonial powers were aware that there could be no return to the pre-war situation. After the expulsion of Italy from Ethiopia (to which Eritrea was federated in 1950) there could be no question of the resumption of colonial rule there. Italian Somaliland, after some futile British pressure for the creation of a greater Somalia that would include the Somali districts of Ethiopia, was restored in 1949 to Italian administration, but it was only a temporary trusteeship granted by the successor to the League of Nations, the United Nations. France was also in a delicate position because of its defeat at the hands of Germany and its internal dissensions. In Algeria, De Gaulle in December 1943 promised Muslims the franchise and in early 1944 the Brazzaville Conference in the French Congo accepted the principle of colonial representation in the metropolitan legislature. The colonies were no longer to be subordinate to a French Empire but partners in a French Union. In British West Africa new constitutions were introduced in the Gold Coast in 1946 and Nigeria in 1947. African majorities were installed in the legislative councils. In the Belgian Congo representatives of African interests were brought into the Conseil du Gouvernement and by 1951 all the members were African.

There were in Africa some who did well out of the war, e.g. firms exporting raw materials and importing scarce consumer's goods at no risk and with comfortable, even exorbitant, profits, industrial workers in South Africa, mine-owners on the Copper Belt and clove planters in Zanzibar, suddenly affluent enough to pay off heavy debts. Among the mass of the population, in contrast, there were growing signs of discontent and restlessness. In British West Africa the post-war constitutions were out of date even before they were implemented, such was the volume of dissatisfaction which sustained new political leaders. In 1945 rebellions were suppressed with great loss of life in Algeria, while in neighbouring Tunisia the nationalist leader Habib Bourguiba left for self-imposed exile in Egypt. In Egypt itself there was agitation for the withdrawal of Britain altogether from the country. In Uganda in 1945 there were riots. These had something to do with the heavy burden of taxation in the form of export taxes, a poll-tax and import duties which put up the cost of consumer's goods, purchases of which were made additionally expensive by the disappearance of cheap Japanese imports during the war. In neighbouring Kenya in 1946 Jomo Kenyatta returned home after an absence of fifteen years and built up the Kenya African Union as a mass political movement aiming at the end of colonial rule.

In parts of Africa there was rapid growth of trade unionism, stimulated by rising prices, lagging wages and the increased demand for labour. In Nigeria only nine unions existed in 1941; by 1946 there were a hundred with a membership of over fifty thousand. Everywhere strikes became more frequent and more serious, sometimes leading to riots. Peasants, too, expressed in rioting or absconding their discontent with the rising cost of living and compulsory delivery of produce. In South Africa there were 183 strikes between 1941 and 1945, involving 36 000 workers, the largest number drawn into industrial action since the early 1920s. In West Africa there were thirteen big strikes in Sierra Leone in 1942 and ten in the Gold Coast. A general strike was mounted in Nigeria in 1945, when seventeen unions stopped work for more than a month. Some strikes were successful, e.g. the Gold Coast strike of 6 000 men of the Ashanti Goldfields Company in 1945, when the unions were awarded a pay increase. But industrial action was generally brief and unsuccessful, as employers were unsympathetic to unions and funds were insufficient to sustain long strikes.

The momentum was maintained after the war. There were big strikes in Egypt in 1946 and 1948. In Nigeria in 1949 there were disorders at the government coal mines at Enugu, resulting in twenty-one deaths. By the end of the 1940s trade union membership in the colony was well past 100 000. Trade unions were very often bound up with growing political ambition, the vehicle for nationalist feeling. Strikes were sometimes aimed at embarrassing colonial governments, and many trade union officials were really politicians, not suited by temperament or training for trade union work. In the Gold Coast in 1950 there was a general strike for political ends, and in Eritrea, where the railway workers were well organized and able to stage a strike in 1947, the unions were opposed to federation with Ethiopia. In the 1950s there was less violence as employment opportunities improved and real wages went up, though the greater sharing of political power must also have had an influence. How far the improvement in real wages resulted from trade union pressure is uncertain. More certain is that what they lacked in size of membership, financial resources and quality of leadership, they made up in capacity to mobilize formidable, though unstable, support.

Some enterprises tried to put industrial relations on a better footing by recognizing company or house unions. These were unpopular, thought to be too much under the influence of management. Governments tried to make unions more responsible by giving them help and recognition. Nigeria provided education facilities for trade union officials. Unions received legal recognition in Egypt in 1942 and arbitration procedure for labour disputes was established in 1948. In the Belgian Congo black unions were permitted from 1946, though they were subject to close supervision. In the French Empire the legalization of unions and collective bargaining in Equatorial Africa came in 1944, though only for those Africans literate in French. In AOF literacy in French ceased to be required, but an educational test for union officials was demanded, as well as an annual government inspection of union accounts.

Craft unions were rare in Africa because of the small number of artisans. Industrial unions were found in industries where the labour force was large, especially mining, the railways and the docks. But even where one big industrial union was possible, advantage was not always taken of the situation and the work force was divided up among a number of unions. In the 1950s there were no fewer than eight railway unions in Nigeria. The typical African union was small, sometimes ludicrously small. But general unions were common, bringing together workers of different skills and industries and with different employers. These had the advantage of avoiding absurdly little unions, but even so tended to be poor and badly run. They laboured under serious disadvantages. It was difficult for heterogeneous unions to negotiate with employers. At the same time union members worked for a very wide range of employers and it was difficult to negotiate with a large unorganized mass of small employers, especially in the handicraft trades. The negotiating weakness of the general unions made them very dependent upon the colonial governments, since they had to resort to government machinery, such as wage boards, to get minimum wages fixed or adjusted. This dependence upon government was increased by the fact that the colonial authorities were usually the biggest employer and their wage policies tended to act as the standard for the whole of commerce and industry.

There was a trend towards co-operation among unions. Trade union federations were established. A Trades Union Congress was set up in Nigeria in 1943 and another in the Gold Coast. These were particularly prone to getting mixed up in nationalist movements. Both the Nigerian and the Gold Coast TUCs split over political disagreements. Federations, like big unions, suffered from the inadequacy of transport and communications.

In East Africa the growth of trade unions was slower than in West Africa. In Uganda as late as 1957 only a third of 1 per cent of the total labour force was unionized. Yet here also unions were encouraged and assisted by the colonial authorities. Uganda was not typical of East Africa. The nationalist movement there was late in developing. Unions were more powerful in Tanganyika and Kenya, where they performed political rather than industrial functions. This was also true of the Anglo-Egyptian Sudan, where the Workers Affairs Association, formed in 1946 among railway workers, was a quasi-political organization. By means of strikes it secured official recognition in 1947 and an official enquiry into wages in 1948, but its successor, the Sudan Workers Trade Union Federation, was refused recognition and, though not connected with the political parties that were formed, was as much concerned with frustrating government as remedying industrial grievances.

Northern Rhodesia was a special case because of the large labour force engaged in copper-mining and the presence of a European union. The African Mineworkers Trade Union was not uninfluenced by politics, but seemed more dedicated to improving the position of its members. It soon showed signs of pressing for sectional interests at the expense of the African working class as a whole.

The trade union movement in French and Belgian Africa lagged behind development in British Africa. In the Belgian Congo African trade unionism was never much of a force in the colonial period, perhaps because of the high level of welfare services provided by the state and Union minière and other companies, and it tended to be political. In the French colonies, despite the grudging nature of official recognition, numerous trade unions were formed, mostly small but of some significance among railway workers and seamen. They attracted their greatest support among government employees of all sorts and white-collar workers, and they were strongest in Senegal and Dahomey, later in Guinea. Francophone unions encountered the same sort of difficulties as anglophone ones – fragmentation, inexperienced leadership, inadequate financial backing and hostile management. But a complication in the case of the French colonies was the introduction of trade union rivalries from France. Most African unions were affiliated to the Communist CGT (Confédération générale du Travail), the Socialist FO (Force Ouvrière) and the Catholic CFTC (Confédération française des Travailleurs croyants). These contacts were useful because they provided financial help, aid in training officials and expert advice. They tended to act as a unifying force, bringing together trade unions irrespective of territorial boundaries. These advantages, however, were gained at the expense of the intrusion of ideological conflicts that did not suit the African context. Communists talked in terms of the class struggle, but it was doubtful how far class had any meaning in Africa. The cleavage was rather between European employer and African employees, separated by race and a different relationship to a colonial government rather than by a different relationship to the means of production. In Africa a close link existed between rich and poor through the extended family and through the tribe. European communists attached much importance to the revolutionary rôle of the proletariat, but in Africa the proletariat was tiny and the distinction between workers and peasants or subsistence farmers was blurred by the migratory labour system. The Marxian model of a class struggle also required a bourgeoisie, but in Africa the development of an indigenous bourgeoisie was hindered by the influence of foreign capital. Sékou Touré of Guinea and other left-wing unionists recognized this and aimed at mobilizing all Africans, rural as well as urban, on non-tribal lines in a national struggle against foreign capital, regarded as the real enemy. It is doubtful how closely Sékou Touré adhered to that ideal.

Trade unions in the French colonies aimed at getting a labour code that would give equality of racial opportunity. A series of strikes and demonstrations was organized to that end, beginning with a prolonged railway strike in 1947-1948 and ending with a general strike throughout French West Africa in 1952. The Overseas Territories Labour Code was promulgated by the metropolitan government at the end of 1952. This did not end strikes, but changed their objectives. The Code laid down standards governing wage rates and hours of labour that were superior to those currently prevailing, and there was a campaign of strikes to force the state and private employers to conform to them. The French government gave way and a marked improvement in real wages followed.

The war disrupted established commercial ties and distorted existing trading patterns. After the German conquests most of the European continent lost contact with the rest of the world. Similarly the great extension of Japanese power severed the links between a large part of Asia and the world economy. Africa, which had conducted a brisk and growing trade with Germany and Italy, could no longer buy from or sell to these countries and for a large part of the war ties between the French colonies and their chief trading partner, France, were broken. Britain, with the elimination of so much competition, was able to increase its share of colonial trade (three-quarters of the total overseas trade of the West African colonies in 1945). Being engaged, however, in a struggle for survival, it was unable to take full advantage of the situation. The allocation of resources, including shipping, to war purposes left little capacity for the production of goods required in Africa. Even essential commodities were in short supply and rationing was introduced. In places there were food shortages because the imported foodstuffs, e.g. rice, on which dependence had grown, were no longer so readily available or because, with fuel shortages, transport was crippled. There was renewed emphasis upon the compulsory cultivation and delivery of food crops and upon the direction of labour into work thought to be in the interests of furthering the war effort.

The British colonies in Africa, as well as South Africa and Egypt, belonged, like most other countries of the British Empire, to the sterling area, the members of which kept a large part of their monetary reserves in London in the form of sterling and collaborated in financial policy. In the interests of prosecuting the war, foreign exchange was strictly controlled and used as sparingly as possible. During the war large sterling balances were run up in London as members of the sterling area provided Britain with supplies for which full immediate payment was not made. But to some extent Britain's pressing need for raw materials was relieved by the American lend-lease scheme of 1941. Goods to the value of thousands of millions of dollars were sent to Britain without payment, though partly offset by the provision of goods and services to the United States without charge. Britain, the largest international trader in 1939, could concentrate its resources on manufacturing war supplies without the urgent necessity of keeping up its exports to pay for its imports. British exports were drastically reduced in volume.

In the 1930s the chief economic problem of Africa was finding consumers able to pay for the volume of goods being produced. During the war it was often a question of trying to satisfy the insatiable demands of economies working at full capacity to produce war supplies and meet the basic needs of civilian populations. The gradual economic recovery of the 1930s sharply accelerated, though it was a recovery of government finances more than of the general standard of living. In some cases transport difficulties or labour shortages hindered the assembling and exporting of commodities. This was especially true of the French colonies after the defeat of France in 1940. Algerian exports grew in volume in the early years of the war, but were badly disturbed by the fighting of 1943–1945. After rising in value from 5 000 million francs in 1939 to 7 600 million in 1941, they fell to less than a 1 000 million in 1943. The value of exports from AEF fell in 1940, but soon recovered and passed the 1939 level. The exports of Senegal fell in value from 775 million francs in 1939 to 390 million in 1943, then recovered strongly. Its ground-nut exports, usually well over half a million tons a year in the later 1930s, were less than 200 000 tons in 1941. Egyptian exports declined in value until 1942, but recovered by the end of the war. They were worth £E 33 million in 1939. only £E 19 million in 1942 and £E 45 million in 1945. Nigerian exports consistently grew in value throughout the war, but only slowly compared with the leap of the post-war years – £10 million in 1939, £14 million in 1942, £18 million in 1945, £90 million in 1950. Transport was often the key. The number of ships entering ports in the Gold Coast fell from over 800 in 1938 to fewer than 500 in 1944 and the volume of cocoa exports fell at least partly because of that. Until 1945 the total value of Gold Coast exports fell but never below the 1938 level. Imports also fell off because of the shipping shortage, but this meant that there was a favourable balance of trade.

Sometimes the increased demand for African foodstuffs, industrial crops and minerals resulted in bigger output. Maize production in Uganda doubled during the early years of the war, at least partly to satisfy the needs of the Allied forces in the Middle East. Colonial governments used both persuasion and compulsion to secure expanded output. In the French colonies production targets were fixed for the various administrative districts. It did not follow, however, that an increase was achieved, either there or elsewhere. The value of Ugandan cotton exports during the war rose from £3,7 million in 1940 to £7,0 million in 1945, but output was lower at the end of the war (41 000 metric tons in 1945) than it was before it (54 000 metric tons in 1939). Production was as high as 67 000 metric tons in 1940, as low as 21 000 in 1942. But in 1949, 71 000 metric tons were produced. In Egypt the 1940 output of cotton was not recovered for the rest of the decade and production in the Sudan was irregular during the war and in the immediate post-war period. Egyptian output stood at 412 000 metric tons in 1940 and 400 000 in 1948, but in the intervening years it fell as low as 160 000 in 1943 and was well below 300 000 metric tons between 1942 and 1947. 1947, as in Egypt, was a bad year in the Sudan, with production at 40 000 metric tons, but in 1942 (64 000 metric tons) and 1944 (68 000 metric tons) the pre-war level was passed. In 1950 it was as high as 100 000 metric tons.

Coffee production was much better maintained during the war by African peasants in Uganda than by white planters in Kenya. In the former output reached 20 000 metric tons for the first time in 1943; in the latter output fell as low as 5 100 metric tons in 1944. In Angola output increased, exceeding 30 000 metric tons in 1945. Portugal was one of the few neutral countries in Europe in the war. Madagascar, the biggest pre-war producer, suffered a fall in output as it was drawn into the fighting. In most of the African coffee-producing countries there were clear signs immediately after the war of that great expansion of production that was to make Africa the source of 13 per cent of the world's coffee in the early 1950s. Ivory Coast was in the forefront of that expansion.

Throughout the war ground-nut production in Senegal was below, sometimes well below, the 1939 level – 560 000 metric tons in 1939, 110 000 in 1942 and 350 000 in 1945. There was a similar pattern in the case of Algerian wine production – 17,8 million hectolitres in 1939, 6,5 million in 1943 and 9,5 million in 1945. On the other hand, Nigeria's output of 210 000 metric tons of ground-nuts in 1939 increased to 560 000 in 1946, surpassing the output of Senegal, always previously Africa's biggest producer. By the end of the war African output of ground-nuts was about a quarter of total world production. The output of rubber in Liberia expanded rapidly, from 5½ thousand metric tons in 1939 to 20 thousand in 1945. That was in response to the loss by the Allies of the rubber plantations of South-East Asia. The collection of wild latex was resumed, sometimes after a lapse of twenty years. Output in the Belgian Congo and

Nigeria of wild and cultivated rubber fluctuated, but towards the end of the 1940s began a strong expansion which was to make their production rival that of Liberia in the following decade. The Belgian Congo produced 1,1 thousand metric tons in 1939 and 8,0 thousand in 1945; Nigeria 1,1 thousand in 1939, 10 thousand in 1945. Cocoa was less necessary for the war effort and its price fell after 1938 and stabilized at a lower level during the war. None the less, despite too the continued ravages of swollen shoot disease in the eastern Gold Coast and the Ibadan region of Nigeria, total output increased over the decade and Africa maintained its two-thirds share of total world production.

What the Gold Coast lost on the value of its cocoa exports it made up for to some extent in exports of gold and manganese. Minerals did well both during the war and in the post-war reconstruction. The chief ones produced by Africa before the war, in order of percentage of total world production (in 1937), were as follows: diamonds (97 per cent), cobalt (89 per cent), gold (47 per cent), chromite (43 per cent), vanadium (42 per cent), phosphate rock (40 per cent), manganese (24 per cent), copper (19 per cent), asbestos (16 per cent) and tin concentrates (11 per cent). By the end of the 1940s Africa had increased its share of total world production of many of these: chromite up to 52 per cent, copper to 22 per cent (overwhelmingly from Northern Rhodesia and Katanga), gold to 56 per cent (apart from South Africa, the most important producers being the Gold Coast, Southern Rhodesia and the Belgian Congo), manganese to 52 per cent (Gold Coast, South Africa and Morocco the biggest producers) and tin concentrates to 13 per cent (the Belgian Congo and Nigeria the leading producers). Africa's share of antimony production rose from 5 per cent of the world's total in 1937 to 29 per cent in 1950, South Africa being the principal source (8 000 metric tons in 1950), smaller quantities coming from Algeria and Morocco (just over 1 000 metric tons each). The African share of world diamond output remained much the same, but there was a change in its distribution. The Belgian Congo became the biggest producer, with an output of 10,1 million carats in 1950 (compared with 1,7 million from South Africa). Tanganyika was beginning to become a significant producer, following the discovery of important deposits in 1940. With an output of only 70 000 carats in 1950, it was a very small producer, but even then its output made a valued contribution to export earnings and government revenue. As early as 1946 its diamonds, which were both gem and industrial stones, were worth £1½ million.

Africa was not an important producer of iron – only 4 per cent of world output – but in some countries it made an important contribution to the economy. In 1950 Algeria's output of iron ore was 1,3 million metric tons, that of Morocco, South Africa and Sierra Leone 0,7 million and that of

Tunisia 0,4 million. After the war Southern Rhodesia began to exploit its ore deposits, but output was very small until the 1950s. Morocco experienced a very remarkable increase in phosphate production. During the war it fell sharply, from 1,7 million metric tons in 1939 to only 493 000 in 1941, but after the war it rose from 1,6 million metric tons in 1945 to 3,8 million in 1950. Tunisia was left behind, Algeria far behind.

During the war the colonial powers greatly increased their economic controls. The French government took over the functions of the various funds and boards which existed in the colonies and assumed complete control of trade. Expatriate firms were used as its agents. The British government bought the colonial products it required in bulk and the colonial governments made the arrangements for the purchase of the local output. Centralized marketing organizations were established by law and these had the power to fix prices. In East Africa there were separate bodies for the different products; in West Africa the Produce Control Board (1942) handled all the main export crops. A place was found for the trading firm, in both East and West Africa, in the marketing system, buying and exporting on behalf of the government, and in Kenya the Farmers Association, representing white farmers, became a recognized link between government and producers. Farmers were assured a stable market and guaranteed prices. That was an advantage. On the other hand, prices were set lower than prevailing world prices, an advantage to the authorities because inflation was curbed and the undistributed proceeds of sale could be used as a loan for war purposes. These balances accumulated and were available for future development projects, but growers were faced with hardship as prices of imports and taxation rose. Cotton growers in Uganda were receiving in 1942-1944 less than a third of total export proceeds. This was partly to encourage farmers to go in for food production rather than cotton when poor weather conditions posed the threat of famine. The effect, however, was rather to turn cultivators to coffee, also subject to controls but more profitable. White farmers in Kenya did not suffer this disadvantage, receiving the full price for their exports. Indeed, for their maize they got payment above world prices. This concession was to encourage maize production to meet domestic needs after a shortage in 1942 and 1943.

The Second World War, just as the First had done, gave a stimulus to industrialization, even reindustrialization in the sense that craft industries, such as weaving and metal working, revived. Modern industrialization took the form either of the processing of primary products to save shipping space or import substitution to make good the decline of imports. Governments previously indifferent to local manufacturing began to give encouragement, and, with wartime shortages, trading firms saw some advantage in colonial-made goods. To economize on shipping capacity the French authorities permitted ground-nut oil producers to send large quantities of oil to North Africa. After the defeat of France and the restriction of the market for ground-nuts, and amidst increasing shortage of fuel oil, the oil manufacturers at Dakar produced a substitute, though an expensive one, for diesel oil. The colony was far ahead of Gambia and Nigeria in ground-nut oil extraction. Palm oil extraction greatly increased in Cameroun, rising from 5 to 12 thousand metric tons, but in Nigeria, by far the biggest producer, production fell off and did not recover until the late 1940s.

In the Belgian Congo production of palm oil rose from 65 000 metric tons in 1940 to 88 000 in 1946 and 110 000 in 1948. Exports of oil cake increased from 2 000 metric tons in 1940 to 18 000 in 1946 and 25 000 in 1947. Sugar production declined rather than rose during the war, but the output of cement more than quadrupled between 1940 and 1947 (to 115 441 metric tons), that of soap more than trebled (22 776 metric tons in 1947) and that of textiles almost doubled (22 million metres in 1947). There was substantial growth in the manufacture of sulphuric acid and compressed oxygen.

In Kenya an Industrial Management Board was established by the government to promote local manufacturing and the range of manufactured products was extended. The preparation of pyrethrum extract was started and the manufacture of some building materials, such as roof tiles and cement tiles. At the end of the war East African Industries Limited, financed by the British government and Unilever, was set up to produce soap, detergents and margarine. Other overseas companies set up East African subsidiaries, especially in the Nairobi area, attracted by the services and facilities it could offer and, to some extent, by the low cost of labour. In addition many companies were started by Europeans and Asians resident in the colony.

Similarly, in Southern Rhodesia there was government encouragement of manufacturing during the war and, indeed, the colony went through a phase of state-directed development. In 1940 the government set up an Industrial Development Advisory Committee and from 1942 went in for state ownership of basic industries, with the aim of compensating for the reluctance of private capital in Rhodesia to participate in such investment and for the shortage of local entrepreneurship and with the aim of forestalling foreign, particularly South African, dominance. The industries affected were iron and steel (put under the Rhodesian Iron and Steel Commission, RISCOM), the processing of meat and dairy products and cotton spinning (run by the Cotton Research and Industries Board). A further manifestation of government intervention was the nationalization of Rhodesia Railways in 1947. Rhodesian manufacturing output, measured in constant prices, doubled during the war and doubled again between 1945 and 1952. In 1953-1954 there were 70 000 persons employed in manufacturing, compared with 18 000 in 1937-1938.

In Egypt the Allied military establishment was a source of new demand for locally produced goods. The Middle East Supply Centre was set up and gave assistance to Egyptian industry. Big profits were to be made and these encouraged small workshops to spring up. Large-scale manufacturing expanded by at least a third during the war. Most of the growth occurred in the early years. After 1941 the difficulty of importing capital goods inhibited further development. There was some improvement in productivity, but even so the net output per person employed in manufacturing in 1947 was estimated to be less than an eighth of the American level of ten years earlier. The industrial labour force increased, as many as 200 000 workers being employed directly by the military. In 1947, $8\frac{1}{2}$ per cent of the economically active population were employed in manufacturing and the small mining sector, 722 000 people in all. The spread of industrial skills and the accumulation of capital during the war permitted further industrial development after it. New industries were started, including canning, jute processing and the manufacture of rubber goods, spare parts and tools. The chemical and pharmaceutical industries expanded and diversified their output and the production of foodstuffs, textiles, glass, leather and cement increased. At the end of the decade food processing was still the biggest industrial sector, accounting for two-fifths of the total value of industrial output, spinning and weaving providing a further quarter. However, engineering and electrical equipment (9,8 per cent of the total value of industrial output in 1952) and chemicals and pharmaceuticals (6,5 per cent in 1952) were not significant, with an output worth £E 30 million and £E 20 million respectively in 1952.

Industrial development in French North Africa made little progress during the war. No attempt was made in the early part of the war to strengthen it industrially, with the result that it was unable to provide a base for the continuation of the struggle against Germany after the defeat of the metropolitan country. The Vichy government made plans for industrial expansion to remedy the heavy dependence upon imported manufactures, which had caused such hardship when supplies were cut off, and also to find employment, especially in Algeria, for the growing numbers which could no longer be supported on the land. Little could be done in wartime. Some progress was made in Morocco, relatively unaffected by the war, by way of expanding existing light industry, e.g. textiles. In contrast, in Tunisia industrial capacity was reduced by war damage in the fighting of 1942-1943.

In South Africa there was a certain adjustment to wartime needs in production and an increased use of local materials. The growth industries were munitions, clothing and footwear, foodstuffs, chemicals and explosives. The share of manufacturing's contribution to GDP continued to rise rapidly. In 1940 it was 12,5 per cent, in 1945 15,3 per cent and in 1950 18,4 per cent. The total value of manufacturing output by the end of the war exceeded that of agriculture and that of mining. More important, however, was the improvement in engineering standards, associated chiefly with the government manufacture of small-arms ammunition, beginning in the 1930s. The state Mint Ammunition Factory turned out, not only ammunition, but also precision tools and skilled toolmakers. The manufacture of munitions and armoured cars contributed to the expansion of the iron and steel and engineering industries. Difficulties, however, were experienced: shortages of imported raw materials and equipment and, with 300 000 men in the forces, a shortage of labour. More white females and more black male workers were drawn into industry, many blacks into skilled and semi-skilled jobs formerly performed by whites. During the war the white labour force in industry grew by 21 per cent and the black industrial labour force by 74 per cent.

South African industry remained very dependent upon state support in the form of tariff protection and wartime import control that continued into the post-war period. In 1940 the Industrial Development Corporation was constituted and, by making loans and investing in various undertakings, it strengthened state influence. Industry also relied on the foreign exchange earnings of other sectors of the economy, since the value of its exports was exceeded by that of the imported equipment and materials it needed. It still faced difficulties in the form of a narrowly restricted, though growing, internal market. Effective demand was curtailed by the poverty of the majority of the population and the emergence of a national market was hindered by high transport costs in a big country with distinct regional markets. Skilled labour was in short supply and expensive.

Like most other countries South Africa suffered during and after the war a shortage of hard currency. It had to introduce exchange control and conform to the arrangements made by the sterling area. Owing to the wartime restrictions on imports the balance of payments was in surplus, thus posing a problem of excessive domestic liquidity. To give it more power to mop this up, through open-market operations, the Reserve Bank was allowed by the Reserve Bank Act of 1942 to hold a larger amount of short-dated government securities. At the end of the war South Africa faced the typical post-war problems of high inflation and large government budgetary deficits. Although taxation and saving increased, wartime expenditure was financed largely with help of bank credit, which greatly increased the money supply without a corresponding increase in the availability of goods.

By May 1945 the war in Europe was over. In the Far East, Japan, after being pushed back on all fronts by the Americans and British armies that included troops from West and East Africa, surrendered after the dropping of the atom bombs on Hiroshima and Nagasaki in August 1945. In October 1945 the United Nations Organization was founded and its first session in January 1946 was attended by fifty-one nations. Already, however, the wartime alliance was beginning to break down. Because of their size and power the USA and the USSR dominated international relations and the mutual distrust engendered by their irreconcilable social systems created a new international tension, the 'Cold War'. Europe was divided into western and eastern spheres, separated by an 'iron curtain', which ran through defeated Germany. Two German states emerged, the western German Federal Republic and the eastern German Democratic Republic, each eventually drawn into a military alliance, the western North Atlantic Treaty Organization (1949) and the eastern Warsaw Pact (1955). In the Far East a communist régime was set up in China in 1949 and in Korea, formerly a Japanese colony, pro-communist and anti-communist governments faced each other along a frontier that originated simply as the boundary line between the post-war occupation zones of the USA and the USSR. In 1950 war broke out between the two Korean states. All these events, apparently so remote from Africa, had their repercussions upon Africa. International rivalries were transferred to Africa and the economic condition of Africa was influenced by the effects of war and cold war upon the economies of countries that had close ties with Africa and upon the international economy as a whole.

The international economy that emerged after the war was very different from the pre-war one. Among the colonial powers Britain, though undefeated, was exhausted and heavily in debt, its export markets neglected. France and Belgium had been defeated and occupied. Italy had been defeated and deprived of its colonies except Italian Somaliland. In contrast the USA was an economic power immeasurably stronger than any other country. Its productive capacity grew during the war and by the end of it was producing half the world total of manufactured goods and was the owner of half the world's shipping. It was the world's creditor and the rest of the world craved the goods that almost only America could supply because of the widespread devastation and exhaustion brought about by the war and the division of Europe into communist and non-communist blocs. The chief world economic problem was the rebuilding of the shattered economies of Europe and the Far East. The biggest obstacle to recovery was the shortage of dollars. This was remedied by the United

States through the Marshall Plan and the European Recovery Programme (1948-1951). International trade began a long-term expansion. It was assisted by the creation of a world monetary system at the Bretton Woods Conference in 1944, its twin pillars the International Monetary Fund and the World Bank, while the General Agreement on Tariffs and Trade (1947) helped to free world trade from the restrictions characteristics of the pre-war period.

By the end of the 1940s the economies of western Europe had recovered or passed pre-war levels. Reserves of foreign exchange, however, particularly dollars, were still inadequate and that had its effects on the economies of the colonies. Gold and foreign exchange controls and import quotas restricted the entry of foreign goods into the colonies to conserve stocks of gold and dollars and to help the metropolitan countries to achieve a balance of payments equilibrium. In other ways too the latter sought a solution to their economic problems in their empires. A shortage of dollars encouraged them to look for supplies from sources which they controlled themselves or which, at least, fell within their economic sphere of influence, the sterling area in the case of Britain. At the same time there was an intensified emphasis upon colonial development. This was further encouraged by concern for colonial welfare, not a new interest, but one which attracted more generous financial support than before the war. In the British colonies the proportion of expenditure going on development and social services grew at the expense of administration and defence, and there was an appreciable decline in debt charges. If one compares the situation in the early 1950s with that of the mid-1930s, one finds that the percentage of colonial expenditure going to debt charges fell in Nigeria from 21,4 per cent to 3,6 per cent, in Northern Rhodesia from 21,4 per cent to 3,5 per cent and in Nyasaland from 15,8 per cent to 5,1 per cent. The proportion of the budget devoted to defence and administration fell from 55,6 per cent to 16,2 per cent in Gambia, from 35,9 per cent to 14,2 per cent in Nigeria, from 43,4 per cent to 18,5 per cent in Northern Rhodesia, from 40,3 per cent to 17,4 per cent in Nyasaland, from 38,5 per cent to 15,5 per cent in Sierra Leone, from 52,3 per cent to 25,7 per cent in Tanganyika and from 44,9 per cent to 14,9 per cent in Uganda. The share of expenditure taken by development and social services rose from 33,4 to 73,4 per cent in Gambia, from 44,3 to 62,6 per cent in the Gold Coast, from 32,2 per cent to 66,9 per cent in Nyasaland, from 35,3 per cent to 67,9 per cent in Sierra Leone and from 31,8 per cent to 50,4 per cent in Tanganyika.

More encouragement was given to self-help. Colonies passed ordinances setting up machinery for the registration and supervision of co-operative societies. By the end of the colonial period there were several hundred societies in each of the British East African territories. They replaced to a considerable extent Asian middle-men. In Southern Rhodesia the government Land Bank in 1945 began to make low interest loans to African farmers in the so-called purchase areas, where they were able to pledge land, though in the first decade of the scheme only £6 000 was lent to some seventy farmers. However, the more pressing problem in Southern Rhodesia was thought to be that of black urbanization. Housing for African town residents received little attention before the war and provision was made at its end for the extension of urban accommodation. The obligation was placed upon employers to find accommodation for their workers, either by building their own, which big enterprises like Wankie Colliery did, or by paying rent to local authorities for housing in locations built and administered by them. Between 1946 and 1953 local authorities spent £3,7 million on African housing, and other houses were put up by the central government in what were called native village settlements, where residents were allowed to buy or lease their own homes. Urbanization threw some doubt upon the earlier assumption that the settler and native economies were to develop separately. The position, however, was ambiguous. Africans were still subject to residential restrictions and required to carry passes. In South Africa the trend was decidedly in the direction of clarity rather than ambivalence. In 1948 the National Party under D.F. Malan was elected to office pledged to implement uncompromising apartheid.

In dependent Africa the return to peace permitted the implementation of ambitious developed projects. Conceived in Europe and administered from there, they were too often characterized by enthusiasm rather than prudent planning. They included a British scheme to grow ground-nuts on a large scale in Tanganyika. It was undertaken in the late 1940s by the British Ministry of Food, at a time of continuing world food shortage, to meet a large part of Britain's requirement of edible oil, thus a scheme built on British needs rather than on African possibilities. It was inspired by the faith, fostered by very different wartime conditions, that mechanization could achieve anything. Unfortunately no proper examination of the soil or climatic conditions was undertaken and no consideration given to the problem of training drivers, maintaining tractors a long distance from the coast and using them for bush clearance. The land chosen was densely covered with thorn bushes, and the soil, with its high clay content, turned out to be unsuitable. By 1948, 20 000 hectares had been cleared and half planted, but the harvest was blighted by disease and poor rains. In 1951, after an expenditure of £25 million, the scheme was brought to an end. That was a quite spectacular failure. Other colonial ventures attracted less attention but did not enjoy much more success, such as the French Niger irrigation scheme, which by 1953 had still resulted in the irrigation of only

25 000 hectares of the original 800 000 planned before the war. Agricultural modernization schemes in Madagascar from the late 1940s appear to have had a limited impact upon Malagasy prosperity.

A more judicious development was the long-established Gezira scheme in the Sudan, which entered upon a new lease of success after the war as disease was overcome and cotton prices rose. The Syndicate was wound up in 1950, the shareholders having received over the years an average annual return of 6 per cent on their capital. The government of the Sudan also did well from its share of the investment, as well as from the greater use of the railways and from the increased tax revenue.

The Gezira scheme was a good example of a development project conceived and operated locally. In most cases development in the British colonial empire was left to local initiative. This did not preclude planning at colonial level. Planning was fashionable after the war, partly the legacy of wartime planning, partly the result of development experience in the West Indies during the war and partly the result of the prestige of Soviet and German planning in the 1930s. In the French empire there was coordination of all local plans into an overall programme for the whole empire; in the British colonial empire the different colonies were left to devise their own plans without any attempt at producing a master plan for the whole and with little interference from London except to the extent that local plans drawing upon British grants and loans needed approval. The plans of the British and French colonies allocated investment in broadly similar ways. Substantial sums were set aside for the social services, especially health and education. For economic development priority was given to transport, especially road building. Agriculture took second place, mining and manufacturing third.

Just before the end of the war a new Colonial Development and Welfare Act (1945) was passed, providing for the expenditure of £120 million by the United Kingdom within the ten year period ending in 1956. Colonial administrations were invited to furnish ten-year plans to assist the British government in apportioning the Colonial Development and Welfare Fund among the receiving territories. Owing to the shortage of trained officials and the unsettled post-war conditions, development plans of an acceptable type began to come forward only in the late 1940s and early 1950s. One of the earliest was the Worthington Plan of Uganda, which was to run from 1946 to 1956. Some colonial governments complained of the difficulty of drawing up plans without the necessary basic information, staff and money. Others drew up plans that displayed enthusiasm and imagination rather than research and thought. Some territories called in outside experts, e.g. Sierra Leone in 1947 and Uganda and Somaliland in 1951.

In 1948 the Colonial Development Corporation was set up, with the right to borrow for the projects in which it participated. Through its operation and the fund established by the 1945 Act, overseas British public investment in the colonies increased markedly after the war, and a substantial proportion took the form of grants rather than loans, which meant that the recipients carried proportionately lighter burdens of repayment than in the pre-war years. In the French Empire Algeria benefited from an influx of public capital. For West and Equatorial Africa, even before the end of the war, ideas were mooted among the Gaullists for promoting colonial development with the help of large-scale contributions from the metropolitan country. These ideas were embodied in the ten-year overseas plan of 1946, the Plan de Modernisation et d'Equipment, which was revised in 1953. The main French development agency was FIDES (Fonds d'Investissement pour le Développement économique et social des Territoires d'Outre-Mer), which was established in 1946. Annual subsidies were made available from the metropolitan budget, supplemented by smaller contributions from the colonies. FIDES money was distributed by the Caisse centrale de l'Outre-Mer (CCOM), which issued the CFA (Colonies françaises d'Afrique) franc. In addition to distributing FIDES sums it granted long-term, low interest loans from other public funds to both public and private bodies. The French invested in their colonies in the post-war period considerably larger public funds than the British did in theirs. Most public investments were not entirely disinterested, but owed something to hopes of political and economic advantage for the metropolitan country. The Belgians, too, put large sums of public money into their colony after the war. A ten-year development programme was introduced in 1948-1949, prepared by the Belgian government with the assistance of local officials.

British colonies were able to draw on sterling balances accumulated in London and also had access to funds derived from local sources. With the expansion of demand for primary products and the consequent increase in imports more revenue was yielded by taxes on trade. In Uganda, after years of stagnation, ordinary revenue doubled during the war and increased even more rapidly after it. Revenue also more than doubled in Egypt, where the Allies spent heavily during the war. In Zanzibar, where income tax was brought in, revenue rose from below half a million pounds a year to over £600 000 by the end of the war. Fully progressive income tax was introduced into Nigeria too during the war as a consequence of the contraction of trade which reduced revenue from taxes on imports and exports, and as an anti-inflationary measure. It applied only to non-Nigerians and to people living in Lagos. Outside the capital Nigerians had to pay the native authority tax. Total revenue rose from £5,8 million in 1939 to £11,4 million in 1945. In French West Africa, after falling heavily in the early stages of the war and unable to cover expenditure, revenue doubled, then trebled, then quadrupled by 1944 its 1941 level and continued to grow rapidly in the post-war years, outstripping expenditure. Revenue rose from 293 million francs (expenditure 470 million) in 1941, to 13 974 million francs (expenditure 11 769 million) in 1949.

Apart from their income through regular taxation, funds were built up by colonial authorities through their marketing boards, which were retained and elaborated after the war. In British West Africa the Produce Control Board was replaced by separate commodity boards in each colony. In East Africa a Lint Marketing Board and a Coffee Board were set up in Uganda to succeed the more informal bodies that handled marketing in wartime. In Tanganyika the Lint and Seed Marketing Board concerned itself with marketing, but other official boards in the territory – for coffee, cashew nuts, tea, pyrethrum and seed – served only an advisory purpose. Kenya had no government marketing boards for the export staples, but white farmers' organizations – the Kenya Farmers Association and the Kenya Co-operative Creameries – undertook marketing. Even in the colonies where there were boards, expatriate firms were still used as buying agents. Prices continued to be fixed officially, the declared policy being to set the price below the world price during prosperous times and to build up a reserve from the extra earnings to be used for supporting prices when world rates became depressed. In practice the funds were raided for development schemes. Some £21 million were taken from the Uganda cotton and coffee funds between 1945 and 1954 for that purpose. In the French colonies a different method was adopted to bring about price stability. Caisses de Soutien – support funds – were formed, getting their money from export levies. These were unpopular with the farmers despite the minimum produce prices guaranteed.

Private investment in Africa, more interested as it was in quick returns, remained modest compared with private capital imports elsewhere, but it rose after the revival of the export market. Most of it went into territories with a substantial European population, especially South Africa. These attracted immigrants as well as capital. In the post-war years there occurred the last of the waves of white immigration into East and Central Africa. Although decolonization was much nearer than these settlers imagined, they went in relatively large numbers to Kenya and even to Uganda, in both the upward trend persisting throughout the 1950s. Some immigrants went to Kenya under the auspices of the Agricultural Settlement Board, set up in 1946 with the help of a British loan of £1½ million. By 1960 the number of European farmers had reached 3 600. European agriculture enjoyed a period of expansion and well-being, helped by government credit and guaranteed prices. Fertilizer was used in increasing quantities and oxen were replaced with tractors. A good deal of capital went into white farming after the war, not only into machinery, but also into roads and dams. There were big improvements in coffee and milk yields, though not in maize and wheat.

European immigration into Southern Rhodesia, which had averaged 4 000 a year just before the war, was about 14 000 a year in the post-war period. The white population rose from 83 500 in 1946 to 138 000 in 1951. Immigrants came from both Britain and South Africa. The number of white South Africans moving into Rhodesia grew from 2 501 in 1945 to 12 917 in 1951. South Africa itself was getting immigrants in the years after the war, their numbers reaching a peak in 1948, 36 631. With the victory of the National Party in the general election of 1948 immigration declined drastically and in 1950 emigration (14 000 departures) exceeded immigration (12 000 arrivals). Most migrants took with them some capital, supplementing the post-war movement of business capital to South Africa and Southern Rhodesia and from South Africa to both Rhodesias, mostly for the establishment of subsidiary companies. It is estimated that £233,7 million was invested in Southern Rhodesia between 1949 and 1953, 70 per cent from external sources. Most of the capital and the immigrants went into the towns, especially Salisbury and Bulawayo, but agriculture also attracted both. The Southern Rhodesian government spent £26 million on European farming between 1949 and 1954. As in Kenya there was rapid mechanization and increased use of chemical fertilizers. In South Africa, where numbers were so much greater, whites were moving out of agriculture at a faster rate than before. The total number of white rural residents fell from 696 000 in 1936 to 653 000 in 1946 to 571 000 in 1951. As elsewhere, mechanization and fertilization were increasing, the number of tractors more than doubling in the second half of the 1940s.

Although a good deal of investment in South Africa continued to go into gold-mining, foreign capital became more diversified in its origins and purposes. While British interests continued to predominate, the USA became an important creditor and there was increasing investment from France, West Germany and Japan. Many British and other foreign manufacturing firms opened subsidiaries. But in the immediate post-war period South Africa found itself in balance of payments difficulties. The wartime surpluses ended and reserves ran down because of the import of capital goods, the rise of the prices of imports and the fixed price of gold. Crisis developed despite an influx of sterling from Britain, pulled by the apparent stability and soundness of the South African economy and pushed by reaction against the policies of the post-war Labour government. With a high level of domestic liquidity there was pressure of demand for imported goods. Consequently in November 1948 import controls were imposed on goods from both the sterling area and countries outside it. Exchange controls were introduced, not only to restrict non-sterling imports but also to restrict capital transfers from Britain to genuine long-term investment. In September 1949 the South African pound was devalued by 30,5 per cent, the same percentage by which sterling was devalued shortly before. Such methods of correcting the balance of payments deficit were preferred to measures to restrict demand, which would, it was felt, slow down growth.

Conditions favoured a continued industrial expansion: pent-up consumer demand that could not be satisfied quickly enough by imports, rising prices and a high rate of domestic and foreign investment, e.g. in the newly opened gold-fields of the West Rand and the Orange Free State. Manufacturing expanded particularly in metals and engineering, textiles and the chemical industry. A plant to extract oil from coal mined in the Transvaal and the Orange Free State was established. The value of the gross output of secondary industry at constant prices doubled between 1938–1939 and 1949–1950. The proportion of manufacturing output that was exported rose to 7,7 per cent in 1950, compared with 4 per cent in 1939.

In Southern Rhodesia the wartime experiment in state enterprise was not a complete success. In the face of difficulties that included the small size of the domestic market RISCOM rarely made a profit in its first years, but was able to undercut duty-free imported products. Government-owned cotton spinning was rather more profitable, but on the whole, because they were not run with great efficiency, the state's industries were a burden on revenue, and it soon disposed of them to the foreign interests from which it had hoped to escape. In 1957 the iron and steel industry was handed over to private British and South African control, and cotton spinning was sold off in 1960.

In North Africa after the war, through loans and subsidies, eighty or so successful new enterprises, subsidiaries of French firms, were established, bringing the industrial labour force up to about 80 000 in 1949, employed in some 800 factories and workshops, though these were mostly small and concentrated near the ports. Relatively large investments were made in Morocco in the five years from 1948 to 1953, enabling it to catch up with Algeria, especially in the production of foodstuffs and in light engineering. Industrial production in Tunisia multiplied two and half times during the period 1944–1949. In Algeria the rate of growth in industry between 1948 and 1954 was about 6,6 per cent a year.

Urbanization in North Africa required very high rates of growth of electrical power generation. In 1948 the total production (in millions of kilowatt-hours) in Algeria was 461, in Morocco 410 and in Tunisia 127. This compared very favourably with the situation south of the Sahara, where, apart from South Africa, the only countries producing more than 100 were the Belgian Congo (497), the Gold Coast (171), Nigeria (108), Southern Rhodesia (330) and Northern Rhodesia (877 in 1951–1952). A measure of the greater economic development of South Africa was the immensely bigger output of electricity – 9 259 million kilowatt-hours in 1948. Per capita production in South Africa was 814,4, in Southern Rhodesia 165,0 and in Uganda 1,6. In Egypt output rose from 288 million kwh in 1938 to 978 in 1951 giving a per capita consumption of 50, much the same as that in Turkey and Syria.

The increase in Egypt's electricity consumption was one indication of industrial expansion. Another was growing use of iron and steel. Imports doubled between 1947 and 1950, to 348 000 tons. In 1949 small-scale production or iron and steel began, using scrap, a good deal of which was inherited from the wartime belligerents. Coke was imported. Other developments in the immediate post-war period included the foundation of a fertilizer company in Suez, a small plant for assembling Ford cars and factories for assembling refrigerators and the manufacture of plastics. By 1950 industry accounted for about 15 per cent of GDP, employing about 8 per cent of the labour force and contributing 9,6 per cent of foreign exchange earnings from visible exports. Industries producing consumer's goods were predominant, especially those manufacturing non-durables. It is estimated that in 1950, 51 per cent of the gross value of manufacturing production came from five categories – food products, beverages, tobacco products, textiles and some kinds of hardware and electrical appliances. Most industrial establishments were still very small, though by the end of the war there were about fifty that were very big, employing 500 or more workers each. After 1947 foreign investment was discouraged. An attempt was made to restrict foreign ownership by means of exchange controls and a prohibition of foreign participation greater than 48 per cent in newly-founded companies. In 1954 only 14 per cent of the total number of larger industrial establishments was owned by foreigners, a further 1 per cent by joint foreign and Egyptian interests.

CHAPTER VIII

1950-1960 (DECOLONIZATION)

After the Second World War African decolonization became part of the larger process of imperial disengagement that saw the British withdrawal from India, Ceylon and Burma and, with a great deal more reluctance and in the face of much more resistance, that of the French from Indo-China and of the Dutch from Indonesia. The collapse of France in 1940, the British defeats at the hands of the Japanese in South-East Asia in 1942, the exhaustion of Europe in two world wars, the increasing influence of the political left in Europe and the shift of economic and political power in the world to the superpowers, who were hostile to empires other than their own, as well as awareness that the African contribution to the war effort had to be suitably rewarded, all these factors in varying degree contributed to the liquidation of colonial rule. Even though it was the decisive influence only in a few cases, hostility to colonial rule was not without importance. Dissatisfaction in the colonies became vocal and sometimes violent, originating perhaps - at least in West Africa - in the world depression of the 1930s and the hardships of the Second World War, especially rising prices and falling incomes, and the post-war period, when colonial governments were unable to offer much in the way of alleviation.

Land hunger among subsistence farmers was sometimes a contributory, even dominant, factor in national self-assertion, as in Kenya's Mau-Mau rebellion of 1952. The nationalist movement, however, drew support primarily from those caught up in the exchange economy, as peasant farmers, traders and wage-earners or members of the professional classes. There had been a considerable extension of the money economy as a result of the development of a growing road transport network, the spread of European education and the development of industry and modern services. There were more and better educated workers and more farmers with money in their pockets. From the professional classes in Africa came the leaders of the political parties which were founded at the end of the war. Felix Houphouët-Boigny, the founder of the Parti démocratique de la Côte d'Ivoire, was a well-to-do farmer; Sekou Touré of Guinea was a trade union leader; Hastings Banda of Nyasaland a physician. For people in the money economy the war had presented the opportunities of an expanding economy, as well as grievances, especially rising prices.

The black nationalism of francophone Africa in the 1950s had important effects upon the labour movement. The relationship between the two varied. In the West African Federation the principal political movement was the RDA (Rassemblement démocratique africain), a federation of territorial parties founded in 1946. At first under the influence of the communists, it broke ties with them in 1950. Since the Communist CGT was dominant in the trade union movement, a coolness arose between the RDA and a large section of the industrial labour movement. Individuals were members of both the RDA and CGT unions, but trade unions as such were outside the mainstream of nationalist movements in all colonies except Guinea. Here the dominant figure was Sekou Touré, a leader of the CGT who also controlled the Guinea section of the RDA. Therefore, here there was a very intimate relationship between the industrial and political movements. A similar situation existed in Soudan, where there was a close link between the Union générale des travalleurs de Soudan (affiliated to the GGT) and the Union soudanaise.

The rise of African nationalism had the effect of bringing about a rupture between the African trade unions and the metropolitan trade union federations. African nationalism was unwelcome to the CGT. The French Communist Party distrusted it and considered that the liberation of colonial peoples could only follow the victory of the French proletariat. To Africans this subordination of events in Africa to events in France seemed a type of imperialism. As early as 1953 Leopold Senghor of Senegal called for the formation of an autonomous African industrial labour movement, but in the event it was Sekou Touré who took the most decisive step. He did not cease to be a Marxist, but considered that African socialists must determine their own policy. Consequently in 1955 he proposed to the RDA leadership the disaffiliation of African unions from the metropolitan organizations. In this he was supported by Senghor and by Houphouët-Boigny of the Ivory Coast section of the RDA. In 1956 the Confédérération générale des Travailleurs africains (CGTA) - later the Union générale des Travailleurs d'Afrique noire (UGTAN) - was formed. After some resistance the CGT came to accept an autonomous black trade movement affiliated directly to the communist-dominated World Federation of Trade Unions. The rupture with the metropolitan organizations spread to the confessional and non-Marxist socialist unions affiliated to the CFTC and the FO.

A number of factors determined the pace of decolonization - the strength of demand for independence among the colonized, the realism of the colonial power, the existence of special European interests, the extent of white settlement and, where there was such settlement, the degree of autonomy enjoyed by the white settlers. Furthermore, there was a distinction between super-Saharan and sub-Saharan Africa. In the British tropical colonies internal self-government was given shortly after the war, e.g. Gold Coast in 1951 and Nigeria in 1952. France was slower in coming to terms with such an outcome in its black colonies. In 1956, however, the metropolitan government, with its *loi cadre*, reconciled itself to internal self-rule for the separate colonies within the French Union. Two years later the French government went further, offering a choice to the colonies between total independence and autonomy within a French Community. It was scarcely a free choice: Guinea, the only colony to elect for independence, was deprived of all aid. In the event France proved unable to breathe life into the Community and political independence was accorded to all the colonies, including Madagascar. On the whole, in the absence of extensive European settlement, the British, French and Belgians, while they did not succumb to pressure without some resistance and sometimes put nationalist leaders into prison – Kwame Nkrumah, leader of the Convention People's Party in the Gold Coast, was imprisoned in 1950 – for the most part resigned themselves to abandoning, sometimes somewhat – and, in the case of the Belgian Congo in 1960, more than somewhat – precipitately, empires which they had come to recognize as anachronisms. The precedent was the metamorphosis of the Gold Coast into Ghana in 1957. Nkrumah was the most enthusiastic protagonist of pan-Africanism and when Guinea chose total independence from France, Nkrumah and Sekou-Touré declared the union of their countries, though in practice this meant little.

Decolonization was much more painful where there were considerable European interests or where there were sizeable white settler communities not lacking in influence in the metropolitan country. The most intractable problem was that posed by Algeria. Whereas the other countries of the Maghrib, Tunisia and Morocco, could be freed (in 1955 and 1956) with comparatively little difficulty, Algeria not merely had a substantial French-speaking population, but also was considered a part of the metropolitan country. There began in 1954 a revolt that cost a million lives and ended only after seven years of conflict had convinced France that decisive military victory was impossible. In 1958 General de Gaulle was called from retirement and made head of state, following a military revolt in Algeria. Convinced of the futility of attempting to maintain French rule, he alone had sufficient authority and prestige to force upon the colonies a settlement that gave independence to the nationalists in 1962.

The granting of independence to Kenya was less bloody, though it took place only in 1963 after the suppression by 1957 of the Mau-Mau and increasingly unrealistic attempts to secure for the white settlers a special political status. Southern Rhodesia presented a difficult problem that was similar to, but more thorny than, that of Kenya. Not only did it have a more substantial white minority, but it also had internal self-government. In 1953 it was joined to Northern Rhodesia and Nyasaland in a federation designed to form a viable economic entity in British Central Africa and to relieve Britain of the burden of the economic development of the poorest component, Nyasaland. It was a political solution entirely unacceptable to the nationalists of the two northern territories, appealing to white settler rather than to African interests. The Europeans of Northern Rhodesia saw association with Southern Rhodesia as a means of securing continued white predominance, threatened by an imperial declaration of 1930 of the paramountcy of African interests. For the Southern Rhodesian whites the virtue of association with the northern territory was its implicit claim of independence from excessive South African influence. Added to that was the post-war desire to exploit the revenues of the prosperous Copper Belt. The scruples of the British government, unwilling to see an amalgamation of the two Rhodesias because the so-called Native policy of the south was in conflict with the 1930 declaration, were allayed by the safeguards that could be written into a federal constitution, and advantage was taken of the establishment of the Federation to provide for the future of Nyasaland. It was the intention of the imperial government that the federation should function in a spirit of partnership between black and white. In practice it was run by the white community, which did not share London's views on racial collaboration. African opinion was not canvassed. Nor was there a full investigation of the economic implications of federation. It was commonly assumed that there was already existing a high degree of economic inter-dependence and that closer union must inevitably be advantageous, protecting and widening the market for local industry, giving the benefits of greater economic diversification, pooling revenue, promoting joint planning, and encouraging foreign investment.

Like Southern Rhodesia – and also partly for the benefit of its white minority – Kenya was closely linked to its two neighbours, Uganda and Tanganyika. The inter-territorial relationship was made more formal after the war, with the establishment in 1948 of the East Africa High Commission. This was responsible for administering certain services which were common to all three territories. Some were self-contained, self-financing services, other services that were financed from revenue and known as General Fund Services. The self-contained services were Railways and Harbours, Posts and Telecommunications and, later on, Airways. The General Fund Services were more numerous than the self-contained ones, but were much less important in terms of investment and income. East African Railways and Harbours Administration represented a very large investment and was the largest employer in East Africa. The High Commission was made up of the three governors assisted by a Secretariat and a Central Legislative Assembly, partly appointed and partly indirectly elected.

In Egypt, Britain and other western countries felt that European control of the Suez Canal was essential to their interests and decolonization was not completed until after a number of radical nationalist officers in the Egyptian army seized power in 1952. Independence was consummated by the assumption of authority by Colonel Gamal Abdel Nasser in 1954 and the humiliation of Britain and France in 1956, when they were compelled by the superpowers to accept Egyptian nationalization of the Canal. In 1956, too, the Anglo-Egyptian Condominium over the Sudan was brought to an end. Sudan elected to be free of Egypt, but Egypt itself formed a union with Syria in 1958, the United Arab Republic, joined also by Yemen; but it had little vitality.

TABLE OF DECOLONIZATION

Year
1951   Libya
1956   Tunisia, Morocco, Anglo-Egyptian Sudan (Republic of Sudan)
1957   Gold Coast (Ghana)
1958   Guinea, Madagascar (Malagasy Republic)
1960   Federation of Nigeria, Federation of Mali (Senegal and Soudan, soon separated as Senegal and Mali), Dahomey (later Benin), Niger, Upper Volta (later Burkina Faso), Mauritania, Ivory Coast, Cameroun, Chad, Gabon, Belgian Congo (Congo-Leopoldville, Congo-Kinshasa, Zaïre), French Congo (Congo-Brazzaville), Central African Republic, Togo, British and Italian Somaliland (Somali Republic)
1961   Sierra Leone, Tanganyika (later Tanzania)
1962   Ruanda-Urundi (Rwanda and Burundi), Algeria, Uganda
1963   Kenya, Zanzibar (united with Tanganyika as Tanzania in 1964)
1964   Northern Rhodesia (Zambia), Nyasaland (Malawi)
1965   Gambia
1966   Basutoland (Lesotho), Bechuanaland (Botswana)
1968   Swaziland, Mauritius, Spanish Guinea (Equatorial Guinea)
1975   Moçambique, Angola, Portuguese Guinea (Guinea-Bissau)
1979   Southern Rhodesia (Zimbabwe)

To draw up a balance sheet of the costs and benefits of colonialism, both for colonies and for colonizers, defies human ingenuity because of the impossibility of their quantification or even of identifying their nature. It is an emotive subject that is scarcely susceptible of objective appraisal. While no doubt the imposition of political control was thought by the occupying powers to serve their economic interests, directly through immediate economic advantage or indirectly through the protection of strategic interests or the furtherance of national prestige, both of which have an economic aspect, it does not follow that the allocation of human and material resources to empire brought greater gain than would have accrued to their use in a different way. The only certainty is that some groups and individuals did very well out of imperialism and that equally others lost their money or their lives. Thousands were killed in the conquest of African colonies (notably French in Algeria and British in South Africa) and in wars of liberation (once again particularly in Algeria).

In the last years of their rule the colonial powers consciously did a great deal for their colonies that was disinterested. France shouldered a large share of the burden of public investment in its colonies. In the poorer ones it contributed also to normal budgetary expenditure. It maintained a large body of technical assistants of all types, as many as twenty thousand at a time, in the Maghrib and tropical Africa. In addition France supported the prices of African agricultural products and provided guaranteed markets. But in return for this expenditure there were considerable compensations. There were direct payments for services rendered and preferential treatment of French firms and French exports. Africans had to pay substantially above world prices for French imports, especially for capital goods.

Even the good intentions of the colonizers did not escape obloquy. French colonial planning, with its emphasis upon imperial co-ordination was condemned as a device for strengthening the dependence of the colonial economies upon the metropolitan economy. The kind of planning that was implemented in both British and French colonies was subject to much criticism, even contempt: plans were said to have no central strategy, assigned no positive functions to government beyond the pro-vision of law, order, transport and tax incentives, and made no attempt to direct the future course of action of the private sector. Undoubtedly the first colonial plans had fairly modest aims and consisted mainly of lists of desirable items, but with the approach of independence at the close of the 1950s more complex plans dealing with the economy as a whole, co-ordinating development between sectors and prescribing growth rates, were introduced. Although in practice the plans brought in around the time of independence proved to be often over-ambitious, based on questionable statistical data and frequently overtaken by political events and although they sponsored some ill-judged projects, they were probably at least as effective as later ones. A specific criticism was that only a comparatively small proportion of investment went into industry. It was not, however, negligible. Official enterprise was important in encouraging industrial development. Government involvement of an indirect kind included the assistance of private manufacturers in the establishment of import-substituting and export-processing industries. Help took the form of protective duties and quotas, grants and cheap loans, guaranteed purchases and tax relief. Considerable public investment went into utilities, notably electricity.

Development was hampered by a shortage of skilled workers. Education for Africans tended to be inadequate and of the wrong kind. Dominated by missionaries, it was more likely than not to be academic and non-vocational, producing too many aspiring clerks. Although in the last years of colonial rule there was a rapid expansion of school and university enrolment, there were still relatively few university graduates and the proportion of children and young people receiving formal education was far smaller in Africa than in, for example, Latin America. Business enterprises were slow in establishing proper selection procedures and providing training schemes. Government education lagged behind because of the shortage of money. In British West Africa there was some vocational training from the end of the First World War, but then there was retrenchment during the depression. Owing to the shortage of skilled labour there was a tendency everywhere for a very wide gap to appear between skilled and unskilled rates of pay, especially when, as was often the case, skilled workers had to be attracted from abroad. In the public service and commerce administrative posts were filled by expatriates who were paid at rates far higher than those obtaining in the metropolitan country. In the absence of extensive university education graduates could command a level of income that set them far above the mass of the population.

In those parts of the continent where there were considerable non-African populations, skilled work in industry, transport, commerce and government tended to be monopolized by whites (newcomers rather than the long settled) or, in East Africa, Indians. It was arguably easier to employ high-priced immigrant labour or to train industrious and reliable Indians than to cope with an unstable labour force ignorant of the simplest techniques of commercial and industrial employment. In South Africa it was Europeans who received preference, to the detriment not only of Africans, but also of Indian and mixed race workers. After the National Party came to power in 1948 the discriminatory legislation of the past was made more comprehensive and doctrinaire.

There were early signs that the decolonized parts of Africa could have governments as authoritarian as South Africa's and as dogmatic in a different way. Paternalism did not vanish with the colonial rule. The revolutionary government in Egypt outlawed strikes. Unions were permitted and membership was even compulsory for some categories of workers, but they were strictly controlled by the government's Advisory Council for labour. The policy was to anticipate workers' grievances by government-offered concessions, such as minimum wage and maximum hour regulation, sickness and unemployment insurance, security of employment, compulsory profit sharing and worker participation in management. Employees were apparently satisfied with the gains that accrued to them under the régime's labour legislation. At all events there was little serious industrial discontent.

One of the first acts of the revolutionary government in Egypt was land reform. At the time of the revolution some two thousand landowners possessed almost one-fifth of the total cultivated area, while over two million smallholders owned only 13 per cent. Many of the latter group had holdings so small that they either rented additional land to make farming worthwhile or, renting out their own small plots, took other employment. There were in addition well over a million peasants who had no land of their own at all. Under the Land Reform Law of 1952 no individual was permitted to own more than 200 feddans (and under an amendment no family more than 300) and those who possessed more were required to sell the surplus to their tenants in plots not exceeding five feddans in area. Land not disposed of in this way was liable to expropriation in exchange for 3 per cent non-negotiable thirty-year bonds and its distribution in small plots among the landless, who were in turn required to make redemption payments over a period of thirty years, to undertake not to sell, let or subdivide their plot and to join a co-operative society. The 1952 Law also fixed minimum rents, minimum periods for leases and minimum wages.

In Egypt the intention was to preserve a class of small peasant proprietors. In Southern Rhodesia and in the Portuguese colonies it was to build up such a class. In the former they were to be black, in the latter both black and white. Organized government-sponsored immigration in Angola reached its climax after the Second World War. Families were brought out from Portugal at government expense, settled on farms, provided with buildings, stock and implements, paid for partly by the government, partly by interest-free or low-interest loans. To preserve the peasant character of their settlements the colonists were not permitted to employ Africans either as farm labourers or as domestic servants; nor could the farms be sold. Such systematic settlement was not, however, very successful despite the very large state investment. There was a considerable wastage of settlers, a rapid turnover of owners, and a high proportion of vacant farms. The settlers displayed the same old predilection for trade and found it difficult to market low-value produce. The settlements were not always well-sited with respect to soil fertility and water supply and the administration was unsatisfactory, a combination of detailed rules governing cultivation and inadequate provision for their implementation.

In Moçambique too, there were post-war government settlement schemes, Africans being involved as well as Europeans. As in Angola, in so far as the object of such land schemes was to bring in as many white settlers as possible, they were not conspicuously successful. Africans held on average smaller holdings and supplemented the income derived from them with wage labour on white farms. The Colonato do Limpopo, planned as early as 1924, but not implemented until the 1950s, involved the construction of a dam and a railway from Lourenço Marques to Southern Rhodesia, both of which were finished in 1956, and an irrigation scheme. Colonization began in 1954 with European families brought out from Portugal and African families. By the end of 1960 over 3 000 white and black families were settled in the *colonato*. Credit with long repayment periods was granted, and the purchase of inputs, cultivation and marketing were all strictly controlled by the co-operatives which each settler had to join. By the middle 1960s the white settlers were enjoying a relatively good return on their plots, but most of the African settlers had difficulty in wresting a livelihood from their much smaller holdings.

Not all white farming in the Portuguese colonies was small-scale. In Moçambique commercial agriculture was mostly in the hands of big companies, though there were some small farmers settled along the Beira-Umtali railway, around Lourenço Marques and elsewhere, for the most part growing maize for the internal market. Of the farms and plantations owned by firms, some were immense. The Companhia Colonial do Buzi, for example, owned about half the total area (40 000 ha) under sugar cane, while the Companhia do Madal ran a coconut plantation that contained more than two million trees. In the 1950s some 420 000 hectares of land were set aside for coffee plantations in Angola, mostly on a strip of high land in the north-east producing robusta. Here too there were enormous plantations. The Companhia Agrícola do Angola (CADA) had over 17 000 hectares under coffee. But the typical plantation was more like 250 hectares, and some were smaller.

Coffee production in Angola expanded from an average of 56 000 metric tons a year during 1948-1952 to 132 000 tons in 1960. The colony benefited from the great expansion of demand for robusta for the manufacture of soluble coffee. Prices were high in the early 1950s and peasant farmers in Uganda also responded to them. In Buganda a quarter of all cultivated land came under coffee and the overwhelming majority of the farmers there grew some. There was no shortage of land, nor of labour from Ruanda. Savings accumulated through the sale of cotton were used to plant coffee bushes. In neighbouring Kenya an important development was the expansion of production by African smallholders. Government policy changed and peasant cultivation was encouraged. The area planted by Africans increased ten-fold to 20 000 hectares in the 1950s. It was the Ivory Coast, however, that was Africa's biggest producer and the third biggest in the world. Robusta was the most favoured variety and almost all of the 600 000 hectares under coffee were African. Total coffee production in Africa rose from an annual average of 280 000 metric tons over 1948–1952 to 730 000 in 1960. In 1956 Africa's production made up of 20 per cent of world production, subsequently falling to a slightly lower level. In 1954 world coffee prices started to decline and in 1958 an International Coffee Agreement tried to stabilize them by restricting exports.

Another crop in which Africa increased its share of world output in the 1950s, though even in 1960 its contribution was still less than 5 per cent, was tea, prices of which rose markedly in 1953. It was mostly a European plantation crop, requiring a large investment. The chief producing areas were Nyasaland and Kenya. In the former it contributed between 40 and 50 per cent of total export earnings.

Africa's share of world production of long-established cash crops remained at much the same level: palm products about 80 per cent (though a growing proportion was being consumed locally), ground-nuts about 30 per cent, sisal about 65 per cent and cotton about 12 per cent. Cocoa experienced more vicissitudes. Production in the early 1950s was still affected by earlier ravages of swollen-shoot, but new planting in the late 1940s once again raised output, especially in Ghana. In 1960 Africa grew three-quarters of the world's supply. There was some change in distribution of the production of the staples, e.g. Angola becoming an important sisal producer, catching up with Kenya and surpassing Moçambique, though Tanganyika remained by far the biggest producer (208 000 metric tons in 1960).

By the end of the 1950s there were ominous signs that total agricultural production was beginning to increase at a slower rate than population. After 1958 per capita production was falling, while that of the world as a whole continued to rise. South Africa was exceptional. From the end of the 1940s there was a sharp increase in total farming production. The output of maize for the first time exceeded 3 million metric tons in 1953, a level which was maintained throughout the decade. The total gross value of agricultural production, which was R447,2 million in 1950, was R814,6 million in 1960. This improvement was associated with mechanization (48 000 tractors in 1950, 119 000 in 1960) and increased inputs of artificial fertilizer (which trebled to over a million tons a year over the period 1945-1960); but it was an improvement with disquieting features, mono-culture in some areas and soil damage (not at all a new problem) and the continued degradation of farming in the black reserves.

The 1950s were a period of remarkable economic growth in the world. With the end of the dollar famine it became possible for Europe to relax the restrictive trade practices of the immediate post-war period. In any event these practices conflicted with the freer trade sought by the international community and the new international organizations, the General Agreement on Tariffs and Trade (GATT) and the Organization of Economic Co-operation and Development (OECD), to which the colonial powers were party. Liberalization of imperial trade proceeded faster in the British Empire than in the French. As a result, by 1960 Britain's 1945 share of the overseas trade of its West African colonies fell by a quarter, with Japan gaining ground at its expense. In contrast France's share of the external trade of its colonies fell by only 5 per cent. It was not until the development of the European Economic Community in the 1960s that bilateral links weakened noticeably. In the case of Portugal there was a distinct fall in the proportion of Angolan exports going to the metropoli-tan country from the end of the war. To some extent the changed situation could be attributed to a change in the character of Angola's products, with a growing emphasis on exports of coffee and minerals, which could not be absorbed by the Portuguese economy.

Trade relations between Africa and Europe were affected by the establishment of the European Economic Community by the Treaty of Rome, signed in 1957 by France, Italy, Belgium, Holland, West Germany and Luxemburg. The Netherlands, France and Belgium at that time still had colonies, the most extensive being the French and Belgian colonies in Africa. During the negotiations leading to the Treaty the relationship between the EEC and the colonies of its members was discussed. France wished to bring the colonies into the Common Market, West Germany to keep them out. The compromise that emerged gave them an associate membership, which aimed to eliminate gradually tariffs between the Common Market and its associates and among the associates themselves, in so far as this did not conflict with international obligations, the protection of infant industry and raising revenue. A European Develop-ment Fund was set up but financial aid was implicitly dependent upon access of EEC nationals and companies to associated territories.

The EEC was the most important source of multilateral aid to Africa. It started making aid available after the Treaty of Rome. But this was not altogether new aid. To some extent it replaced aid hitherto given by France to its colonies. France channelled through the EEC some of the aid previously given directly. During the initial period of its association with the colonies and ex-colonies between 1958 and 1961, the EEC made available $581 million in aid. Of this, substantial amounts went to Algeria and Dutch New Guinea.

The effect of the establishment of the EEC was to diversify the European relationship with parts of Africa that had hitherto experienced strong bilateral relations. This did not occur all at once, nor did it alter the colonial legacy of relatively little trade between one part of Africa and another. Some of the old inter-regional trade, notably the trans-Saharan trade had been ruined and there had been little new to replace it. Such new internal trade as emerged in the colonial period was almost entirely in foodstuffs and few African countries earned more than a fraction of their income by the sale of commodities and services to others in Africa. In the 1950s the amount of recorded trade amongst African countries was estimated at about 10 per cent of the total value of Africa's import and export trade with the whole world. Regions which had above average levels of intra-continental trade were the old AOF, Moçambique, Sudan, South Africa and the Federation of Rhodesia and Nyasaland, where inter-territorial trade amounted to about a quarter of the Federation's total trade.

In the Central African Federation there were free movement of persons, capital and goods, a common currency, common economic policies and a common tariff. To some extent these pre-dated the Federation. There was already a free movement of labour among the three territories, and Southern Rhodesia and the more prosperous part of Northern Rhodesia already virtually constituted a free trade area. The inclusion of Nyasaland and the north-eastern part of Northern Rhodesia, which came under the Congo Basin Treaties and had to have their withdrawal from the application of the treaties negotiated, in the federal tariff system made little difference to the size of the market because of their poverty and remoteness from the centres of production. The benefits of the pooling of revenue proved to be of doubtful value for Northern Rhodesia. No doubt it gained from the stabilization of its revenue, but it lost more through the redistribution of federal income amongst the members. The effect of federation, even if that was not the intention, was to subsidize the European settler-dominated colony of Southern Rhodesia and the indigent protectorate of Nyasaland with the copper revenues of Northern Rhodesia. There was little joint planning among the territories and it was virtually impossible to alter the pattern of revenue allocation established at the time of the Federation owing to the distribution of powers enshrined in the federal constitution. The major achievement of federation, the construction of the Kariba hydro-electric scheme, was implemented in preference to an alternative scheme on the Kafue River that may well have been of greater benefit to Northern Rhodesia.

Among the East African countries of Uganda, Tanganyika and Kenya only about 8 per cent of total trade was with one another or other African territories. This was somewhat surprising given that they had a common currency and formed a customs union. Kenya differed from the others. Commerce and banking developed much more there than in Tanganyika and Uganda, partly because it provided services, including transport services, especially to Uganda, and, to some extent, processing facilities for the other two, and partly because the substantial European and Asian population, with income levels higher than those of the bulk of the population throughout East Africa, set up a significant demand for services and commercial facilities, which in turn attracted further European and Asian immigration. Kenya, having a highly developed service sector, had an unusually low dependence upon agriculture for a country with a population overwhelmingly rural. Three-fifths of GDP was derived from services, only a little more than one-fifth from agriculture, whereas half of GDP in Uganda originated in agriculture, less than two-fifths in services. Similarly Kenya was much less dependent upon overseas export earnings than Uganda and Tanganyika, where overseas exports amounted to about two-fifths of GDP, and yet it required a greater volume of imports from overseas than they did. Nevertheless, Kenya too was highly dependent upon coffee exports and its economic prosperity was indirectly tied to the export earnings of the other two East African countries, to which it furnished meat and dairy produce, industrial goods and services.

The East African customs union benefited Kenya most, especially the white farming community, which was assured of an enlarged protected market for their products. Kenya maintained a favourable balance of trade with Tanganyika and Uganda which enabled it to carry a less favourable balance of trade with the rest of the world. The balance on invisible account was also in Kenya's favour because of its favourable geographical position and because of the services it offered. Nairobi developed as the commercial centre of East Africa. Most inter-territorial trade was made up of Kenyan exports to Uganda and Tanganyika and of Ugandan exports to Kenya. The economies of Uganda and Kenya were especially closely interrelated. To a considerable degree this was the result of their geographical relationship. Uganda's purchase of services from Kenya consisted of the transport of its exports and imports via Mombasa, the marketing services of Kenyan importers distributing to the Ugandan market and commercial and other services supplied to Ugandan residents.

Tanganyika was at a particular disadvantage. Between 1922 and 1949 Tanganyikan exports to Uganda and Kenya actually declined from 25 per cent to 5 per cent of its total exports and remained at that level throughout the rest of the colonial period, though its imports from the other two increased. One cause of complaint in Uganda as well as Tanganyika was the location of the headquarters of the common services in Nairobi. Kenya was alleged to be unduly favoured in such things as railway development and employment and to benefit from the high proportion of Kenyans on the staff.

In 1960 the Colonial Office appointed an Economic and Fiscal Commission (the Raisman Commission) to enquire into the working of the customs union and reported that, although it was beneficial to the whole of East Africa, compensation for their disadvantages should be made to Tanganyika and Uganda. Consequently a proportion of the revenue derived from company taxation and from customs and excise was paid into a 'distributable pool', one half of which was used to finance the non-self contained common services, i.e. all those except Railways and Harbours and Posts and Telecommunications, and the other half shared equally among the three. In its report on Uganda and Tanganyika that appeared shortly afterwards (1960-1961) the World Bank considered that the disadvantages of the common market for these countries were not outweighed by the advantages, but that there were potential advantages and that the common services had an undoubted value. The Economic Commission for Africa of the United Nations came to the same conclusion in 1962 with respect to Tanganyika.

In the later colonial period it proved to be very difficult to formulate a common economic policy in the East African customs union. In spite of disagreements, collaboration in fixing external tariffs through the Tariff Advisory Committee was fairly successful, but friction developed over the allocation of industry. In 1948 an Industrial Council was set up to license firms in scheduled industries, but it was largely ineffective, and in any case there was only a small number of scheduled industries. Since there was no overall plan or direction of the location of industry, excess capacity resulted in some sectors, including paper, cement and oil refining. Ambitions and jealousies were particularly apparent in Tanganyika. Various attempts were made to secure equitable allocations of industries, including the appointment in 1962 of an economic adviser to the Common Services Organization, but with little success.

The strain within the colonial-arranged common markets of East and Central Africa did not diminish the theoretical approval among African leaders and their sympathizers and advisers of economic collaboration. This was urged by the United Nations, particularly its Economic Commission for Africa, established in 1958. A pan-African conference at Accra in 1958 resolved to set up an All-Africa People's Conference to promote intra-African trade by removing restrictions and improving transport and communications and by joint development projects. The chances of such co-operation were slight. Heavy dependence upon the export of a limited range of primary products was characteristic of African economies. In the mid-1950s well over three-fifths of the value of the combined exports of the three mainland members of the East African customs union was made up of coffee, cotton and sisal. In some cases over a third of the value of total exports came from a single product: Egypt (cotton 84 per cent), Ghana (cocoa 63 per cent), the Federation of Rhodesia and Nyasaland (copper 54 per cent), Angola (coffee 42 per cent), Madagascar (coffee 42 per cent), Cameroun (cocoa 38 per cent), Dahomey (palm kernels 43 per cent), Gambia (ground-nuts 93 per cent), Ivory Coast (coffee 59 per cent) and Niger (ground-nuts 81 per cent) (in 1957). Although the trend was towards a greater diversification, it was of a somewhat limited scope, dependence upon three or four primary products instead of one, e.g. Moçambique (cotton 25 per cent, sugar 17 per cent, cashew nuts 13 per cent, copra 9 per cent), Nigeria (cocoa 21 per cent, palm kernels 14 per cent, ground-nuts 16 per cent, palm oil 11 per cent). The Belgian Congo owed much to copper (32 per cent of exports) but also exported considerable quantities of palm oil, coffee, cotton and rubber, and South Africa had a wide range of exports. Even in those two cases, the situation was not entirely satisfactory because prices of primary products tended to move together in world markets. In the early part of the 1950s they were high, under the influence of the Korean War.

Relatively few people, however, were concerned directly with the production of export commodities. In some expatriate enterprises there was a large labour force, e.g. in copper-mining in Northern Rhodesia and Katanga, but such activity was confined to a limited area. Even crop production for export was relatively concentrated. In the 1950s Nigeria accounted for 37 per cent of the total value of West African exports and the Gold Coast, much smaller and less populous, 20 per cent, while Senegal and the Ivory Coast accounted for three-quarters of the total exports of French West Africa, which amounted to a quarter of total West African exports.

In return for exports of primary products Africa imported mainly manufactured consumer's goods. After the Second World War an increasing proportion of imports was composed of machinery, transport equipment, mineral fuels for use in transport and electricity generation, building materials and chemicals. More countries in Africa were making their own textiles and processing their own foodstuffs and beverages or at least buying their needs from cheaper sources. None the less, in 1960 manufactured consumer's goods and foodstuffs made up about 60 per cent of the value of all imports into French West Africa and 45 per cent of all imports into British West Africa. Textiles accounted for 23,3 per cent of Ethiopia's imports, 21,4 per cent of Sudan's.

Between 1948 and 1960 the total exports of the non-Communist world grew at an average annual rate of rather more than 6 per cent. From 1953 to 1963 trade in primary products increased by 44 per cent and trade in manufactures by 83 per cent. Africa shared in that expansion of trade, but its share of total world trade did not increase. Whereas in 1937 its share was 5,7 per cent, in 1960 it was 5,5 per cent (3,9 per cent sub-Saharan, 1,6 per cent super-Saharan). In the 1950s the exports of industrial countries grew much faster than Africa's and in the latter part of the decade Africa's exports grew faster than those of the rest of the developing world only because by then it was becoming an important source of petroleum. Over the period 1956-1961 world exports grew by 26 per cent, those of the industrialized countries by 34 per cent, those of Africa by 15 per cent (7 per cent excluding petroleum) and those of the rest of the developing world by 11 per cent.

South Africa remained much the biggest trader in Africa. In 1960 it imported goods to the value of $1 555 million, far outstripping the imports of the next two biggest African markets, Egypt and Nigeria, which bought $667 million and $604 million worth of goods respectively. Algeria was importing heavily in the later 1950s, with imports valued at $1 265 million in 1960, but that was due at least partly to an inflow of military equipment. Compared with other countries South Africa was importing machinery and transport equipment, accounting for 40,2 per cent of total imports, on a much greater scale. Only 5,3 per cent of its imports in 1960 were composed of food, drink and tobacco, compared with 21,4 per cent of Egypt's imports, 19,6 per cent of Tunisia's, 19,5 per cent of Angola's and 19,2 per cent of Ghana's. Southern Rhodesia, with a relatively big European population, was a comparatively big market, and among the West African countries Nigeria and Ghana predominated. The Federation of Rhodesia and Nyasaland imported $429 million worth of goods in 1960, Ghana $362 million.

South Africa was also the chief exporter in Africa. Its exports were worth $1 238 million in 1960. Its nearest rival was the Federation of Rhodesia and Nyasaland, which exported goods to the value of $576 million. Egypt's exports earned $568 million in 1960, the highest since 1951. For most of the decade Egyptian trade did rather badly, exports consistently below $500 million a year and imports falling to $472 million in 1954. Between 1950 and 1959 Egypt's share of total African imports fell from 14 per cent to 7 per cent and of total African exports from 14 per cent to 9 per cent. The other substantial exporters were the associated territories of East Africa, Kenya, Tanganyika and Uganda ($387 million), Nigeria ($475 million), Ghana ($294 million) and Morocco ($354 million). Algerian exports amounted to $394 million in 1960, but these were the lowest since 1951, a decline due to the unrest in the country. Most countries recorded considerable increases in exports in the 1950s. In East Africa exports doubled, in South Africa and the Federation of Rhodesia and Nyasaland they increased by three-quarters.

Relying upon foreign aid or their reserves some African countries in the 1950s were importing more than they were exporting, e.g. Egypt, Morocco, Tunisia, Liberia, Ghana and Nigeria. Algeria, because of the political situation, had a very large trade gap. Most other African countries for most of the decade usually exported more than they imported, but an adverse trend set in towards the end of the 1950s. Commodity prices started to fall from their Korean War heights in 1952, as industrial activity slowed down and industrial countries ceased to accumulate reserves of primary products. The long-term trend after the war was for Africa's terms of trade to deteriorate as prices of manufactures were maintained. It is estimated that the terms of trade of the underdeveloped countries as a whole worsened by about 11 per cent between 1950-1955 and 1962-1963, after which they stabilized for the rest of the 1960s, though at a relatively low price level, with Third World manufactures rather than primary products benefiting from stabilization. The deterioration of the terms of trade between primary products and capital equipment was particularly severe and therefore put an additional obstacle in the way of industrial development. Loss of foreign earnings through worsening terms of trade was sufficient to neutralize in large measure grants of aid from the developed world. It was unfortunate that this occurred at the very time that colonies were being liberated and expectations of economic improvement were therefore rising among the newly independent peoples.

The deterioration of terms of trade varied from country to country according to the composition of its exports. Egypt and the Sudan, depending on cotton, and Tanganyika, an important sisal exporter, did badly. Egypt also suffered from an indifferent cotton crop during most of the 1950s. Copper exports from Northern Rhodesia and the Belgian Congo did well until 1956. Cocoa prices were also maintained until the middle of the decade, but then fell sharply, though very unevenly. By the middle of the 1960s twice the volume of cocoa exports of ten years earlier earned about the same amount of foreign exchange. From 1956 Ghana was, with the exception of 1958, consistently in deficit on the current account of the balance of payments.

When world prices fell after the Korean War, the marketing boards of the British West African and East African colonies fixed their prices at a still lower level and continued to accumulate funds, though on a reduced scale. When they were disgorged in the late 1950s and 1960s, they were used mostly, though not entirely, to finance government development projects and not, as originally planned, to compensate the producers. Marketing boards were controversial in aim and purpose, certainly unpopular among farmers receiving less than world prices for their products and they sometimes provoked violent protest. They may have discouraged production and given rise to smuggling and illicit trade. It is commonly agreed than one of their purposes was to achieve price stabilization, though it is apparent that this was often subordinated to their revenue collecting function and there is some dispute whether they succeeded in stabilizing prices. It has been argued that, while they virtually eliminated intra-seasonal price fluctuations, they had very little success in levelling out prices from season to season and totally failed to stabilize incomes, which depended as much upon volume of production as upon price, and no attempt was made to control output. It has even been contended that incomes were more unstable under the marketing board system than they would have been in its absence and that the boards had a generally depressing effect on the economy by dampening down demand and possibly blunting the incentive to invest in productive enterprises within and outside agriculture. On the other hand, it has also been argued that the funds accumulated by the boards were invested usefully in various government-sponsored projects, notably agricultural research, education, road construction and local industries, and that the boards proved to be effective in mobilizing savings for investment which would otherwise not have been made. If the reserves had been paid out directly to the farmers, the greater part of the additional income would have been spent on imported consumer's goods. But this argument has been questioned. It has been suggested that the investment of marketing board surpluses was not always well-advised and that the boards simply led to a proliferation of bureaucracy subject to political manipulation.

In the French colonies marketing became confused as the powers of the various caisses were reduced. Between 1954 and 1956 a series of price stabilization funds (caisses de stabilisation) were created for the principal French West African exports, financed by levies on exporters, by export duties and by a central fund in Paris (Fonds national de Régularisation des Cours des Produits d'Outre-mer). They seem to have had a considerable success in fixing producer prices well above world prices. Unlike the marketing boards in the British colonies they made serious efforts to influence incomes by trying to control the volume of produce placed on the market, and they also used their reserves to support prices when the market weakened.

Most of Africa experienced balance of payment difficulties, which were sometimes grave, and these imbalances were corrected only by the import of public and private capital, sometimes in the form of government aid, and by running down the sterling balances built up during the war. Kenya would have had an even more serious balance of payment problems had it not been for its relationship with Tanganyika and Uganda. In North Africa the exports of Algeria and Tunisia amounted to only 70 per cent of imports, of Morocco only 65 per cent. South Africa had an unfavourable balance of payments on current account from 1946 until 1958. This was made good by capital inflow, but there was always the danger of an outflow of funds attracted by higher interest rates elsewhere. Exchange control prevented the movement of funds to non-sterling countries and in the 1950s the government extended exchange control to transactions within the sterling area.

During the 1950s the local South African money market expanded and diversified. In 1949 the National Finance Corporation was established with government sponsorship and this attracted call money that had hitherto been invested in London. Subsequently a number of discount and accepting houses was established. This development strengthened the power of the Reserve Bank to control credit through the bank rate and through its position as lender of last resort. In 1956 it was given the power to impose additional reserve requirements upon the commercial banks, thus restricting their ability to extend credit. However, the tendency of the government to borrow heavily, especially overseas, to make good budgetary deficits had the effect of promoting inflation.

Capital imports into South Africa, used principally to develop the Orange Free State gold-mines and to extend infrastructure, continued at a high level until 1954, thereafter tailing off. In 1957, 1959 and especially 1960, there was a net outflow. In 1960 the total foreign liabilities of South Africa were R3 077 million, R1 972 million to the sterling area (mostly Britain), R623 million to the dollar area and R429 million to European countries other than Britain. South Africa itself, however, had investments outside its frontiers, totalling R772 million, mostly in the Federation of Rhodesia and Nyasaland. South Africa and the Federation, together with the Belgian Congo, were the chief beneficiaries of Africa's rather modest share of World Bank loans in the 1950s, most of the money being devoted to the development of electricity-generating capacity and transport. South Africa was the chief outlet in Africa for exports of British private capital. French exports of private capital went chiefly to its colonies or former colonies. France was also an important source of foreign aid. Of the $26 000 million granted as aid throughout the world between 1945 and 1960, $16 000 million came from the USA. Of the world total Africa obtained $6 700 million. Most of France's $4 500 million in aid went to its colonies or ex-colonies.

A good deal of imported capital was used to build roads. Between 1948 and 1957 the length of roads in the Gold Coast increased 242 per cent and the Gold Coast had one of the highest ratios in Africa of commercial vehicles to population (3,1 per thousand in 1958). In French Equatorial Africa the length of roads increased 270 per cent between 1948 and 1954 and most African countries recorded substantial, though not so startling, improvements. South Africa with 14,0 commercial vehicles per 1 000 people, was best off, followed by Algeria with a ratio of 5,9 and Southern Rhodesia with a ratio of 5,4 per thousand people. Expansion of road services constituted a post-war transport revolution. There was, however, also some railway construction, e.g. a connection between Lourenço Marques and the Rhodesian railway system to relieve congestion at Beira (1955). Existing railways were much more intensively used. Passenger kilometres in the Belgian Congo and Moçambique increased well over 200 per cent between 1948 and 1958 and metric ton kilometres in Moçambique increased more than 700 per cent.

The expansion of road networks and road transport enlarged the market for domestically produced foodstuffs, grain, root crops, vegetables, fish and meat. In 1964 no fewer than 300 000 head of cattle were imported into southern Nigeria from the savanna, together with 118 000 sheep, rams, goats and pigs. The railway captured a good deal of this traffic, though substantial numbers of livestock were driven to market. The trade in kola nuts (a regional delicacy) likewise increased. The volume sold for external consumption by the Ivory Coast rose to some 30 000 tons in 1954, making them the territory's most valuable export after coffee and cocoa. About a third of that total was sent to Senegal either by road to Bamako in Soudan, then by rail or by sea to Dakar. Northern Nigeria was another major market. In 1964, 54 000 tons were sent from southern Nigeria to the north. Ghanaian producers found new markets for themselves in Upper Volta, Soudan and Niger.

There were changes in agricultural techniques, such as the introduction of chemical fertilizers, better seeds and pesticides. Storage facilities were made better. On the whole, however, peasant production, whether of export staples or of foodstuffs for the local market, made use of traditional methods. Production was increased by the application of more labour to land. Moreover there was little transfer of entrepreneurial skills from agriculture. Although the pioneers of cocoa farming in the Gold Coast displayed considerable resourcefulness, even there little branching out into commerce and industry was found. In the case of foreign enterprise, local opportunities for acquiring skills were limited by the competition of, and preference for, expatriate personnel. However, traditional trading people, like the Hausa and Dyula, were shrewd at finding new outlets for their accumulated experience and capital and at meeting new competition in fields in which they had long established their dominance. Entrepreneurs, with trading traditions or not, found openings in construction, processed foods, books, cinemas, motor servicing and road haulage. The trading firm was, as in the past, normally a family firm with all the advantages that came from pooled labour and capital, but operating within narrow limits to growth, not least because of inheritance laws.

In West Africa, even in the import-export business, dominated though it was by a few expatriate firms, there was a growing number of small middlemen. Thousands of petty traders or agents went in for purchasing small quantities of cash crops from producers for re-sale to substantial African brokers who dealt with the big foreign firms. On the import side, besides a host of small traders dealing in the cheapest of manufactured goods, there were African merchants who acted either as independent wholesalers or as agents selling goods on commission for manufacturing firms in Europe. In Nigeria the African share of the import trade rose from 5 per cent in 1949 to 20 per cent in 1963, partly the result of the decision of the big trading companies, in the face of competition on the one hand from small businesses with low overheads and on the other from overseas industrial concerns, to concentrate on wholesaling a more limited range of products, thus leaving the field clear in some areas, especially retailing, to local businessmen. Government policy was also changing, influenced by increasing African participation in administration. In Nigeria the official approach after the war was not only to promote the development of the economy, particularly manufacturing, but also to increase the degree of Nigerian participation in trade and industry. It was not thought that this would be harmful to British economic interests as there was ample scope for British investment and enterprise. In the 1950s the government became increasingly interventionist. Public corporations were established to enlarge the Nigerian share of the economy. Although socialist sentiments were expressed, this public activity was not intended to supplant indigenous private enterprise but to fill a vacuum that Nigerian businessmen were unable to fill themselves. It was not a success. The public corporations failed to make a profit and the government, implicitly acknowledging a dependence on foreign enterprise, chose rather to rely upon persuading foreign-owned firms to give management jobs to Nigerians and to sell shares to local investors and to itself.

It sometimes happened that new opportunities in trade and industry were seized by ethnic minorities. This was especially true where the indigenous merchant class was weak. Indians and, to a less extent, Chinese were quick to take advantage of openings in retail trade, e.g. in Madagascar. Even in West Africa the so-called Syrians, mostly Lebanese families which had arrived in the 1920s, by hard work and self-denial established themselves in trade and later motor transport. Although they numbered only a few thousand, they had an influence disproportionate to their numbers and aroused some hostility among native Africans. In South Africa the Indians engaged in a much wider range of economic activity and were very much more numerous than the West African Syrians. Long subject to discrimination, they found their position deteriorated with the advent of the National Party to power. The Group Areas Act of 1950 was one of the chief means by which apartheid was to be implemented. In East Africa there were fewer obstacles in the way of Asian entrepreneurs. Often coming from families which had had a mercantile background in India, industrious, thrifty and clannish, they played an important part in marketing peasant agricultural produce and, in Uganda, in cotton ginning.

Asian investment came to predominate in the new industries that developed in Uganda in the later colonial period, often in association with the Uganda Development Corporation, set up by the colonial government in 1952. Coffee processing, sugar production and refining and the manufacture of industrial alcohol were Asian-pioneered activities of great importance. The Uganda Development Corporation invested in the manufacture of cement and cotton textiles, the latter protected by a substantial tariff in 1958. In 1962 it joined with Asian enterprise to set up a steel rolling mill using scrap metal.

In West Africa after the war, particularly after the Korean War, the expatriate firms began to display an interest in promoting industry that they had never shown before. Their earlier reluctance was due to lack of incentive. They were doing very well as general merchants, while manufacturing was risky, especially during the depression, when demand was so restricted. During the greater post-war prosperity, they were more willing to consider investment in industry, especially as the import trade had become more competitive and profits were not what they had been. As manufacturers, they could, with their lower production and transport costs, hope to undersell overseas industry. Processed food and drink, textiles, clothing and footwear, furniture, utensils and construction materials accounted for the biggest share of import substitution in West Africa during the 1950s and 1960s, concentrated chiefly in Lagos and Dakar.

At the end of the colonial period Nigeria had the biggest industrial sector in tropical Africa in terms of total industrial production, but this may be attributed primarily to the size of its population, large enough to provide a market for a local manufacturing plant. In terms of the share of manufacturing in GDP it fell far short of the Belgian Congo and Southern Rhodesia and appreciably short of Senegal and Kenya. All four latter countries had substantial European populations. European settlers were able to contribute savings, skills and entrepreneurship and were able to obtain government sympathy. Exports from Kenya to Uganda and Tanganyika, which in the early post-war years were still largely agricultural products, by the end of the colonial period were more than half made up of manufactured goods. Although even in Kenya manufacturing and repairs represented by the end of the colonial period only 10 per cent of GDP, this compared favourably with the situation in Uganda and Tanganyika. Kenyan industry was concentrated upon the processing of food, drink and tobacco, but also included soap, miscellaneous chemicals, leather and leather goods, furniture and forestry. By the end of the colonial period there was a further group of industries that, though still small, was potentially of great importance. This included the manufacture of textiles, clothing and footwear, shipbuilding and repair, rolling stock manufacture and the production of industrial chemicals and light machinery.

In Southern Rhodesia industry was increasingly diversified and more complex. There was substantial production of metalware, textiles and chemicals, as well as a growing engineering industry. At the conclusion of the rather brief period of state intervention in industry firms from Britain and South Africa, Southern Rhodesia's principal trading partners, predominated. White settlers tended to display more interest in commerce and land speculation as fields of investment and enterprise, leaving industry to foreign investors and managers. Yarn and clothing were exported to South Africa, but the chief markets for Southern Rhodesia's manufactured exports were its partners in the Central African Federation, Northern Rhodesia and Nyasaland. At the outset of federation, manufacturing contributed 13 per cent of Southern Rhodesia's GDP. Under federation this increased to 16 per cent, an increase that was modest in relative terms, but of significance in absolute terms. Manufacturing in Southern Rhodesia forged ahead of industry in Northern Rhodesia in range and volume of production. To some extent this superior performance can be explained by the external economies to be gained by the expansion of manufacturing in an area where industry was already relatively highly developed. As, however, the Copper Belt, with its concentrated and comparatively well-off population and its infrastructure developed for the mining industry, could offer similar advantages, the explanation may lie in the political influence exerted by Southern Rhodesian interests in the federal government.

The Belgian Congo also developed into one of the more industrialized African territories at the end of the colonial period. The progress of the 1920s, interrupted by the depression, was resumed and from 1950 there was rapid development. This second phase ended within less than ten years as imports of capital goods outstripped the colony's capacity to pay for them. The index of industrial production more than doubled between 1950 and 1959. As elsewhere, industries were of two types, processing raw materials, such as palm fruit and palm kernels, timber and minerals, and import substitution, such as foodstuffs, textiles, cement and other building materials.

In Egypt the wartime and post-war industrial spurt suffered a temporary setback after the Korean War as cotton prices began to fall. The easier opportunities for import substitution were becoming exhausted. After the revolution of 1952 the state took a more direct rôle in industry, though intervention occurred relatively gradually. The state sector expanded through selective nationalization. The process began with the national-ization of the Suez Canal in 1956, apparently in response to the decision of Britain and the USA not to help finance the construction of a High Dam at Aswan. Following an Anglo-French attack on Egypt and war with Israel, British, French and some Jewish property was also seized (and in 1961 Belgian assets as an Egyptian protest against Belgian policy in the former Belgian Congo), giving the Egyptian government a very large stake in banking and insurance. In 1957 all remaining foreign-owned banks and insurance and trading companies were required to dispose of the majority of their shares to Egyptians and bring in Egyptian managers. The state exercised its powers through a body set up in 1957 called the Economic Organization, the responsibilities of which continued to grow through further nationalization and the establishment of new state enterprises. To begin with nationalization was inspired chiefly by nationalism, but the movement to greater state ownership had a momentum of its own and the government was strongly influenced by its autocratic character and its desire to hasten the process of development. Nationalization was extended to entirely Egyptian-owned businesses when, in 1960, the Bank Misr was taken over. Planning became increasingly comprehensive, with an in-dustrial plan introduced in 1957, superseded by a First Five-Year General Plan in 1960.

After 1954 there was rapid industrial growth in Egypt, nearly 10 per cent a year in the next ten years. The immediate cause of expansion was not so much state investment, which did not become effective until late in the 1950s. Rather output was attributable to increased domestic demand as the level of income rose and government restrictions kept out imported goods. A great deal of industrial capacity previously not fully employed was brought into production. The importance of textiles, already the chief contributor to value added in manufacturing, grew. In the late 1950s and early 1960s there was a sharp increase in the number of cotton spindles (1,1 million in 1960). Egypt was far ahead of its nearest African rival, South Africa (0,1 million spindles in 1960). Cotton manufacturing was favoured by the availability of locally grown raw material, whereas the importance of food processing decreased as Egypt imported more and more of its foodstuffs. The growth industries, apart from textiles, were chemicals, paper, metals and metal products. Egyptian industry became more diversified, but there was still no significant production of capital goods.

Industry in Algeria developed rapidly in the 1950s. The index of industrial production, excluding building, rose from 100 in 1950 to 132,9 in 1954 and to 152,4 in 1957. In 1954 there were 264 000 persons employed in industry, 117 800 of them engaged in public works and construction. In the Second Four-Year Plan of 1953–1956 the emphasis was on labour intensive enterprise in an effort to solve the ever more pressing problem of finding employment for the increasing numbers going on to the labour market. The first Four-Year Plan of 1949–1952 had concentrated more on infrastructure. Despite industrial growth, even in 1955 large-scale industry still contributed only 10 per cent to GDP. A significant indication of comparative industrial backwardness was that a third of all low-tension electric current was consumed by householders and public lighting. Elsewhere in the Maghrib, Tunisia and Morocco became independent in 1956 and inevitably political disturbances in the 1950s affected the economy. The evidence is somewhat conflicting, but both appear to have enjoyed a steady growth.

In South Africa in the 1950s metals, engineering and chemical production expanded. Metals had the advantage of access to cheap coal and local raw materials. South Africa became competitive in price and quality on world markets. Although the older industries of food, beverages, tobacco, clothing, textiles and furniture also grew, their share of total output began to shrink. The canning industry enjoyed considerable expansion. The textile industry benefited much from the import restrictions imposed between 1948 and 1957. Franchise rights were acquired from overseas suppliers whose access to the local market was blocked, and several foreign manufacturers became directly involved in local production. The establishment by the South African Coal, Oil and Gas Corporation (Sasol) of a plant in 1955 for extracting oil from coal had an important effect upon the chemical industry. Sasol plants supplied chemical by-products as inputs, especially for the fertilizer industry. Production of hardboard and rayon pulp was begun from local raw materials, mostly for export. At the same time there was a great expansion of the paper and printing industries.

South Africa accounted for 40 per cent of the industrial output of sub-Saharan Africa, though only 6 per cent of its population. The net value of total industrial output of the rest of sub-Saharan Africa was less than that of Sweden. It is in that light that the impressive performance of industry in Africa in the 1950s must be seen. Growth rates were high – 7,4 per cent a year in manufacturing and 6,7 per cent a year in mining in Africa excluding South Africa in 1948–1960 – but the base was low and little was achieved in narrowing the industrial gap between the developed and developing countries in the world. Africa was overwhelmingly a continent of small farmers producing mostly to meet their own needs. Excluding South Africa, it produced only half per cent of the machinery it required. In most African countries the contribution of industry, including mining, to GNP was only about 10 per cent and the contribution of agriculture about 40 per cent. Within the industrial sector mining predominated. A far larger share of industrial output came from mining than was the case with developed countries. If mining was excluded, the contribution of industry to GNP reached 10 per cent only in Kenya, Southern Rhodesia and the Belgian Congo. These had a large inflow of private capital and European technicians into industry after the war. Elsewhere the proportion was less than 5 per cent, only 1 per cent in Nigeria.

Almost half of all industrial production in Africa, excluding mining, came from handicraft industries, such as spinning, weaving, basket making and pottery. Outside South Africa and Egypt the engineering industry was made up of small workshops doing repairs and maintenance on bicycles, railway rolling-stock, motor vehicles, agricultural equipment and river boats. Southern Rhodesia manufactured some machinery. Outside North Africa and South Africa there was little production of chemicals. East Africa exported soda ash and wattle bark and Southern Rhodesia chemical fertilizers. Most African countries manufactured textiles, especially cotton goods, but only Egypt was approaching self-sufficiency in cotton, rayon and woollen fabrics.

The mining industry continued its rapid development. By the end of the 1950s it provided direct employment for over a million workers. About half of these were in South Africa, where the chief exploited minerals were gold, diamonds, uranium, coal, asbestos, iron ore, manganese and chrome. South Africa accounted for over two-fifths of the total value of mineral output in Africa. New gold fields were opened in the Orange Free State and the original Witwatersrand fields were extended eastwards and westwards. By the 1960s new fields were accounting for over 85 per cent of total production. Gold output rose from 11,6 million ounces in 1950 to 21,3 million in 1960. By then South Africa was producing 63,1 per cent of the world's output of gold.

South Africa was outstripped in value of per capita production of minerals after the war by Northern Rhodesia and South-West Africa. Other important producers, either in aggregate or per capita value or both, were the Belgian Congo, Morocco, Algeria, the Gold Coast, Nigeria, Southern Rhodesia, Sierra Leone, Swaziland, Egypt and Tunisia. The most important minerals for Egypt were manganese (though its output could not compare with that of the Gold Coast, South Africa or Morocco) iron ore and petroleum.

In the late 1950s oil production began in various parts of the continent. It was destined to challenge gold, diamonds and copper as the biggest contributors to the total value of mineral production in Africa. Egypt had oil deposits that had been worked long before any others in Africa and was the biggest producer for most of the 1950s. Until 1957 it produced over 90 per cent of Africa's petroleum. There was rapid development in Algeria in the latter part of the decade and in 1960 Algerian production (8,7 million metric tons) was twice that of Egypt (3,3 million metric tons), and Angola was beginning to exploit its resources. Morocco produced 0,1 million tons in 1955, but after that production declined.

The exploration for oil and the exploitation of oil-fields were undertaken by a mixture of state and private capital. The French government was particularly keen to develop sources of oil which were not controlled by the big British and American companies that dominated the Middle East, and therefore in Algeria and Morocco the prospecting for and production of oil were state enterprises. The industry in Egypt was run by the Anglo-Egyptian Oilfields Company, largely owned by Shell with a small government share. It was nationalized in 1956. The first refinery was at Suez but two more were built in the 1950s, at Alexandria and Cairo. In Angola the Companhia Concessionária de Petróleos de Angola (Petrangol), established in 1957 to exploit the deposits discovered in 1955, was owned jointly by Portuguese and, more especially, Belgian private interests and by the colonial government. A refinery was constructed near Luanda. In Nigeria Shell-BP was first in the field, but was subsequently joined by American companies. Exploration costs were particularly high in Nigeria, where the deposits were situated in the difficult Niger Delta region.

In West Africa, apart from oil, there was a sharp increase in the output of bauxite (for aluminium) in the late 1950s in Guinea and Ghana (though even in the 1960 Africa's share of world production was still only 7 per cent) and iron ore in Liberia. Knowledge of the existence of bauxite deposits in the Gold Coast went back to at least the 1920s, when the possibility of damming the River Volta to provide hydro-electricity for developing them was first considered. They were not worked until after the war, when a railway line was constructed to facilitate exports. The Volta River project was not started until the late 1950s, and the dam was completed only in 1966. In the meantime the Gold Coast was overtaken by French Guinea as a producer. In 1952 a small deposit on one of the Los Islands off Conakry was developed and much larger deposits subsequently worked at Fria and Boké.

Interest in Liberian iron ore was shown in the 1930s, but nothing came of it. After the war American firms secured a contract from the government for the exploitation of the newly-discovered Bomi deposits, and operations began in 1950 on the strength of a loan from the Republican Steel Corporation of the United States. In 1951 the first shipment was sent to America and in 1953, 0,8 million metric tons were produced. Subsequently other American companies were attracted, in 1958 the National Iron Ore Company and in 1961 a consortium called Lamco Joint Ventures, the former operating on the River Mano in the west, the latter in the Nimba Mountains. Output increased rapidly – 2,1 million metric tons in 1960. The economy of the country was revolutionized. The mining companies built roads and railways for their own purposes, but the whole economy benefited, since the movement of labour was facilitated and the develop-ment of local industry stimulated. By the mid-1950s Liberia was already the biggest producer of iron ore in Africa, surpassing South Africa, which itself outstripped Algeria by the end of the decade. Output in Algeria, Tunisia and Morocco fell in the late 1950s but picked up again in 1960.

In 1960 the proportion of the world's metallic minerals produced in Africa was as follows: antimony 39 per cent, bauxite 7 per cent, chromite 44 per cent, cobalt 73 per cent, copper 27 per cent, gold 69 per cent, iron 4 per cent, manganese 45 per cent (the African contribution had fallen to only 19 per cent in 1957. The Gold Coast was the most important source and its output was reduced in the early 1950s by the difficulties of deeper mining.), silver 4 per cent, tin concentrates 13 per cent, tungsten ore 5 per cent and vanadium 21 per cent. The African share of world output of the non-metallic minerals was: asbestos 20 per cent, coal 2 per cent, diamonds 94 per cent and phosphate rock 33 per cent (mostly by far from Morocco, where output was 7,5 million metric tons, with Tunisia the second biggest producer, having an output of 2,1 million tons).

Greater industrialization meant more urbanization. Familiarity with wage employment, the spread of knowledge of job opportunities and the development of transport that presented the means of taking advantage of such opportunities, all contributed to the growth of permanent commitment to wage-earning. In Northern Rhodesia by the 1950s from 20 per cent to 30 per cent of the black population of the copper-mining towns had lived away from the rural areas for over ten years. The trend towards permanence was welcomed by mine managers, who responded by providing married quarters. Health and efficiency improved and training schemes became more worthwhile.

The stabilization of the African labour force in Northern Rhodesia inevitably raised the question of the white monopoly of skills and high wages. The majority of Europeans in mining came from South Africa, though there were some specialists from Britain and the United States. With the growing cost of European labour and the growing efficiency of African labour, the mining companies tended to substitute African for European labour in semi-skilled work. After the Second World War African wages began to rise appreciably. Real wages increased 300 per cent between 1940 and 1960. The mines therefore started to economize on African labour by using it more efficiently and by mechanization. It became worthwhile to train Africans to take over from Europeans. The employers were also influenced by the growing stability of the black labour force and the approach of African independence. White labour was hostile to black advancement and its union insisted on a colour bar, which they called a safeguard against dilution of labour. In 1955 a compromise was reached with the management. Certain categories of employment were turned over to Africans. The compromise was by no means the final solution, but only the first stage of a long process of Africanization.

Throughout Africa an increasing range of employment opportunities became available. In the early days the chief demand was from plantations and mines and development projects, such as railway construction. For a long time the industrial sector was negligible, as industry was mostly small-scale and mostly of the handicraft type. Trade was handled, apart from the expatriate firms, by individuals who employed no labour. But gradually new labour needs appeared. Colonial governments were important employers of labour, both for administration and for public works and transport. Towards the end of the colonial period about half the total employed workers in British West Africa were working for the government. But the expansion of trade also set up a demand for labour, for marketing and transporting cash crops and for the distribution of imported goods. New tastes in manufactured goods were acquired. Towns became more attractive, representing an escape from tribal discipline and family obligations, even though it might be possible to earn more money at home producing for the market. The spread of western education produced a class which wanted permanent employment in the clerical and higher levels of business, industry and government service and which had no intention of returning to rural life. Towns, where there were hospitals and schools and there was more entertainment, were thought to provide a better and more prosperous life. During the colonial period movement to the towns was also an escape from the obligations imposed by colonial authorities, e.g. enforced cultivation of cash crops in the Belgian Congo, where movement to the towns was especially marked.

Thus the attraction or supposed attraction of urban life exerted a pull into the towns. Sometimes rural emigration deprived agriculture of the labour of the sound and fit; and an enlarged urban population had to be fed by an agriculture that, even where it was not short of workers, suffered under some other disability, such as government neglect. It was not only the lure of the towns that influenced migration. The urban pull was reinforced by the push of population growth, which became stronger as Africa began to feel the full effects of the revolution in medicine and public health and which in some parts of Africa resulted in an intolerable pressure upon land, causing soil erosion and falling agricultural output. In 1955 three-quarters of the population of French North Africa lived on the land, but produced only 30 per cent of GDP. In many places demographic saturation point was reached and the problem was less one of a labour shortage than of unemployment as growth in employment creation throughout Africa lagged behind growth in output and growth in population. Even as late as the 1950s population data were far from reliable. But it is evident that by 1960 eight countries in Africa each had a population greater than ten million – Algeria, Morocco, Egypt, Sudan, Ethiopia, Nigeria, the Belgian Congo and South Africa – and that the annual rate of population growth was commonly more than 2 per cent, in some cases more than 3 per cent. The most populous countries were Egypt and Nigeria. Density of population varied widely. The Nile Valley, the palm belt of Nigeria, and Ruanda-Urundi were particularly thickly populated. Egypt, the Maghrib and South Africa were the most urbanized parts of the continent.

Except for a privileged minority urban life proved to be not nearly as attractive in reality as it seemed to be in anticipation. Rural immigrants who flocked to the towns in increasing numbers found living in town expensive and, to say the least, uncomfortable. Not all of them found work. Casablanca, Algiers, Oran, Tunis, Tripoli, Cairo, Alexandria, Brazzaville, Leopoldville, Dar es Salaam and Nairobi all had a large floating population of unemployed as early as the 1950s. Housing construction did not keep pace with the influx and shanty towns and bidonvilles sprang up. Inadequate, often insanitary, accommodation, an alien and sometimes hostile environment and the tendency for males to be separated in the towns from their families that remained on the land, created grave social problems.

The extent to which towns expanded and African workers became more permanent and skilled depended on a variety of factors that included the ratio of land to population, the capacity of agriculture to support population, the type of land tenure, the rate of growth of commerce and industry, and the policy of government and employer. In South Africa everything favoured a rural exodus and a growing permanence and skill of these rural migrants. Opportunities for employment of all types grew fast, extensive and subsistence agriculture was reaching the limit of its capacity to support the growing population and the hold exercised by communal land holding upon the country dweller was slackening or did not even exist. It was in South Africa, however, that these pressures were most resisted. The policy of the government, which, on the one hand, increased the push of Africans into the towns by its land policy, which confined them to less than 13 per cent of the country, on the other, seconded for the most part by both capital and white labour, thwarted the trend towards a growing, stable and skilled urban black population, by its industrial policy. The typical worker was still the unskilled contract labourer. The social evils that stemmed from the migrant labour system were all too plain, both for the men cooped up in barracks away from their families for months on end and for the catchment areas of such labour recruitment – Moçambique, Nyasaland, Basutoland, the Transkei and so on – where the absence of a high proportion of the adult males reduced some districts to depression and demoralization.

In the interests of the National Party's policy of apartheid, the government tried to turn back the tide of blacks flooding into the modern sector of the economy. Since the logic of economic development could not be refuted, however, the authorities relied increasingly on the fiction that black workers in the so-called white areas were there only temporarily, denied them permanent residence rights, and prevented their escape from the demoralizing migratory system. Such attempts as employers made to encourage stabilization – by, for example, the provision of married quarters in the Orange Free State gold-fields – came into conflict with government policy. In 1951 there were more than half a million African migrant workers from the South African reserves, together with some 400 000 from outside South Africa's borders. But even the size of this army did not suffice and permanently urbanized blacks settled increasingly in the industrial centres in the white areas. Partly to reduce the numbers and partly to raise living standards in the reserves (or homelands as they came to be called) the government appointed a commission (the Tomlinson Commission) to investigate and make recommendations. The suggestion that was made in its report (1954) was the offering of incentives to entrepreneurs to set up businesses in the reserves. The government preferred to begin a policy of encouraging the location of industry along the borders of the homelands to employ commuting labour.

CHAPTER IX

1960–1970 (THE FIRST DEVELOPMENT DECADE)

In the 1960s the process of decolonization was all but completed. Britain recognized the impracticability of preserving the Central African Federation and dismantled it in 1964, granting independence to Northern Rhodesia as Zambia and Nyasaland as Malawi. It felt powerless, however, to act with any effectiveness against a white community in Southern Rhodesia that had enjoyed internal self-government for fifty years and was not dependent upon metropolitan support against armed nationalism. In 1965 Southern Rhodesia declared itself independent and, despite economic sanctions imposed by Britain and the United Nations and armed incursions into its territory, managed with the connivance of South Africa and Portugal to survive and even prosper. The Portuguese, established in Africa longer than any other European people, displayed the greatest obstinacy in clinging to their colonies, not only where there was considerable white settlement, as in Angola, but also where it was negligible, as in Guinea-Bissau. They faced uprisings in all three of their mainland colonies.

Africa emerged into independence as a collection of many, mostly small and more or less poor and undeveloped states whose frontiers bore no relation to linguistic boundaries. For administration and education they used the European languages which they inherited from their colonial rulers. Undesirable as that was, these foreign tongues, as well as the cultures they expressed, constituted one of the few unifying forces within the new states, providing a lingua franca for the educated. African states were small in population rather than in geographical extent and by that same criterion some were tiny, e.g. Gabon, with its half million people. Since they all produced similar commodities, there was little scope for trade among themselves. Besides, the transport system was not designed to facilitate that. Each colonial power built its roads and railways, with their varying gauges and operating practices, to meet its own needs. What local industry had grown up during the colonial period was dependent on tariff protection and this the newly-independent states were determined to retain. Enthusiasm for pan-Africanism, popular among nationalists during the colonial period, waned after independence. Separate states were unwilling to submerge themselves in a greater whole. Even the existing states sometimes found it difficult to maintain their unity. Two of the biggest, Congo-Leopoldville and Nigeria, had civil wars. The former had to suppress with United Nations help the secession of Katanga (1960–1963) and the latter had to fight to preserve the federation bequeathed to it by the departing British against a secessionist movement in its eastern region, which called itself Biafra (1967).

Though the national movement in AOF led by the Rassemblement démocratique africaine had been inter-territorial and some African politicians, notably Leopold Senghor, had expressed themselves in favour of federation, the federation broke up in 1958, when the territories were offered independence within the French Community. Wealthier states, such as Ivory Coast, did not want to be saddled with the support of their poorer neighbours; poorer states wanted to develop their national economies free from the domination of their more advanced neighbours. It was perhaps French policy itself that was responsible for loosening inter-territorial ties. The *loi cadre* of 1956, though retaining federal control over defence, foreign affairs and finance, allocated specific responsibilities to the separate colonies.

The pan-African movement split up into competing groups – the moderate Monrovia group (1961), composed of both English and French-speaking states favourably inclined to the west; and the radical Casablanca group (1961). The latter's members were Morocco, Egypt, Guinea, Ghana and Mali (formerly Soudan), their rulers radical in foreign policy and authoritarian in domestic policy. The personal ascendancy exercised by these political successors of recently departed colonial administrators and the monopoly of power of their parties set a trend that was to become typical of Africa. Another feature of independent Africa which soon became apparent was the coup détat, the result of frustrated opposition denied other means of expression or of protest against the excessive ambition and ineptitude that was displayed by some of the early leaders or of the sheer self-interest of cliques out to secure the fruits of government. An early victim of instability was Kwame Nkrumah, ousted in 1966 by the army and police. In that same year there was a military coup in Nigeria.

The chief legatee of pan-Africanism was the Organization of African Unity (1963), which agreed to the inviolability of the frontiers inherited with independence. It was a political body, though it called upon member states to 'co-ordinate and harmonize' their policies in the field of 'economic co-operation, including transport and communications'. The only other organization working on a continental scale was the United Nations Economic Commission for Africa, whose activities were largely confined to research, advice and the organization of conferences. It set up an office in each of four sub-regions, North, West, Central and East Africa, with an administrative team to give technical advice and help to African governments and to organize training courses. The OAU and the ECA jointly sponsored periodical conferences on trade and development.

On becoming independent, the ex-colonies had to negotiate their economic relationship with the European Common Market. The Convention of Yaoundé, Cameroun, came into force in 1964. There were 18 associated members, Guinea being the only francophone country that stayed outside, apart from the countries of the Maghrib. Under the Convention the exports of the associated states to the EEC were to benefit from the same gradual elimination of duties and quotas as the full members. The agricultural products from the associated states that did not compete with EEC products were to be subject to the common external tariff at reduced rates. Those agricultural products that did compete with EEC products, notably oilseed and sugar, were to receive favourable consideration under the EEC common agricultural policy. The associated states agreed to remove customs duties and quota restrictions on imports from the six members of the Community except in special cases. Customs duties were allowed for the protection of infant industries and for fiscal purposes. Quantitative restrictions were allowed to solve balance of payment difficulties. The EEC undertook to finance schemes to facilitate the marketing of African products throughout the Community.

Britain was not a founder member of the EEC and some of its chief trading partners in Africa made their own arrangements with the Community before Britain's entry in 1973. Nigeria made an agreement that came into force in 1967, granting preferential tariffs to the EEC for a substantial list of products already primarily imported from the Community and not likely to be manufactured in Nigeria for some time. The agreement introduced a new discriminatory element into the Nigerian tariff structure. In 1968 Kenya, Uganda and Tanzania concluded the Arusha Convention, which, though more limited than Yaoundé, gave preferential treatment to the trade between the European Community and the East African Community.

The Yaoundé Convention was subject to much criticism for alleged trade restrictions and discrimination. This came from African and other Third World countries which were not associates and from GATT members, especially the USA. There was also complaint about neo-colonialism, economic dependence on former metropolitan countries. The chief trading partners of Africa remained much as they had been before independence. Francophone Africa continued to trade with France, anglophone Africa with Britain, and Liberia with the USA. Intra-African trade was negligible. After more than a decade of independence intra-African trade accounted for less than 10 per cent of total trade and was mainly in primary products. Although for historical reasons the East African countries of Kenya, Uganda and Tanganyika did a fair amount of trade with one another, their exports in the 1960s to the rest of Africa amounted to less than 5 per cent of their total trade and their imports less than 2 per cent. Guinea and, to a lesser extent, Mali developed ties with the Soviet bloc. But trade with Britain and the rest of Western Europe was most important, accounting for two-thirds of total trade. In the 1960s the European Economic Community countries accounted for about a fifth of East African exports and 17 per cent of imports. EEC preference for some of the products coming from associate members – coffee, cocoa and palm oil – was reduced to disarm international criticism.

Negotiations for the renewal of the Yaoundé Convention, which expired in 1969, began in 1968 but were not successfully completed until shortly after the first Convention had already expired. African states were dissatisfied and there were some disagreements among the Six. Associated states complained that their exports to the EEC had increased by less than 1 per cent in value during 1964–1966 and had fallen by 1 per cent in 1967. But exports from the EEC to the associated states rose by 10 per cent in 1966–1967. Some members of the Community, especially the Netherlands, were unhappy about giving a privileged position to a minority group among developing nations and wanted to extend trade preferences and aid more broadly, whereas France was anxious to keep to the existing arrangements and even tie the African associated states more closely to the Common Market. At all events the Second Yaoundé Convention was signed in 1969 and ran to 1975. It gave more favourable treatment than before to the agricultural exports of the associates. As the Arusha Agreement had not come into force before the expiry of the first Yaoundé Convention, a new agreement had to be negotiated, providing for EEC suspension of customs duties and quantitative restrictions on imports of all East African products except for cloves, coffee and tinned pineapples, for which quotas were imposed. In return Kenya, Uganda and Tanganyika granted the EEC tariff preferences on 58 products. The Agreement affected 6,5 per cent of the total imports of the East African Community and 10 per cent of its imports from the EEC. It was to expire at the same time as the Second Yaoundé Convention.

Like the Treaty of Rome, the Yaoundé Convention aimed at the eventual elimination of tariffs between the EEC and its associates. The establishment of free trade areas of the associate states ceased to be an objective, but no obstacle was put in the way of their participation in other customs unions or free trade areas, and a wide variety of groupings was established with varying degrees of effectiveness. Some of these organizations originated in colonial times, such as the East African Community, but others were completely new. At the same time some of the colonial forms disappeared, such as the Federation of Rhodesia and Nyasaland. The pattern of economic ties existing in south Central Africa persisted after

1963, however, and even survived to some extent Southern Rhodesia's declaration of independence. Rhodesia continued to import and export, though clandestinely, through South Africa and Moçambique. Zambia (formerly Northern Rhodesia) continued to export copper through Rhodesia to Beira in Moçambique until Rhodesia closed the border in an abortive attempt to force Zambia to desist from harbouring guerillas fighting against the Rhodesian régime.

In 1961 the East Africa High Commission became the East African Common Services Organisation, the chief ministers of the members replacing the colonial governors. During the last years of the colonial period there was criticism from African leaders, uneasiness about the common services, which put limitations upon national sovereignty, especially in the sensitive areas of fiscal policy, communications and power, and complaints in Uganda and Tanganyika that Kenya was getting most of the benefits. Consequently, after the granting of independence, although there was some talk of political federation, the bonds of the association were loosened rather than tightened. Uganda and Tanganyika tried to redress the balance of advantage in their own favour. The 1964 Kampala Agreement greatly reduced the effectiveness of the common market by permitting the deficit countries to impose quota restrictions on imports from those in surplus. Tanzania (as Tanganyika had by then become) and, to a lesser extent, Uganda took advantage of the agreement to place restrictions on imports from Kenya, thus slowing down the expansion of inter-territorial trade. Then in 1966 the three members of the association adopted separate (but mutually convertible) currencies and set up three central banks, each with its own reserves, to replace the East African Currency Board. There were some departures from common tax policies, with the introduction of unilateral levies and excise taxes. However, there was reluctance to abandon the association altogether and in 1967 a Treaty for East African Co-operation was signed, establishing the East African Community. It was a change of name rather than a change of substance. There was no supranational authority. Every decision was the result of negotiation among the three governments. Each of the common services was under the supervision of a triumvirate of ministers. To correct the continuing imbalance in trading advantage between Kenya on the one hand and Tanzania and Uganda on the other without recourse to the quantitative restrictions permitted by the Kampala Agreement, a system of transfer taxes was introduced and the East African Development Bank established in Kampala to direct investment into Tanzania and Uganda, which were each to get 40 per cent of the total loans. The headquarters of the common services was moved from Nairobi to Arusha in Tanzania.

Despite these efforts to distribute benefits more equitably friction remained, particularly over a mutually acceptable commercial policy. The need, imposed by the existence of a common market, to co-ordinate commercial policy limited the freedom of members of the Community to manipulate it in the interests of national economic growth. Trading agreements that were concluded in particular by Tanzania with overseas countries, Czechoslovakia, Japan and China, led to recrimination. The balance of advantage continued in Kenya's favour. In 1970 Kenya's exports to Uganda were worth £16½ million, those of Uganda to Kenya only £10 million; Kenya's exports to Tanzania were worth £14¾ million, those of Tanzania to Kenya only £6 million. Comparatively little trade was done between Uganda and Tanzania. Uganda exports to Tanzania were worth only £2 million and its imports from Tanzania worth even less, £1½ million. However the Community was surviving, apparently the most successful example of inter-regional co-operation in Africa, and a possibility existed that it might be expanded to include some of the neighbouring states.

In former French Africa something was salvaged from the co-operation that had existed in the colonial period. Most of the former French colonies concluded agreements of co-operation with France and most made use of French technical experts, who tended to give an element of uniformity to the policies and administration of the various independent states. When AOF was dissolved in 1959 the former members, with the exception of Guinea, attempted to maintain a customs union (Union douanière entre les États de l'Afrique occidentalé, UDAO), but it failed because of inter-state rivalries and jealousies. It attempted too much and its procedures and machinery were complicated and faulty. It proved to be impossible to establish a common external tariff. The member states were unwilling to relinquish their right to determine their own import taxes in the interest of raising revenue. All were heavily dependent upon such taxation. Direct taxes were more difficult to collect and much less profitable. It even proved to be impossible to achieve free movement of goods among the members: duties were imposed even upon products imported by one member state from another. There was no provision for adequate consultation and no secretariat. There was a Customs Union Committee, but it was too inflexible. The members were unwilling to submit to the decisions handed down by a supranational body. There was no common customs service for the collection of import duties and no proper machinery for redistributing the revenue for the benefit of the less developed members of the Union. Existing arrangements were unsatisfactory.

Four of the former French colonies in West Africa formed a looser union, the Conseil de l'Entente in 1959, Dahomey, the Ivory Coast, Niger and Upper Volta. It was reorganized in 1966 with the addition of Togo. To stabilize revenue it established a solidarity fund into which each state paid a tenth of its budgetary receipts. One-fifth of the total was held in a reserve and the rest distributed among the states in inverse proportion to their contribution. From 1966 it guaranteed external loans contracted by any member and tried to co-ordinate the efforts of the members in promoting development. The Conseil built up considerable reserves, but the association was an uneasy one. There was fear of the domination of the Ivory Coast, and the organization had as much to do with politics as economics. It was founded in rivalry to the proposed (and short-lived) Mali federation of Soudan and Senegal.

In 1966 the UDAO was replaced by the UDEAO, the Union douanière des Etats de l'Afrique de l'Ouest. The idea of an immediate customs union and common market was given up, though it remained an expressed aspiration, and the external tariff varied considerably from country to country according to revenue requirements. The products of one member remained subject to import duties imposed by another for fiscal, and sometimes even for protective, purposes. Although there was supposed to be no other restrictions placed on the free movement of goods produced by the member states themselves, provision was in fact made for the imposition of quotas during emergencies. The only decision-making body was the council of ministers, composed of the finance ministers. It was to meet annually and majority decisions were to be binding. There was also a council of experts, an advisory body of delegates representing the member states and meeting twice yearly. A general secretariat was set up, based at Ouagadougou in Upper Volta. After its formation, however, the UDEAO made little progress towards harmonizing the fiscal policies of its members. It was reported at the meeting of the council of ministers in 1969 that trade among the members had increased by only 1 per cent in the case of imports and 2 per cent in the case of exports. The general secretariat was understaffed and ineffectual. Eventually the 1966 convention broke down.

The four members of the old AEF – the Central African Republic, Chad, Congo-Brazzaville and Gabon – established in 1959 a customs union, the Union douanière équatoriale (UDE), providing for the free movement of goods and capital between member countries, a common external tariff, a solidarity fund and a single tax system. The solidarity fund was made up of contributions from member states and shared between the two less prosperous states, the CAR and Chad. Under the single tax system a tax was levied on the manufactured products of one member state destined for another member state. This tax was to be lower than the import tax upon the comparable product imported from a non-member state and it was paid to the account of the importing country. In 1961 Cameroun became an associate member with separate import duties and taxes. In 1962 the four original member states and Cameroun achieved a common external tariff.

In 1964 a treaty was signed broadening the original customs union into an economic union, the Union douanière et économique de l'Afrique centrale (UDEAC), which came into effect in 1966. In addition to the earlier objectives of the UDE, those of the UDEAC included the establishment of a common customs service, periodically sharing out the revenue collected; the co-ordination of industrial development planning; and the establishment of uniform codes to facilitate the inflow of foreign private investment by means of fiscal and other benefits such as protection, the allocation of foreign exchange, loans and government contracts. To run the Union a council of heads of state was set up, meeting twice yearly, determining general policy and making final decisions in the event of dispute. An executive committee, composed of ministers of finance and ministers in charge of economic development, was to determine the rate of common duties and harmonize industrial projects, development plans and transport facilities. A General Secretariat was situated at Bangui, the capital of the Central African Republic. But the course of the UDEAC did not run smoothly. It was gravely weakened by the withdrawal of Chad in 1968, followed by the departure of the Central African Republic. The two defectors joined with Zaïre (formerly the Belgian Congo) in a new common market, the Union des Etats de l'Afrique centrale, which, however, scarcely survived the departure of the Central African Republic, which decided to return to the UDEAC. The UDEAC survived and was reformed in 1974.

The former French colonies and mandated territories in West and Central Africa became members of the franc zone, and a monetary union was set up in both regions. The West African Monetary Union was composed of seven countries, Togo and all the former colonies except Mali and Guinea, and the Central African Monetary Union had five members, the four ex-colonies together with Cameroun. A common currency, the CFA (Communauté financière africaine) franc, was issued by the Banque centrale des Etats de l'Afrique de l'Ouest (BCEAO) and the Banque centrale des Etats de l'Afrique equatoriale et Cameroun (BCEAEC). These monetary arrangements were criticized on the ground that they gave France virtual control of the money supply and policies of its former colonies. The two central banks had their headquarters in Paris and a substantial proportion of each board of management (*conseil d'administration*) was French, one-third in the case of the BCEAO and a half in the case of the BCEAEC. There were eight French directors of the latter, while Cameroun had four and the other four member states only one each. Even in the BCEAO the French had a veto over all important decisions, since these required the support of three-quarters of the *conseil*. The banks kept their reserves in French francs at the French Treasury. The provision of credit was decided by a national monetary commission in each member state, but it had to conform to the rules and limits determined by the board and the French government was able to punish infractions by withholding loans and aid. There were French representatives even on the national commissions, sometimes constituting a majority. The compensation for this strong French influence was that local currencies had the support of the French Treasury and the African states could within limits overdraw their accounts.

Apart from these unions and associations two other more comprehensive organizations were formed for more general economic co-operation. Firstly, there was the Conference of East and Central African States, which originated in inter-governmental discussions aimed at co-ordinating support for nationalist movements in southern Africa. Its interest subsequently shifted to economic co-operation. In 1967 the Economic Commission for Africa was asked to suggest fields in which economic collaboration was suitable. It was a loose organization, not founded on treaty. Its supreme organ was composed of the heads of state and government, who met annually in conference. Five committees were set up to discuss various sectors of the economy. Secondly, in 1960 the francophone countries set up the Union africaine et malgache (UAM), which, before its dissolution in 1963, formed the Organisation africaine et malgache de Co-opération économique (OAMCE), which was supposed to co-ordinate development plans and aid investment and the free flow of goods. It had no power to enforce common action. In 1965 it was renamed the Organisation commune africaine et malgache (OCAM) with fourteen francophone members, including Zaïre and Rwanda but excluding Guinea. Mauritius joined in 1970. OCAM aimed at economic co-operation and established a development bank. It also aimed at maximizing intra-African trade. The OCAM Sugar Agreement was one of its achievements, but there were few others and there were a number of defections.

Organizations for the development of specific areas included the following:
1. the Organisation of the Senegal River States (OERS), Guinea, Mali, Mauritania and Senegal, which originated in a committee appointed in 1963 with the limited aim of encouraging the joint development of the River Senegal and was set up in 1968 to promote trade and common projects.
2. the Lake Chad Basin Committee, created in 1964 by Cameroun, Chad, Niger and Nigeria to promote the joint utilization of Lake Chad, to co-ordinate efforts for the social and economic development of the

surrounding area, to co-ordinate the development of transport and communications and to eliminate livestock diseases.

3. the Niger River Basin Commission, which was established in 1965 by those countries with interests in the River Niger to ensure the joint development of river navigation and the joint exploitation of the river's resources.

Organizations for specific purposes were of three kinds. The first kind was made up of those concerned with loans, money and banking. The Association of African Central Banks co-ordinated the banking and monetary activities of African states. The African Development Bank, founded in 1964, aimed to raise money entirely from African sources to finance approved development projects. It enjoyed limited success. Member states fell behind with their subscriptions and difficulty was experienced in finding suitable projects to finance.

The second group was composed of those organizations concerned with the production of cash crops – cocoa, coffee, ground-nuts, rice and sugar. The Cocoa Producers' Alliance included Brazil as well as the African producers and aimed at maintaining and stabilizing cocoa prices. Other bodies, notably the Inter-African Coffee Organisation and the African Ground-nut Council, existed merely to exchange information. No effective international co-operation in raising raw material prices emerged before the Organisation of Petroleum Exporting Countries and prices continued to be fixed chiefly by the level of world demand.

The third group was made up of miscellaneous organizations for consultation and collaboration in such matters as the study of endemic diseases, tsetse fly and locust control, siting of industry, ports, civil aviation, post and telecommunications and tourism. Some common services were set up, e.g. Air Afrique, founded in 1961 by the Union africaine et malgache, and the Zambia-Tanzania Rail Link and Road Services; and, finally, from time to time bilateral agreements were made, e.g. governing the supply of electric power and the development of international transport links.

Some co-operation was unofficial and unwelcome, such as the smuggling of goods into neighbouring French-speaking states from Ghana.

African attitudes to international co-operation were ambivalent. Because the chances of successful development were thought to be facilitated by the widening of markets, there were these attempts at co-operation; but the fact that there was at the same time a fear that co-operation substituted a new type of dependence, that of less developed upon more developed, for the old kind, or a reluctance of the stronger economies to subordinate their interests to those of weaker neighbours helps to explain why co-operation was not remarkably successful. Attempts at international co-operation had only the slightest of effects upon the economic and social problems the new states all faced at home. The problems were obvious: how to feed, educate, clothe, shelter and find jobs for a rapidly growing population. Although one of the Malthusian checks upon population had been largely removed (disease), another (famine) became more threatening. Population pressure was relieved slightly by the emigration of Africans to work, mostly as unskilled labourers, in the prosperous industries of Europe, and by the repatriation of European settlers. The numbers of departing settlers were small in relation to the native population, even in the case of Algeria, from which the great majority of Europeans left soon after independence. This relief was purchased by the loss of the skills which the emigrants possessed and which could hardly be made good quickly even with the introduction of facilities for the rapid training of indigenous replacements. The departing colonists took with them a great deal of capital as well, e.g. from Kenya in the early 1960s.

Unemployment became the predominant economic and social problem in independent Africa. The shortage of applicants for wage employment characteristic of the early colonial period had long since ended. A shortage of unskilled labour existed only in South Africa in certain areas and for certain types of work because of the policy known as influx control, i.e. regulating the movement of blacks into towns. Throughout Africa the increase in the number of jobs in fact lagged behind the growth of both output and population. Needless to say, although there was no lack of unskilled labour, the shortage of skilled labour persisted, the result partly of the continued practice of migration, partly of inadequate training facilities.

Although Africa was the least urbanized continent, its town population grew at an accelerating pace because of natural increase and rural emigration. The movement of people from country to town accelerated with independence, partly because of the removal of colonial restrictions upon migration. The urban population of Ivory Coast, one of the more successful countries in maintaining a high economic growth rate, increased from 160 000 in 1950 to 650 000 in 1965. The urban population of Algeria grew at an estimated annual rate of 6,6 per cent during the 1960s, though this was by no means the fastest rate of urban population growth in Africa. A movement of peasants into the towns strained urban amenities to the limit and beyond, and a large, vociferous and riotous urban population presented a threat to public order. Attempts were sometimes made, e.g. in Tanzania and Tunisia, to check the inflow by the expulsion of the unemployed or the destruction of shanties.

Peasants too often moved from underemployment on the land to unemployment in the towns. Employment in industry, large-scale commerce and government service grew slowly, if at all. It is estimated that rather fewer than two million people were in regular industrial employment in tropical Africa in 1960, about 2 per cent of the total labour force. By 1970 the number of industrial workers had grown to only between 2,5 and 2,8 million. Given the increase in population, the percentage of the total labour force remained much the same. At most the industrial work force expanded by 45 per cent in the 1960s, while during the decade manufacturing output increased more than 100 per cent. The United Nations Economic Commission for Africa attributed the disappointing amount of job creation to the following factors.

1. The comparatively small amount of investment. Though some $7 000 million were invested in the 1960s, it represented only about $2 a year for each person.
2. The increasing expense of job creation. The UN estimated that by 1970 it was necessary to invest at least $15 000 to create one additional job.
3. The expansion of highly capital-intensive industry. Petro-chemical plant, aluminium smelters and engineering factories, for example, did not create much direct employment.
4. The increasing productivity of labour. This was partly the result of more inputs of capital, partly the result of increasing efficiency on the part of labour growing more accustomed to industrial work.
5. There were not the people available to set up small businesses using obsolete machinery discarded by large enterprises or providing repair facilities.
6. Many businesses were owned by expatriates who were not interested in job creation and, indeed, preferred techniques that simplified their labour management problems.
7. The increasing cost of labour encouraged economy in its use.
8. The costs of implementing projects in developing Africa were much higher than the costs of establishing similar plant in developed countries, and these costs were increasing constantly.
9. The bias towards the consumption of imported goods among the élite of the newly-independent countries which inherited the salaries as well as the jobs of the departing Europeans.

Despite the surplus of labour that appeared, wages did not fall. Governments and private employers were forced to pay wages much higher than the average income of those engaged in farming and handicrafts. African governments were subject to numerous pressures both urban and regional. Government investment programmes and other economic policies often reflected the interests of groups with the greatest political power rather than those of the majority of the population. Government spending tended to increase the supply of surplus labour in the towns rather than absorb it. Disproportionately high wages were paid to government employees. At the same time the relatively high rate of investment in education resulted in an increase in the number of people seeking non-manual employment in the towns. Rural immigrants attracted by higher urban incomes joined the ranks of the unemployed, went in for petty trading or domestic service or lived off employed relatives. The only solution open to governments was rural development, but that would have required the diversion of resources from industry. Growing social tensions and frustration resulted from urban unemployment and the growing income gap between those in regular industrial employment and the rest of the population, urban and rural. Just as the gap between rich and poor nations inexorably widened, so did the gap between privileged and unprivileged.

One of the reasons for the gap was the strength of the trade unions, which, in the colonial period, achieved for themselves in some countries and some industries a wage structure related, not to the state of the colonial economy, but to the remuneration that could be commanded by expatriates. Where this happened their members constituted a privileged élite. It was particularly noticeable in Zambia, where, at the end of the colonial period, 12 per cent of the 225 000 workers employed in the modern sector of the economy received 50 per cent of the wages paid. The mining industry was so vital for the economy that the mine workers were in a strong bargaining position, able to hold the economy to ransom. The high wages secured in mining then had repercussions upon the wage level in other industries. There were traditionally two separate wage structures in the mining industry. While the wages of expatriates were determined by the wage levels for comparable work elsewhere, plus inducement pay, the wages for Africans were determined by the level of local unskilled wages. The African trade unions demanded the Africanization of employment, at the same time demanding that Africans moving into white jobs be paid white salaries. The situation was made worse by the fact that white salaries were themselves forced up by independence and consequent Africaniza-tion. The Northern Rhodesia Mine Workers Union (renamed the Mine Workers Society in 1964) had to be bribed with higher salaries to accept job fragmentation and to train and make way for Africans. The white union was in a very strong position, since it controlled the supply of indispensable skills. It accepted conversion of permanent employment into fixed-term contracts only in exchange for substantial privileges. Africans taking over white jobs wanted the same wages. That did not meet the approval of the United Nations Economic Survey Mission which in 1964 reported on the economic development of Zambia. It took the view that the existence of a privileged group would prejudice economic progress and political stability. But this view did not commend itself to the Zambian Mine Workers Union (ZMU), which expressed dissatisfaction with the dual wage system and demanded increased wages. Although it won a substantial increase in 1966, it still called a strike shortly after. A commission appointed to inquire into the mining industry rejected the dual wage system in the interests of improved labour relatiohs and criticized the high wages of expatriates on the ground that they were inflationary and damaging to the economy of the country. It recommended new wage rates somewhere between local rates and expatriate rates. Future expatriate employees were to receive the locally determined rates plus inducement allowance.

In Zambia the strength of the black mine workers was reduced somewhat by a split in their ranks. For the Zambian Mine Workers Union was challenged by the Mines African Staff Association, which like its rival, claimed to represent all mine workers. Then within the ZMU there was a further struggle for leadership that was to some extent politically inspired. After independence, as before, the trade union movement was weakened by incompetent leadership and the proneness to internal dissension. Most unions were poor and unable to afford the salaries that men of ability and education could command elsewhere. The Kenya Federation of Labour was £5 000 in debt by 1962–1963 despite a subsidy of £1 000 a month from the International Confederation of Free Trade Unions. In Zambia union leaders tended to lose control over their own membership and wild-cat strikes were common. The typical trade union tended to be small and weak. Generally the trade union movement was narrowly based, largely confined to the towns and displaying a tendency to fragment. Fragmentation was sometimes due to ideological splits and the intrusion of international politics, namely the cold war between the ICFTU and the communist World Federation of Trade Unions. In Nigeria two national organizations existed, the left-wing Nigerian Trade Union Congress, which was supported by the WFTU and the right-wing Trade Union Congress of Nigeria, supported by the ICFTU and the American labour movement. Attempts at reunification in the 1960s were short-lived. In Liberia, Sierra Leone and East Africa the unions were affiliated to the International Confederation. This was so also in the case of Senegal, where the influence of the socialist Force Ouvrière was still felt, and of Madagascar, French Equatorial Africa and Zaïre, where confessional unions were strong.

After independence there was a tendency for the trade unions to clash with the government and dominant party, which did not like their pursuit of sectional interests or their persistent internal dissensions. Although governments and parties were reluctant to quarrel with them because of the prestige which they had acquired in the cause of African nationalism, sometimes, indeed, supplying the very personnel of the new independent government, and because of the pressures they were able to exert, especially the unions of government employees and of the employees in the important occupations, such as railways and harbours or mining, tension there was and a fundamental divergence of interest and aim. Under colonial rule the split did not appear because pressure upon colonial governments and expatriate employers was compatible with the nationalist struggle for independence, but when, contrary to expectations, economic and social problems were not solved by political independence, trade unions were troubled by divided loyalties, to the nation as a whole and to their own special interests.

Broadly speaking there were three views on the rôle of the trade unions in the independent states. One, expressed by Tom Mboya, himself a trade unionist who had entered the Kenyan government as minister of labour, was current in the anglophone countries, where the influence of the more pragmatic approach of British trade unionism was felt. Unions, it was argued, should, now that independence had been gained, remain aloof from politics, concerning themselves primarily with the defence of the economic and social interests of their members, but none the less recognizing their duty to promote long-term economic development. Sekou Touré, on the other hand, who had risen to power in Guinea through the industrial labour movement, took the view that a political rôle for the trade union movement remained, a part in the struggle against neo-colonialism and imperialism, and that it should submerge itself into a greater unity. The former view was more tolerant of a decentralized organization of the trade union movement, once again in accordance with British trade union practice; the latter required a united, centralized movement working in close collaboration with the government. A third view was that held by radical trade unions operating in opposition to conservative or, at least, non-socialist governments, the view that their task was to bring about a far-reaching change of society in the interests of egalitarianism.

The relationship between the labour movement and the state ranged from cordial, if short-lived, co-operation through various degrees of conflict to outright confrontation resulting in either the captivity of the trade unions or the overthrow of the government. The situation was in constant flux as governments changed or simply changed their policy. In Morocco after independence the chief trade union federation, the Union Marocaine du Travail (UMT), which was affiliated to the governing party, the Istiqlal, supported the government of Muhammed V, working for increased national production, and was rewarded by being consulted and gaining for its members legal and social benefits. When, however, Istiqlal split and Muhammed V died, the new king, Hassan II, based his government upon his personal adherents and adopted a much more conservative policy, abandoning, for example, schemes of land reform and social security proposed by Istiqlal. The UMT increased its membership, in particular by extending its activities to agricultural labourers and, excluded from the counsels of the government, became much more militant. In 1961 the number of man-days lost through strikes were two and a half times as much as they had been in 1960. By 1965 the trade unions and the government were in open conflict. In March of that year at demonstrations staged by students and trade unionists in Casablanca and other cities, police and soldiers opened fire, killing and wounding hundreds of people. Large-scale arrests and imprisonment followed.

In the Sudan the trade unions, or at least those representing the majority of trade unionists, engaged in a running battle with the government from independence onwards. The Sudan Workers Trade Union Federation (SWTUF), of left-wing persuasion, in the first years of independence had to fight to preserve its existence, then in 1958, when a military coup d'état overthrew the government, was, in common with the entire trade union movement, suppressed, several of its leaders being arrested and imprisoned. In 1960 the government permitted trade unions to function once again, though under severe restrictions imposed by the Trade Union Ordinance (Amendment) Act, which prohibited the federation of unions, the formation of any union except where more than 50 workers were employed in the same firm, and the organization of white-collar workers and government employees, and which required government registration of all unions. Since about half of all wage earners worked for enterprises employing fewer than 50 workers and the other excluded groups were substantial, the majority of workers were deprived of the right to join trade unions. In 1961 an anti-government strike of railway workers brought only slight concessions but in 1964 a repetition forced the military government to accept a return to civilian rule. In the ensuing elections a conservative government was elected and the trade unions found themselves in opposition again.

In Kenya the relations between unions and government were much less bitter, though even here Tom Mboya threatened in 1962 to take away their right to strike. The secretary-general of the Kenya Federation of Labour ran as an independent candidate against the nominees of the government party, the Kenya African National Union. In Zambia in 1967 the government issued the Preservation of Public Security Regulations making it an offence to withdraw labour in the mines. Union leaders were torn between a desire to respond to the government's plea for wage restraint and higher productivity and the desire to satisfy their members. These tended to look for support to local officials of the governing party, the United National Independence Party, rather than to trade union officials, thus further reducing their authority. Trade union officials complained about the failure of the government to consult them in formulating economic policy. In Tanganyika there was a series of strikes following independence, culminating in a railway strike in February 1962. The government felt that trade union action was a threat to economic development. An Act was passed outlawing strikes and lock-outs except in certain circumstances. Union leaders were placed in restriction. In January 1964 there was an army mutiny and the government took advantage of its suppression to deal with the trade unions once and for all. It dissolved the Tanganyika Labour Federation and its affiliated unions and set up a new government-controlled union affiliated to the dominant political party, the Tanganyika African National Union. In some of the former French colonies the UGTAN was generally too radical and revolutionary for many new African governments. In the Ivory Coast in 1959 there was a particularly violent clash between the government and the trade unions. In 1959 a government-controlled trade union was established and made responsible for all workers in the country. Similarly in Senegal a national union was established firmly under the control of the dominant political party. Even in Guinea friction occurred between the unions and the government. The economic policies of the latter led to inflationary price rises and union discontent. In 1962 the government imposed greater restrictions upon trade union activity.

More than one government was brought down through trade union recalcitrance (e.g. in Congo-Brazzaville, Dahomey and Upper Volta) and sometimes replaced by a military régime called in by trade unions able to destroy the politicians but unable to take their place. Not everywhere, however, was the trade union movement able to make the government dance to its tune. In some countries the trade unions were defeated in a trial of strength and incorporated into the machinery of the one-party state (e.g. Ghana, Guinea) or, at least, compelled, as in Kenya and Tunisia, to accept arbitration as a necessary solution to industrial disputes.

The best construction that could be placed on the motives of governments unable to tolerate free trade unions was that they were impatient of obstacles in the way of economic progress. Most nationalist leaders, Afrikaner as well as Arab or African, shared a determination to foster economic development, in particular to promote industrialization, thought to be the key to economic independence, wealth and power. It was

supposed that that required far-reaching state intervention in the economy. Even in South Africa, to appearances a typical market economy,
the rôle of the state was of great importance, although the pursuit of
development was inseparable from the implementation of a racial ideology. Such a mixture of political and social dogmatism with economic
objectives was found throughout Africa. Only the dogma varied. Some
states attempted to set off down the road pioneered by the USSR,
following a policy of extensive nationalization of industrial, commercial
and financial undertakings and the collectivization of agriculture, but not
necessarily subscribing to Marxist-Leninist socialism. In 1960 Algeria
nationalized foreign-owned mines, land abandoned by departing Europeans and the insurance companies. The great mining companies were
commonly nationalized, criticized on the ground that they were a state
within a state and contributed nothing to the economic development of the
countries in which they operated. Throughout a large part of Africa the
received ideology, while tending to reject capitalism, frequently embraced
a kind of socialism which was thought to conform with either Arab or
African traditions and provide a genuine alternative to European ideo-
logies, considered inappropriate to Africa. The proponents of Arab
socialism were mostly young radical army officers, Gamal Abdel Nasser in
Egypt, Muammar Gadaffi in Libya and Jaafar Nimeiry in Sudan, the last
two moving to power as the result of coups d'état in 1969. Their
instrument was the Revolutionary Command Council, their policy nationalization of foreign assets and internal reform. They were firmly anti-
communist, though not necessarily unwilling to receive help and support
from the USSR, and sometimes savage persecutors of local communist
parties, e.g. in Sudan after an abortive communist uprising against
President Nimeiry in 1971.

   To some extent African socialism was a logical continuation of anti-
colonial ideas and was permeated by pan-African ideals, though it was
rejected as unscientific by some of the most important nationalist leaders,
Kwame Nkrumah, Sekou Touré and Mobido Keita. It aimed to avoid
what were thought to be the mistakes of both capitalism and communism
and make use of the best elements of traditional society, which was thought
to have pronounced socialist features – communal land ownership,
egalitarianism and co-operation in the performance of social obligations. It
was virtually unknown before the 1960s. The first attempt at defining its
content was made at a conference in Dakar in 1962. It was not attended by
much success and African socialism remained somewhat amorphous, the
product of ideas thrown out by African leaders, not a consistent body of
thought. It meant different things in different places. Nevertheless, certain
common characteristics emerged. There was a strong hostility to élitism,

disapproval of those who took advantage of their superior education, talents or opportunities to pursue their own selfish interests without thought for the welfare of the majority. Self-reliance was another feature, a desire to make do as far as possible without foreign grants and loans. Yet implicitly there was the intention to promote economic development. Inevitably this led to an emphasis upon public planning and investment. African entrepreneurs were a subject of distrust, because, it was thought, they would introduce an element of selfishness and greed. Indeed, private investment from abroad was less unwelcome to some than native private enterprise, because it was assumed to be less dangerous. But all private investment should, it was argued, come under state control.

African socialists were anxious that the economic development so much desired should not disturb communal harmony. The aim was the preservation of a classless society and avoidance of extremes of wealth and poverty in the interests of ensuring post-independence national unity and common endeavour. African socialism should, it was thought, hold out hope to those whose economic condition had not been improved by the ending of colonialism. It rejected individualism and, while stressing the traditional subordination of the individual to the group, sought to enlarge the boundaries of group loyalty beyond the clan and locality to encompass the nation. Large-scale economic enterprise was held in suspicion because it was thought to be socially divisive and destructive of personal satisfaction in the exercise of a craft, subverting the communal spirit whatever form of ownership, whether state or private, was adopted. It might be added that no African government, whether it thought of itself as pursuing African socialism or not, was likely to admit that it was not aiming at equitable distribution of income, however glaring economic differences actually were.

Nowhere was African socialism taken more seriously than in Tanzania, independent in 1961, a one-party state in 1963 and composed from 1964 of two parts, Tanganyika and Zanzibar, following a revolution in the latter. The socialism of Tanzania was elaborated in a number of policy statements issued by the Tanganyika African National Union and President Nyerere from 1962 onwards, especially the Arusha Declaration of 1967. Its positive content seemed small, its chief component a collection of moral precepts. Socialism was seen, not as a particular organization of society, but as an absence of exploitation, as hard work, self-reliance, selflessness, co-operation and equality. All party and government officials were exhorted to be workers or peasants, which, for practical purposes, meant to refrain from becoming company directors, shareholders or landowners. More practical proposals were advanced in the realm of agriculture. But in time other features of Tanzanian socialism emerged. These included

deportation of urban unemployed to the countryside and state participation in commerce, industry and banking. In 1967 some enterprises were
nationalized, banks, insurance companies and export-import firms and a
60 per cent state interest obtained in others. Rural socialism clearly did not
preclude industrialization, economic planning and foreign investment.
Like all other African states after independence Tanzania adopted comprehensive planning as a means to rapid economic development.

For most African states, even the most conservative, national planning
was the continuation of the struggle for independence transposed from the
political to the economic plane. It was encouraged by the United Nations,
which, in declaring the 1960s the First Development Decade, set as a
minimum objective a 5 per cent annual growth rate of GDP. Optimism
abounded. There was not uncommonly a belief, explicitly stated in the
Tanzanian plan, that post-colonial development was a relatively simple
process, a question of identifying 'structural deficiencies in the economic
and social fields', with the prospect of 'relatively rapid growth once the
impediments of a structural nature' were eliminated. The 1960s were the
golden age of the economic planner. Even South Africa had its Economic
Planning Office of the Prime Minister, which issued regular Economic
Development Programmes to encourage investment in such a way as to
bring about balanced growth. Most other African governments had very
comprehensive plans covering a period of years.

AFRICAN DEVELOPMENT PLANS AND PROGRAMMES

North Africa

Algeria	1963-1964 (capital expenditure programme)
Libya	1963-1968
Morocco	1965-1967
Sudan	1961/1962-1970/1971
Tunisia	1962-1964, 1965-1968
Egypt	1963-1965, 1965-1970

Eastern Africa

Burundi	None
Ethiopia	1958-1962, 1963-1967, 1968-1972
Kenya	1957-1960 (abandoned), 1965/1966-1969/1970
Madagascar	1960-1962, 1964-1968
Malawi	1962-1965, 1965-1969
Rhodesia	1965-1968
Rwanda	1964-1970
Somalia	1963-1967

Uganda	1966-1971
Tanzania	1961/1962-1963/1964, 1964/1965-1969/1970
Zambia	1965, 1966-1970

West Africa

Dahomey	1962-1965, 1966-1970
Gambia	1967/1968-1970/1971
Ghana	1957-1958, 1959-1964, 1963/1964-1969/1970 (abandoned)
Guinea	1960-1963, 1964-1970
Ivory Coast	1962-1963, 1965-1969
Liberia	None
Mali	None
Mauritania	1960-1962
Niger	1961-1963, 1965-1968
Nigeria	1962-1968
Senegal	1961-1964, 1965-1969
Sierra Leone	1962/1963-1971/1972
Togo	1966-1970
Upper Volta	1963-1967, 1967-1970

Central Africa

Cameroun	1966-1971
Central Af. Rep.	1960-1962, 1967-1970
Chad	1964-1965, 1966-1970
Congo-Brazzaville	1961-1964, 1964-1968
Congo-Leopoldville	1965-1969
Gabon	1963-1965 (abandoned), 1966-1970

Southern Africa

Botswana	1963-1969
Lesotho	None
South Africa	1964-1969

(Source: Secretariat of the Economic Commission for Africa, 'Development planning and economic integration in Africa', *Journal of Development Planning*, 1, 1969, p. 108.)

The results of the plans were disappointing. Although Africa did achieve its 5 per cent annual increase of GDP in real terms, there were disquietening features in this achievement. Growth was won largely by expanding exports of primary products, with few signs of greater economic diversification, and it barely kept ahead of growth of population. Performance varied, with some economies coming near to collapse, e.g. in Guinea and Ghana. In the late 1960s in only seven countries was annual per capita income higher than $200, in fifteen less than $70. Political readjustment after decolonization was partly to blame. But there was some disillusionment with planning itself, though implementation was perhaps rather the culprit. Drawn up often by foreign experts with a high degree of sophistication, plans were frequently either ignored or implemented for a short time, then replaced by new ones or constantly changed or only nominally put into operation. They were subject to political pressures and interdepartmental rivalries and excessively optimistic about the funds available to support them. At best they drew attention to problems and suggested possible solutions and desirable projects. It was sometimes alleged that they were remote from, and meaningless to, the mass of the population or even the civil service and the dominant party, ignoring non-economic factors of importance. Foreign economists worked in a vacuum, with little contact with politicians or administrators, assuming that what they themselves thought desirable was the preference of the people whose future they were planning. Governments lacked data and the ability to carry out plans of great complexity, especially when these coincided with a policy of rapid Africanization, itself disruptive because it introduced into high positions men lacking proper experience or even training. Given the resources available many plans were over-ambitious, attempting too much too quickly, though only modest given the growth of population and the growing expectations of newly independent people. Six countries in the 1960s were anticipating per capita GDP growth rates of between 2 per cent and 3 per cent, five of between 3 per cent and 4 per cent, seven of between 4 per cent and 5 per cent and four of more than 5 per cent. Nor did they aim only at growth. They sometimes had egalitarian objectives as well, aiming at the transformation of society and perhaps expropriation of foreign and domestic businesses.

Most development plans were based on an assumption of substantial foreign investment, especially investment in the public sector, though there were considerable variations. Much hope was put in foreign aid, though the attitude of Third World countries to aid was ambivalent. 'Trade not aid' was the *cri de coeur* of the 1960s, expressing a belief that the primary producers were victims of discrimination. Implicit was a certain distrust of foreign aid. At the same time there was criticism that aid was inadequate and declining. Certainly from the end of the 1960s it fell in real terms, partly because of disillusionment with its effectiveness experienced by western governments beset with fiscal problems of increasing difficulty and less able to justify it to their electorates and partly because of depreciation of the currencies of the industrial nations.

Aid took a variety of forms, determined to some extent by the receiving country's level of development. Most was in the form of loans with considerable variations in the period of repayment – from a few years to fifty or a hundred years. Interest rates also varied widely. The loan might be repayable in foreign currency or in local currency. Aid might be outright grants or take the form of technical assistance. It might be made available through single donors or a number acting together or through international agencies. In 1961 donor countries set up consultative machinery, the Development Assistance Committee, to introduce a measure of co-ordination. By the end of the 1960s over $3 000 million were being granted annually in aid in one form or another. But it was subjected to much hostile criticism. It was suggested that much aid was ineffective on the ground that it was given in an *ad hoc* way without regard to overall needs, allocated according to the political or commercial advantage of the donors. Undoubtedly little foreign aid was entirely disinterested. Ulterior motives ranged from providing industry in the donor country with guaranteed orders, where aid was conditional upon the purchase of goods and materials from that country instead of the cheapest and most suitable source, to a desire to support a particular region politically or secure its political support. Aid was sometimes motivated by a wish to off-load surplus products or to establish a sphere of influence or to corner a market. Some argued that it was desirable to channel all aid through international agencies, but there was no evidence that it was more wisely administered in that way than through bilateral arrangements.

Africa became somewhat less dependent upon capital imports, notably those countries with oil revenues, Libya and Algeria and, to a smaller extent, Nigeria. In the 1950s non-African sources of capital accounted for over half Africa's total capital formation. By 1970 this had fallen to 20 per cent. By 1972 gross capital formation in developing Africa in real terms as a percentage of GDP reached, though with wide variations from country to country, 19 per cent compared with 17 per cent in 1960. But in many African countries at least half the investment in the public sector came from abroad. Dependence upon foreign capital was not unique in the history of development. The United States in the 19th century developed with the help of European capital. None the less, African countries were more heavily dependent than most on foreign help. Private consumption in Africa took a larger share of GDP than was the case in the rest of the Third World. Though declining in the 1960s, it was still some 65 per cent in the early 1970s. Africa was also exceptional in the amount of technical aid it received. Something like 80 000 experts, many of them teachers, and volunteers were working in Africa, half of them in sub-Saharan Africa.

The biggest donor to Africa was France, which gave to its former colonies. Its aid averaged 0,6 per cent of its GNP. Britain was the second most important donor, giving chiefly to former colonies. The USA began to aid Africa after independence, but a good deal of American aid reached Africa before that through assistance to Europe for post-war reconstruction. Initially the Americans gave impartially to all African states, but after the mid-1960s their aid was directed according to three criteria – the need of the recipient, its effective use and the amount of political support to the United States in the Cold War. Algeria, Ethiopia, Liberia, Morocco, Nigeria, Tunisia, Libya and Zaïre were the chief beneficiaries, though grants and loans to Algeria and Libya tailed off towards the end of the 1960s. Total US government grants and credits to Africa fluctuated, $180 million in 1960, rising to $412 million in 1966 and falling in 1970 to $275 million. These sums represented a relatively small fraction of total American aid to developing countries, $3 208 million in 1970. Soviet bloc aid to Africa was comparable with the American. The amount varied: $870 million in 1964, less than $60 million in some years in the 1960s. It concentrated upon a few selected countries – Ghana, Guinea, Ethiopia, Mali, Somalia and Tunisia. China gave aid to the Algerian nationalists and subsequently to Guinea, Mali, Somalia and Tanzania. By far its biggest aid project was a railway linking the Zambian Copper Belt with Dar es Salaam (the Tan-Zam Railway). Aid also came from West Germany, Sweden, the Netherlands, Canada and Israel. In the 1960s West Germany spent about DM14 000 million on development aid. A further DM1 000 million was given in military aid, which at that period accounted for most of its arms exports. But in 1965 the West German government decided against supplying arms to areas of tension and after that military aid dwindled.

The most important source of multilateral aid was the EEC, chiefly in the form of grants, the rest as either soft loans through the European Development Fund or ordinary loans through the European Investment Bank. The bulk of the aid was earmarked for capital investment, the balance for assisting the cheaper production of agricultural goods, agricultural diversification, price stabilization measures and technical assistance. The associated states were dissatisfied with the way in which aid was allocated during the period of the first Yaoundé Convention and, during negotiations in 1968–1969 for its renewal, the eighteen demanded increased aid, complaining that during the first five-year period only 4 per cent of European Development Fund investments had gone into industrial projects and that not enough had been done to promote self-sufficiency in agriculture and to train technical personnel. Furthermore too much of the aid took the form of loans rather than grants, and the Development Fund took too long to get approved projects started. $1 500 million were demanded for the next five years, $1 000 million the amount finally granted. France and Germany contributed about one-third each of the money made available. The aid programme for 1964–1969 worked out at about 0,1 per cent of the combined GDP of the members.

Another important international donor was the World Bank. Its early loans were chiefly to Europe for post-war reconstruction, but in the 1960s its loans to the Third World greatly increased. In 1966 loans to Africa totalled $1 224 million. Most of the money was provided by the United States and critics claimed that the Bank was too much under American influence. Under its first president, Eugene Black, the Bank's policy was high interest rates, investment only in private enterprises and unwillingness to invest in agricultural schemes owing to the difficulties of supervision and the higher risks involved. Policy became more liberal under the second president, George Woods.

The Bank was organized into three sections.

1. The International Bank for Reconstruction and Development (IBRD), the original and principal section, established in 1945, had over a hundred members, Yugoslavia the only communist one. It made loans on a standard commercial basis, with high interest rates, and obtained its money chiefly by borrowing on the international money markets and to a lesser extent from members' subscriptions.
2. The International Finance Corporation (IFC) invested in private undertakings either by making loans at commercial rates or by acquiring shares.
3. The International Development Association (IDA) was established in 1960 to make very long term loans at nominal interest rates ($\frac{3}{4}$ per cent), but was sometimes hampered by lack of funds.

Planners had extravagant expectations of foreign capital and too sanguine hopes of a high level of domestic saving. Aims did not take enough notice of the realities of the situation and money was sometimes lavished on projects for prestige rather than real national benefit – a charge commonly made against Nkrumah. Many countries got hopelessly into debt. It was estimated that debt charges amounted to 26 per cent of gross inflow of capital into Africa in 1966 and 53 per cent in 1975. The extravagance of Nkrumah was partly responsible for his overthrow by a military coup d'état in 1966. Poor countries pressed for a lightening of their debt burdens. The attitude of the creditors was ambivalent, on the one hand reluctant to accept what they regarded as an undesirable principle, on the other not wholly unsympathetic to the plight of debt-ridden countries.

Independent African states were forced to grapple with the same problems that had beset colonial administrators, the excessive dependence upon exports of a limited range of primary products. In 1965 six primary products - petroleum, copper, cotton, coffee, cocoa and ground-nuts - accounted for 52 per cent of African exports, and the dependence of individual countries upon one, two or three products was notorious. A quarter of all African countries were still substantially dependent upon one major export staple and another quarter upon two. These earnings were in some cases supplemented by tourism (Moçambique, Kenya), taxes on the earnings of migrant labour (Moçambique, Malawi, Lesotho) and the profits of transit traffic (Kenya, Moçambique).

The railways, ports and cities were oriented towards foreign trade flows and the needs of production for export. A large proportion of GNP was exported - 33 per cent in the case of Ivory Coast, 40 per cent in the case of Zambia, 50 per cent in the case of Liberia and 25 per cent in the case of Senegal and Cameroun. The days when specialization in the export of primary produce would lead to development seemed long passed. Before the First World War such specialization may well have maximized benefits and trade may have been the 'engine of growth' in underdeveloped countries. There was a rapid growth in world trade in food and industrial crops at that time because of growing population and increasing industrialization in Europe. Yet it is doubtful whether all round development has ever followed from foreign demand for primary products. Australia, New Zealand and Argentina, all primary product exporters, experienced considerable growth until the Second World War, but not much development of manufacturing.

So many primary products in Africa came from enclaves dominated by foreign capital. As foreign firms were dedicated firstly to the interests of their shareholders and employees, they were uninterested in the rounded development of the countries in which their subsidiaries operated or even in their political stability. The aluminium smelter run by the Kaiser Corporation in Ghana processed imported ore, though there were large local deposits of bauxite. It took advantage of the cheap electricity afforded by the Volta River scheme, the cost of which contributed to Ghana's economic plight in 1966 and the overthrow of Dr. Nkrumah. Bauxite was brought from Guinea, the development of which would have been better served by local smelting. The activities of foreign firms like Kaiser tended to be isolated from the rest of the economy either economically or geographically or both. There were few forward linkages, as products were mostly exported in a raw state. It was not normally to the interest of expatriate firms to process minerals before export, with the result that African countries gained little from value added to their natural resources when they were exploited. There were few backward linkages, as machinery, if any was used at all, was imported because there was no African machine-tool industry. Profits were exported as dividends to foreign shareholders, and managerial and technical personnel were expatriate and their income was spent either on imports or repatriated. The only influences from the enclave were the low wages paid to unskilled labour, the rent of the land used and export taxes and royalties. A classic example of unbalanced growth was Liberia. Here there was an independent country where foreign concessions secured an enormous growth in primary production exports with only slight benefits for the economy as a whole. Independent African governments could perhaps have derived greater advantage from enclaves if they had exerted enough pressure, but their power to do so was probably greater in theory than in practice.

The independent African states relied overwhelmingly upon taxes on trade for their revenue, as much as 60 per cent in the case of Uganda, which depended particularly heavily upon export taxes. In Ghana cocoa alone accounted for 25 per cent of government revenue. Government income, like export earnings, was unstable because of dependence on particular commodities and perhaps only a single trading partner. Although this was not universal and not all countries showed a marked earning instability, undoubtedly some commodities were highly volatile in their earnings. Their prices fluctuated wildly. Economic development could be jeopardized in the event of concentration upon unstable commodities, such as sisal. In such circumstances a budget could be badly affected. Above all there was the long-term deterioration in the terms of trade for primary products exchanged against manufactured goods.

For the most part there was expansion in primary production for export. Tanzania in its first decade of independence doubled or more than doubled its production of cotton, coffee and pyrethrum and trebled its production of sisal. In spite of that, exports at the end of that decade were worth only 73 per cent more than they had been at the beginning. Moreover, there was a sharp decline in the price of sisal in 1965. Similarly Uganda was sensitive to the volatility of coffee prices and its cotton output was disturbed by climatic factors. Fluctuations in copper prices had a severe effect on the economies of Zaïre and Zambia.

Primary producers were trapped. The more prices fell, the more they produced, and the more they produced, the more prices fell. While primary products were becoming cheaper, industrial products were growing more expensive in spite of a vast increase in industrial productivity. It is estimated that at least half as much primary produce again, as a century earlier, was needed by the 1960s to buy the same amount of manufactured goods. The benefits of increased productivity were passed on to capital in the form of increased profits and to labour in the form of increased wages, but not shared with the poor countries. The primary producers were largely dependent upon the markets of the industrialized countries. There the demand for tropical food was inelastic and the demand for industrial raw materials did not rise as rapidly as incomes. While the value added to raw materials by manufacturing increased all the time, the raw material component in total costs decreased. There was a tendency in the industrial countries for the proportion of income spent on services to increase and that spent on manufacturing to decrease, thus causing a decline in relative expenditure on raw materials. The purchase of the latter was also threatened by technological improvements that economized on their use and by the introduction of synthetic substitutes. The upshot was that a growth of 5 per cent a year in the industrialized countries meant an increased demand for African products in the order of $2\frac{1}{2}$ to 3 per cent, and a growth rate of that size was cancelled out by the growth of population. Per capita GNP thus remained the same and the income gap between poor countries and industrial ones tended to widen at an accelerating pace. It was therefore difficult to pin hopes on to trade as an 'engine of growth'.

For these reasons those newly-independent African countries which thought of themselves as progressive and socialist, put their trust in industrialization as the source of future prosperity and economic independence. Industry was to be the means by which the social structure and attitudes were to be altered in the interests of economic development. It was thought that the demand of industry for foodstuffs, raw materials and labour would have a stimulating effect upon agriculture, and the higher incomes of the farmers would in turn enlarge the market for manufactures and provide the savings for further investment. Socialist countries naturally saw a much greater rôle for the state in the economy and attached importance to comprehensive planning. They included Tanzania, Guinea, Ghana and Uganda in black Africa and Tunisia and Egypt (then the United Arab Republic) in Arab Africa. Uganda assigned an important rôle to the Uganda Development Corporation, not only because it preferred state action, but also because private enterprise in the past had concentrated its attention much more on Kenya. Egypt had probably the most purposeful industrialization policy, with tariff protection for industry, financial incentives and state enterprise. Private enterprise was distrusted because it was thought to be responsible for maldistribution of income and because it was so frequently foreign. Colonial government seemed to have shown that industrialization would never take place spontaneously and without state encouragement; and yet it bequeathed a tradition and apparatus of state intervention: state-controlled and state-run transport systems, rudimentary planning, marketing boards, etc. None of the instruments of government intervention, however unpopular they may have been under colonial rule, especially marketing boards, was discarded by the successor states. Given the shortage of capital, entrepreneurial skill and infrastructure, governments thought themselves compelled to act. The question was not whether the state would be involved, but the degree of its involvement, and that was determined largely on political or ideological grounds. There was large-scale expropriation of private business, which took the form of outright nationalization or state participation in private companies.

That was not the universal view. Kenya was disposed to favour private enterprise both from choice and from its experience of considerable private investment in the colonial period, which it had no reason to suppose would not continue. Some African countries were content to leave foreign enterprise alone or even, e.g. in the case of the Ivory Coast, Kenya, Ethiopia, Cameroun, to encourage it as much as possible; and to give priority to agriculture (e.g. Kenya, Senegal) or infrastructure (e.g. Nigeria) rather than manufacturing. The first stage (1960–1965) of the Ivory Coast ten year development plan concentrated on increasing the volume of traditional agricultural exports in order to earn foreign exchange and extract higher savings from farmers for public investment in infrastructure and agriculture. The second stage (1965–1970) sought to diversify agricultural exports and raise the value added content of exports by carrying processing further. Proclamations of socialist principles did not necessarily mean dogmatic socialism in practice. For all its socialist proclivities, the Republic of the Congo (Congo-Brazzaville) did not disturb foreign private enterprise. His ideological protestations did not prevent President Sekou Touré of Guinea from giving a free hand to foreign interests exploiting bauxite deposits. Despite President Nkrumah's similar leanings towards 'scientific socialism', which led him to the commencement of a number of development projects with the help of China, the USSR and eastern European states, subsequently abandoned when he was overthrown, he co-operated with multi-national corporations.

African countries varied very widely in the industrial legacy that they inherited from their colonial past and in their industrial potential, which depended, not only on their existing industrial structure, but also upon resource endowment, size of the internal market and the state of their infrastructure, and these factors influenced policy as much as ideological commitment. National differences also sprang from the amount of import substitution already developed. In most countries there was still plenty of scope for simple consumer's goods industries; in others the limit of that sort of development was soon met or had already been reached. Egypt, Morocco, Tunisia, Kenya and Congo-Leopoldville already had a great

deal of light industry and for further advances private investment could
not be depended on. In several countries which were avowedly not socialist
or were only nominally so, the government went in for state enterprise
simply to promote industrial diversification or it nationalized (or transferred the ownership of) foreign enterprises to prevent the export of capital
or to ensure Africanization of management. Morocco in its plan of 1960-
1964 aimed to diversify its existing industrial base by introducing an iron
and steel industry and developing its engineering and chemical industries.
Tunisia's second development plan of 1965-1968 assumed a considerable
diversification and state intervention. The Ivory Coast had a high rate of
state expenditure (up to about 20 per cent of GDP in the early 1960s), a
considerable public sector (railways, ports, palm oil processing) and a wish
to advance industry. In Ethiopia the state was dominant in banking and,
from 1970, in insurance, and it had shares in a range of enterprises. In
Congo-Leopoldville the assets of the Union minière du Haut Katanga
were taken over by the state in 1967. In Kenya, though direct state
participation remained limited, the government introduced a measure of
control in important sectors, such as banking and oil refining. Africanization was a particularly powerful force there. The transfer of white land to
black ownership and, in general, the fostering of indigenous capitalism
were important features of government policy.

There was significant industrial growth in the 1960s. This was not only
due to state action. In the first flush of independence international
companies were willing to invest in African manufacturing. The United
Africa Company, for example, which had hitherto supplemented its
primarily commercial interest only with planting and timber extraction,
branched out into industry, and by the end of the decade it owned, wholly
or partly, or acted as agent for, a large number of industrial enterprises.
The industrial output of developing Africa in 1969 was worth $11 900
million, compared with an output worth $2 771 million in 1950 (at
constant prices). Some countries made determined efforts to reduce
imports of consumer's goods in the interest of purchasing more capital
goods. In Tanzania, for example, the proportion of imports composed of
consumer's goods fell from 45 per cent to 9 per cent between 1961 and 1970
and the share of capital goods rose from 31 per cent to 53 per cent.
Domestic production of manufactured goods in Africa grew at an annual
compound rate of 8,5 per cent from 1950 to 1969. $3 000 million were
invested in the 1950s and $7 000 million in the 1960s, and industrialization
was no longer confined to small and medium-sized enterprises. By the end
of the 1960s at least six enterprises under construction or recently
completed required an investment of more than $100 million each. The
expansion of output was accompanied by considerable diversification and

by the end of the 1960s industries included oil refining, manufacture of petro-chemicals, metallurgy (with small iron and steel mills in Tunisia, Rhodesia, Kenya and Uganda), heavy engineering and vehicle assembling and the manufacture of tyres, textiles, cement and various consumer's goods, including processed foodstuffs, textiles and shoes. Increases in the output of textiles, beer and cement were particularly great and an increasing number of countries was engaged in their production, though Africa still imported half its textiles and its own production was mostly cotton. There was also a rapid expansion of the clothing industry, though the average unit of production remained small. The brewing of beer became almost universal throughout Africa, which became virtually self-sufficient in its production. Output rose from 3,6 million hectolitres in 1960 to 8 million hectolitres in 1970. There were three oil refineries in Africa in 1950, 18 at the end of 1966 and 26 in 1970. The output of petroleum products, estimated at nearly 5 million metric tons in 1961, rose to nearly 20 million in 1968, though many refineries were small, serving only small local markets and little refined petrol was exported except from North Africa. A large volume of agricultural produce was processed and pro-cessing was carried further, especially in cocoa and chocolate in West Africa, sisal in Kenya and Tanzania, cashew nuts in Kenya and Tanzania and wood pulp in West, Central and East Africa.

There was throughout Africa an appreciable increase in the production of power. Tunisia, for example, increased its output from 144 million kilowatt hours in 1961 to 380 million in 1971. Next to liquid fuels the most important source of energy was hydro-electricity. The initial investment was much greater than with thermal generation but the production costs were considerably lower. It is estimated that in 1970, 65 per cent of electricity produced in the developing countries of Africa came from hydro-electric power stations. There was a rapid growth of hydro-electricity production after 1965. Important projects came into operation or increased their production during the 1960s, including the Volta River (Ghana). The Volta River scheme, though envisaged as early as the 1920s and its possibilities investigated just after the war, was very much the child of Dr. Nkrumah. Altogether £50 million was invested by the United States government and American private interests (especially the Kaiser Cor-poration) and a loan was obtained from the World Bank in 1960. The work began in 1963 and the project was inaugurated in 1966. Power was supplied to the Kaiser Corporation's smelter at Tema on the coast near Accra and to the towns of southern Ghana, as well as exported to Togo and Dahomey (Benin) after 1971. A lake of nearly 8 500 square kilometres formed behind the dam, giving birth to an important fish industry. Agriculturally the scheme was rather less successful. 80 000 people had to be resettled owing to the flooding of their homes and the resettlement schemes encountered considerable difficulties.

Other hydro-electric schemes in Africa were the Aswan High Dam (Egypt), Kainji (Nigeria), which was completed in 1969, Kariba (Rhodesia and Zambia), Edea (Cameroun), chiefly for aluminium, Kindaruma (Kenya), Inga (Zaïre) and Carbora Bassa (Moçambique). When the Carbora Bassa scheme was first begun, the intention was to introduce Portuguese smallholders for the sake of strengthening the hold of the colonial power. The contract was awarded in 1968 to a consortium of South African and European firms. A considerable share of the power was destined for South Africa, which was also associated with Portugal in a scheme on the Kunene River on the South-West Africa border with Angola. But electricity consumption continued to be low in Africa. It was highest in North Africa and lowest in West Africa. The biggest consumers were Zambia (for copper), Liberia (for iron) and Ghana (for aluminium). There was a tendency in the 1960s for power stations to run at less than full capacity, for example, Owen Falls at Jinja in Uganda.

There was a steady growth of education and medical facilities during the 1960s, though sometimes quantity was purchased at the expense of quality. Tanzania was able to claim an advance in life expectancy from about 38 to 41 over the decade 1957 to 1967, chiefly through the decrease in infant mortality. More doctors, nurses and health centres became available. Throughout Africa the rate of growth of primary school enrolments between 1965 and 1970 was 5,2 per cent a year, of secondary enrolments 11,7 per cent a year and of higher education enrolments 7,1 per cent a year. In 1968, 125 Egyptian engineers graduated for every million of the population, a ratio that compared very favourably with that of other developing countries (e.g. 20 per million in India), though naturally inferior to that of industrialized nations (e.g. 265 per million in the United States). At the end of the 1960s Congo-Leopoldville and Gabon claimed that all the children of primary school age were at school. Three-quarters of that age-group in Zambia were receiving schooling. On the other hand, only 28 per cent of primary school age children were at school in Nigeria, 16 per cent in Ethiopia and 15 per cent in Mauritania.

The school population growth rate began to slacken off in the later 1960s as the sections of the population still to be brought within reach of education were progressively more difficult to incorporate, people in remote areas or people too poor to send their children to school. There was also a growing shortage of qualified teachers, especially in the rural areas. There was not enough money available for education to keep pace with increasing needs. In Nigeria students in institutions of higher education numbered only 7 000 out of a total population of 55 million and in Congo-

Leopoldville only 4 000 out of 21 million. An additional burden was the tendency for highly qualified men and women to move to more lucrative posts abroad. In some countries tension arose about the nature of education and the medium of instruction. This was particularly true in the Maghrib, where the claims of French, the language of administration, commerce and industry, conflicted with those of Arabic, favoured for nationalist and religious reasons. In Tunisia President Bourguiba waged war against the confessional schools, but in Morocco and Algeria there was compromise and the education system was linguistically divided. Students trained in French had better employment chances than the Arabists, but too often throughout Africa school and university-leavers were difficult to employ in economies not expanding fast enough to absorb them or requiring different skills from those commonly acquired. A great deal of capital was misallocated, invested in the wrong sort of education. African university students had little taste for science and technology, and the spread of elementary education frequently only aroused dissatisfaction with rural life. The problem of the shortage of skilled workers tended to become more acute as the requirements of industry and commerce became more pressing.

Another problem met by the newly-independent countries was poor transport. Railways inherited from the colonial period were far from adequate. Total length open was about 50 000 kilometres, excluding South Africa, which had almost half as much as the rest of Africa put together. Germany had as extensive a railway network in 1900 as Africa (excluding South Africa) had in 1960. After independence railways were often neglected. Nigeria Railways were perhaps an extreme case, with their reputation for accidents, slowness and inability to keep schedules and plagued by strikes. There was a regular deficit and nothing for investment. Because of the indifferent service provided by the railways, the roads were congested. Railway freight volume carried and the number of passengers declined. But that was not typical. Africa's growth rate for railway goods traffic in the 1960s was the highest in the world, though the level of traffic in 1960 was very low. Important railway projects after independence included the Trans-Cameroun Railway and the 1 810 kilometre-long Tan-Zam Railway, the latter financed by an interest-free loan of $400 million from China, to be repaid over a period of thirty years beginning in 1985, and built by Chinese and African labour. Originally scheduled to be completed in 1976, the Tan-Zam Railway was finished sooner. It was designed to solve a political problem, to enable Zambia to escape from its dependence upon Rhodesia and Portugal. In 1964 Zambia was dependent on Rhodesia for two-fifths of its imports and almost all of its exports. The new railway had little economic justification, since it was only slightly

shorter than the existing route to Beira. It was for that reason that the
World Bank declined to finance it. The route lay through barren land in
northern Zambia, unlikely to be able to take advantage of the railway to
produce foodstuffs for the market, and the gauge was not the standard East
African one. For more than half its distance it ran alongside the new
Tan-Zam Highway, an unnecessary duplication. This was financed partly
by the World Bank and partly by the United States. It was one of the most
important road developments of the period. Others included the Nairobi-
Addis Ababa road, originally scheduled for completion in 1973, and the
Freetown-Monrovia road of 500 kilometres. Two trans-Saharan highroads
were planned. In the Somali Republic the Chinese undertook to build a
road linking the northern and southern centres of population.

The volume of cargo loaded and unloaded at African ports increased
strikingly, requiring considerably more investment in harbour facilities.
The traffic at Dar es Salaam doubled from half a million to a million tons
between 1963 and 1969. A good deal of harbour development took the
form of oil and natural gas terminals in North Africa and Nigeria. Other
harbours were constructed for the export of solid minerals, for example,
Tema in 1961 for the export of aluminium ore from the Volta River, or
existing ones were extended, such as Monrovia for the export of iron. In
the Horn of Africa new port facilities were developed at Assab in Eritrea
and at Berbera and Kismayu in the Somali Republic, the former provided
by the Russians, the latter by the Americans. Airports were also built in
large numbers, so that many towns hitherto difficult to reach by road or
rail were brought into easier contact with the outside world.

It was the exploitation of minerals that was the fastest growing industrial
sector, above all oil. Growth was particularly marked during the first half
of the decade, when in North Africa the annual rate of growth of mining
was 38,5 per cent and in West Africa 21,7 per cent. Exports of minerals
could be invaluable if the proceeds of their sale were used wisely. But they
could not provide the jobs that were so urgently needed. For them Africa
pinned its hopes to manufacturing, only to be largely disappointed. Per
capita consumption of iron and steel in the countries of developing Africa
in the mid-1960s was less than 2 kilograms for more than half of them and
exceeded 20 kilograms in only six. In the industrialized countries per
capita consumption ranged between 250 and 300 kilograms. Most of the
iron and steel used in Africa went into building rather than into
engineering. Yet despite low per capita consumption of basic materials
African countries were frequently cursed with excess industrial capacity,
e.g. in the production of plywood, cement and petrol. The national
markets were unable to absorb even the small amounts produced. The
performance of Africa during the first decade or so of independence was

inferior to that of Asia and Latin America. It was estimated that the value added contributed by the manufacturing sector to GDP in 1970 ranged from 1 per cent in countries with the worst performance to 20 per cent in those with the best. In Latin America in 1965 the range was between 12 per cent and 34 per cent and developing Asia 6 per cent to 28 per cent. The overall contribution of manufacturing to GDP was less than 12 per cent in 1970. Africa remained largely dependent upon agriculture. Even in South Africa in 1970, 28 per cent of the economically active population were engaged in agriculture, though this was to an extent a reflection of the policy of apartheid, which confined to the overcrowded reserves Africans who might otherwise have found employment in industry. The UN Economic Commission for Africa attributed Africa's poor industrial performance to, among other things, lack of entrepreneurs and trained personnel, the inability of governments to formulate, evaluate and implement projects effectively, inadequate local technology and the high installation and running costs of industrial plant.

Economic performance varied. The Ivory Coast was one of the most successful and its experience seemed to lend support to the argument that growth was possible through trade. The development plan of 1960-1970 aimed at an increase of 7,2 per cent a year in GDP in the first half of the decade. The actual growth rate was 10 per cent a year and it was a plan based on the export of primary products, principally coffee and cocoa. However, the Ivory Coast was favoured by exceptional circumstances, such as abundant land for expansion, being as big as France with a population of fewer than 4 000 000. There was ample foreign migrant labour and that kept wages down. Egypt could also claim progress. At least it was able to reduce its dependence on cotton exports (49 per cent of total exports in 1970). None the less it encountered severe difficulties, not least its persistent state of hostility towards Israel, which meant large military expenditure and in 1967 brought open warfare, resulting in the loss of Sinai and its oil, hitherto a significant export, and the closing of the Suez Canal, an important source of revenue, though the loss was compensated to some extent by subsidies from other Arab states.

During the 1960s South Africa retained, indeed increased, its industrial lead, though the celebrated winds of change that blew away so much colonial rule from Africa from the late 1950s did not leave it unruffled. Private capital began its flight from the country, the result partly of fears for its political stability, partly of anticipation of devaluation of the South African rand (which had superseded the pound when the country went on to a decimal currency). After a serious civil disturbance at Sharpeville in March 1960, when police fired on a black crowd, the flight was accelerated. During the following months capital was leaving at the rate of 12 million rands a month. The government's first attempts to stem the flow by increasing the bank rate and taking other measures to raise interest rates and by tightening up import and exchange controls, were ineffective, and so unrestricted repatriation of non-resident owned capital was suspended and the rand ceased to be freely convertible. The outflow of capital dried up and from the middle of 1961, assisted by a favourable balance on current account, resources of foreign exchange rose rapidly. When Britain devalued the pound sterling in 1967, South Africa did not find it expedient to conform, despite its informal membership of the sterling area and the pound-rand link, and in 1969 import controls were ended as a means of securing a balance of payments equilibrium. In 1972 South Africa's foreign liabilities stood at R7 786 million, but an increasing proportion of South African assets were owned by residents. Whereas in 1917 more than 85 per cent of gold-mining dividends went to foreigners, in 1963 this proportion had fallen to 27 per cent. South Africa was also a capital exporter, with investments in Rhodesia, Zambia and Malawi.

Under the stimulus of reduced interest rates, of modest inflation (the average annual percentage increase in the retail price index being only 2,2 per cent in the period from 1958 to 1969) and of substantial state investment, made available partly through the Industrial Development Corporation, South Africa experienced a new prosperity comparable with that of the 1930s. There was a tendency for the economy to become overheated, and the government tried to restrict credit through the Banks Act of 1965, which gave the Reserve Bank the power to vary liquid asset requirements and, when that proved ineffective, by fixing credit ceilings.

Public investments included the Orange River Project, which aimed at, among other things, an increase of 40 per cent in the area under irrigation, and a new steel plant at Newcastle in Natal to supplement existing steel works at Pretoria and Vanderbijl Park. By the end of the 1960s the parastatal Iron and Steel Corporation was producing ingot steel at a rate of more than 5 million metric tons a year and was able to supply 65 per cent of the local market for steel and, favoured by the cheapness of its product, attributable to low-cost local raw materials and labour, was exporting to - or, as it seemed there, dumping in - Europe significant quantities of steel. A new ore field was exploited at Sishen and new harbours were planned at Richards Bay and Saldanha Bay.

In spite of a severe drought in 1964-1965 which was damaging to agriculture and the food processing industry, including canning, in the 1960s GDP at current prices more than doubled, growing at an average rate of 8,9 per cent a year. In real terms the growth rate was 5,9 per cent a year and 2,9 per cent a year per capita. By 1965 the railways were carrying over 64 million tons of goods and 425 million passengers a year and ocean and coastal shipping some 60 million metric tons of goods. There were over 184 000 kilometres of roads and 1½ million motor vehicles in use. The transport system kept pace with economic expansion except during periods of rapid growth.

The contribution of manufacturing to GDP exceeded that of agriculture and mining for the first time in 1965, though the value of industrial output, which increased 81 per cent between 1959-1960 and 1966, grew more slowly in the second half of the decade, 52 per cent between 1966 and 1970. Secondary industry remained heavily dependent upon those other sectors for the foreign exchange earnings that made possible the import of raw materials and capital equipment. Although in terms of employment agriculture, forestry and fishing remained the most important sector of the economy, in terms of contribution to GDP their share was in 1972 only 9,9 per cent compared with manufacturing's 22,4 per cent and mining's 11 per cent. In 1972 more than 1½ million workers were employed in manufacturing industry. In the 1960s employment grew at a rate of 6,1 per cent a year. As a result of increasing productivity the physical volume of production grew at an appreciably faster rate, 8,5 per cent a year. In terms of size of labour force and value of output the manufacture of metal products and engineering were the most important industrial activities. Also important were vehicle assembly (nearly 300 000 of all types in 1972) and clothing and textiles (supplying respectively 90 per cent and 60 per cent of local demand in 1972). To qualify for tariff concessions vehicles assembled in South Africa incorporated a large proportion of locally manufactured components, which, however, could not be produced so cheaply as the motor industries of the major industrial countries, taking advantage of economies of scale, could turn them out.

South Africa's foreign trade became less dependent on the British connection, though Britain remained the chief trading partner. Wool, fruit and fish were important exports. Gold remained the main earner of foreign exchange, but its relative contribution to total exports declined. During the 1960s the fixed price was under pressure. The attempt between 1961 and 1968 to keep the price down by means of an international gold pool (formed under American influence) which intervened in the gold market had to be abandoned and in 1968 a two-tier marketing scheme was inaugurated, separating the price of gold on the free market from the fixed price of monetary gold.

The geographical distribution of South African economic prosperity was extremely uneven. Industry was concentrated very largely in the southern Transvaal (Pretoria, Johannesburg, the Rand and Vereeniging), accounting for about a half of total industrial output. The Cape Peninsula and Durban and Port Elizabeth and their environs accounted for a further 30 per cent. The rural areas and country towns stagnated, particularly the African reserves. In the 1960s the government pressed ahead with its policy of encouraging a wider dispersal of industry through the establishment of 'border industries'. In 1968, in an effort to touch the hard core of poverty, it broadened the scope of its policy to permit the penetration of the so-called homelands by white entrepreneurs and capital, and in 1969 it extended to the reserves the concessions previously granted in the border areas.

Between 1960 and 1972 the decentralization programme resulted in an increase in employment in the special areas of rather more than 100 000 workers, three-fifths of them Africans. But the impact upon the depressed reserves was much less marked than these figures would indicate. The areas which benefited most from new development were close to the existing industrial areas of Pretoria and Durban-Pinetown-Pietermaritzburg .

Though in comparison with the rest of Africa an advanced industrial state, by some criteria South Africa remained distinctly underdeveloped. Not only were there very marked regional disparities, which are characteristic of underdeveloped countries, but there was also a low per capita income in the case of the majority of the population. The fact that South Africa had an overall per capita income in 1970 substantially greater than any other African country except Libya, with its small population and large production of oil, was misleading. In 1973 the average European worker in manufacturing earned five and a half times as much as the average black worker, and in mining and quarrying fourteen and a half times, though up to a point the disparity would be explained by the greater productivity of white workers, who were usually better skilled. Another sign of the underdevelopment of the South African economy was the burden imposed upon it of absorbing into industry an influx of unskilled recruits from a primitive agricultural background in conditions of rapidly growing population. In the period 1957–1967 the African labour force in industry increased by 55 per cent, and the magnitude of the problem could be gauged from the fact that, as early as 1964, there were some 200 000 new entrants to the labour market every year, nine-tenths of them black. By 1970 the total population stood at 21 million (compared with rather less than 6 million in 1911) and the black population was growing considerably faster than the white. The white proportion of the population in 1911, 21,4 per cent, had fallen to 17,8 per cent in 1970. The white rate of increase in the 1960s, including immigration (some 24 000 in 1973), at 2 per cent a year was appreciably lower than the black rate of increase, also including immigration, of 3,2 per cent a year.

Better paid employment, the skilled and managerial jobs, continued to be largely reserved for whites and legislation and convention continued to hinder the vertical mobility of black workers. To some extent the rigidity of a racial division of labour was softened as African and Indian workers were permitted to move into more highly skilled jobs in manufacturing and distribution, and during the boom of the 1960s the real earnings of black urban workers rose significantly, partly because of the activities of the government-appointed Wage Board, the minimum wage determinations of which were racially non-discriminatory, but affected blacks more than whites and covered nearly all African employees in the manufacturing sector. The average wage received by an African industrial worker compared very favourably with that current elsewhere in Africa. But there were disquieting features. The African reserves benefited only in so far as they received the remittances of migrant workers. Even among the industrial workers themselves relatively few earned more than what welfare organizations, using far from extravagant criteria, considered was necessary for the support of an average-sized family in the bleak conditions of a black suburb. Moreover, while undoubtedly the trend was for the gap between white and black earnings to narrow in relative terms, in absolute terms the trend was for it to remain as wide as ever, if not to widen still further.

The relative poverty of some three-quarters of the total population restricted the size of the domestic market, hampering the exploitation of the economies of large-scale production and discouraging the installation of more highly specialized machinery. At the same time the restrictions placed upon the acquisition of skills by black workers exacerbated the shortage of skilled workers. A relatively small proportion of African workers was held back from advancement by legal job reservation (as distinct from other impediments), but the existence of such discrimination was a source of resentment, as was the withholding of legal recognition from black trade unions. The conciliation and negotiation machinery for Africans and the minimum wage powers of the Wage Board were not regarded by articulate black workers as an adequate substitute for the free collective bargaining of properly constituted trade unions.

The manifest injustice of South African society, the persistence with which the government pursued its policy of apartheid and the universal condemnation it incurred brought not only internal frustrations and tensions, but also external pressures. Boycotts and threats of boycotts did not, however, prevent the expansion of South Africa's foreign trade, except in the case of the African continent; and, even here, the decline was partly due to a slowing up in the rate of growth in some African territories. It would be wrong to say that the embargoes had no effect, because, had it not been for them, trade expansion might have been even greater. Sanctions and the threat of them also played an important part in stimulating the domestic economy, because they accelerated the development of import-substitution industries like armaments, car manufacturing, the aircraft industry, shipbuilding and chemical manufacture (including synthetic rubber); and they stimulated the search for oil.

Two other parts of Africa with a political situation not dissimilar to South Africa's ended the decade in a strong economic position on the surface, the Portuguese Empire and Southern Rhodesia. In 1964 Portugal removed restrictions on foreign investment, and the share of foreign private investors in gross fixed capital formation in Angola rose from 15 per cent in 1963 to 25 per cent in 1969. Investment by Gulf Oil and Krupp led to a rapid development of mineral production. The value of mineral exports doubled between 1965 and 1970, to reach a level of £170 million. Industrial output grew at the rate of 17 per cent a year between 1962 and 1969 and cotton exports increased four-fold between 1967 and 1970.

Too much hope was attached to industry as an economic panacea. The 'myth of the steel works as a symbol of independence and economic progress' found many believers, convinced that profitability was irrelevant and that any industry, whatever the opportunity cost of its establishment, was desirable as the stimulus to ever more industrialization. The hope that agriculture would be uplifted by industry proved to be unfounded. It stagnated and the rural demand for manufactures was small. Africa was unable to match the remarkable achievements of some Asian countries, such as South Korea and Taiwan, in the creation of urban employment. Industrialization turned out to be no solution to the problem of rural overpopulation and to the extent that it substituted capital for labour actually reduced employment opportunities. At the same time it attracted into the towns people in search of jobs, so that rural unemployment was transmuted into urban unemployment.

Agriculture was not altogether disregarded. Endeavours were made to raise the level of productivity and the range of products within the peasant farming sector by means of extension services, the use of insecticides, the encouragement of fertilization, the provision of improved seed strains and the introduction of more advanced, though still simple, technology, such as the ox-plough. There were also attempts to improve the quality of local livestock by cross-breeding and by the introduction of better methods of animal husbandry. African rural society remained generally resistant to change and innovation as a result of prevailing religious beliefs, pagan and Muslim, the existence of communal rights in land, the raising of cattle for ostentation rather than consumption, the distribution of output to fulfil obligations to the extended family rather than to accumulate capital for investment and a sexual division of labour that overburdened women and made inadequate use of male labour. The value of the extended family lay in its capacity to furnish a social security that only a wealthy economy could afford for the mass of society, and in its capacity to mobilize resources for common endeavour. Security was purchased at the price of inhibiting the initiative of the individual, who was deterred by the prospect of the dispersal of the fruits of his effort, and common endeavour might well be directed towards a non-economic end.

With increasing population pressure and expanding market opportunities agriculture was becoming more intensive and there were signs that the extended family was breaking up, at least as far as the pooling of labour was concerned, throwing the nuclear family upon its own resources of labour and thus encouraging the adoption of improved technology. But the employment of better implements, especially the plough, was a cause as much as an effect of the tendency of the extended family to lose influence, adding also to the pressure upon land, as more could be cultivated, and reinforcing the trend towards consolidation of fragments of land into compact holdings. Inevitably the trend towards individual farming and the introduction of new technology, even something as simple as a plough, promoted the inequality that socialists and rural conservatives for different reasons deplored. However, such tendencies as these were only beginning to make themselves felt. The introduction of new technology made slow progress and increased output was achieved largely, though not entirely, by the cultivation of additional land (increasing in Tanzania, for example, by something like a quarter in ten years by the reduction of fallow) and African states were prone to trust to panaceas rather than more modest small-scale methods. The result was that few of the many projects and schemes aiming at improved farming practices enjoyed much success. The naïve trust in large-scale mechanization characteristic of the Tanganyika ground-nuts scheme survived decolonization and where it was introduced under the influence of experience in the very different conditions of Russia, in the case of the state farms of Ghana, not only was the initial investment large, but the unit costs of production often higher than they would have been with the labour intensive methods that were supplanted, a result all the more absurd where there was land hunger.

Big agricultural schemes entailed land reorganization, but they represented only one aspect of state intervention. There were also found land-reform programmes and the encouragement of co-operation in the spheres of marketing, credit and purchase of inputs. Sometimes land-reform was influenced, though not solely inspired, by political motives. It sometimes ran into difficulties and met peasant resistance, whether it aimed at individualization of tenure, which was resented by the migrant labourer, who saw his ultimate social security threatened, and by the community at large, hostile to the ambitious individual or nucleated family, or whether it aimed at more rigid collectivization; whether it was as modest as in central Malawi in the 1950s and early 1960s or as spectacular and ideologically inspired as in Tanzania.

In Egypt land-reform had gone on since the revolution of 1952. The intention was not collectivization or the destruction of communal land-holding, but partly to reduce the power of the big landowners by breaking up their estates, partly to provide a solution to the problem of rural poverty and compel a small group of conspicuous consumers to disgorge its misused wealth. In 1961 individual ownership was reduced to 100 feddans and in 1969 to 50, and foreign landowners were deprived of their holdings in 1963. In the meantime interest payments upon compensation bonds were reduced, then brought to an end in 1964, and the bonds became irredeemable. At the same time redemption payments were progressively reduced and were spread over a longer period. The requisition and distribution of land was carried out with some vigour by the Agrarian Reform Authority. This body also had the power to fix minimum wages, rents and tenancy agreements. In practice its wage regulations were never enforced and its rent and tenancy regulations sometimes evaded. By 1970 817 000 feddans of land had been distributed, plus public land and reclaimed land, to the benefit of more than a third of a million families. This was quite apart from land sold in the early days of the reform by those landowners who took the opportunity to dispose of land in excess of the legally permitted maximum. Plots distributed under the land laws were on average very small, less than half the statutory maximum of 5 feddans, but the trend throughout the country was for the average size of the smallest farms to increase, chiefly because of the sale or redistribution of land by those possessing more than the legal maximum and of government land. Since even the maximum holding of 50 feddans fixed in 1969 was still some forty-seven times bigger than the average smallholding, it is clear that land-reform did not get rid of agricultural inequality. None the less, the very large estates were eliminated.

Land awaiting distribution was administered by the Authority, which rented it out or, less often, cultivated it itself. The Authority was also responsible for the General Co-operative Society, under which were grouped the co-operative societies which farmers of redistributed land had to join and which organized production and marketing. In 1962 the power of the co-operatives was extended, when they became the sole suppliers of agricultural credit, seeds and fertilizers and the sole marketing outlet for cotton and onions. In 1970 there were more than 5 000 co-operatives with 3,1 million members.

Although supervision by co-operative societies introduced a large measure of control from above in Egypt, land-reform remained founded upon private ownership. That was also true of Kenya. There the land settlement programme of 1961-1966 was a means of transferring to African ownership land which European farmers were anxious to sell in order to recover their capital. Commercial farming was becoming difficult because of illegal squatting and cattle thefts, but land prices had fallen and only government intervention could ensure adequate compensation. The government wanted an orderly transfer to ensure continued production for the market, though as the chief beneficiaries were intended to be farm labourers and the landless unemployed, the hopes of continued high productivity was over-optimistic. The scheme, both the purchase of land and the provision of working capital, was financed by loans and grants from Britain (£18 million up to 1966), the World Bank, the Commonwealth Development Corporation and the West German government. There was a High Density scheme, which provided plots that would give a net cash income of between £25 and £40 a year, and a Low Density scheme, which for the most part was intended to provide a net cash income of some £100 a year. The size of farms, all intended to be worked by family labour, varied according to fertility, climate and situation. Part of the money advanced to the new owner was repayable over a period of thirty years, but was a heavy burden of debt from the outset and necessitated the production of commercial commodities – mostly dairy produce, maize and pyrethrum – to pay off what was owed. It was a very ambitious programme, involving an enormous amount of surveying and legal work, and it went hand in hand with a programme of land consolidation, the extension of cash crop farming into areas hitherto confined to subsistence farming and a proposed introduction of rural training schemes.

In Kenya membership of co-operative societies was encouraged. In its neighbours collective solutions were imposed. The Group Farm programme in Uganda aimed to persuade peasant farmers to pool at least some of their land and utilize machinery in the interests of making the best use of available labour during periods of heavy demand. It enjoyed doubtful success. In Tanzania at least one object of reform was the destruction of the influence of prosperous farmers, who, it was feared, had the makings of an anti-social élite, especially as many of them had family and political links with people in the government. Land reform was an integral part of the ruling party's ideological programme aimed at socialism and egalitarianism. Its practical objectives were an increase in agricultural productivity and the best use of limited national resources in the provision of rural health, education and technical and extension services. Agriculture was the predominant economic activity. At the time of independence 90 per cent of the population was directly dependent on the land, most engaged in subsistence farming. Agriculture contributed 60 per cent of GNP, compared with the contribution of 5 per cent from mining and 3 per cent from manufacturing. The keystone of Tanzanian socialism was the agricultural co-operative, the ujamaa village, the name of which was derived from the Swahili for familyhood. Cultivators were to be encouraged to migrate to new villages in new areas, where sufficient people would be concentrated to justify the provision of services. President Nyerere was convinced that traditional rural society was socialist and he did not think of the ujamaa village as an innovation, but as an age-old institution adapted to the production of cash crops and modified by the granting of equal rights to women.

The ujamaa was subjected to much criticism and scepticism from the beginning. The Tanzanian people were not in the main village dwellers. Before the ujamaa experiment began only just over a million peasants, it is estimated, lived in a village of some sort, and in fact the government programme created thousands of non-ujamaa villages in addition to the co-operative villages. Whether or not the new rural socialism conformed to the traditional pattern of rural life, that pattern had long since been upset by the spread of farming for the market. There was some doubt too, whether co-operatives necessarily promoted equal distribution of wealth, since they could be prosperous or poor, successful or failures.

The typical ujamaa, containing up to three thousand people, resembled the Israeli moshav (rather than the kibbutz, where everything is communally owned, the land worked communally and the proceeds equally distributed), with the villagers retaining their land rights, but holding all basic goods in common and marketing their crops through marketing boards. The system of official marketing boards was extended. In 1962 the coffee board, which had existed in the colonial period, extended its functions to marketing and new boards were established to control the marketing of wheat, sugar and papain. A National Agricultural Products Board, set up in 1963, handled the marketing of maize, paddy rice, oilseeds, cashew nuts and copra. Locally, marketing was handled by co-operatives. The sale of crops to those boards was statutory in some instances (e.g. cotton), but in others not (e.g. tea). The proceeds of sales were divided among the members of the co-operatives according to the contribution, measured in task hours, to the communal effort. Therefore it was possible for economic differences to appear, though there was felt to be a moral duty to eliminate poverty as far as possible. In theory each ujamaa was formed spontaneously and governed democratically, and the only means used to ensure that ujamaa projects worked together to promote the well-being of the whole nation were persuasion and advice from the development council of each village, which was representative of the central government. No compulsory targets were fixed.

People in the poorer regions, particularly the dry central plains, and the landless from the better endowed areas were enthusiastic or at least open-minded, though some became disillusioned by the inadequate housing and the absence of promised services at new village sites. Those better placed on fertile land were reluctant to give up their traditional settlements, and the very fact that ujamaa villages tended to be composed chiefly of the poorest people in the worst-off districts prejudiced their chances of success. Some criticisms were well-founded. Co-operative marketing was costly and inefficient. Farmers got less from the marketing boards than from private traders, and the co-operative movement expanded so rapidly that it outstripped the supply of trained and experienced staff. Another difficulty was a lack of skilled and enthusiastic agronomists and other experts to provide technical help. Tanzania was exceptionally short of technical resources and local capital. Many ujamaa projects were weakened by sheer ignorance. There was a tendency for officials of central or regional government to be interfering and overbearing. In the more advanced co-operatives the members were reduced to the status of directed labour with little influence on administration.

If there was any country with a crying need for land reform, it was Ethiopia, where the diversion in the southern provinces of an agricultural surplus from an oppressed peasantry to a parasitic landowning class co-existed with considerable land hunger. Though endowed with some of the most fertile soil in Africa, Ethiopia had a per capita income which was very low even by African standards. Only a relatively small proportion of the country's arable land was actually under cultivation and on smallholdings there was little incentive to increase production when the major portion of any extra was appropriated as rent or tax or went as tithe to the Church, which set its face against any change in the *status quo*. After an abortive coup d'état in 1960 the government accelerated the distribution of some of its own land which had begun as early as the liberation in 1941, and up to 1970 had granted nearly 5 million hectares. Only a small proportion of it, however, about a quarter, went to the landless and the unemployed. Most went to gentry, civil servants and officers, with the aim of attaching them to the régime. As for the existing landowning class, there was no hint of concession. In the province of Harrarge three-quarters of the arable land was owned by two men, one of whom paid taxes on only a hundredth part of his estate. 62 per cent of all arable land in Ethiopia was owned by large landowners.

CHAPTER X

1970-1980 (THE SECOND DEVELOPMENT DECADE)

Politically Africa moved in the 1970s perceptibly nearer to the goal dear to the hearts of most of its inhabitants, the total removal of foreign rule from the continent. In 1974 the people of Portugal revolted against the task imposed on them by their government and hastily cast the colonial burden off. Portuguese Guinea, Angola and Moçambique obtained their independence. The white government of Rhodesia, after making futile attempts to arrive at an accommodation on its own terms with the black majority, was compelled to submit to nationalist forces after a long and damaging war. The small French colony of Djibouti, with its population of fifty thousand, joined the ranks of the free, and Spain, after the death of General Franco in 1975, divested itself of its colonies (apart from four enclaves on the African Mediterranean coast, if these can be counted as colonies). The Spanish Sahara was ceded to Morocco and Mauritania. There was, however, a powerful demand for self-determination and, with the support of Algeria, the nationalist Polisario Front waged war against the successor states, forcing Mauritania in 1978 to relinquish its share, which was taken over by Morocco. Relations between Algeria and Morocco were embittered and the whole issue proved to be very divisive within the Organisation of African Unity. For Muslim Africa it was of less importance than developments in Arab-Israeli relations. In 1973 Egypt fought a war against Israel which did not bring victory, but was sufficiently successful to restore Egyptian self-esteem. Colonel Nasser had died in 1970 and his successor, Anwar Sadat, felt confident enough after the 1973 war to brave the opprobrium of the rest of the Arab world to make peace with Israel in 1978. Of greater significance perhaps for Africa was, however, the conduct of Somalia, which broke the fundamental rule of the OAU, respect for the colonial boundaries. Its irredentism brought it into dispute with Kenya and an unsuccessful war with Ethiopia in 1977-1978 for possession of the Ogaden territory, ruled by Ethiopia but inhabited by Somalis. Ethiopia was rescued by the intervention of the troops of the USSR and Cuba, itself a sign of Africa's growing involvement in super-power rivalry.

Within African states military coups d'état continued to be commonplace and there were few signs of a decline of authoritarianism. New revolutionary governments in Ethiopia, Angola and Moçambique had doctrinaire Marxist policies and were in close alliance with the Soviet

Union. Attempts to restore civilian governments in Nigeria (1979-1983), Mauritania (1980) and Ghana (1979-1981) failed. Civil wars of varying length and causing varying amounts of damage, springing from ethnic and religious differences or simply from the ambitions of warlords, abounded: in Ethiopia, which faced after its military revolution in 1974 new independence movements as well as the old-established one in Eritrea; in Zaïre; in Sudan; in Chad; in Angola; and in Uganda.

The biggest single obstacle to the attainment of complete decolonization was South Africa. For most of its white people the process of decolonization had been completed in 1910 by the Act of Union, or at least by 1961, when the country became a republic; most of the much more numerous black inhabitants were convinced that decolonization was yet to come. Although the second of these irreconcilable views seemed the juster one, it could not be disputed that, unlike the European community in Algeria, Angola, Moçambique, Kenya or Southern Rhodesia, the European population in South Africa could look back on an effective presence stretching over a period of three centuries and had been responsible for its own destiny for at least half a century. But South Africa could not remain immune from the effects of the Portuguese revolution. Its black population became increasingly restive and dissatisfied with its share of national income and of opportunities for advancement. In 1974 strikes occurred throughout the country following the example of peaceful protest among migrant labourers from Ovamboland in South-West Africa in 1973. In 1976 internal unrest became acute, with bloody riots among Africans in the black suburbs of Johannesburg and Cape Town. The migratory labour system, which was entrenched in the mining industry, was widely admitted to be a deep source of grievance among blacks, but the removal of the system was as far off as ever. The policy of the government was not the only obstacle to reform. The gold-mining companies argued that the creation of a permanent labour force was beyond their financial means.

External hostility to South Africa reached a new pitch and it found itself temporarily embroiled in 1975 in the civil war in Angola, subject to international demands for withdrawal from South-West Africa, Namibia, and on uneasy terms with the post-colonial régime in Moçambique. The government came to recognize the wisdom of giving up Namibia, without, however, mustering sufficient resolution to do so; and the beginnings of an accommodation, timid and treated with great suspicion by almost everyone except its active proponents, were attempted in South Africa itself with the Coloured and Indian communities. The process of transforming fragmented and indigent African reserves into petty states, unrecognized anywhere in the world, and of the removal of long-settled black communities from areas assigned to white residence continued.

A contributory factor in the growing turmoil in South Africa was the increasing unemployment among blacks. This was the result of a high rate of population growth and a much more uneven economic performance in the 1970s. To some extent South Africa shared the economic misfortunes that afflicted the whole of the western world. The favourable international economic climate of the 1950s and 1960s came to an end. One cause (or perhaps only a symptom) of this was the confusion into which the world economy was thrown in the early 1970s. In August 1971 the convertibility of the dollar into gold at a fixed rate was abolished, terminating the system of fixed currency parities which had characterized international payments since the Second World War and replacing it with fluctuating exchange rates. Although currencies did not float freely in accordance with market forces but were managed by national governments as part of their monetary strategy, the earlier certainties of the post-war world disappeared. But monetary instability was not the only problem. Another influence was American inflation induced by budgetary and balance of payment deficits. The very sharp rise in the price of oil was yet another.

The prosperity of the industrialized world in the 1950s and 1960s owed very much to the cheapness of oil. In the early 1970s, however, this situation was profoundly changed. The very cheapness of energy had encouraged the growth of fuel-intensive industry and the extravagant use of oil. In 1970, as a result of that long-term trend and a combination of short-term factors, such as the closure of the Suez Canal after the Arab-Israeli War of 1967, there was an oil shortage in the West and its price began to rise. The new revolutionary government in Libya was determined to exploit the advantages of Libyan oil, its high quality and, more particularly, its comparative nearness to European markets, Middle Eastern oil having to go round the Cape. To increase pressure upon its customers Libya cut production, which fell from 159,7 million metric tons in 1971 to 71,5 million in 1975. Libya was an important producer, with an output in 1970 more than three times that of Algeria, itself one of the leading world sources of oil. The private campaign waged by Colonel Gadaffi merged into two other international developments, which were to bring a profound change to the world oil market. One was the new outbreak of fighting between Egypt and Israel in 1973, which united Arab oil producers in an attempt to force western countries to lessen their support for Israel, and the other was the new cohesion and effectiveness of the long-established cartel of oil producing countries, the Organisation of Oil Exporting Countries (OPEC). In 1973 oil prices quadrupled. Recession spread throughout the non-communist world, bringing a decline in the volume of world trade of some 6 per cent in 1975. The recession in turn, together with economy in the use of oil, brought about a decline in the demand for oil. When, after 1978, it picked up again, it brought on a fresh round of price increases in 1979-1981, to be followed by yet another fall in demand and a glut of oil. Africa's total output of crude petroleum fell from 425,0 million metric tons of coal equivalent in 1970 to 350,6 million in 1975, rose to 469,8 million in 1979 and fell again to 330,9 million in 1981.

What affected South Africa more than the price of oil, though dependent upon oil imports despite its large investment in plant for extracting oil from coal, was the price of gold. Its economy was in recession in 1971 and most of 1972, but was helped out by the rising price of gold after the United States abandoned the fixed price. From the end of 1972 to late in 1974 it went through an upward phase. There followed a prolonged recession, accompanied by double-figure inflation, i.e. the 'stagflation' characteristic of the West during a large part of the decade. Moreover, in the midst of recession the government, beset by external threats and internal strife, felt compelled to allot a bigger share of its budget to defence. In 1975 defence, which had accounted for 5,7 per cent of state expenditure in 1970, rose to 10,1 per cent though it subsequently fell to 8,7 per cent in 1980.

Actually real GDP in South Africa increased 2,5 per cent in 1975-1976 and manufacturing output 3,1 per cent, but GNP fell as a result of a decline in the price of gold and other exports. The price of gold, its fall accelerated by the large-scale auctioning of its stocks by the IMF, reached its lowest point of little more than $100 an ounce in August 1976, with adverse effects upon the country's balance of payments and upon the government's revenue at a time of heavy imports of capital equipment for public enterprise. Little comfort could be derived from manufacturing, which could still cover with its exports only a fraction of the imports it required. It was becoming increasingly obvious that the domestic market was too small for it. Perhaps the needs of industrialists for export markets and of South African investors for investment outlets influenced the government's so-called outward-looking foreign policy in the early 1970s. There was speculation on the possibility of forming a Southern African common market. The Portuguese revolution and the deterioration of international relations in Southern Africa which followed, put paid to those hopes.

South Africa's deficit on current account was 6,6 per cent of GDP in 1974-1975 and 7,2 per cent in 1975-1976. Gold and foreign exchange reserves fell despite considerable capital imports by public corporations and, to a lesser extent, by the government. In September 1975 South Africa was compelled to devalue by 17,9 per cent and impose tighter controls on foreign exchange dealings. Relief was only temporary. By the end of 1976 it became apparent that domestic and foreign investors were losing confidence in the stability and profitability of the national economy. There was a tendency for foreigners to divest themselves of their South African holdings either because they distrusted the country's future or because they had, or felt obliged to have, moral scruples about its racial policies. In 1977 and 1978 there was an outflow of capital and South Africa was compelled to borrow heavily abroad. The decline in gold and foreign exchange reserves, large-scale borrowing by public authorities and measures to bring down the rate of inflation and cut expenditure on imports, such as a rise in the bank rate, led to markedly higher interest rates, which in turn hampered recovery. But recovery did come as the price of gold again went up and world economic conditions improved. 1979-1981 was a period of rapid growth and over the years 1976 to 1981 GNP increased by 22 per cent in real terms. In 1979-1980 the country's current account was in substantial surplus. Then, from the end of 1980 it was again in deficit, the rand depreciating and the rate of inflation reaching 15 per cent in 1981. By the end on 1981 the upward phase in the business cycle was over.

The international economic crises had a varying effect on other African countries. Naturally those that had oil resources benefited considerably from the successes of OPEC. Government oil revenues in Libya jumped from $1 598 million in 1972 to $3 000 million in 1973 and $6 000 million in 1974; those in Algeria rose from $700 million in 1972 to $1 100 million in 1973 and $3 500 million in 1974. Nigerian crude petroleum exports earned 1 893 million naira in 1973 and N5 359 million in 1974. In 1970 state income from Nigerian oil amounted to $350 million, in 1980 to $16 000 million. Nigeria accounted for $3\frac{1}{2}$ per cent of total world production, Libya 3 per cent and Algeria 1,7 per cent in 1980. In addition Gabon produced 10,2 million metric tons and Angola 8,5 million in 1974 and Tunisia 5,6 million in 1980. The rest of Africa was in a less fortunate situation, though a few countries could meet their domestic needs partly themselves.

Non-oil producing countries were afflicted not only by the increased price of oil but also by the rise in prices of manufactures from inflation-ridden industrialized countries. African countries found their industries damaged by a shortage of foreign exchange for inputs and their import bills greatly increased. The cost of Ghana's imports of oil quadrupled. The Ivory Coast spent 3 809 CFA francs on crude petroleum imports in 1971 and 31 043 million in 1974. Zambia paid 26,5 million kwacha for imports of mineral fuels and electricity in 1972, K57,4 million in 1974. Fortunately for Zambia the price of copper strengthened in 1973-1974 and earnings from that, by far its principal export, rose over these years (from K490,9 million to K836,5 million). Kenya had no such assistance, and its oil import bill in 1974 was more than double that of 1973. Yet, self-sufficient in food, it was better off than Tanzania, in trouble because of a decline in agricultural produce. Uganda, though receiving considerable financial help from Libya and Saudi Arabia, also found itself in deficit in its balance of payments, partly because of the difficulties facing the cotton growers, who were responsible for the country's chief export. It was already under severe distress owing to the maladministration of General Amin and the damage done to the country's commerce and industry by a precipitate expulsion of the Asian community. Countries without oil intensified their search for it, promising favourable terms to oil companies in the event of a successful outcome to their costly explorations and surveys, or tried to conclude bilateral agreements with individual oil-producing countries.

The oil-producing countries, amidst mounting criticism from African non-producers, declined to make any distinction in oil prices for the benefit of poor countries, taking the view that their troubles were at least partly due to the selfishness of the industrialized countries, which were said to control international economic relations to their advantage. Unlike that of the developed nations, the wealth of the oil-producers came from the sale of a depletable resource and, in any event, was needed for the development of the OPEC countries themselves. They did, however, assist oil importers who were in difficulties. Of particular value to Africa was the Special Arab Assistance Fund for Africa (SAAFA), which disbursed over $200 million in emergency oil aid among thirty-seven countries between 1974 and 1978. OPEC as a whole established the OPEC Fund for International Development (OFID), also known as the OPEC Special Fund. It lent money both for development projects, particularly in the field of energy, and for imports of oil and other essential commodities by countries in balance of payment difficulties. In 1979 it made forty-eight loans, totalling $230,5 million, and in 1980 fifty-four loans, totalling $250,77 million, many of the borrowers being African states. Another body which helped developing countries with their oil imports was the Islamic Development Bank, the capital of which was furnished chiefly by Arab oil exporters. Although most of its loans went on financing foreign trade, including oil imports, it also lent money for development projects, which were intended to be its primary objective. Help was confined to members of the Islamic Conference organization, some in Africa. A third body making loans for oil imports was the Arab Bank for Economic Development in Africa which took over the rôle of the discontinued SAAFA. It also gave help to development projects. A similar institution was the Iraqi Fund for External Development, which lent money to buy Iraqi oil and later started to give aid for various development projects, some in Africa. Finally, a good deal of Arab aid was given bilaterally, particularly, though not exclusively, to Islamic countries. The Arabs, much criticized for their parsimony towards the poor, claimed that their aid in fact represented a much greater sacrifice than that of the developed countries. Certainly as a percentage of GNP Arab aid was much larger. In the mid-1970s OPEC aid was some $2\frac{1}{2}$ thousand million dollars a year, Western aid rather more than $8 000 million and Soviet bloc aid about $500 million.

Purposeful economic development through planning remains the chief objective of state policy throughout Africa, despite earlier disappointments. The 25th session of the United Nations adopted an International Development Strategy for the Second Development Decade that aimed at a 6 per cent overall rate of growth, a 3,5 per cent per capita growth rate and an annual increase of 8 per cent of value added in manufacturing output for forty-one independent developing African countries (excluding South Africa and Rhodesia). Even if such growth rates had been consistently achieved, the gap which separated Africa from the developed world would have defied closing except in the very remote future. In 1976 Africa (excluding South Africa) contributed 0,7 per cent of world manufacturing value added, compared with 4,8 per cent for Latin America and 3,1 per cent for Asia. The remaining 91 per cent or so came from developed countries, capitalist and communist together. Three-quarters of Africa's 0,7 per cent was produced by eight countries – Algeria, Egypt (which accounted for nearly half of the output of the northern region), Morocco, Tunisia, Nigeria (which produced about half of West Africa's output), Zaïre, Kenya and Zambia.

Industrial objectives were accorded priority in those countries which could afford to pursue them, mostly, but not solely, those which exported oil. Morocco made strenuous efforts in its 1973-1978 plan to develop a capital-intensive industry based on phosphates (e.g. the manufacture of phospheric acid and fertilizer), with exports in view rather than import substitution, and paid for out of the profits from the export of phosphates, the price of which went up almost five-fold over a period of eighteen months. A second great leap forward was attempted in the early 1980s, this time to exploit the country's reserves of shale-oil and natural gas. Libya, with its small population and immense oil deposits, opted in its so-called transformation plans for capital-intensive industrial and agricultural projects, with the aim of escaping from dependence on oil exports, which accounted for almost all export earnings and half of GDP. As late as the 1981-1985 Plan, when there was every sign of over-capacity in the world production of petrochemicals and iron and steel, and new projects had to meet keen competition from Taiwan and South Korea, thousands of millions of dollars were allocated to the manufacture of such products.

The influence of oil was amply shown in Nigeria's Third National

Development Plan of the second half of the 1970s, after the steep increase in its price. The expenditure of the Second Plan, though itself enlarged towards the end of the plan period, was eclipsed by that of the Third Plan, which looked forward to spending as much every year as was spent throughout the entire period of the Second Plan, and all the money was to come from Nigeria's own resources. Understandably oil revenues engendered much optimism and the failure of earlier plans to achieve more than partial success did not discourage even more hopeful targets. The Third Plan aimed at an industrial revolution or at least the beginning of Nigeria's transformation into a modern diversified state, an ambitious aspiration for a country where in 1975 manufacturing represented only 8 per cent of GDP. The emphasis was upon engineering and chemicals and the aim was to make Nigeria self-sufficient in petrochemicals and some other products (e.g. pulp and paper and sugar) and to develop a motor industry (and not merely a motor assembling industry) and remedy the shortcomings of the iron and steel industry inherited from earlier plans.

Throughout the 1970s Algeria's plans similarly emphasized the capital-intensive petroleum, iron and steel, chemical and engineering industries. Investment absorbed a very substantial proportion of GDP, 40 per cent in the 1974-1977 Plan. The production of steel, plastics, chemicals, fertilizer, tractors, farm machinery and industrial vehicles was either started or expanded during the 1970s. For vehicles the aim was 75 per cent locally manufactured content. Industry was allocated 43,5 per cent of total investment in the 1974-1977 Plan. Good intentions were expressed regarding agriculture and housing, but in effect they were neglected. Whereas in 1960 agriculture accounted for 21 per cent of GDP, by 1979 this had fallen to 7,5 per cent, when the contribution of industry and construction reached 55,5 per cent. However, with the death of President Boumedienne in 1978 and a certain relaxation introduced by his successor, President Chadli Benjedid, the 1980-1984 Development Plan gave more serious attention to housing, health and education, and this bore some fruit, especially through the use of prefabricated building techniques to provide houses, hospitals and schools. But industry still took 38,6 per cent of total investment.

The plans of countries without oil (or phosphates) were less ambitious. Self-sufficiency in oil-refining, cement or sugar was as much as some could hope for. In Somalia in the 1970s meat and dairy factories were put up, but the biggest development project was the Juba Sugar Project, the refining of sugar from locally grown cane. Sudan had a similar project, at Kenana, started in 1976.

Some of the most ambitious industrialization plans did little to mitigate the problem of unemployment because they were so capital intensive. This was a cause of concern in some countries. Egypt, with its dense and rapidly growing population and with an industrial sector longer established and more diverse than was typical of Africa, attached great importance to job creation. Like the contemporary Algerian plan, the Egyptian 1980-1984 Development Plan devoted resources to making good past neglect of housing, providing jobs as well as meeting an urgent social need. The Maghrib had to some extent always exported its unemployment when the European economy, especially the French, was absorbing North African labour. With the harsher economic climate of the 1970s this was no longer possible. On the contrary France began to offer inducements to North Africans to return home. A partial remedy was at hand in the import of workers – from Egypt and elsewhere as well as from the Maghrib – by Saudi Arabia and the United Arab Emirates.

In all countries, oil producers or not, the development of transport and communications received a great deal of emphasis. 45 per cent of the investment proposed in Zaïre by the Mobutu Plan of the late 1970s was to go on transport, mostly paid for from foreign aid. The Nigerian Third National Development Plan of 1975-1980 allocated its biggest single investment of funds to transport, ₦7 300 million, for improvements in roads, railways (including conversion to standard gauge), air services, ports and telecommunications. Zambia's Second National Development Plan of 1972-1976 assigned K716,5 million to 'economic facilities and transport', more money than was devoted to any other sector.

The 1970s were not particularly successful even in the sphere where most effort was made, industry. Although it is true that the relative contribution of manufacturing and mining to GDP was growing at the expense of that of agriculture, that shift was attributable as much to poor performance in agriculture as to the growing significance of industry. In 1972 an overall industrial growth rate of 5,4 per cent was achieved, but in 1973 only 4 per cent. Over the whole decade developing Africa experienced an annual industrial growth rate high enough to maintain its existing share of world industrial production, but only because western industrial growth was slowing down. The rest of the Third World increased its share. Developing Africa's share of world exports of manufactures declined from 1,12 per cent during 1970-1971 to 0,6 per cent during 1975-1976. In contrast the share of the rest of the developing world increased. Most of the decline was due to diminished exports of non-ferrous metals, partly because of falling world demand, but partly also because African exports tended to be less competitive than those of Asia and Latin America owing to the relatively high cost of labour, given its low productivity. Between 1970 and 1976 manufacturing value added (MVA) in developing Africa grew at a rate of 5,3 per cent a year, but this fell short of the UN target and in some countries the contribution of manufacturing to GDP declined.

Industrial output in Moçambique fell after independence by a third or even a half because of the emigration of experts, shortage of funds, disorganization of transport, loss of outlets, falling productivity and general confusion. In contrast in South Africa, despite increasing economic difficulties, the pace of industrial expansion picked up in the 1970s. In 1976 the contribution of manufacturing to GDP reached 24,5 per cent.

Manufacturing continued to be very unevenly distributed. Apart from South Africa and Rhodesia, Egypt was still the most industrialized country in Africa, though its share of total African output had been falling since 1960. Nigeria and Algeria increased their share. In 1975 these two and Egypt contributed two-fifths of developing Africa's total manufacturing output, three-quarters of which came from ten countries. At the other end of the scale 24 African countries together contributed less that 10 per cent. Manufacturing remained largely processing of food, beverages and tobacco and, to a smaller degree, textiles, clothing and leather goods. Altogether such light industries accounted for nearly three-quarters of total MVA and industrial employment. The bulk of manufacturing employment was in small and medium size establishments. Although such enterprises played an important rôle in the economy, they found little favour with most governments and in fact were subject to discrimination. The leading heavy industries were chemicals, petroleum, coal, rubber products and metal products. Algeria, with its oil and bias to heavy industry, and Zaïre, with its copper and other non-ferrous metals, had a higher than average proportion of heavy industry in their industrial structure. Growth rates in metal products, machinery and electrical goods tended to be high in many African countries, especially Mauritius, Nigeria, Tanzania and Zambia. Although these growth rates were less remarkable than might have appeared at first sight, because they started from a low production base, none the less they were signs of growing diversification. The share of Africa in world output of metals and engineering products, however, was well below 1 per cent and Africa was more dependent upon imports of these things than any other part of the Third World.

Although there appeared to be more scope left in Africa for further processing of exports than in other developing regions, there were obstacles in the way of that particular avenue to development. Developed countries were thought to give unsympathetic treatment to Third World exports, their tariff rates tending to rise with the degree of processing undergone by raw materials. Import substitution remained the chief source of industrial growth, a strategy often pursued in countries where the internal market was not big enough to give the advantages of economies of scale. The market was narrow not merely because of small population but also because only a relatively small proportion of that population was able to afford the products of the typical import substitution industry, which assembled imported components of such luxuries as cars and refrigerators or produced expensive textiles or foodstuffs.

Owing to loss of economies of scale, the textiles, chemicals, fertilizers and other products that were manufactured in Africa were often more expensive than foreign products, even taking into account transport costs, so that they could compete with imports only behind high tariff walls. Higher costs were passed on to other industries, such as clothing, road transport and farming, which used the products, and ultimately to the consumer. Such import substitution had other disadvantages. Many industries, because they were concerned only with assembling imported components, did not bring much manufacturing value added or employment, and imports of intermediate products and machinery imposed burdens on foreign exchange reserves. But the most obvious shortcomings of these new industries were low productivity and excess capacity. In the late 1970s some of Algeria's state-owned manufacturing enterprises were operating at only 15-25 per cent of design capacity. One plant which was working at far below its potential was the steelworks at Annaba, opened in 1972. Yet this did not deter the government from embarking upon an enlargement of capacity from 400 000 tons a year to 1,8 million tons. A similar course of events occurred in the fertilizer industry. In Morocco, according to the World Bank the phosphoric acid making plant of Maroc-Phosphore operated at barely more than half its full capacity.

Africans were for the most part worse off in 1980 than they had been in 1970. Some newly acquired wealth filtered down to the mass of the population in the oil producing countries, e.g. Nigeria, where univeral primary education was introduced in 1976 and university education made free in 1977, but on average African people were worse off than those in developing countries in other parts of the world with respect to life expectancy and literacy. Egypt in 1975 (with a population of 38 million) had an adult literacy rate of only 44 per cent (slightly less than that of Libya, which, however, had a population of only 3 million), Tunisia 38 per cent (despite a campaign which had begun in 1969 to eliminate adult illiteracy), Algeria 35 per cent, Morocco 28 per cent and Sudan 20 per cent. India's adult literacy rate was 36 per cent. Life expectancy in northern Africa was as follows in the late 1970s – Egypt 54, Morocco 55, Tunisia 57, Algeria 56 and Libya 55. Though far lower than that of the USA (73), it was better than India's (46), but India's was better than that of some countries in Africa (e.g. 39 in Ethiopia, 42 in Mauritania, 42 in Burundi). In most African countries it was below 50: 46 in Sudan and Zaïre, 48 in Zambia, though 52 in Uganda. Infant mortality was appreciably higher in Africa than it was elsewhere.

During 1970-1976 Africa's GDP grew 4,4 per cent a year, but a population growth of 2,7 per cent a year brought the annual per capita increase down to 1,7 per cent a year. Per capita GDP stood at $194 in 1976 (in 1970 values). Thirteen countries had in 1976 per capita incomes of less than $100 in 1970 values. During the period 1970-1976 twenty African countries experienced falling per capita GDP. Over the whole decade GNP per head in developing Africa declined by about ½ per cent a year, largely because of the continued rapid growth of population. In 1976 the population of developing Africa reached 381 million. As much as 40 per cent of the total population of Africa was under working age, representing a very heavy burden upon economy and society. Algeria at the end of the 1970s had something like a fifth of its labour force out of work, with the ranks of the unemployed being swollen all the time as more and more young people went on to the labour market.

With population growing at an average rate of 2,7 per cent a year and food production at 1,5 per cent a year, Africa was increasingly less able to feed its population. Nutritional standards were among the worst in the world. Although local shortages of foodstuffs had appeared as early as the 1930s, as late as the first half of the 1960s it was possible to say that, despite a doubling of population from the beginning of the century and a vast expansion of cash crop production, Africa could still feed itself. By the end of the 1960s the Ivory Coast, Ghana and Nigeria were being compelled to meet substantial and increasing food bills. In 1969 Algeria provided 73 per cent of its domestic food requirements; by 1980 this had fallen to 30 per cent. In Mauritania agriculture, confined to the banks of the Senegal River and the oases, failed to respond to the relatively small-scale urbanization that followed the granting of independence and the consequent growth of a national administration and to the development of iron-mining from the end of the 1950s. Rice had to be imported, though cattle farmers did well. Madagascar, an exporter of rice in colonial times, had to start importing it from 1973. From 1961 to 1972 Africa's food imports grew at a rate of 3,0 per cent a year; in the 1970's wheat and rice imports grew at a rate of more than 11 per cent a year, partly because of changing tastes, partly because of unrealistic exchange rates, which made imports cheap, and partly because of decreasing domestic production of maize and other traditional foodstuffs, which in turn was discouraged by imports of competing cereals.

The rate of growth of agricultural production in Africa, which ever since independence had been lower than that anywhere else in the Third World, was actually negative in the 1970s. The decline was more marked in per capita production (with a fall of almost 3 per cent in 1972), but was also true of aggregate output. Decline in output was noticeable in Algeria in the 1960s, falling at an annual rate of 1,6 per cent. In 1970-1976 output fell faster, at 8,7 per cent a year. Agricultural production in Moçambique declined after independence as white farmers, the chief source of the surplus for the market, left the country. This deterioration throughout most of Africa affected not only foodstuffs for domestic consumption, but also cash crops for export. There was a sharp drop in the output of cocoa, palm kernels and, above all, olive oil. In Nigeria the output of palm produce fell throughout the 1960s and ground-nut production fell from 1967, ever more being consumed at home. Nigerian ground-nut exports fell to almost nothing in 1975 and in 1976 exports were prohibited, ground-nut oil being imported from Niger and Senegal. In the middle 1970s Senegal displaced Nigeria as the leading producer in Africa, surpassed in turn by Sudan. In the later 1970s Senegal's output was particularly poor, partly because of drought, but partly also because the producers were discouraged by low profits. There was some recovery in the early 1980s but output was still below the levels of the mid-1960s. Cocoa was ceasing to attract the sharecropper and those who remained in the industry mostly employed casual labour. In Algeria the production of wine, which was 18,6 million hectolitres in 1960, fell to 2,7 million by 1979. That was largely due to government policy, which regarded exporting wine as somehow implying a neo-colonial dependence.

The agricultural situation was gloomy, but not entirely so. In Egypt in the late 1970s increasing mechanization and the use of fertilizers had some impact upon output. In 1980 production actually increased by more than population did, though only slightly. None the less, with agriculture confined to 4 per cent of the total land area and productivity generally considered low, the cost of food imports mounted. The net deficit on trade in foodstuffs amounted to $1 700 million in 1980. Malawi, one of the more thickly populated countries of Africa (50 per square kilometre), was able in most years to feed itself and sometimes have a small surplus of maize for export. Its chief export earners were tobacco and tea, in both of which output increased.

In those parts of Africa where there was white commercial agriculture, production levels were maintained in normal circumstances. In Rhodesia agriculture was adversely affected by the civil war, but with the return of peace there was recovery and a record output in the first year of independence. Sales of livestock and crops reached just over Z$700 million in 1981, an increase of 44 per cent over 1980. There was a maize surplus of a million metric tons, part of which was exported. A proportion of it came from black farmers. The tobacco crop earned Z$220 million in 1981. Prolonged drought, however, from early 1982 brought a setback. Drought also affected South African agriculture, but, subject to fluctuations, total volume of production continued to grow. This increase was partly attributable to the introduction of high yield varieties of maize. Annual maize output, which in the 1950s usually exceeded 3 million metric tons and in the 1960s 4 million, in the 1970s mostly was over 7 million tons and sometimes well over that.

Africa has more than a fair share of environmental obstacles to agriculture. A large part of the continent is unsuitable for farming, more particularly cultivation. Flood and, above all, drought are widespread and frequent hazards. Especially severe drought in 1973-1974 affecting the Sahelian lands and Ethiopia, Somalia, Tanzania and parts of Kenya, was to a considerable degree responsible for dearth in the 1970s. In the 1980s dearth became widespread famine. But food production was diminishing even in the absence of exceptionally bad weather. Clearly the failure of rain only aggravated a situation which quite different causes had created. Indeed, drought itself, as well as soil erosion, was brought on to some extent by deforestation resulting from population expansion, land clearance and destruction of trees for fuel and fertilizer. The Sahara was relentlessly encroaching on usable land both north and south. Another plausible explanation for poor agricultural performance was inadequate investment in the land and, related to that, low prices fixed by government for produce and the inefficiency of state-run marketing. Much of what was grown was lost because it was poorly harvested and badly stored. Agriculture simply had a low level of productivity. In Algeria in the early 1980s 42 per cent of the workforce were engaged in agriculture, but accounted for only 7 per cent of GDP.

Stemming desertification is a long-term process. In some parts of Africa there were afforestation schemes (e.g. Algeria, Angola, Zambia and Moçambique) to arrest the process of erosion and also to provide wood for pulping and other industrial purposes. It is doubtful how far such planting offset the loss of indigenous trees. A quicker remedy to Africa's food problem was more consideration for farmers. In the 1970s some African governments, though not giving up their hopes of industrial development, at least recognized the magnitude of the rural problem. The Zambian Second National Development Plan of 1972-1976 gave priority to agricultural improvement, particularly in the 'traditional farming sector', and allocated K152,5 million to that end, though in fact the sum fell far short of the funds allocated to investment in industry (K655,0 million). In Nigeria's Third National Development Plan ₦1 000,6 million was set aside for agriculture, not a small amount, but insignificant compared with the money assigned to infrastructure and industry and a great deal less than the sum to be devoted to defence (₦2 827 million). Only a third of the total cultivable land in Nigeria was in fact under cultivation and in 1978 all unused land was placed under state ownership. In Sudan an even larger proportion of the cultivable land was unutilized and in the 1970s there were hopes of using Arab oil money and western technology for turning the country into 'the breadbasket' of the Middle East and Africa, an objective that the famine of the 1980s was to show wildly optimistic.

In 1972 the military government of Ghana began 'Operation feed yourself' and in 1975 proposed as part of its new plan the provision of rural services for the equalization of rural and urban living standards. Food imports continued. Inducements were offered to foreign companies to use their blocked profits for the large-scale production of non-export crops. But the decline of export crops was also a cause of concern. To restore cocoa output the government set up a National Cocoa Production Committee, increased Marketing Board prices to the farmers and went in for extensive replanting, using high-yield varieties. This was evidently no great success because in 1982 a new military ruler, Flight-Lieutenant Jerry Rawlings, announced that the rehabilitation of the cocoa industry was his government's primary consideration.

One of the priorities of the independent government of Zimbabwe was the restoration of the rural areas devastated or neglected during the civil war. Services were revived as soon as possible, such as education and veterinary attention. In 1980 it embarked on a programme of transferring land from white to black ownership. Already in 1977 under the Rhodesian government the law had been amended to permit African purchase of land in the white area, and after independence the British government made available £30 million for the purchase of European-owned land. By the middle of 1982 some 12 000 black families had been settled on former white land.

In Algeria land reform was initiated in 1971 to redistribute land for the formation of co-operatives. During the 1970s some 6 000 of these were established on some 650 000 hectares of land taken from big landowners. The members of the new co-operatives were formerly landless peasants and they received state assistance in the form of loans and grants in kind. Absentee landlords were required either to undertake cultivation themselves or to dispose of their land to peasants. In 1980 enforced collectivization was begun of livestock farming on the steppe. State policy, however, went beyond institutional and organizational changes. The Five Year Plan of 1980-1984 provided for the rehabilitation of derelict cultivable land, the construction of dams and irrigation projects, and increase in agricultural investment, improvements in the wages and conditions of work of agricultural labourers and the relaxation of price and marketing controls. In 1982 the Banque d'Agriculture et Développement rurale (BADR) was set up to make loans to all types of farm – state, co-operative and private. Rural development was not inspired only by the desire to increase food output. There was also the question of trying to stem the rural exodus. Some $1\frac{3}{4}$ million persons migrated from country to town between 1967 and 1977 and the population of the capital, Algiers (or El Djezaïr) had swollen to about two million by the end of the 1970s. In the first half of the decade the rate of urban population growth was 5,7 per cent a year.

Collectivist solutions to the agricultural problem continued to be favoured not only in Algeria. In Moçambique state farms were established and the big sugar companies were nationalized. This policy had mixed results. By 1980 sugar production under Cuban supervision was more or less back to its 1975 level of 250 000 metric tons and cotton production rose from 28 000 metric tons in 1975 to 80 000 in 1977-1978. On the whole, however, state farming was a failure and after 1978 the emphasis was placed instead upon co-operatives, though the collective farms which had already been established had not had a very encouraging output. President Nyerere of Tanzania persisted with his ujamaa experiment and, indeed, expressed dissatisfaction with the rate at which villages were being organized. By June 1971 there were some 2 700 involving some 840 000 people, less than one-tenth of the total rural population, and by early 1974 there was still less than a quarter of the people drawn in. Officials, therefore, in some instances used force to get people into villages, ujamaa and non-ujamaa, destroying houses and ploughing in crops to prevent people returning to their old homes. The acceleration of this concentration in villages coincided with drought, so that agricultural production and, consequently, raw material exports were adversely affected, and Tanzania was compelled to import food, for which, foreign exchange reserves being exhausted, the government had to obtain overseas credits, from Sweden and Canada. Coercion, however, was not applied on a large scale, nor was it long sustained, since the consistent application of force lay beyond the government's powers. Opposition came mainly from malcontents in the towns and the government service itself. In rural education and health, upon which government expenditure was lavish in relation to its small resources, notable advances were made.

Another sort of populist socialism was practised in Madagascar after the 1972 revolution. Village councils were given greater and greater responsibility over rural administration, land reform, irrigation, roads and the marketing and processing of agricultural products. They were far from becoming the motor of economic progress, for the most part incapable of filling the rôle assigned to them. Contrasting with this decentralization was the scientific socialism of Ethiopia. There, after the revolution of 1974, the military rulers proclaimed public ownership of rural land in 1975, executing or imprisoning some of the biggest landowners. Co-operatives were formed among the poorest farmers and state farms were set up to grow cotton and sugar. Progress was slow. After ten years there were still fewer than two thousand co-operatives with 60 000 members and only 2 per cent of the cultivated land was farmed by state enterprises. But bold claims were made for rural health and education programmes. 5,5 million people were said to have learnt to read and write between 1974 and 1982 and the percentage of the population with access to health services to have increased from 15 to 50 per cent.

Where state action did seem appropriate was in the spread of irrigation and fertilization and the use of high yield seeds. Although these were beset with the dangers of waterlogging, erosion and soil exhaustion, they were capable of remarkable results. Chemical fertilizer, being derived chiefly from oil, became very expensive in the 1970s, but its use continued to grow. In Egypt the completion of the High Dam at Aswan in 1970, at the cost of more than $1 000 million, extended the cultivated area and changed the entire character of Egyptian agriculture, no longer dependent upon the annual floods. Libya too went in for irrigation projects, using water pumped from underground reserves. Unfortunately it was used so prodigally that by the end of the 1970s in some places the water table had fallen very low and was being contaminated by the sea. The schemes mostly produced food at very high cost and relied very heavily on foreign experts and workers. The similarly ambitious projects started in Sudan were just as disappointing. In 1980 $76 million from the World Bank was needed to finance essential capital inputs to keep them in operation. Inefficient management seemed to be the chief problem. The Kenana Sugar Estates, said to be the largest irrigated sugar plantation in Africa, was in the early 1980s still far from giving Sudan self-sufficiency in sugar.

African governments sank ever deeper into debt and their foreign reserves were run down. In 1978 Sudan was $3 441 million in arrear in debt repayment and in 1980-1981 had a balance of payments deficit on current account of some $1 000 million. By the middle of 1979 Zaïre's indebtedness amounted to some $4 600 million. There were repeated currency devaluations and at the end of 1979 a currency reform which replaced old banknotes with new in order to reduce the volume of notes in circulation and thus curb inflation and speculation. This caused chaos in the rural areas and its effects were largely evaded in the towns. Even oil-producing countries borrowed heavily in the 1970s for development projects. In 1979 Algeria's public external debt stood at some $19 000 million, with interest payments amounting to $2 125,9 million that year, not far short of its total foreign exchange reserves at the time. The total external debt of Africa south of the Sahara was $8 000 million in 1970 and $36 000 million in 1978. As a proportion of GNP in the 18 (including

South Africa) middle income countries of sub-Saharan Africa external debt rose from 11 per cent in 1970 to 18 per cent in 1979; and in the 30 low income (less than $340 per capita GNP) countries from 16 per cent to 29 per cent. Current account deficits for the whole of developing Africa grew during the decade from $1 500 million a year to $8 000 million a year and the cost of servicing the mounting debt doubled as a proportion of foreign exchange earnings, which themselves declined as the result of a 20 per cent fall in the production of agricultural exports. Even before the end of the 1960s the situation had arisen where in some years more capital, in the form of debt charges and repatriated profits, was leaving Africa than entering it. This became a source of growing resentment and increasing demand at UN Conferences on Trade and Development (UNCTAD) for debt rescheduling.

There was no mass defaulting on interest payments, but most debtors could not contemplate repayment of the principal and some borrowed afresh to service old debts. Wherever the situation became hopeless creditors were sympathetic if only to obviate financial collapse. When Ghana in 1972 repudiated or unilaterally rescheduled some short and medium-term commercial debts, the Western creditor countries, though retaliating by ceasing to grant any new long-term credits and by withdrawing all official export credit guarantees, made no attempt to impede the continued granting of multi-lateral loans to finance development projects and in March 1974 agreed at Rome to a rescheduling of outstanding medium-term debts on terms that were not ungenerous, allowing for a grace period of ten years, a repayment period of twenty-eight years at an interest rate of 2,5 per cent and the payment of arrears of interest in instalments. The creditors did not press for payment of the debts that had been repudiated. In November 1974 the United States made a low-interest loan of $10 million repayable over forty years, including a ten year grace period, to finance imports of machinery, fertilizers, etc. In 1979–1981 Sudan was engaged in negotiations for rescheduling $500 million of official debt due for repayment in 1981, $420 million of debts to commercial banks and $450 million of trade credits. Part of the agreement with foreign commercial banks in 1981 was the promise of a further loan of $75 million over seven years to finance essential imports. The American and West European governments were swayed by fears of disastrous political as well as financial effects resulting from too much pressure on debtors like the Sudan. Whatever reservations they had about governments like those of Presidents Nimeiry and Mobutu of the Sudan and Zaïre, the alternative possibilities were more unattractive. It was not only a question of sympathy over debt rescheduling; substantial sums in development and military aid were also forthcoming.

Countries heavily in debt and balance of payment deficits could have recourse to the International Monetary Fund, but only on terms which developing countries found hard to accept. The IMF demanded balanced budgets and austerity. One of the biggest items of government expenditure was subsidies on basic goods and these could be reduced only at the cost of social disturbances. The IMF's insistence on the reduction of food subsidies as a condition for a loan to Egypt led to food riots in Cairo in 1977; a partial reduction of oil and sugar subsidies in Sudan in 1979 caused riots, a rail strike and a government retreat; and food price rises in Morocco in 1981 had similar effects. Budgetary deficits were one cause of high rates of inflation: 20 per cent in Morocco and Egypt in 1980, 25 per cent in Libya in 1980-1981, 40 per cent in the Sudan in 1980, 60-70 per cent in Somalia in 1979-1980.

Not all African countries fared badly in the 1970s. There were wide variations. Five countries accounted for about half the GDP of developing Africa: Nigeria, Egypt, Algeria, Libya and Morocco. Two countries, Libya and Gabon, both oil exporters, had annual per capita incomes in 1976 of more than $1 000 in 1970 values ($2 480 and $1 540 respectively). Over the decade among the nations of sub-Saharan Africa, excluding South Africa, nine had annual growth rates of more than 2½ per cent in per capita income, compared with an annual decline of ½ per cent over the whole region. In 1976 four countries – Egypt, Nigeria, Algeria and Morocco – accounted for about 53 per cent of African industrial production, excluding South Africa's. In North Africa Algeria achieved an annual industrial growth rate of 9 per cent during its first Five Year Plan of 1970-1973 (inclusive) and an annual growth rate of GDP of 6,2 per cent in real terms during the period 1970-1976.

Although the rapid growth of industrial output in Rhodesia came to an end in 1974 and there were balance of payment deficits from 1973 (with the exception of 1978), there were signs of economic recovery as early as the later 1970s when the internal political setlement was patched up, and these signs were confirmed after the ending of the civil war. The Zimbabwean government inherited a strong and versatile economy which had been strengthened by sanctions rather than weakened, having been compelled to achieve a large measure of self-sufficiency. Rhodesia had become able to produce even some industrial equipment and machinery and had become much less dependent on oil for energy. After independence sanctions were lifted, usual trading relations were resumed, restrictions on exports were removed and more foreign exchange was available for the purchase of raw materials, capital equipment and spare parts. Exports grew and in March 1981 a Conference for Reconstruction and Development resulted in promises by overseas countries and agencies of

Z\$917 million in aid. Real growth in GDP in 1980 was 14 per cent. Domestic consumption rose by 40 per cent after the introduction of a minimum wage, the reduction of prices of some basic commodities, the incorporation of more people into the cash economy and a growing budgetary deficit. The fixing of minimum wages aimed to reduce the white-black income ratio of nearly eleven to one.

The early promise of unimpeded economic advance in Zimbabwe soon became less rosy. Inflation was made more severe by higher wages, increased government expenditure and expanded bank credit to private enterprise. The growth rate fell in 1981 to 8 per cent and would have been lower had it not been for a good performance in agriculture. The volume of mineral output in 1981 was the lowest for ten years and world prices of minerals were weakening, especially the price of gold. Expenditure on consumer's goods leapt up and foreign exchange reserves were badly depleted by increased imports. The government was forced to seek short-term loans overseas. At the end of the financial year 1979-1980 the budget deficit was Z\$350 million and in 1980-1981 Z\$254 million, despite tax increases. The shortfall was financed mostly by domestic borrowing. More and more recourse to the banks for loans contributed to the acceleration of the growth of the money supply and to inflation. In order to slow down the rate of inflation the government was forced to restrict its borrowing, raise interest rates, discourage consumer credit and restrict imports. There was a dearth of foreign exchange and a shortage of skilled labour and the perennial problem of inadequate transport facilities was as intractable as ever. Foreign private investment was disappointing, discouraged by the absence of a clear investment code and fear of political instability. Although the transition to independence was effected smoothly, it was not long before political tension became apparent between the country's two chief peoples, the Shona and the Ndebele, and fears were entertained of state expropriations. Mineral prospecting, which had been more or less in abeyance during the civil war, was resumed, but the setting up of a state Minerals Marketing Corporation to control all sales of minerals caused some apprehension among foreign and local companies.

Many of the countries with the best economic performance owed their success to oil. Of these Gabon and Libya had only very small populations. Even where there was no oil, a favourable population/resource ratio was a powerful aid to prosperity, e.g. in Botswana. The terms of trade for oil exporters generaly much improved over the 1970s, but there was a fall in demand in 1977-1978 and another in 1981-1983, adversely affecting the producers. Algerian output fell from 54,0 million metric tons in 1978 to below 40 million in 1981, partly because of deliberate conservation policy, but largely because of declining world demand. Even Algeria, ever insistent on maximizing prices, was forced to reduce the price of its crude in 1982-1983. Nigeria, which was in crisis by the end of the 1970s, was permitted by OPEC to lower its price slightly more than other members. Algeria managed to safeguard its position to some extent by concentrating more on the export of natural gas, much of it liquified, to the USA and Europe, but from 1983 by pipe-line to Italy. France and Italy were prepared to pay above world market prices for Algerian natural gas for the sake of political goodwill and trade opportunities. Three liquification plants were completed in the 1970s and early 1980s and two pipe-lines to take gas to the coast, as well as the 2 400 km pipe-line to Sicily via Tunisia and the Mediterranean, which was finished in 1981 at a cost of $2 500 million, mostly granted or lent by Italy.

The terms of trade for other primary products also improved over the course of the 1970s. This, however, excluded metals, prices of which fell in the latter part of the decade because of the recession in the developed world, while costs of production rose. Africa did not on the whole respond to falling prices or take advantage of rising prices by increasing exports. On the contrary, the volume of exports diminished, aggravating balance of payment deficits. Foreign enterprise became more reluctant to invest in mining in Africa because of the Africanization and nationalization policies commonly pursued.

Heavy dependence on a few export staples continued. In fact, the situation worsened to the extent that the oil producing countries relied almost entirely upon oil revenues, on the strength of which after the sharp increase in oil prices in 1973 they embarked on ambitious development programmes or, in some cases, wasted their revenues on imports of foreign manufactured consumer's goods at the expense of domestic investment. Algeria, from being an exporter of wine, citrus fruit and iron ore in chronic foreign trade deficit, began to have very large foreign earnings from oil exports. It was exceptional in imposing strict import controls except in food, raw materials and capital goods, imports of which, however, were sufficient to cause frequent deficits, depending upon demand for petroleum. One of the biggest disadvantages of oil and other minerals as earners of foreign exchange was that they contributed little else to the economy. In 1979 the mining industry was responsible for nearly one-half of Zimbabwe-Rhodesia's export earnings, but accounted for only 8 per cent of GDP and employed only about 6 per cent of the labour force.

The trade pattern inherited from colonial times proved to be resilient. Portugal remained the chief buyer of Moçambique's sugar and cotton and accounted for a third of its total exports in 1980. Moçambique, however distasteful it found it, was compelled to maintain economic relations with South Africa, which supplied 20 per cent of its imports in 1978, and the remittances of workers in South Africa continued to be an important source of income, though the numbers of Moçambicans working in the mines fell from 100 000 to some 30-40 000. Another tie which was difficult to escape was the Cabora Bassa hydro-electric scheme. The lake began to fill up in 1974 but the supply of power to South Africa, which was planned to begin in 1975, started only in 1977 and was subject to disruption through sabotage by Moçambican dissidents. In 1978 it provided about 9 per cent of South Africa's electric power needs. These ties with the capitalist world were reinforced by the aid which Moçambique received from the West. Despite Moçambique's ideological preference for the Soviet bloc, most aid came from Western countries and international organizations, about $310 in 1975-1978.

Algeria too traded mostly with the capitalist countries. It is true that deteriorating relations with France, especially over the nationalization of French oil interests in 1971, brought the French share of Algeria's exports down from a pre-independence 81 per cent to only 12,7 per cent in 1977 and of imports from 82 per cent to 24 per cent, but from 1979 Franco-Algerian trade began to recover, more especially from 1982 when an agreement was concluded for the French purchase of natural gas. There was also a preferential trade agreement with the EEC. Although there was a tendency for trade with the members of the EEC to decrease at the expense of trade with the USA, Japan and Latin America, the Common Market was the chief trading partner of Africa as a whole, accounting for more than half of total trade. Relations between the two were altered by the adherence of Britain to the EEC in 1973, which meant that special arrangements had to be negotiated by the anglophone Commonwealth states to ensure continued preferential access to the British market. Mauritius anticipated the others by entering into association in 1972. Its agricultural produce (excluding sugar, the sale of which was governed by the Commonwealth sugar agreement) received preference in the EEC and its manufactured goods entered duty-free. EEC goods imported by Mauritius were treated the same as Commonwealth goods. On Britain's entry into the EEC developing Commonwealth countries were offered a choice of a trade agreement or limited association (like that of Kenya, Uganda and Tanzania under the Arusha agreement) or full association in accordance with the Yaoundé Convention. They all chose full association. By then negotiations were already underway for the renewal of the Yaoundé Convention.

Negotiations opened in the middle of 1973. The African participants were the nineteen associated with the Community under the Yaoundé Convention together with the twelve Commonwealth countries. The only OAU countries not present were Libya, Guinea and Equatorial Guinea.

Negotiations lasted eighteen months. Many problems were outstanding, including the objections of the United States and other countries to preference hitherto granted to the EEC members in the markets of its associates. The USA threatened retaliation against developing countries which gave special treatment to EEC products. The Common Market gave way on that point and restricted itself to requiring most favoured nation status in the associated states.

The new convention between the EEC, now with nine members (Ireland and Denmark having acceded as well as Britain), and forty-six African, Caribbean and Pacific (or ACP) countries – the term associate was no longer used – was signed at Lomé in Togo in 1975, two more countries, Seychelles and the Comoros, joining in 1976. It covered trade and co-operation in general, and more specifically export earnings from commodities, industrial co-operation, financial and technical co-operation, capital movements, and institutions. The most important aspect of the new agreement was the free access to the Common Market from the ACP countries of most agricultural products and all their industrial products. Special agreements were reached on sugar, rum and bananas. To help stabilize the export earnings of the ACP nations, a scheme was in-augurated known as Stabex. This was applicable to twelve basic products, including coffee, tea and bananas, and provided for a payment to any ACP country whose earnings from the export of one of the specified products represented at least 7,5 per cent of its total export earnings, of compensation in the event of its income from that specified product falling by 7,5 per cent below a level (the reference level) calculated on the basis of the average of the four previous years, For twenty-four of the least developed countries, such as Tanzania and Upper Volta, the dependence upon such exports would have to be only $2\frac{1}{2}$ per cent before they qualified for help. The EEC put money into the Stabex fund and those ACP countries which had received compensation from it were also required to contribute five years after receiving aid. The EEC also agreed to provide about £1 000 in development aid during the Convention's five year life span. In real terms it represented a fall in the amount of aid compared with the provisions of the Yaoundé Convention, but assistance came in other forms as well. Two-thirds of the development aid was to consist of outright grants, the rest of loans.

The Lomé agreement was renewed on 1st January 1981 with some amendments. It set up an Industrial Co-operation Committee representing both the EEC and the ACP countries to oversee the progress of industrial co-operation and a Centre for Industrial Development, run by officials from both sides, to gather and disseminate information, encourage the development of new enterprises and provide technical advice. Provision was made for the joint public and private financing of enterprises. European private investment in Africa, deterred by political instability and constrained by recession, had been largely confined to Mediterranean Africa and oil producing countries. African countries having investment agreements with one EEC member now undertook to give similar treatment to other Common Market members. The list of products benefiting from Stabex was extended and a new scheme for mineral exports (Sysmin) was implemented. Loans at an interest rate of 1 per cent were offered to mineral exporters whose production or exports declined by at least 10 per cent. Producers of copper, cobalt, phosphates, bauxite, and manganese qualified on condition that the mineral exported accounted for more than 15 per cent of a country's exports (or 10 per cent in the case of the poorest ACP nations). An attempt by the EEC to insert a human rights clause into the Convention failed. After the renewal of the Convention the ACP group was brought up to sixty in number with the adherence of Zimbabwe.

After 1980, with the fall of commodity prices, there was such demands on Stabex that its resources were exhausted. This was a cause of dissatisfaction among ACP countries, which in the negotiations for the 1985 renewal of the Convention demanded more generous treatment from the Community. The latter, however, was more interested in emphasizing agriculture and rural development, the plight of the poorest ACP countries, regional co-operation, the conservation of natural resources and human rights.

The pace of nationalization in Africa kept up in the 1970s and even where there was no outright nationalization, state intervention in the working of the economy increased. The revolutionary government of General Muhammad Siad Barre in Somalia nationalized banks and the oil companies soon after a coup d'état in 1969 and greatly extended state ownership in 1972. In 1972 the military government in Ghana took a 55 per cent shareholding in a number of foreign-owned companies, mostly in mining and timber, including Ashanti Goldfields and Consolidated Diamonds (previously British Consolidated African Trust), and in 1975 it announced its intention of capturing 'the commanding heights of the economy' during its five year development plan. Nigeria also followed a policy of selective nationalization of foreign assets. In Madagascar after the 1972 revolution the government nationalized or imposed state participation in a wide range of economic activities: banking, insurance, transport, foreign trade, power generation, mining and the pharmaceutical industry. Wholesale nationalization followed the revolution of 1974 in Ethiopia, where, however, there was already a considerable state sector. Some of the strongest bastions of capitalism fell, the oil companies in the biggest oil producing countries, Algeria, Libya and Nigeria. The Algerian national hydrocarbon corporation SONATRACH controlled 31 per cent of oil production in 1970, 77 per cent by 1980.

Yet there were growing signs of relaxation of hitherto inflexible policies. Tunisia abandoned its policy of state directed industrialization in favour of inducements to foreign private investment. In Egypt, President Anwar Sadat, greatly modified the socialism of his predecessor and broke off relations with the USSR. Closer ties with the West encouraged a return of foreign private investment. But the Egyptian economy remained heavily dependent upon foreign subventions. Sudan too turned to the West and the OPEC countries after the failure of a pro-communist coup in 1971, and the socialism of President Nimeiry was somewhat modified. In Algeria the succession of Chadli Benjedid presented an opportunity for a measure of liberalization aimed at increasing the production and distribution of consumer's goods, of which there were chronic shortages. There was some relaxation of the state's international trade monopoly to permit some imports of manufactures. The small private sector of light industry (some 5 000 firms with about 60 000 workers) was given more sympathetic treatment under a new investment code of 1982, and in the same year encouragement was given to foreign investors to enter into private joint ventures. From 1983 foreign and domestic manufacturers were being urged to sub-contract for the state corporations, with local businessmen eligible for credit from state banks. It was only a cautious shift in policy, permitting the state to buy out foreign participants more or less when it felt so disposed. However, in the building industry private enterprise, with or without official permission, helped to reduce the housing backlog. In the public sector reform proceeded in the direction of decentralization, which, it was hoped, would increase productivity and efficiency. Other expedients to improve output included profit-sharing and more rational salary scales for state employees. The big state corporations were split up in the early 1980s into smaller units. At the same time the 1980–1984 Five Year Plan provided for greater emphasis upon housing, health, education and light industry, especially food processing, building materials and textiles.

In Moçambique a state bank, the Banco de Moçambique, was set up in 1975 and in 1978 all but one of the private commercial banks and credit institutions were nationalized. From 1977 state enterprises were established in most sectors of the economy. A state company was given the monopoly of the production and distribution of electricity. The oil refinery at Maputo (formerly Lourenço Marques), the cement industry and the coal mines were all nationalized. In 1981 a state enterprise was granted exclusive rights to oil prospecting and drilling. In the late 1970s, however, the economic situation became so serious that the government not only introduced rationing and froze imports and salaries, but also allowed a limited return to private enterprise. The retail trade was denationalized. The escudo was replaced by a new currency, the metical, in 1980 to destroy the value of hoards accumulated illicitly. Wage incentives were brought back in some industries and plantations. In February 1979 Moçambique made an agreement with South Africa to increase South African exports through Moçambique, making a valuable contribution to foreign exchange reserves. In the same year there were hints of reopening the country to tourists, but tourism became less likely as travel became increasingly dangerous.

Except in the Marxist states and Tanzania egalitarianism was not a priority in Africa and there was still a trend towards economic differentiation. This was noticeable in agriculture, increasing concentration of landownership and growing landlessness. Such slow change, however, had little impact compared with the disparities of wealth which resulted from the distribution of political power. The continent-wide policy of indigenization was very often the avenue to wealth for those with influence in government circles. In its economic form indigenization meant the fostering of a class of local capitalists. When Uganda expelled its Asian community in 1972, it handed over the businesses to Africans. In 1973–1974 virtually all foreign-owned enterprises in Zaïre were transferred to some two thousand Zaïrians who had political influence. Less crudely, in some countries state backing was given to local entrepreneurs to acquire businesses by purchase. In Nigeria this policy was greatly helped by the influx of wealth from oil exports. The Nigerian Enterprises Promotion – or Indigenization – Decree of 1972 ordered twenty-six activities, mostly in small-scale industry, services and retail trade, to be reserved to Nigerians after 1974, and foreign-owned firms engaged in any of twenty-seven other economic fields, in which larger organization or more complex technology were required, were instructed to sell 40 per cent of their equity capital to Nigerians or, in the case of the smaller ones, to sell out completely. Not all economic activities were covered by the decree. In these either the government itself took substantial holdings – 40 per cent of the equity of the three big commercial banks, up to 40 per cent of the equity of the chief foreign insurance companies and a minimum of 55 per cent of the equity of the oil companies; or they were left untouched, and these included some of the most important manufacturing sectors – textiles and tyres. Some of the shares thus compulsorily sold were bought by state governments and institutions, the rest by a relatively small number of Nigerians who were best placed to seize the opportunity, frequently on credit advanced by the State Bank for Commerce and Industry or by the commercial banks or by the firms themselves. Many shares were undervalued or were sold on favourable terms that left control of the firms in foreign hands. Therefore, to make foreign firms more accountable to Nigeria, the government began to require African participation in company decisions and to insist upon approving agreements between firms based in Nigeria and overseas partners. In Kenya foreign firms were urged to sell shares to Kenyans and state loans were granted to African businessmen. Between 1973 and 1977 Africans bought 57 per cent of Kenya's foreign-owned coffee estates and they also moved into manufacturing and urban property.

Indigenization had limited success. Indeed, it sometimes looked as though there were a correlation between the degree of indigenization, which sometimes gave responsibility to the incompetent and the corrupt, and the extent of economic deterioration. The administration of President Tsirinana in Madagascar was much criticized for its subservience to France, but it is undeniable that after the 1972 revolution and the indigenization that followed, the economy of the country declined lamentably. Economic chaos descended on Uganda and Zaïre. In the latter country some of the foreign firms were returned to their original owners, others nationalized. Plantations Lever au Zaïre, the old Huileries du Congo belge, nationalized in 1975, was given back in 1977. Africanization often led simply to the enlargement of the public sector. Large-scale state ownership remained characteristic not only of those states which were dedicated to socialism of one form or another and of those which spoke the language of socialism without taking it very seriously, such as Zambia, but also of those states which were favourably disposed to capitalism. In the Ivory Coast indigenization was official policy, but little was done to assist African entrepreneurs or to reduce foreign investment. The state, anxious to increase the industrial processing of Ivorian raw materials, itself played an expanding part through its own corporations. In the late 1970s 32 per cent of Ivorian industry was state-owned and only 13 per cent privately owned by citizens of the country. Foreign ownership of the economy was declining, but at the end of the 1970s three-quarters of trade was still foreign owned and 55 per cent of industry.

Everywhere, even in the face of economic stagnation, governments spent more and more. The share of government consumption in total GDP in developing Africa, which had been slightly more than 13 per cent in 1960, reached about 20 per cent in 1975. Inefficient industry was over-protected by tariffs or import controls and agriculture neglected, even subjected to discrimination through taxation, underpricing of its products by the state and high marketing costs. Too much scarce skilled labour was absorbed into the bureaucracy, interfering rather than producing. Currencies were consistently overvalued, cheapening imports and making exports either unprofitable or uncompetitive. Government enterprises in transport, manufacturing and marketing were not centres of growth but burdens upon consumers and taxpayers, especially farmers. More sympathetic observers point to the difficult political situation in which most African countries find themselves. Influence is weighted in favour of the towns, and the higher agricultural prices necessary to entice greater agricultural production are difficult to enforce because of the urban protest likely to follow. Another extenuating factor is that in backward countries skills and savings are in short supply and state action is perhaps the only kind of development action which can take place and is preferable to foreign enterprise, which is selfish and even unscrupulous. On the other hand, Africa has become notorious for the dishonesty and rapacity of its politicians, soldiers and administrators. The opportunities and temptations for malfeasance and embezzlement were great. In Zaïre a large proportion of the state budget was at the disposal of the presidency and an even larger proportion of revenue was not used for purposes for which it had been assigned. In Nigeria in 1975 the military government dismissed 11 000 civil servants for corruption and forced the retirement of many military commissioners and governors. This at least demonstrated an awareness of the problem and a determination to remedy it.

If development could be ordained by conferences, Africa would soon have made rapid strides forward. At the continental level the decade opened with a conference of ministers of industry at Addis Ababa in May 1971. It issued a Declaration of Industrialisation, which was adopted by the OAU Council of Ministers in June 1971. Member states were exhorted to be guided by certain principles that were laid down. No machinery was set up to implement them. However, an African Development Fund came into operation in 1973 with the aim of channelling soft loans from the developed countries to the developing countries of Africa.

At the regional level organizations for co-operation continued to proliferate. In 1970-1971 the Senegal River States agreed upon the establishment of a common market and the harmonization of development plans; in 1970 the Liptako-Gouma Development Authority was set up by Mali, Niger and Upper Volta for the joint development of that area, in partcular its mineral resources, with a secretariat and consultative machinery to co-ordinate activities in the field of hydro-electricity, transport (especially railways), forestry and the eradication of livestock diseases; in 1973 a Committee to Combat Drought in the Sahel was set up by Chad, Niger, Upper Volta, Mali, Senegal, Gambia and Mauritania; in 1974 the old UDEAO was replaced by the Communauté économique de l'Afrique de l'Ouest (CEAO), composed of the Ivory Coast, Mali, Mauritania, Niger, Senegal and Upper Volta. Rather than a full customs union it merely sought to encourage intra-regional trade through a regional co-operation tax, which gave preference to industrial products emanating from within the Community. It had a secretariat, a Community Development Fund to compensate members for losses incurred through the working of the Community and a Solidarity and Intervention Fund to make grants and loans for projects in the less developed areas. Another organization was set up in 1983, the Communauté économique des États de l'Afrique centrale (CEEAC), while the Organisation commune africaine et malgache (OCAM) underwent a series of changes. In 1971 OCAM was joined by Mauritius and became OCAMM: but reverted to OCAM (Organisation commune africaine et mauritienne) again in 1974, when Madagascar withdrew. Cameroun, Chad, Congo, Gabon and Zaïre all left and in 1985 the organization was disbanded.

West African organizations were overshadowed by a very ambitious attempt at promoting economic co-operation among all West African states, the Economic Community of West African States (ECOWAS or CEDEAO), perhaps the most comprehensive and ambitious of the Third World's regional economic groupings, with sixteen members of which four were Commonwealth, nine francophone, two lusophone (Cape Verde, which joined in 1977, and Guinea-Bissau) and Liberia. It was formed by the Treaty of Lagos in 1975. This was not an organization set up hastily and without preparation. Its origins went as far back as the Lagos Conference on Industrial Co-operation in West Africa of 1963, which began a long period of negotiations and meetings. It was not intended to annul the rights and obligations contracted under existing multilateral and bilateral agreements and organizations, provided they were not in conflict with the terms of ECOWAS. A secretariat was established in Lagos and staffed on the principle of equitable distribution of appointments among the member states. It was responsible to a Council of Ministers, composed of two representatives of each state and meeting twice a year. Four Technical and Specialized Commissions were to make recommendations on such matters as trade and customs, industry and agriculture, transport and energy and cultural affairs, and a tribunal was to adjudicate on disputes. The Community was committed to the elimination of internal customs duties within fifteen years, a common external tariff within fifteen years and the eventual free movement of capital and labour. In such conditions industry would tend to concentrate in the more industrially advanced country, at coastal locations or in the country less prone to government intervention. Measures were necessary to counteract excessive concentration and ensure the wide distribution of benefits. Therefore collaboration in agricultural, industrial, monetary, fiscal and infrastructural policies (including the formation of a joint airline), the establishment, with its headquarters at Lomé, of a Fund for Co-operation, Compensation and Development (to promote development projects in the less developed territories of the Community and to compensate member states suffering loss as the result of Community policies) were provided for. Member states were to contribute to the Community budget. Shortly before the signing of the Lagos Treaty a Committee of West African Central Banks was set up to work out a West African clearing system.

Although Morocco, Algeria and Tunisia were linked in a Maghrib Permanent Consultative Committee, there was little economic co-operation in North Africa, chiefly because of poor international relations, especially between Egypt and Libya and between Algeria and Morocco. Libya formed unions with Egypt (1973) and Tunisia (1974). Neither brought anything except acrimony. In 1984 there was a union between Libya and Morocco proclaimed. Less spectacularly there was some border region co-operation between Algeria and Tunisia, and the possibility of collaboration between Algeria and both Morocco and Libya grew in the early 1980s. In 1982 Algeria signed an economic agreement with Libya.

The first Southern African Development Coordination Conference was held at Arusha, Tanzania, in 1979. It was attended by representatives of Angola, Botswana, Moçambique, Tanzania and Zambia and its object was to harmonize development plans and reduce economic dependence on South Africa. Zimbabwe joined the Conference in 1980 and Lesotho, Malawi and Swaziland also acceded. In April 1980 a meeting in Zambia issued the Lusaka Declaration, an agreement to allot special responsibilities to member governments. Moçambique, for example, was entrusted with the task of setting up a regional transport commission. Particular importance was attached to developing a transport system which would enable the member countries to do without the South African ports. In June 1980 Zaïre, Zambia, Zimbabwe and Moçambique agreed to a ten-year programme to develop Moçambican railways and harbours for joint use. The second SADCC, held at Maputo in November 1980, was attended by representatives of the EEC, various development agencies and thirty-five industrialized countries, who promised financial aid to a number of development projects.

How effective these organizations were remained open to doubt. There was much mutual distrust and there were many obstacles to co-operation, not least sheer inadequacy of the necessary infrastructure and the continued dependence of African countries upon the developed world. ECOWAS was weakened by the persistent gap between Nigeria and Ivory Coast on the one hand and the remaining members on the other, and also by rivalry between anglophone West Africa, led by Lagos, and francophone West Africa, led by Lomé. Nigeria did not endear itself to its partners by its policy of expelling illegal immigrants, especially from Ghana, attracted by the greater economic opportunities in an oil-producing country. Contributions to the Community soon fell behind ($12 million out of $50 million in December 1981), as well as to a special fund which was supposed to finance a telecommunications project. However, a start was made on the reduction of tariffs and the introduction of the free movement of persons. In 1977 tariffs on raw materials and traditional handicraft products were abolished. The markets of the strong states (Ghana and Senegal in addition to Nigeria and Ivory Coast) were opened at a faster pace than those of the weak. In May 1981 tariffs on the products of companies with Community status were abolished. The minimum indigenous ownership required for companies to qualify to participate in intra-Community trade was fixed at 20 per cent for 1981-1983 and 35 per cent for 1983-1989. A number of joint projects was begun: a cement works (CIMAO) in Togo with the participation of Ghana, Ivory Coast and Togo and a fertilizer factory in Senegal with the participation of Ivory Coast, Nigeria and Senegal.

International disputes, sometimes the result of ideological differences, tended to cause either the breakdown or the atrophy of these organizations. The Organisation of the Senegal River States disintegrated and three of the four members set up a Senegal River Development Organisation without Guinea. A more important casualty was the East African Community, which had achieved considerable success. Tanzania's refusal to recognize the government of General Amin hampered the machinery of co-operation and led even to outright political and military conflict. In this ill-feeling between Uganda and Tanzania, Kenya acted as negotiator, but at the end of 1974 new bitterness welled up between Kenya and Tanzania, already divided by ideology. Zambia, in an effort to reduce its trade with South Africa, which had increased after Rhodesia had declared independence, started importing more food from Kenya by road across Tanzania and exporting some copper through Kenyan ports, which were operating more efficiently than Dar es Salaam. This caused anger in Tanzania, adding to the existing resentment at Kenya's already disproportionate benefit from the Community, and the result was the closing of Tanzanian roads to heavy vehicles from Kenya and a retaliatory closing by Kenya of rail crossings and the expulsion of Tanzanian workers.

Africa did not, then, get much further along the road to economic unity. This was hardly possible as long as rivalries persisted, and these themselves were a heavy burden upon national economies. Very large sums of money were spent on armaments to combat internal opposition or external enemies. The arms traffic accelerated in the 1970s. The value of West German arms sales alone to Africa, which in 1965-1974 had amounted to $73 million, rose in 1974-1977 to $425 million. Between 1974 and 1978

West Germany sold $280 million worth of arms to Algeria, $140 million worth to Libya. Total arms sales to sub-Saharan Africa by the West (chiefly the USA, France, Britain, Italy, the Federal German Republic and Canada) were worth $1 345 million during that period. That was modest compared with arms transfers to states in sub-Saharan Africa from the USSR, China, Czechoslovakia and Poland in 1974-1978, worth $3 065 million. In 1956-1964 the value of Soviet arms transfers to sub-Saharan Africa was about half of economic assistance and about the same in 1965-1974, but in 1975-1979 economic credits equalled only 28 per cent of the value of arms transfers. Soviet arms went chiefly to Angola ($410 million) and more especially Ethiopia ($1 300 million) for the sake of political influence, but also to Nigeria ($80 million in 1975-1979) for the sake of earning hard currency.

The gap between poor and rich nations remained as wide as ever, if not wider than before. Within Africa itself there was a big and growing disparity between the oil-exporting countries (which accounted for a third of developing Africa's GDP) and the dozen or so countries with per capita incomes of less than a hundred American dollars in the late 1970s (countries which accounted for a ninth of developing Africa's GDP), not only poorly endowed landlocked countries, e.g. Chad and Upper Volta, but those which had great economic potential, e.g. Ethiopia and Zaïre. However, it was not the intra-African gap which attracted attention, but the discrepancy in wealth between the industrialized countries of the First World and the developing nations of the Third World. In 1975 a Conference on International Economic Co-operation opened in Paris, the so-called North-South Dialogue between the rich countries and the poor. It was the result of pressure from the OPEC countries to force the developed countries into accepting the necessity for what was called a new international economic order, by which was meant principally fair and stable prices for Third World exports and their free entry into the developed markets. As the demand for oil declined the pressure became less effective and the conference came to nothing. The next initiative came from the Brandt Commission, an independent, self-appointed but distinguished body of politicians and experts which wanted the setting up of a World Development Fund. It led to another conference, in Mexico in 1981, with similarly disappointing results.

Some argued that the less developed countries of the world were trapped in a vicious circle of poverty: low income and indebtedness, therefore little saving and investment and so low income. It was for that reason that foreign aid was necessary in generous amounts. Others argued that foreign aid was merely a euphemism for charity and was much more likely to do harm than good. If the necessary conditions for economic development were present in the recipient country, foreign aid was not required; if they were not, it was worthless. Any country willing and able to develop would be able to accumulate capital for itself. The problem was not that African countries were so poverty-stricken that development efforts were doomed to failure, but rather that resources were misallocated, lavished on armaments and imported luxuries. Others stressed entrepreneurial inadequacies and reluctance of private capital to invest in manufacturing. Although investment in cattle declined in favour, investment in land retained its popularity among the wealthy. Able entrepreneurs were not lacking in trade and the provision of transport services, but the successful tended to prefer to keep their businesses small enough for personal management and to invest in land rather than industry. It was partly because of the shortage of suitable entrepreneurial talent that the independent states relied so heavily on state enterprise in their planning. That in turn was much criticized. The state sector was said to be too large and often too inefficient, with altogether too much interference in the running of the economy. Foreign investors were deterred by insecurity and restrictions on the repatriation of profits.

Except in South Africa and Algeria (where petrochemical and electrical and mechanical engineering research institutes were founded) the parastatal enterprises so widespread in Africa paid little attention to research and development, preferring to call in foreign consultants to solve local problems. In 1980 there were more people engaged in scientific and technological research in South Africa than in all the other countries of Africa, including Egypt and the Maghrib, put together, and South Africa spent twice as much, though including substantial expenditure on weapons research. Much of the research and development carried on in developing Africa was provided through foreign aid, and although South Africa remained heavily dependent upon imported technology and was therefore vulnerable to economic sanctions, it was almost alone in Africa in having an indigenously developed science and technology programme. Few of the recommendations of international conferences organized by the OAU, the United Nations and its agency, UNESCO, to foster science and technology in Africa were implemented.

One of the biggest obstacles to the development of science and technology was the shortage of skilled scientific and technical manpower, and that was sometimes attributed to the poor quality of the primary schools, where science and mathematics were either not taught or mistaught. Partly for that reason the failure rate in these subjects was very high in the secondary schools and few students went on to take them at university level. Many of those who obtained high qualifications and were able to go into research preferred to move overseas where facilities, rewards and political stability were so much greater. There were plenty of universities in Africa but except in some countries, notably South Africa and Egypt, student numbers were small and scientific and engineering faculties were not used.

Those who subscribe to the neo-colonialist explanation, to the belief that the independence granted to the ex-colonies was spurious, argued that Africa was kept in subjection through the machinations of the former colonial powers. These sought to tie the ex-colonies closely to the former metropolitan power and to promote maximum disunity by fostering the pseudo-nationalism of subservient élites. The ties between Africa and the EEC represented one aspect of the continent's continued subjection. All poor countries were in debt peonage to the rich industrial nations. Inextricably caught up in a system not of their own devising, the primary producers had to give more and more for less and less reward in order to service debts incurred, unable to escape from dependence upon one or two staples. Industrialization was precluded through loss of capital abroad and overwhelming foreign competition. Agriculture was in a parlous state because food crops were sacrificed to cash crops demanded by inexorable and avaricious creditors and cultivated by traditional, unimproved methods. Foreign aid was a mockery, at worse a device for perpetuating dependence, at best a palliative, diminishing in quantity and cancelled out by increasing export of capital to service debts and pay dividends to foreigners. The poverty of the developing countries, socialists suggested, was an inevitable outcome of capitalism, as colonial authorities, it was argued, left behind them a social structure that gave power partly to discredited traditional authorities, chiefs, emirs and kings, partly to an élite which, in selfish pursuit of its own interests, reproduced in Africa the social injustice of Europe and at the same time acted as lackeys to international capitalism. Even the military régimes that were the scourge of Africa were part of the colonial heritage, an all too likely outcome of the political, economic and social malaise that followed the realization that political independence was not real freedom. There arose no true native capitalist class, for which neither the capital nor the incentive existed. The nearest approach was the detestable group of kulak cultivators, like the members of the Muslim Mourides brotherhood, whose fortunes were founded on low wages and poor working conditions for their labourers. The multi-national company safeguarded its interests with cynical disregard for the prospects of local development. For its operations in any one state were merely a part of a complicated process of production, and intervention by the state was likely to prove of marginal benefit to itself and of comparatively slight inconvenience to the company.

The implication of the neo-colonial argument is that Africa has only to recover control of its own resources for development to leap forward. In fact Africa is not well endowed with natural resources. Just over a quarter of African countries have valuable minerals, fewer than a tenth have considerable deposits of oil. Above all, well-watered and fertile soil is lacking. A further implication is that dependence is inescapable, whereas, although there are numerous examples in history of suppressed and exploited societies, there are, too, examples of nations, and those also overshadowed by the West, that have asserted their economic independence and won prosperity, even affluence, for their peoples. The possibility of escape is recognized by some African economists. It is a question of breaking away from the policies and theories inherited from the developed world. But it is more commonly argued that the solution to Africa's problems lies in a change of heart of the rich countries of the world.

It is possible that Africa has been either so concerned with equal shares or such a battlefield for groups contending for the lion's share of what there is, that it has not bothered enough about enlarging the distributable surplus. Between 1960 and 1975 there were twenty successful military coups in Africa and others that failed. Soldiers were transformed overnight into administrators, legislators and economists, a metamorphosis no more to be commended as a solution to economic and social problems than would be similar protean feats by the butcher, the baker and the candlestick maker. During the same period any opposition to the established régime in most cases was eliminated or absorbed by the ruling group. It is difficult to escape the conclusion in most cases that the capture of government was an end in itself, a seizure and redistribution of wealth and privilege mostly for the benefit of the soldiers and of the civil servants on whom they rely. To the neglect of science and technology, industry and agriculture, frequently abandoned to foreigners, the able and the ambitious were drawn into politics, the army or the bureaucracy, because they could offer the rewards. Africa, even if cursed so often with leaders who were incompetent, uncouth and self-indulgent, also had a fair share of those who were energetic, devoted, honest and selfless. The latter wore themselves out in a frenzy of activity to stimulate the apathetic and curb the self-seeking and the corrupt. The problem that faced them was immense, but it would be hypocritical to suggest that none of its difficulties was of Africa's own making and futile to deny that their solution lay in the hands of its own people. Wherever industrialization has taken place in the world, somebody has had to pay the price, voluntarily or, much more often, involuntarily. It seems that Africa is making the sacrifice without enjoying the growth, and only Africa can ensure that the rewards are commensurate with the sacrifice. The 1980s were declared the African Industrial Development

Decade by the United Nations Organization and the Organization of African Unity. Few can be confident of rapid progress. Even the target of a modest 2 per cent African share of world industrial production by 2 000 would require an annual growth rate greater than that ever achieved so far.

SELECT BIBLIOGRAPHY

1. STATISTICS
Mitchell, Brian, *International Historical Statistics* (Macmillan, London and Basingstoke, 1982).

2. GENERAL ECONOMIC HISTORY OF AFRICA
Duignan, Peter and Gann, E.H., *Colonialism in Africa 1870-1960*, Volume 4 (Cambridge University Press, Cambridge, 1975).
Munro, J. Forbes, *Africa and the International Economy 1800-1960* (J.M. Dent & Sons Ltd., London, 1976).
Munro, J. Forbes, *Britain in Tropical Africa 1870-1960* (Macmillan, London and Basingstoke, 1984).
Pim, Alan, *The Financial and Economic History of the African Tropical Territories* (Clarendon Press, Oxford, 1940).

3. REGIONAL ECONOMIC HISTORY
Herschlag, Z.Y., *Introduction to the Modern Economic History of the Middle East* (Brill, Leiden, 1964).
Hopkins, A.G., *An Economic History of West Africa* (Longman, London, 1973).
Issawi, Charles, *Economic History of the Middle East and North Africa* (Columbia University Press, 1983).
McPhee, A., *The Economic Revolution in British West Africa* (Routledge, London 1926).
Owen, Roger, *The Middle East and the World Economy 1800-1914* (Methuen, London, 1981).

4. NATIONAL ECONOMIC HISTORY
Coleman, F. L., ed., *Economic History of South Africa* (HAUM, Pretoria, 1983).
Crouchley, A.E., *The Economic Development of Modern Egypt* (Longmans, Green and Co., London, New York and Toronto, 1938).
De Kiewiet, C. W., *A History of South Africa, Social and Economic* (OUP, London, 1941).
De Kock, M. H., *Economic History of South Africa* (Juta, Cape Town and Johannesburg, 1924).
Ehrlich, Cyril, 'The poor country: the Tanganyika economy from 1945 to independence' (D. A. Low and A. Smith, eds., *History of East Africa*, Volume III, Clarendon Press, Oxford, 1976).
Ehrlich, Cyril, 'The Uganda Economy 1903-1945' (V. Harlow & E. M. Chilver, eds., *History of East Africa*, Vol. II, Clarendon Press, Oxford, 1965).
Ekundare, R. Olufemi, *An Economic History of Nigeria: 1860-1960* (Methuen and Co., Ltd., London, 1973).
Houghton, D. Hobart, 'Economic development, 1865-1965' (M. Wilson and L. Thompson, eds., *The Oxford History of South Africa*, Volume II, Clarendon Press, Oxford, 1971).
Lury, D. A., 'Dayspring mishandled? The Uganda economy 1945-1960' (D.A. Low and A. Smith, eds., *History of East Africa*, Volume III, Clarendon Press, Oxford, 1976).
Mabro, Robert, *The Egyptian Economy 1952-1972* (Clarendon Press, Oxford, 1974).
McWilliam, Michael, 'The managed economy: agricultural change, development and finance in Kenya, 1945-1963' (D. A. Low and A. Smith, eds., *History of East Africa*, Volume III, Clarendon Press, Oxford, 1976).
Manning, Patrick, *Slavery, Colonialism and Economic Growth in Dahomey 1640-1960* (Cambridge University Press, Cambridge, 1972).
Mosley, Paul, *The Settler Economies, Studies in the Economic History of Kenya and Southern Rhodesia 1900-1963* (Cambridge University Press, Cambridge).

O'Brien, Patrick, *The Revolution in Egypt's Economic System; from Private Enterprise to Socialism 1952-1965* (Oxford, 1966).
Pankhurst, Richard, *Economic History of Ethiopia 1800-1935* (Addis Ababa, 1968).
Schumann, C.G.W., *Structural Changes and Business Cycles in South Africa 1806-1936* (P.S. King and Son, Ltd., London, 1938).
Stewart, Charles F., *The Economy of Morocco 1912-1962* (Haruaro U.P., Cambridge, Mass., 1967).
Szereszewski, R., *Structural Changes in the Economy of Ghana 1891-1911* (London, 1965).
Van Zwanenberg, R.M.A., *An Economic History of Kenya and Uganda 1800-1970* (Macmillan, London and Basingstoke, 1975).
Wrigley, C.C., 'Kenya: the patterns of economic life, 1902-1945' (V. Harlow and E.M. Chilver, eds., *History of East Africa*, Volume II, Clarendon Press, Oxford, 1965).

5. ECONOMIC HISTORY OF SMALLER AREAS
Baier, Stephen, *An Economic History of Central Niger* (Oxford, 1980).
Fearn, Hugh, *An African Economy; a Study of the Economic Development of the Nyanza Province of Kenya 1903-1953* (London, 1961).
Lawson, Rowena M., *The Changing Economy of the Lower Volta 1954-1967* (Oxford University Press, Oxford, 1972).

INDEX

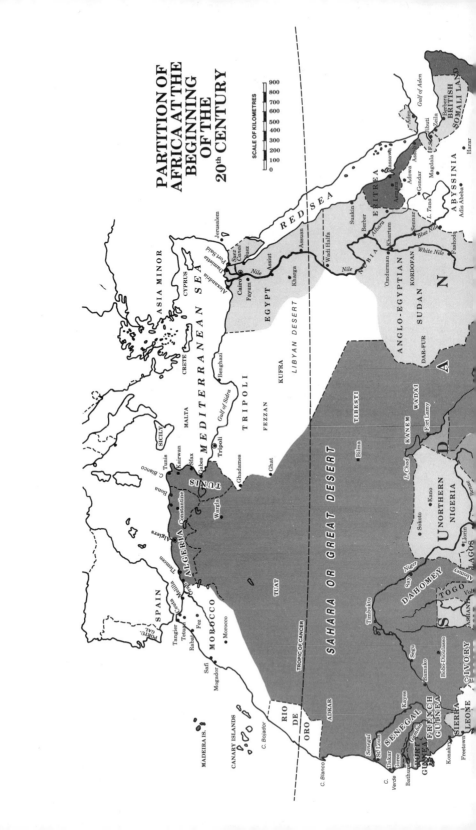

PARTITION OF AFRICA AT THE BEGINNING OF THE 20th CENTURY

SCALE OF KILOMETRES

900
800
700
600
500
400
300
200
100
0

ASIA MINOR

CYPRUS

CRETE

MEDITERRANEAN SEA

MALTA

SICILY

Jerusalem

Damietta
Port Said
Suez Canal
Suez
Alexandria
Cairo
Fayum
Nile
Assiut

EGYPT

LIBYAN DESERT

RED SEA

Aden
Gulf of Aden

Berbera
BRITISH
SOMALI LAND
Zeila
F. Somali
Djibuti

Harar

ABYSSINIA
Adis Abeba

Magdala
Adowa
Gondar
L. Tana
Argo
ERITREA
Massawa
Asseb

Suakin
Berber
Atbara
Khartum
Blue Nile
Sennar
Fashoda
White Nile

NUBIA
Wadi Halfa
Assuan
Nile
Kharga
Omdurman

ANGLO-EGYPTIAN
SUDAN
KORDOFAN
DAR-FUR

N

Benghazi

Gulf of Sidra

TRIPOLI

FEZZAN

KUFRA

TIBESTI

WADAI
Fort Lamy

KANEM
L. Chad
Bilma

Tripoli
Ghadames
Ghat

TUNIS
Tunis
C. Bianco
Bona
Kairwan
Sfax
Gabes

Constantine
Algiers
ALGERIA
Tlemcen
Wargla

SAHARA OR GREAT DESERT

TUAT

TROPIC OF CANCER

ADRAR

Timbuktu

L. Chad

Kano
Sokoto

NORTHERN
NIGERIA
Ilorin
Say
Niger

DAHOMEY
TOGO

Volta

ASHANTI

S

A

D

U

SPAIN

Ceuta
Tangier
Tetuan
Rabat
Melilla
Fez
MOROCCO
Morocco
Safi
Mogador

PORTU-
GAL

MADEIRA IS.

CANARY ISLANDS

C. Bojador

RIO
DE
ORO

C. Blanco

C.
Verde

Senegal
St. Louis
Dakar
Bathurst

SENEGAL

FRENCH
GUINEA

Kayes

Segu
Bamako
Bobo-Dioulasso

IVORY

SIERRA
LEONE
Freetown
Konakry

PORTG.
GUINEA

Niger

Lagos
Benue